CONVERSATIONS WITH NIETZSCHE

FRIEDRICH NIETZSCHES STERBEHAUS UND NIETZSCHE-ARCHIV ZU WEIMAR.

NIETZSCHE
1844-1900.

Even before Nietzsche's death in 1900, the "Nietzsche House," Villa Silberblick, had become a major tourist attraction in Weimar. After his death it became the center of the "Nietzsche cult." Postcards, printed by Elisabeth Förster-Nietzsche's Nietzsche Archive, were only one sign of the Nietzsche industry which grew up about the dead philosopher's name. *(Source: Private Collection, Gilman)*

Conversations with Nietzsche

A Life in the Words of His Contemporaries

Edited and with an Introduction by
SANDER L. GILMAN

Translated by
DAVID J. PARENT

New York   Oxford
OXFORD UNIVERSITY PRESS

Oxford University Press

Oxford   New York   Toronto
Delhi   Bombay   Calcutta   Madras   Karachi
Petaling Jaya   Singapore   Hong Kong   Tokyo
Nairobi   Dar es Salaam   Cape Town
Melbourne   Auckland

and associated companies in
Berlin   Ibadan

First published in 1987 by Oxford University Press, Inc.,
200 Madison Avenue, New York, New York 10016

First issued as an Oxford University Press paperback, 1991
Oxford is a registered trademark of Oxford University Press

Library of Congress Cataloging-in-Publication Data
Begegnungen mit Nietzsche. English. Selections.
Conversations with Nietzsche.
Abridged translation of: Begegnungen mit Nietzsche.
Bibliography: p.   Includes indexes.
1. Nietzsche, Friedrich Wilhelm, 1844-1900.
2. Philosophers—Germany—Biography.
I. Gilman, Sander, L. II. Title.
B3316.B43213   1987   193   86-33303
ISBN 0-19-504961-6
ISBN 0-19-506778-9 (pbk.)

1   3   5   7   9   8   6   4   2
Printed in the United States of America

In memory of
Mazzino Montinari,[†]
the dean of modern Nietzsche scholars

CONTENTS

INTRODUCTION
TALKING WITH NIETZSCHE
xiii

CHILDHOOD AND SCHOOL DAYS (1844–1858)

Learned to speak late; reading and writing by age of four, 3.   Left birthplace of Röcken on father's death, 3.   Boyhood friendship with Wilhelm Pinder, 4–6. Inspired by Handel's *Messiah*, 6.   Ice-skating; defends deformed boy (anecdote), 6–7.

SCHULPFORTA (1858–1864)

Respectful opinion of teachers and fellow students, 8.   Friendship with Raimund Granier, 9–10.   Excellent student but not leader, 9.   Physical appearance at age of eighteen, 9.   Polish ancestry, 10.   Friendship with Paul Deussen, 10–15. Student-proctor (anecdote), 10.   Love for Anacreon, 10.   Confirmation, 10–11. Piety undermined by historico-critical method, 11.   Member of anti-studious "wild" clique, 11.   Schoolboy quarrel and reconciliation, 12–13.   Shy, reserved temperament, 13.   Piano accompaniment for readings, 13.   Esteem for beauty and contempt for material interests, 14.   Not good as actor or acrobat, 14–15. Danger of eventual blindness, 15.   Writes on Greek poetry, 15.   Comments by former teacher, Otto Benndorf, 15–17.   Attended lectures on Greek sculpture, 16.   Affinity with Goethe, 17.   Friendship with A. Fritsch, 17. Wrote poetry and composed music, 17.

UNIVERSITY AND MILITARY TIME (1864–1869)

Cheerful atmosphere in Naumburg home, 18.   Life-story of Ernst Schnabel, 18–19.   Horseback ride up the Drachenfels; youthful pranks (anecdotes), 20. Arrival at the University of Bonn, 20–21.   Studies Greek lyricists, 21–22.   Joins "Franconia" fraternity, 22.   Fights duel (anecdote), 23.   Accidental visit to a brothel (anecdote), 23–24.   Relations with women and attitude toward marriage, 24.   Classes and theater-going, 24.   Freethinker, but no enmity to Christianity, 25.   Ritschl-Jahn dispute; transfers to Leipzig, 25.   Urges Deussen to give up theology for philology, 25–26.   Forms Philology Club and joins

Ritschl Society reluctantly, 26–28.   High reputation as a student, 29.   Lectures
on Menippus and Homer, 29.   Appointed professor at Basel at the age of
twenty-four, 30.   Rebukes Deussen for lack of respect, 30–31.

PROFESSOR AT THE UNIVERSITY OF BASEL (1870–1878)

1870

Ida Overbeck's first meeting with Nietzsche, 32.   His piano-playing, 32.
Physical description, 32–33.   Nietzsche frequents the Overbeck home, 33.
Attitude toward religion, 33.   Poor eyesight, 33.   Acquaintanceship with Julius
Piccard, 34.   Piano composition (anecdote), 35.   Persecution complex
(anecdote), 35.   As a high-school teacher (three views, with anecdotes), 35–39.

1871

Recommended by Ritschl for professorship, 39–40.   Reaction of Basel public to
his early writings, 40.   Sensitivity to newspaper criticism, 41.   The tragedy of his
life, 41.   Nietzsche's parable on philology, 42.   Friendship with Richard
Wagner, 43.

1872

Jakob Burckhardt's attitude toward Nietzsche (three views), 44–47.   Burckhardt
receives insane letter years later from Nietzsche, 46.   Nietzsche's friendship with
Heinrich von Stein, 47.   Franz Overbeck's comments on Nietzsche's deep, one-
sided friendships, 47–48.   Malwida von Meysenbug meets him in Bayreuth, 48.
Her praise of his friendliness, 49.   Frau Bachofen on Nietzsche's enthusiasm for
Wagner, 49–50.

1874

Nietzsche as pleasant socializer in Miaskowski circle, 50–54.   His manner with
women, 52.   Physical appearance, 53.   His later illness, 53.

1875

Impact of *The Birth of Tragedy* on Peter Gast and his generation, 54.
Schmeitzner becomes Overbeck's and Nietzsche's publisher, 55.   Widemann and
Gast go to Basel to study under Nietzsche, but find him completely unknown
(anecdotes), 56–57.   On Gluck-Puccini dispute, 57.   Praise of Switzerland, 58.
His university lectures, 58.   Pleasant home-life with his sister, 58.   Composes
"Hymn to Solitude," magnificent piano-playing, 59.   Gast copies *Untimely
Meditation* on Richard Wagner and does other secretarial work for Nietzsche, 59–
60.   Physical appearance, 61.   Lectures on the Greeks in a tortured manner, 62.
Burckhardt and Nietzsche, 62.   More on his composing and piano-playing, 62.

1876

Ludwig von Scheffler decides to attend Nietzsche's course, 63.   Scheffler meets
Peter Gast, 64.   Impressions of a Nietzsche lecture, 65–66.   Reinterpretation of

Plato, 66–67. Burckhardt and Nietzsche, 68. Peter Gast's anti-clericalism, 68.
A visit to Nietzsche's apartment, 69–72. On Holbein's self-portrait, 71–72.
Nietzsche's homoeroticism, 72. Lectures on Heraclitus, 73. Invites Scheffler
to accompany him to Italy (anecdote), 74. Compared with Platen as a great
sufferer, 75. Richard Reuter in Basel, 76–77. On the German Reich, 78–79.
Nietzsche's break with Wagner, 79–80. Paul de Lagarde as a source of
Nietzsche's thinking, 80–82.

1877

In Italy with Malwida von Meysenbug and Paul Rée, 83. On striving for truth,
and on suffering, 83. Meysenbug's plans for a community of scholars, 84.
Influenced by Rée's scientific attitude, 84–85. Denies the law of causality, 85.
Rejects transcendentalism, 85–86. On Goethe, 86–87. On other authors, 87–
88. Meysenbug cautions him against Rée's positivism and against premature
criticism of women, 88. Bad state of health, 89. Who should not read
Nietzsche, 89. On Wagner, 90. Writing aphorisms at night between
headaches, 91. Plays church organ (anecdote), 91. On the Catholic
Church, 91. In Sorrento, 91–92. Seydlitz on Nietzsche's character, 93.
Helpful as a critic, 93–95. Attends lecture on Origen's "eternal return of all
things," 95–97. Nietzsche advises a student (anecdote), 97. Pensioned off for
medical disability, 98.

1878

Nietzsche as a broken, lonely man, 99. Object of factionalism in Basel, 99.
Shaken by battlefield experiences, 100. Suffers excruciating headaches, 100.
Sends away his sister and even Peter Gast, 101. His last lecture, 101. Von
Scheffler witnesses Nietzsche's pathetic seclusion, 102–3. Hellenistic
influence, 104. On pity, 105. On morality, 105–6. On psychology, 106. On
the Greeks and Christianity, 107. On religion, 107. Stormy friendships, 108.
Disgust with himself and the world, 109. Mental sufferings, 109. Ida Overbeck
on Nietzsche's philosophy, 109–10.

MIGRANT YEARS (1879–1889)

1880

The ailing Nietzsche visits the Overbecks, 111. His ascetic life, 111.
Philosophical conversations, 112. On French authors, 112. His suffering at
being little known and read, 112–13. On Klinger, Stirner, and
Schopenhauer, 113–14. On Ludwig Feuerbach and Samuel Johnson, 114–15.
On morality and altruism, 115.

1882

Meets Lou Andreas-Salomé and Paul Rée in St. Peter's in Rome (anecdote), 116.
Proposes marriage to Salomé through Rée, 116. Nietzsche seriously ill, Paul

Rée stays in Rome with him, 117.   Second proposal of marriage to Salomé, 117.
Humorous portrait with her, 117.   Spends several weeks alone with her, 117–18.
Aphoristic style, 118.   Deeply religious nature, 118.   Slanders Rée and
Salomé, 119.   "What I have done cannot be forgiven," 119.   Ida Overbeck's
view of the Salomé affair, 120–23.   His "son" Zarathustra, 120.   On
Salomé, 121.   His break with Salomé and Rée, 121.   His sister's role in the
affair, 121–22.   His hopes and mistakes, 122–23.   His terrible loneliness, 123.
His break with Ida Overbeck, 123.   Elisabeth Förster-Nietzsche on his attitude
toward women, 123–25.   Arthur Egidi meets Nietzsche, 125–26.   On Peter
Gast, 126–27.   On Wagner, 127.   On aphorisms, 129.   Tells a Wagner
anecdote, 129.   On punctuality (anecdote), 130.   On the break with
Wagner, 130.   On *The Birth of Tragedy* and Hans von Bülow, 130–31.   On
Beethoven and Bach, 131.   Egidi on Nietzsche's asceticism, 132.   Egidi on the
Wagner case, 132.

1883

Sebastian Hausmann meets him on a walk (anecdote), 133.   On the need for a
formal style in writing, 134.   On "Don't forget the whip!", 135.   On his career
in Basel, 135–36.   On Jakob Burckhardt, 136.   On Richard Wagner, 137–38.
On Jakob Froschammer, and vice versa, 138–39.   Nietzsche's conversational
style, 139–40.   Nietzsche as a secluded scholar in Leipzig, 141–43.   Gives
grapes to children (anecdote), 142.   Conflicts in his thinking, 143.   On
Kant, 143.   On Napoleon and how the strong prey on the weak, 143.   His sense
of tragedy, 144.   On the idea of God, 145.   His high philosophical
ambition, 145.   Franz Overbeck and Nietzsche, 146.

1884

Resa von Schirnhofer meets Nietzsche in Nice, 147.   Her comments on
Salomé, 147.   His sensitivity and courtesy, 148.   On prejudices, 148.   They
climb a mountain and attend a bullfight (anecdote), 149–50.   On Malwida von
Meysenbug and Lou Salomé, 151.   On Sallust, Napoleon, and Corsica, 151.
On Schirnhofer's poems, 151–52.   On Wagner, 152.   On Francis Galton, 153.
On Stendhal and other writers, 153–54.   On Taine, 154–55.   Schirnhofer reads
songs from *Zarathustra*, 155–57.   His scepticism about knowledge of our own
thought processes, 158.   He visits Meta von Salis-Marschlins, 158.   On vanity as
a residue of slavery, 159.   On man's potential, 160.   On dislike for
dialects, 161.   Second meeting with Resa von Schirnhofer, 161.   Stampeded by
a herd of cows (anecdote), 162.   Signed his own prescriptions for drugs, 163.
Schirnhofer on hashish, 163–64.   His fear of mental illness, 164–65.   His sister
disputes her father's brain disease, 165–66.   Helen Zimmern's friendship with
Nietzsche, 166–69.   She vouches for his sanity, 167.   And his courtesy to
women (anecdote), 168.   Pirated translations of his works in the United
States, 168–69.   Dietary problems, 170.   His landlord tells about him
(anecdote), 170–71.   Meeting with Gottfried Keller, 172.   Introduced to the

astronomer Wilhelm Tempel, 172–73.   Paul Lanzky becomes his
companion, 173, 178.   Quest for a suitable place to live, 174–75.   A sad
parting, 176, 182.   His humaneness, 178.   His working and living habits, 179–
80.   Overexertion, 179.

1885

Dietary problems, 180.   Fear of insanity (anecdote), 180–81.   In Sils-Maria with
a musician and an elderly intellectual lady, 182–83.   Physical appearance, 183.
On Chopin, Schumann, Kirchner, and Wagner, 184–87.   Terrible
headache, 187.   Walking, 188.

1886

Meetings with Marie von Bradke in Sils-Maria, 188–92.   Eye for natural
beauty, 190.   Recollects writing *Thus Spake Zarathustra*, 191.   Sensitivity, 192.

1887

On Dostoevsky, 193.   On his own changing personality, 194.   Advice to a
Catholic not to read his works, 195.   His undaunted will, 195.   Summer in Sils-
Maria, 196–97.   Memory of a visit from Heinrich von Stein, 198.   Caution in
forming opinions, 198–99.   Ability to "share joy," 199.   On various
authors, 200–4.   On the French Revolution and Napoleon, 203.   On
conservatives and liberals, 205.   His sanity, 205.   Memories of Schulpforta, 206.

1888

On Wagner, 208.   Nearly drowned (anecdote), 209.   Memories of his childhood
and his mother, 209.   Compared with Murillo's "Christ," 209.   On Wilhelm
II, 210.   Need for independence, 210–11.   His sister warns against errors about
him (tub-of-water and frog anecdotes), 211–12.   Bernoulli refutes her version of
events, 212–13.

Undated

He meets young newlyweds in Venice (anecdotes), 213–16.   His lonely stay in
Turin, 216–18.   Nietzsche's piano, 218–20.

AT THE JENA SANATORIUM (1889–1890)

Nietzsche in the sanatorium, 221–22.   On display to medical students, 222–24.
Syphilis, 224–25.   Left to his mother's care, 225–26.

UNDER HIS MOTHER'S CARE IN NAUMBURG (1890–1897)

Quotations from the sick Nietzsche, 227–28.   Conversation with his
mother, 229–32.   More quotations, 233–36.

ON DISPLAY IN WEIMAR (1897–1900)

Resa von Schirnhofer visits the sick man, 237–40.   A bust of Nietzsche, 240–42. The Archives, 243.   Treatment, 244.   *Dementia paralytica,* 244.   Transfer in special train, 245.   Sketch for a Nietzsche monument, 246.   Physical appearance, 247.   His funeral, 247–48.   A suitcase of manuscripts found in Italy, 249.   A visit to Weimar, 250–54.   Description of him as a patient, 254–55.   Grotesque musical paroxysms, 255–56.   A moment of lucidity? "In vero vinitas," 256.   Medical history, 257–59.   "Mattress grave" and death, 260–61. Death, 262.

BIOGRAPHICAL NOTES
263

SOURCES
268

INDEX OF NAMES AND WORKS
271

INTRODUCTION
TALKING WITH NIETZSCHE

Nietzsche's friend the philosopher Paul Rée once said to the soci-
ologist Ferdinand Tönnies that Nietzsche was more important
because of his letters than his books and yet more important in his
conversations than in his letters.[1] This statement, a report of a conversation, can provide the text for our considerations of the importance, meaning, and function of conversations in general and the
conversations with Friedrich Nietzsche in particular. The tradition
of collecting the spoken discourse of important thinkers is one
which reaches back to classical antiquity. What indeed are the Socra-
tic dialogues but Plato's reports of Socrates' conversations? In the
nineteenth century this tradition reaches some type of height in
Germany with the publication of J. P. Eckermann's conversations
with Goethe.[2] Eckermann's conversations with Goethe share one
feature with Plato's reports of Socrates' dialogues—they were per-
ceived as reliable reports of actual conversations, at least until the
underlying structures of the texts as texts were examined. Once this
was done, it became evident that such "conversations" were elaborate fictions which used the device of the report to create the aura
of reality. The report, with its basic structure of the "talking head,"
the recreation of a first-person representation speaking direct discourse (or reported indirect discourse), mimics our daily experiences of conversing. In this mimetic structure is embedded the possibility of a range of ideological messages, all of which acquire some
believability as they are literally "put into the mouth" of a "real"
individual. What makes this figure real to us, however, is not merely
that the recreation meets our idealized expectations of the nature
of discourse (for who ever spoke like Plato's Socrates or Eckermann's Goethe?) but that it confirms an image of a figure who has
acquired some more general or mythic quality. Thus we expect Eck-

1. Ferdinand Tönnies, "Paul Rée," *Das freie Wort* 4 (1904), 670.
2. See Sander L. Gilman, introduction to *Johann Peter Eckermann: Aphorismen* (Berlin: Erich
Schmidt, 1984).

ermann's Goethe to speak in quotable bons mots because the archetypal image which Eckermann employs is that of the wise old man,
Odin-like, who speaks in gnomic utterances. This is not to deny that
the content of the conversation may have stemmed, at perhaps some
remove, from the historical figure to whom it is attributed. There
is, however, little doubt that the structuring of the literary conversation provides the form and the context even for material which
could be successfully attributed to the actual speaker. Until the
introduction of acoustic recordings of speech in the late nineteenth
century, however, no literary conversation was set down which is not
suspect. In all cases we must consider the author of the conversation
as a more or less creative artist who is shaping (if not inventing) the
conversation.

Does this fact, however, vitiate our use of this material? If we
wish to use the Platonic dialogues, Boswell's conversations with
Johnson, or Eckermann's reports of Goethe's views as the unmediated report of the views and opinions of Socrates, Johnson, or
Goethe, then we are stymied. This material is not original in the
same way as a text ascribed to an author, a letter written or dictated
by him, or even the copy or printing of such material. If we wish to
place this material in the complex reception of the writer, as part of
the mythbuilding which occurs in the creation of a writer's reputation, then we have an extraordinarily rich and complex source. Not
only can we examine the literal recreation of the fictionalized per-
sona of an historical figure, but we can examine it within the bounds
of an identifiable tradition, that of the conversation. The parallel
existence of a genre of clearly fictionalized "conversations," such as
the "imaginary conversations" of Walter Savage Landor, provide
the matrix for the examination of this tradition. Thus we can examine "texts," that is, written documents, to recreate the broader
"text," the reputation of the writer, which is undergoing transmu-
tation and expansion through the generation of texts in which he is
allowed to speak. For the joy of the "imaginary conversation" is that
the mute are given tongue, that the dead are given immortality in
their discourse. In literary conversations much the same illusion is
employed. The mute author, whose presence we sense but cannot
ever truly see behind the work of art, the printed page, the actors
on the stage, suddenly sheds his or her disguise and steps forth and
addresses us directly, without the mediation of the work of art. This
illusion permits us an intimacy with the historical figure impossible
for those of us who know him or her only through the work of art.

We are permitted into the presence of the "great one" and share the sort of intimacy that we desire, but usually cannot hope to have. We see the private life of the creative artist and it reifies our view of his or her greatness. Or, conversely, it reveals the hidden flaws, the feet of clay or goat's feet, enabling us to dismiss the hidden figure behind the book as merely mortal like ourselves.

Having this caveat means that we can begin to seek patterns in the reporting of conversations and the structures which are used by the reporter. We can also call on these accounts in documenting the growth and shaping of a reputation, of our understanding of the dynamic interactions which resulted in our present image of the writer, and in Nietzsche's case, his oeuvre. For Nietzsche is a case study in the power which reports of conversation have to subtly shape our understanding of the man and his work, both altering his image and reflecting the mythbuilding which surrounded the growth of his reputation. This mythbuilding and the resulting attempt to undo it was a conscious and planned act, a rarity in the history of a writer's reception, initially orchestrated by Nietzsche's sister, Elisabeth Förster-Nietzsche, within a specific historical and ideological context, and then expanded by her allies and opposed by her enemies. All of the conversations with Nietzsche reflect this conflicted ideological embeddedness, as indeed they must, but they also reflect an ongoing debate about the use to which Nietzsche and his works were to be put with the rise of the philosopher's reputation and its manipulation during the closing decade of the nineteenth century and the opening third of the twentieth century.

The conversations with Nietzsche reflect a wide range of reporters. Their reflections begin to be recorded only at the point, in the 1890's, when Nietzsche's name literally had become a household word, similar to Freud's or Einstein's in the later twentieth century.[3] They are, by definition, retrospective (except for the accounts of the decade of his illness), unlike Eckermann's daily recording of his conversations with Goethe; and, as such, are both less reliable and more interestingly creative. Some of the reporters knew Nietzsche intimately (such as his sister), while others merely visited the ill philosopher in his home in Weimar, a home which his sister selected so that her brother would, in death, share the glory of the reputation

---

3. On the power of Nietzsche's reputation at the turn of the century, see Sander L. Gilman, "The Nietzsche Murder Case; or, What Makes Dangerous Philosophies Dangerous," in Sander L. Gilman, *Difference and Pathology: Stereotypes of Sexuality, Race, and Madness* (Ithaca, New York: Cornell University Press, 1985), pp. 39–58.

of that seat of the muses, the home of Goethe. Taken all together they give us a sense of the power which the reputation of the philosopher had, and, perhaps, some sense of the residual power which the man himself must have had on those about him.

Some of these reports are "true," i.e., they describe actual events; some are "false," i.e., the events most probably never happened. But most of these reports, the stuff out of which contemporary biographies of Nietzsche have to a great degree been crafted, are neither true or false.[4] They give a single perspective on an event, they report a half-remembered conversation filtered through the growing international reputation of the philosopher/writer. They all, however, capture the image of Nietzsche which speaks to the ideological presuppositions of the author of the memories. They are the realities of mythmaking and must be understood as such. The image they give us of the philosopher is complex. Some of the complexity stems from the author of the memoir, some of it from Nietzsche's own protean self. The ideological bias can be judged from some of the radical positions taken as the writer's reputation was beginning to grow at the turn of the twentieth century.

Friedrich Nietzsche was one of the masters of modern autobiographical self-analysis.[5] Strongly conscious of his own strengths and weaknesses, he submitted the course of his life to constant scrutiny. After his collapse in 1889 this critical distance was surrendered and his life quickly became the object of hagiography. Responsible for this radical change in Nietzsche's image and in public opinion was his sister, Elisabeth Förster-Nietzsche, who soon after her return from Paraguay in 1893 began to establish the legend of Nietzsche as the noble prophet of his time. She worked at this image all her life and defended it stubbornly. The main document of this myth-building was her three-volume biography of her brother. Published in 1895, 1897, and 1904, of all of the memoirs about Nietzsche it contains the greatest number of memories of him.

4. Especially the biographies of Curt Paul Janz, *Friedrich Nietzsche*, 3 vols. (Munich: Carl Hanser, 1978–1979), and Ronald Hayman, *Nietzsche: A Critical Life* (Oxford: Oxford University Press, 1980).

5. See the extraordinary reading of Nietzsche's autobiographical fictions in Alexander Nehamas, *Nietzsche: Life as Literature* (Cambridge, MA: Harvard University Press, 1985). An earlier study of this problem, which reflects on the question of Nietzsche's response to the world of words in which he lived, is Sander L. Gilman, *Nietzschean Parody: An Introduction to Reading Nietzsche* (Bonn: Bouvier, 1976).

The biography was revised in 1913, and the correspondence and extensive quotations from Nietzsche's *Ecce homo* (meanwhile published) removed. The biography was only the peak of a lifelong series of publications devoted to her brother. But this material, whether it be her own memories or her sketches of conversations with people who knew her brother, must be considered suspect. Like all other memories of Nietzsche, his sister's biographical writings represent a specific underlying image, which was created and supported by these very reminiscences. Those among Nietzsche's friends and acquaintances who shared her image of her brother tended to support her work.

The following unpublished letters from acquaintances of Nietzsche to Elisabeth Förster-Nietzsche are a direct echo of the volumes of the biography. Max Heinze, one of Nietzsche's teachers in Schulpforta and Rudolf Eucken's successor as the chair of the philosophy department at the University of Basel, wrote to her in August 1895 after the publication of the first volume:

> "Ungrateful" is probably the word that often came to your mind about me recently in your private thoughts or even in conversations with others, and I cannot deny that you have every right to label me so. But I do not wish to be slow to apologize, since I know—or at least I hope very much—that you will forgive me in the end. From Pentecost until just a week ago I was loaded down with work, and more recently I had hoped to come to Naumburg to express my thanks to you personally. But no opportunity arose, nor probably will any prior to my departure for the South, so I must thank you merely in writing for Volume I of *The Life of Friedrich Nietzsche*. I have read most of the book, and though formerly I was of the opinion that some time should have been allowed to elapse before publication of a biography, I have now changed my mind, since this biography has contributed essentially to knowledge of your brother's early development and hence to an understanding of his later life and achievements. You have earned the thanks of all who honor Friedrich Nietzsche and at the same time you have erected a splendid memorial to yourself as his sister. Writing this book gave you a good deal of joy, though mixed with sadness, may it continue to provide you satisfaction now that it has been published.[6]

6. All unpublished material was found in the former Nietzsche Archive in Weimar, GDR, now located in the Goethe-Schiller Archive, NFG, Weimar.

Nine years later, after the publication of the last volume, he wrote to her:

> After a two-week stay in the green woods, which we enjoyed very much, we are about to return to Leipzig today—until yesterday we had still hoped you might delight us with a visit. Now we can give up the idea completely. Nor had you held out much hope of it in Weimar, and after reading the galley-proofs of your book I can see why you have almost no other thought on your mind than to finish the book. Soon it will have reached that point, and with all my heart I wish you success in finishing this tremendous work. As far as I can judge, the work will bring you many deep-felt thanks. You cast an excellent and bright light on your brother's later development with your mastery of the vast and scattered materials and I appreciate especially Chapter 24, in which you give us a complete explanation of your brother's fundamental ideas and his eventual reconciliation. The intentions he had in writing his great works are now much better understood and evaluated. And what a great deal of new material has come to light! I always said, my dearest friend, that you understood your brother best, and so were most suited to enable others to understand him too, and I understand only too well that one section can still use a few more revisions—as it stands now, some questions remain unanswered. I would have liked to discuss some points with you in person, now perhaps later! I will take note of my concerns! Many thanks for letting me have the galley-proofs, I am sending them back by special delivery.

Wilhelm Pinder, Nietzsche's childhood friend, wrote a long letter to Elisabeth Förster-Nietzsche in July 1895, praising Volume I of her biography:

> Do not be angry with me for sending you my reactions to *The Life of Friedrich Nietzsche* only now. Just as on page 141 of the biography "our friend P." is mentioned as having "trumped up school duties" as an excuse for his apathy as a member of the Germania fraternity, so the aforementioned P. now must bring up business duties as an excuse to obtain your forgiveness for his procrastination in responding to the biography. I have truly been under considerable business pressure until just yesterday evening, when my four-week vacation began. Under such circumstances I must ask you to allow me to express only now my deepest and most heartfelt thanks for the precious gift of the biography which you sent. I have already read about a half of it and can assure you that its

content moves me most deeply and gives me a great deal of joy and happiness. The richest and most moving memories of my youth are linked with the person of my friend Fritz, whom I admired, honored and loved. And you have drawn the image of this friend of my youth, your beloved brother, down to the finest detail with incomparable loyalty, reverence and tenderness! An aura of poetry clings to this image. The portrayal of the youthful years of this great and mighty thinker, who later produced such profound movements through his creations, has an idyllic effect on the reader. But that does not mark the full parameters of the effect produced by the portrayal. For you wrote what you have written with your life's blood, and so the effect of the biography extends far beyond the confines of an idyll.

I will use the leisure of my vacation to finish reading the book and I hope that when I come and visit you briefly in Naumburg in a few weeks, as I intend to do, that I will be able to express my gratitude in person.

Reinhardt von Seydlitz, art critic and author, who had met Nietzsche in 1876, first wrote in 1895:

> Once again it is my liveliest desire not to know at all what you must think of me. For after you had heaped us with precious gifts, my silence must have seemed rather shabby, and your judgment of this silence must be no different than Isolde's: "Can I 'grasp' what you keep silent?"
>
> My laziness is incomprehensible, and only my own indolence can grasp it.
>
> I am very glad to hear that some of the letters from your dear and unique brother will be useful for the second volume of the biography. With the first volume you have erected a heroic monument to himself and yourself (excuse me for naming the great man before the great lady). Everything about this book is delightful, and it should delight everybody. As its creation surely must have had a liberating effect on you, so for the reader it is a copious source of pleasure. You succeeded completely—insofar as that is at all possible—in showing him to us in his developing years. You let him grow up, mature and blossom before our eyes, and the ability to do this is a divine talent. It is an admirable work, which suffers no loss from being written out of genuine most beautiful and purest love. The "reader" as such can thank you only by reading it. But how differently various people read. I can only assure you—*I have* read it! So, a thousand thanks!

Two years later, after Volume II appeared, he wrote to her:

"Of course! When you send people something, then they
finally write, otherwise not at all!" That is what you are thinking,
isn't it? But you are mistaken. One can send people even the nicest
things (especially books!) and they still fail to write. And yet . . .
but no, excuse my boorishness (for excusing myself is my peculiar
type of boorishness), and accept right away my huge sack of gratitude which I've been filling and stuffing ever since the arrival of
the second volume.

Of course I was particularly moved in this volume by learning
how the time when I first met him really was (as seen by him, your
brother). For I met him in the eerie torch-smoke of the Bayreuth
Corybant festival, and under that illumination he seemed to
belong there, "howling with the wolves." Only for that reason, and
of course because the gigantic strides from summit to summit are
so much more difficult for us lesser persons, did our friendship
undergo a brief interruption, which he then ended so beautifully
with his royal initiative of 1885. He was always a king among us,
or rather above us. How he understood the royal art of affability
(to mention just one!).

Now I am thinking primarily of my offenses against him. I have
not yet written my "Nietzsche article." (Incidentally, how he
would laugh at this journalistic expression!) And this sin of omis-
sion seems to turn out to my benefit—everything good is promptly
punished here below, so why should sin not be rightfully
rewarded? For now I will wait until your second half-volume goes
to press, in order not to quote passages from his letters which you
already present; I think it would be better so.

Otherwise, if you wish me to begin *soon*, I need only strike the
rock and a rich stream will pour forth freely. "I sparkle like a
dragon with wit and malice," he once wrote to me from Turin, and
I believe that I too would in turn sparkle right away—not with
malice, for that is the right of kings—as soon as I set pen to paper
in writing this "article," though the sparks might be merely small,
and I feel like Wolf Goethe (the great man's grandson), who once
said: "Yes, my grandfather was indeed a Hun [an imposing figure],
but I am just a hen."

It has been a very long time since your last letter, i.e. since I
failed to answer it. Nothing has changed here since then, except
that I could perhaps mention that Maximilian Street, where you
scraped your knee so painfully then, has now been paved over with
asphalt, so that in the future you will be spared such a fall. But
much has changed with you, as we notice. You are in Weimar! And

where do you have the Archive? And how is your dear mother? I will not ask how *he* is, and will silently wait for you to have some news for us.

(Seydlitz's memories, including those that introduce his correspondence with Nietzsche, are included in the present book.)

Andreas Heusler, Nietzsche's colleague in Basel, wrote to Nietzsche's sister in December, 1896:

> In sending me the first half-volume of Volume II of the life of your dear brother, you have given me a great though melancholy pleasure, and I thank you sincerely with all my heart for it. I was immediately fascinated by the book and I read it from cover to cover in flying haste yesterday and today, only to begin it again from the beginning and reread more carefully at least the main parts, as my free time permits. What interested me most during this rapid reading was more detailed information about his rift with Wagner; for the ideas presented on pages 262–264 from the year 1876 agree astonishingly with objections which your brother himself used to raise even during the time of his greatest enthusiasm for W[agner] (the time of the idyllic days in Tribschen), of course not in as sublime and convincing a manner as they appear in these pronouncements, otherwise he would perhaps have agreed more with me at the time.
>
> Incidentally, I admire your mastery in describing your dear brother's development. You have thereby given him a beautiful and worthy monument.

The last of these letters, dated February 11, 1897, comes from the widow of Nietzsche's teacher F. W. Ritschl, who had known Nietzsche since December 4, 1865:

> When I thanked you several weeks ago for your friendly parcel, dear and respected lady, the book had just arrived and I had read only the preface. Now that I have read the book itself, I feel an urge to thank you again and to express the deep sympathy, the intellectual interest and stirring emotion with which I followed this highly tragic course of life. What a hero full of spiritual power, what a child full of love and imagination your genial brother was! How he struggled with unbroken energy against his cruel disease, always driven restlessly by the feeling of a sublime mission in life! I do not know what false descriptions of his character have been made—but if they resemble Schure's, then your loving, detailed book will dispel this fog for every unprejudiced reader and bring to view his character in its full greatness, boldness, and truthful-

ness. He shines like polished steel. Dear lady, I simply had to write these few words to let you know that you sent your valuable gift to a woman who understands it, who has thought of your brother and "his beloved sister" with unchanging, warm affection, even when he broke with us.

This entire correspondence reflects a general agreement with the heroic image of Nietzsche, as it was later presented in the Nietzsche literature known as the "Weimar school," those unquestioningly positive writings produced by the Nietzsche Archive under the leadership of Elisabeth Förster-Nietzsche.

How cautious one must be with the works of this group is documented in Elisabeth Förster-Nietzsche's two attacks on other authors of accounts of Nietzsche. Both in her "Nietzsche Legends" and in her "Memories," she attacks reminiscences of her brother which run counter to her own.[7] Her own memory is, however, often tendentious, for in fact memories are easier to forge than letters. But even her scholarly accuracy is highly questionable. One example should suffice. In her last book on her brother, *Friedrich Nietzsche and the Women of his Time,* a work intended as an answer to those who wanted to brand Nietzsche as the arch-misogynist, she quotes from an interview with Helen Zimmern, the translator of Schopenhauer into English, whom Nietzsche had met in Sils-Maria, as if she had read this interview personally in the London *Observer.*[8] No such interview was ever published in the *Observer.* What she actually read was a newspaper article in the *Frankfurter Generalanzeiger,* dated November 16, 1926, which claimed to be reporting about an interview published in the *Observer.* Similar inaccuracies are found throughout her works. Her unreliableness as a biographical source is evident. This unscientific tendency, however, fits well with her successful attempt to manipulate the Nietzsche legend during her lifetime (and even afterwards).

The hagiographers of the "Weimar" group found their counterpart in Basel, where a group under the leadership of Carl Albrecht Bernoulli presented a very critical version of Nietzsche's

---

7. Both in *Zukunft,* January 28, 1905 and October 12, 1907. Passages about Salomé in the biography ought of course to be read also in the light of Lou Andreas-Salomé's monograph on Friedrich Nietzsche.

8. (Munich: C. H. Beck, 1935), p. 142. On the question of Nietzsche's image of women, see R. Hinton Thomas, "Nietzsche, Women and the Whip," *German Life and Letters: Special Number for L. W. Forester* 34 (1980), 117–25. On Elisabeth Förster-Nietzsche and her falsifications see H. F. Peters, *Zarathustra's Sister: The Case of Elisabeth and Friedrich Nietzsche* (New York: Crown, 1977).

life. Central figures of this group were Nietzsche's Basel colleague, the theology professor Franz Overbeck, and his wife Ida. Overbeck had been depicted as a "villain" by Elisabeth Förster-Nietzsche. She accused him of having failed to recognize her brother's greatness since he had recommended that some of Nietzsche's papers be destroyed. He was also accused of having ignored the medicine bottles on Nietzsche's night table in Turin. Nietzsche's sister regarded these self-prescribed medicaments as the cause of her brother's collapse. She wanted to use this myth to counter the accusation that Nietzsche's mental illness was either hereditary or of syphilitic origin. Overbeck became fully aware of the Weimar camp's enmity against him when Elisabeth finally published an extract from the third volume of her biography under the title "Friedrich Nietzsche and his Acquaintances" in *Zeitgeist,* an insert in the *Berliner Tageblatt* (October 3, 1904), in which numerous critical remarks against Overbeck could be found. In January 1905, Overbeck wrote to Bernoulli:

> What I believe is that I cannot and do not want to ignore the fact that I no longer have the choice to limit the consequences of this action to the Förster woman's explanations. Even Nietzsche will not remain untouched by the effects of my former indiscretion. For anyone who compares the biography and his letters to me conscientiously and with sharp eyes, a dubious light will inevitably fall also on the unreliability and ambiguity, indeed almost the "lack of will-power" in his behavior toward his sister, and the damage, especially of the position which he occupied between his sister and me (and secondarily also my wife). This will result especially from what my letters will reveal about the "Lou affair," but also from other things. I know this, and by admitting this knowledge, I do not mean to say that I feel sure of my statement in view of the coercion placed on me for my actions by the existence and character of the Förster woman. Unless I meet alone with this hateful person, who moreover is not solely responsible in my eyes, I must resign myself to this totally unintended consequence of my actions; but I still find her obnoxious. And that you had so little understanding for this feeling from the first is what I have to complain about today.[9]

9. Published unabridged in *Zusammenstellung der klägerischen Schriftstücke erster Instanz des grundlegenden Overbeckbriefes vom 3.4. Januar 1905 und der beiden Urteile erster und zweiter Instanz in Klagsachen des Herrn Peter Gast (Heinrich Köselitz) in Weimar gegen Herrn Schriftsteller Albrecht Bernoulli in Arlesheim bei Basel und Herrn Verlagsbuchhändler Eugen Diederichs in Jena wegen Untersagung von Veröffentlichungen. Gedruckt zur Erleichterung der Stoffübersicht für den Privatgebrauch.* (Weimar: R. Wagner, 1908), pp. 67–68.

Overbeck's defensiveness is revealed here. His memories of Nietzsche were published in this defensive, critical mood. After Overbeck's death, Bernoulli published these memories as part of a comprehensive two-volume study on the relations between Overbeck and Nietzsche. After the appearance of the first volume, Peter Gast, Nietzsche's amanuensis who after the turn of the century had again allied himself with the Weimar camp, sought a court injunction against publication of the entire book or the removal of at least the passages which dealt with his correspondence with Overbeck.[10] The court's decision was reached in favor of Peter Gast in the spring of 1908, and long passages of Volume II of Bernoulli's study fell victim to censorship. These passages cast a bad light both on Gast and on Nietzsche's family, while Overbeck was presented extremely favorably. The "Basel group" simply had other prejudices than the "Weimar school"; it too aimed to present a specific image of Nietzsche, one that was far less positive than the one in his sister's hagiographical works, and which implied that Nietzsche's final insanity permeated his entire philosophy.

Other memories of Nietzsche, though not officially of either school, also reflected some type of personal bias. Lou Andreas-Salomé's posthumously published memoirs, Resa von Schirnhofer's sketches, the reports on Wagner's and Burckhardt's criticisms of Nietzsche, all were written down long after the events they describe. The time interval between the events and their written record is in many cases more than fifty years. They were written under the impact of the growing reception of Nietzsche in Europe and must be read in terms of their position in the creation of the various "Nietzsche legends."

Accounts of Nietzsche begin with contemporary depictions of visits with the mentally ill philosopher in the 1890's, when his reputation had begun to spread throughout Europe. Gabriele Reuter's report on her visit with the sick philosopher is perhaps the best known one because of the use Thomas Mann made of it in his novel *Dr. Faustus* (1947), a work redolent with references to Nietzsche's life; but there are many other reports about such visits in the last decade of Nietzsche's life.[11] In addition to his sister's biographical

---

10. A detailed biographical study of "Peter Gast" is available in Frederick R. Love, *Nietzsche's Saint Peter*, Monographien und Texte zur Nietzsche-Forschungen, 5 (Berlin: De Gruyter, 1981).

11. Helmut Kreuzer, "Thomas Mann und Gabriele Reuter: Zu einer Entlehnung für den *Doktor Faustus*," in *Neue Deutsche Hefte 10* (1963), 103–119.

works, the total number of reminiscences of Nietzsche grew continually until the 1930's, especially in the popular press.

While gathering materials for her biography, Elisabeth Förster-
Nietzsche, and later also other collaborators at the Nietzsche
Archive (for example, Richard and Max Oehler, Karl Schlechta),
began to interview or to correspond with many people who knew
Nietzsche. Some of this original material is not accessible (or never
existed in written form) and is therefore taken from the printed
sources. In one case (that of Jakob Wackernagel) two unpublished
memoirs were written down with a thirty-year interval between the
two versions. Other accounts existed apparently until 1945 in written form, but have since been lost. Others were published only in
part until now. This and other unpublished material is presented
here in unrevised form for the first time.

Of some interest, besides, are numerous sources which might
include accounts of meetings with Nietzsche, but fail to do so. Thus,
among others, autobiographical writings of Rudolf Eucken, Gabriel
Monod, Carl Spitteler, Richard Voss, and Ulrich Wilamowitz-Moellendorf do not describe actual meetings with Nietzsche.[12] Eucken,
who wrote an essay about his memories of Nietzsche, mentions him
only fleetingly in his autobiography. Monod's main interest is to
explain Nietzsche's conflict with Wagner. Voss's only remark is that
he avoided visiting the sick Nietzsche.

Many essays with promising titles fall far short of the expectations they raise. S. Zuckermann's article entitled "A Visit to the
Home of Friedrich Nietzsche," in the *Berliner Herold* of December
8, 1897, closes with the paragraph:

> It would of course be of great interest to see the genial man
> even in his helpless state, but such a wish was granted to no one,
> not even to Nietzsche's friends. And if nonetheless such articles
> about personal visits with Nietzsche appear in the newspapers,
> these communications are based, as Frau Förster-Nietzsche
> expressly states, on untruth and stem merely from the fantasies of
> some newsreporter or other. It has been a rule for a long time that
> besides his sister, the nurse Alwine, and at times a servant, no one
> has access to Fr. Nietzsche, since he is able to recognize only his
> sister and the nurse.

12. Rudolf Eucken, *Lebenserinnerungen: Ein Stück deutschen Lebens* (Leipzig: K. F. Koehler,
1921); Gabriel Monod, *Portraits et souvenirs* (Paris: C. Lévy, 1897); Carl Spitteler, "Meine
Beziehungen zu Nietzsche" (1908) in his *Gesammelten Werke* 6 (Zurich: Artemis, 1947);
Richard Voss, *Aus einem phantastischen Leben. Erinnerungen* (Stuttgart: J. Engelhorn,
1920); Ulrich von Wilamowitz-Moellendorf, *Erinnerungen* (1848–1914) (Leipzig: K. F.
Koehler, [1929]).

This statement is an effort to stem the rumors of Elisabeth Förster-Nietzsche's exploitation of her sick brother.[13] Yet such visits continued to take place, as the compendious memoir-literature of that time shows.

The selection of material is taken from the much more extensive *Begegnungen mit Nietzsche* (Bonn: Bouvier, 1981; 2d, rev. edition, 1985), edited by Sander L. Gilman. For the present volume a representative sample of the material has been selected for the English reader. This material supplements (or served as the "source" of) much of what is known about Nietzsche's life. Thus the footnotes to the selections reflect the observations of the original authors of the accounts.

No attempt has been made to clarify contradictions between the various views of specific incidents, as no single view is most probably "correct." *Conversations with Nietzsche* presents (as did its German source) a "new" Nietzsche in that the contradictions in the perceptions of those who knew him are made manifest. Thus the volume can serve as a biography in contradictions of this most contradictory of thinkers.

The material for the original volume was only marginally accessible through existing bibliographies.[14] Much effort and many hours were spent reading European newspapers and journals dating from 1880 to 1980 for any firsthand account of a conversation with Nietzsche. Our thanks for assistance in this go to Ingeborg Reichenbach. The English manuscript was sensitively edited by Susan Meigs, who also has our thanks.

---

13. Similar to Zuckermann's is an essay by Robert de Montesquieu, "Pèlerinage passionné," *Le Gaulois,* October 15–16, 1904.

14. Helpful in locating about one-fifth of the accounts contained in *Begegnungen mit Nietzsche* were the following bibliographies: *International Nietzsche Bibliography,* Herbert W. Reichert and Karl Schlechta, eds., University of North Carolina Studies in Comparative Literature, 45 (Chapel Hill: University of North Carolina Press, 1968), and Richard Frank Krummel, *Nietzsche und der deutsche Geist,* Monographien und Texte zur Nietzsche-Forschung, 3 (Berlin: De Gruyter, 1974). Following the publication of the first edition of the *Begegnungen mit Nietzsche,* Krummel published a second volume of his excellent source study, *Nietzsche und der deutsche Geist,* Band II, Monographien und Texte zur Nietzsche-Forschungen, 9 (Berlin: De Gruyter, 1983), which covers the period from 1901 to 1918. This volume drew heavily on the sources in the first edition of the *Begegnungen.* The German editions of the conversations with Nietzsche (and, therefore, this present selection) contained only memoirs which gave accounts of conversations with Nietzsche. Letters and diary extracts were not included since they will appear in the new critical edition of Nietzsche's work begun by the late Giorgio Colli and the late Mazzino Montinari.

CONVERSATIONS WITH NIETZSCHE

CHILDHOOD
AND SCHOOL DAYS
(1844–1858)

1   Elisabeth Förster-Nietzsche   *1847*

My brother reportedly learned to speak only late, at the age of two and a half, so that our parents were beginning to worry and consulted a physician. This man, a jovial type, gave the following diagnosis: "Little Fritz is being served too solicitously and attentively; all his wishes are being fulfilled without delay, so why should he bother to speak!" Thereafter serious efforts were made, and since little Fritz had always looked at a pastel portrait of Grandma Nietzsche with special delight, he was insistently asked who that was. "Granma," he shouted happily, and that was his first word. In a short time then he was speaking very fluently and clearly. By the age of four he began to read and write. (*13*, 27)

2   Elisabeth Förster-Nietzsche   *1850*

So (after father's death) at daybreak we tearfully left our birthplace, Röcken, which remained all our life the "dear homeland of our loved ones." For us the quiet cemetery with the graves of our father and our little brother was the "quiet isle of graves" to which we bore the evergreen wreath of happy and painful memories. Our family

3

plot in Röcken's cemetery is directly adjacent to the ancient church, one of the oldest in the province of Saxony. The church wall, covered with roses and wild grapevines, forms the back wall of the cemetery. A few paces away is the old schoolhouse where five-year-old Fritz went to school after father's death. Once when my brother and I visited Röcken as adults, the little village children, clattering along in their wooden shoes, happened to be going to afternoon classes. My brother watched all the little blond heads with deep emotion, for he had once sat among them. Of course, now it was children of another generation who were running so eagerly to school, but they still sat on the same uncomfortable old schoolbenches which had already been there in my brother's earliest childhood days.

My brother once stated heart-movingly what he later felt on recurrent visits to our old home: "The sight of our childhood surroundings touches us: the summer house, the church with its graves, the pond and the woods—we always see these again with a painful feeling. Self-pity takes hold of us, for what a great many things we have suffered since then! And here everything still stands, so silent, so eternal." (*17*, 22–23)

3 Elisabeth Förster-Nietzsche *1854*

Here the oldest of these youthful friends, Wilhelm P[inder], who like my brother wrote a biography in his fourteenth year, will now take up the pen to describe in childlike detail their first meeting and our Fritz himself as he then seemed to his friends:

> I must first mention one of the most important events in my life. For by chance I had met in my grandmother's garden a boy who has been my dearest and truest friend ever since and will certainly continue to be so. This boy, Friedrich Nietzsche by name, has since then had a very important and very good influence on my whole life, on all my occupations and my opinions. I want to add here a brief description of his life, since he will be mentioned very often in the course of my sketch and will occupy a very prominent place from now on.

He then recounts the main events in our life, which we have already mentioned, and later returns once again to give a detailed description of my brother:

> He had, as I have already said, had many sad experiences in his life, having at an early age lost his father, whom he loved very

much and of whom he always spoke with great reverence, as well as his little brother Joseph, who had died as a little child shortly after his father's death; and so his basic trait of character was a certain melancholy, which expressed itself in his whole being. From earliest childhood he loved solitude, in which he gave free play to his thoughts, to some extent avoiding human company and seeking out regions endowed by nature with sublime beauty. He had a very pious, tender temperament and even as a child reflected upon matters with which other boys his age do not concern themselves. So his mind developed very early. As a little boy he played various games of his own invention, and this showed that he had a very lively, inventive and independent mind. So he also was the leader in all our games, introducing new methods and making the games more fun and more varied; he was in absolutely every respect a highly talented lad. Moreover he had a very praiseworthy and steady industriousness and served as a model for me in this as in all other things. Very many inclinations were aroused and fostered by him alone; this was especially the case in music and literature. I will have to come back to these two things later.

As already mentioned, he always had a great influence on me and became absolutely indispensable to me. From earliest youth he prepared for the profession he wanted to practice later, namely the office of preacher. He always had a very serious, and yet friendly and gentle nature, and has to this day been a very faithful and loving friend, which I will never forget and which cannot be valued highly enough. He never acted without reflection, and when he did something, he always had a particular, well-grounded reason. This was manifested especially in the works which we wrote together, and when he wrote something down and I could not immediately agree with him, he always managed to explain it to me clearly and intelligibly. Besides this, some of his main virtues were humility and gratitude, which were revealed most markedly on every occasion. This humility often resulted in a certain shyness, and he did not feel comfortable at all, especially among strangers, a characteristic which I fully share with him.

From earliest childhood Fritz had an extraordinary interest in music and literature. How he first was moved by music is told by his friend Wilhelm in his biography of his youth:

This was the time (Spring 1854) when my friends and I began to turn to more serious occupations. It was especially my friend F. Nietzsche who first prompted this. For he had heard a musical presentation in church and this had so moved him that he decided to take up music and to practice it ardently. Through industriousness and great talent he, indeed, soon became very proficient at playing the piano.

My brother himself tells in even more detail of this experience which moved him so deeply:

> On Ascension Day I had gone to the city church and was hearing the sublime Hallelujah from the *Messiah.* I felt like I had to chime in, it seemed to me like the jubilant song of the angels amid whose loud chorus Jesus Christ ascends toward heaven. I immediately resolved to compose something similar. Right after church I set to work and felt childish joy at each new chord I struck. I gained a great deal by persisting at this over the years, for I learned to read music better by mastering the tone-structure.

At any rate his friend Gustav's father, the privy councillor K.[A. Krug], unwittingly had a significant influence on my brother's musical development. (*13,* 31–33, 71)

4   Elisabeth Förster-Nietzsche   *1857–1858*

As that story was being told, a little childhood experience from the winter of 1857–58 came to my mind. My brother loved to ice-skate . . .

Of course, his enthusiasm spread to me, and I wanted nothing more ardently than to learn this beautiful art, which at last I was allowed to do. A few fifth- and sixth-year students were always present at these attempts, and with fatherly condescension they offered to teach me this skill. Once, in the aforementioned winter, we had been skating very energetically, all of us, Fritz and I and a few upperclass students, and were catching our breath a little at one end of the skating rink, when we saw a few younger students teasing a little misshapen, ugly boy. He defended himself with sharp words and blows; but finally their attacks became too rough as they tried to pile a huge heap of snow on the little hunchback, so that he fell over helplessly, whereupon most of the boys burst out in loud laughter, since it must have seemed very comical. I was a passionate child, I stamped my foot and called, "That is too mean!" and broke out in tears. "What's wrong with your sister?" one of the fifth-year students somewhat dejectedly asked my brother, who had hurried to help the little deformed boy. Fritz blushed at this question and then began in his soft voice to explain to the bigger students how wrong it is to make fun of a poor misshapen, helpless boy so modestly and respectfully that they all lowered their eyes in shame. For a moment there was total silence, then the oldest and most sensible fifth-year student cried, "Little Nietzsche is right! Shame on you, you little rascals," he said to the younger schoolboys, "I tell you that whoever lays a hand on the hunchback from now on will get a beating!" After these strong words, the little mistreated boy went home proudly.

Then the fifth-year student took Fritz and me by the hand, skated away with us, and said, "You are good children!" He became so attached to us that every day while ice-skating he brought us some candies, which unfortunately he proffered in a sack of dubious cleanliness, pulled out of a pants pocket where it had been in close proximity to a much-used varicolored handkerchief, so that it cost us two meticulously clean children the greatest self-mastery to accept these favors with the gratitude they deserved. (*13*, 79–80)

SCHULPFORTA
(1858–1864)

5   Elisabeth Förster-Nietzsche   *1858–1864*

I believe my brother was often judged falsely by teachers, although they acted very friendly toward him. I was once told that they had suspected him of having a mocking opinion of them—but nothing was further from his mind. He had the liveliest admiration for their scientific research, he esteemed the stringent truthfulness of their method most highly, and he spoke only with the greatest respect of them, especially of Corssen, Steinhardt, Keil, Koberstein, and Peter. He never made disparaging remarks even about their weaknesses, great or small, but disregarded them; he evidently found it unpleasant to speak about that subject. His respectful heart was practically revulsed by crude jokes to that effect.

In general, my brother was inclined to overestimate rather than to underestimate other people; this trait was shown especially in relation to his fellow students. When I think of the admiration with which he spoke of the talent of a great number of them, I even today ask myself with astonishment: What may well have become of these outstanding young people? I know that at that time I felt that a new world-order would have to begin with them. I recall very clearly an often recurring remark of my brother's: "If I had as much talent as this or that person, what I wouldn't do with it!" (*13*, 171)

6   Raimund Granier   *1858–1864*

Nietzsche and I were friends as pupils in Schulpforta in our youth so long ago. In the scantily allotted free periods when we could stroll around outdoors within the former monastery walls, we discussed many topics, and I believe I recognized some of them again later in his writings. Our relationship lasted until we both graduated in the fall of 1864. In 1865 we still exchanged letters, which unfortunately I have lost. Then we lost sight of each other, as so often happens. Only when the sun of his fame rose, did he reenter my field of view in unsuspected splendor, while I never showed up again for him.

In Schulpforta, Nietzsche was an excellent student, as is well known; but if I remember rightly mathematics was not his strong point. He did not stand out especially among his fellow students, but he immersed himself in his school assignments, especially ancient languages, and in his own particular studies. He did not play a leading role among those who showed intellectual agility; two others, who died long before Nietzsche, played this role. He did not join in the noisy games in the schoolyard, but as a fifth-year student, like we others, he liked to go to the nearby village Altenburg (called Almerich), where he drank not beer but, with great enjoyment, hot chocolate. Already at school he was extremely myopic, and his deep-set eyes had a peculiar gleam. His voice could be very deep; generally it was as soft as his whole being. No one would then have suspected that someday he would attempt the revaluation of all values. His mustache, which later became so extraordinarily prominent, already began to appear in school. But there is still no sign of it in the portrait I am showing you. He was eighteen years old when this photograph was made and we were in the upper fifth term. Nietzsche practiced music zealously already in Pforta and, since I can't play any instrument, he played for me, many a time—a lot of Chopin, if I remember rightly.

I spoke above of a needed apology: I mean by this that I hope not to appear irreverent in permitting publication [of his letters]. I am doing so only because it may perhaps contribute to an understanding of Nietzsche's nature; for one sees from the letters how early he rejected all authority, particularly in giving up the Christian religion, and one sees that even at that time he was filled with a deep pessimism which led him to self-irony.

Not to give the impression of trying to boast of my acquaint-anceship with Nietzsche, I ask expressly that my name not be mentioned. I remark only that the salutation in the letter contains a joking translation of my name which was occasionally used by my fellow students. Nietzsche, as is well known, believed he belonged to old Polish nobility. Thus he signed the letter, as can be seen, half jokingly, half seriously: "Frd. v. Nietzky." (*24*)

7   Paul Deussen   *1859–1864*

Nietzsche had entered Schulpforta as a boarder in 1858, and here I met him in the same class and section in our sophomore year in the fall of 1859. During an intermission, Nietzsche as class-leader at the time was assigned to walk back and forth and prevent us others from getting up from our seats and making too much noise or talking too much. I was sitting quietly in my place, peacefully chewing at my breakfast, a delicious roll. I can still see Nietzsche roaming through the aisles with the uncertain look of a very myopic person, trying in vain to find some occasion to take action. Just then he passed where I was sitting, bent down to me, and said, "Don't talk so loud to your roll!" Those were the first words he ever spoke to me. I no longer know what first brought us closer together. I believe it was our common love for Anacreon, whose poems we both were all the more enthusiastic about as third-year students, since their easy Greek put less difficulties in the way of understanding them. We recited his verses on walks together; we made a friendship pact by coming together in a solemn hour—it was in the dormitory where in my trunk under the bed I kept, among other secret belongings, a packet of snuff—and replacing the polite "Sie," which was customary in Pforta even between the students, by the familiar "du," which was reserved only for closer friends, so that instead of drinking "brotherhood" we "snuffed" it. Our confirmation together on Laetare Sunday of the year 1861 set a new bond between us. As the confirmants walked to the altar in pairs to receive the consecration on their knees, Nietzsche and I, as closest friends, knelt side by side. I still remember very well the holy, ecstatic mood that filled us during the week before and after confirmation. We would have been quite ready to die immediately to be with Christ, and all our thoughts, feelings and actions were irradiated with a superterrestrial joy, which however as an artificially grown little plant could not last and, under the pressure of studying and living, very soon vanished just as quickly as it had come. But a certain devoutness still survived beyond the school-leaving examination. It was undermined unnoticeably by the excellent historico-critical method in which the older students were trained in Pforta, and which quite spontaneously was applied to the biblical field, for example when Steinhart in the Hebrew class at sixth-year level explained the Forty-fifth Psalm completely as a secular wedding song.

My closer friendship with Nietzsche lasted throughout the whole time in Schulpforta, though not without some temporary disturbances. As early as the fifth year a so-called "wild" clique was formed, in which there was smoking and drinking, and studiousness was frowned upon as dishonorable pushiness. We too were drawn into its net, and thereby closer to the others and further from one another. One example may show the strength of these prejudices. On Sunday afternoons we had a study period from two to three o'clock for those who did not want to attend the afternoon religious service. I happened to be reading in Livy about Hannibal crossing the Alps and was so fascinated by it that when the hour struck for recess and the others hurried outdoors, I continued reading for a while. Then Nietzsche came in to get me, caught me reading Livy and gave me a stern rebuke: "So that is what you are doing and those are the ways and means you use to outdo your comrades and put yourself in the teachers' good graces! Well, the others will probably tell it to you even more clearly!" Shamefacedly I admitted my wrongdoing and was weak enough to beg Nietzsche not to tell the others about the event, which he promised; and he kept his word. After that clique broke up, a sort of triumvirate emerged between Nietzsche, me, and a certain Meyer, who was handsome, likeable and witty, also an excellent cartoonist, but forever at odds with teachers and the school system. He had to leave school a year before graduation; Nietzsche and I accompanied him as far as the gate and returned sadly after he had vanished from sight on the country road to Kösen. I saw Meyer once more, some five years later, when he visited me from Neuwied, at my parents' house in Oberdreis, together with Hempel, who later died as a victim of the war. Rarely have I seen such a shattered human heart. He seemed to be broken by all sorts of adverse circumstances, physically and morally ill, at odds with God, the world, and himself. He had worked his way up to the post of a tax supernumerary and later disappeared completely from sight, and he probably is no longer alive. This Meyer was the third man in our alliance until his departure in 1862. Of course, I had to note with pain that what I sought and valued in Nietzsche was quite incompatible with what Meyer was trying to attract him to. This went so far that the two for a time tired of me and broke off with me for no particular cause. The social instrument for this in Pforta, where no one can avoid the other, is the practice of being "mad," a valuable and purposeful means, in its way. One states that one is "mad" at someone, i.e., one considers it a point of honor never and nowhere and under no conditions to speak a word with him. I called this practice valuable because it prevents worse things, e.g. fistfights and the like. So Nietzsche and Meyer were mad at me. This hard time lasted for six weeks, and I joyfully welcomed the first symptoms of a rapprochement from the other side. I was studying Italian at the time with Melzer, who has long since passed away, which study was possible only because we got up an hour earlier than the others, i.e., at five o'clock instead of six. This was, of course, often condemned and mocked as "pushiness." Meyer, if I am not mistaken, at that time wrote a satirical poem against me:

> In early morning at the first dawning,
> When everyone else soundly sleeps,
> Already the philistine is yawning
> As down from the dorm he creeps.

In Pforta "philistine" ("Spiesser," perhaps related to "Spiessburger") is an invective for those who culpably overstudy. At that time one evening shortly before eight o'clock I was sitting in the corridor near the schoolbell, watching the clock. Among the groups walking back and forth were Nietzsche and Meyer. Suddenly they stopped in front of me and asked: "Che ora è?" Surprised, I answered, "Otto ore, in tre minuti," and laughing the two walked on, mocking me for having said "minuti" although "minute" was of feminine gender. Naturally I sought revenge. On one of the following days Virgil was being explained in Steinhart's class. Nietzsche stood up and gave one of those bold conjectures which try to improve not only on tradition but on the author himself. Steinhart refuted Nietzsche's idea in a long Latin speech and finally asked whether anyone had anything to say on the subject, whereupon I got up and said:

> Nietzschius erravit, neque coniectura probanda est.
> (Nietzsche was wrong, and his conjecture is undemonstrable.)

Steinhart chuckled, and the class laughed at this improvised hex-
ameter. After this preliminary skirmish, the main battle was fought
out later one evening. The two parties met by chance with a few
neutral onlookers in one room. Offensive remarks were launched
by both sides, without being aimed directly at the opponent. Rather
one of the observers sitting quietly there became more and more
the middleman to whom both parties directed their complaints, as
if he were supposed to convey them to the opponent though the
latter heard them directly and replied immediately. "Tell
Nietzsche," etc.; "Tell Deussen," etc; "Tell Meyer," etc.—these
words introduced reproaches which each had to make against the
other. This dialogue became livelier and livelier until finally the fic-
tion that one was speaking through a middleman was dropped and
words were addressed directly to one's opponent, which broke the
spell of being "mad" at one another. There now followed a thor-
oughgoing discussion of grievances by both sides and the outcome
of this was a definitive reconciliation.

The Nietzsche was drawn away from me only once more, after Meyer's departure, by an aesthetic coterie, but its inner hollowness
could not alienate him from me permanently. He came back to me
all the more since he then still had a reserved, somewhat shy temperament and found little satisfaction in the activities of the crowd,
and therefore also was not well known to most of them. All they
knew about him was that he wrote excellent German essays and
beautiful poems, was extremely weak in mathematics, and could
improvise fantastically on the piano.

The two of us often withdrew to an empty auditorium, where I
read a poem aloud with pathos and Nietzsche accompanied the
reading, e.g. of Schiller's "The Bell," with the tones of the piano,
while he criticized me repeatedly for reading too loud. By such quiet
entertainments and daily walks alone together, we isolated ourselves
from our companions who, as I mentioned, did not know the quiet,
introverted lad very well and so all the more often misjudged him.
His indifference to the comrades' petty interests, his lack of esprit
de corps, were interpreted as a lack of character and I remember
how one day a certain M., on the "muse's walk" in the school garden, to the delight of the bystanders, indiscreetly made a scarecrow
which he cut out and produced from a photograph of Nietzsche.
Fortunately my friend never learned of it.

When I now contemplate the venerable pastors, teachers, doctors, officers, architects, etc., into which our comrades of that time

developed, and who find the real earnestness of life in caring for their profession and their family, I can understand that most of them even then lacked the sensitivity to understand a Nietzsche. But I find it hard to imagine what would have become of me without him. Esteem for, indeed perhaps overestimation of, everything great and beautiful and a corresponding contempt for everything that served just material interests were probably in my nature; but this glimmering spark was kindled by daily contact with Nietzsche into a flame of one-sided enthusiasm for everything ideal, which was never extinguished even after my ways parted from my friend's. At that time in Pforta, we understood one another perfectly. On our solitary walks all possible subjects of religion, philosophy, literature, the fine arts, and music were discussed; often our thoughts trailed off into obscurity, and when words then failed, we looked each other in the eye, and one said to the other, "I know what you mean." This expression became a familiar saying between us; we resolved to avoid it as trivial and had to laugh when occasionally it nonetheless slipped out. All great names of history, literature and music enlivened our conversation, and while I was more familiar with the ancients, Nietzsche had greater knowledge of German literature and history. As a rule some subject or other stood in the center of his interest and stimulated him to productive treatment, as for a time he toyed with the plan for a heroic poem about Hermanrich. It is remarkable that Nietzsche, who had such a fine and deep understanding of all literature, never was a good reciter. Therefore, as far as I can at all remember he was rarely or never asked to take part in our carnival plays. Our class played Körner's *Night Watchmen* at the 1862 carnival, *Wallenstein's Camp* in 1863, the craftsmen's scenes from *Midsummer Night's Dream* in 1864, but I cannot remember what role Nietzsche played. I do, however, remember that on the tricentennial anniversary of Shakespeare's birth on April 23, 1864, we gave a public reading of *Henry IV* with assigned roles under Koberstein's direction; Nietzsche had to read the role of the firebrand Percy, which he performed in a mellifluous and pleasant voice, but not without false pathos. No matter how often we practiced them together, Nietzsche was never able to read to my liking, especially the words "I'll keep all these," which Percy exclaims when suspected of handing over the prisoners. For Nietzsche's was essentially a deeply serious nature, and all playacting, whether in a blamable or a praiseworthy sense, was completely alien to him; I heard many clever remarks from him, but seldom a good joke. He also cared little for sports and knightly arts; he could not stand acrobatics, since from an early age he was inclined to corpulence and head congestions. If I modeled some acrobatic feat for him, then he too regularly did his only acrobatic trick, to which he jokingly attributed great importance. It consisted in pushing his body through legs-first between the two poles from one side of the bar and coming down on the other side. This simple trick, which a trained acrobat does in a moment, perhaps even without touching the poles, was hard work for Nietzsche, turning his face dark red, making him breathless and sweaty. His achievements were better in swimming. His extreme myopia stood in his way in all sports. He usually wore glasses even then, and once had his eyes examined while in Pforta. The doctor did not find their state to be critical, but called attention to the possibility that he might with advanced age become totally blind. Nietzsche had always disliked smoking, and did it only occasionally out of peevishness. He was also very moderate in drink, but for that very reason one isolated excess was all the more noticeable in its effects; Nietzsche had to pay for it with a temporary loss of his supervisory position and, if I remember right, through this event he lost forever his post as head of our class, which he had held for many years.

Meanwhile the date of our abitur-examination, St. Michael's Day 1864, had been approaching, and the common work and worry about passing it brought the two friends even closer together. For the last semester in the summer of 1864 we had the choice of either doing all the assignments of the fifth-year students or being exempted from them and instead writing a long, scholarly Latin essay on any subject. Naturally, we chose the latter. I investigated Herodotus' religious views and his influence on historiography; Nietzsche treated the literary composition of Theognis' poems, in which the words "good" and "bad" are synonymous with "aristocratic" and "plebeian," respectively. Everyone knows how much these impressions, which were the topic of our daily conversations, influenced Nietzsche's later moral views. (*10*, 3–11)

8   Otto Benndorf   *1862–1864*

Nietzsche received his early education in the age-old princely school in Pforta near Naumburg, called Schulpforta for short, the famous educational and instructional institution which produced Klopstock,

Fichte, Leopold von Ranke; indeed he began his first poetic and philosophical endeavors there. Without a doubt his stay in this "self-contained school-state, which absorbed the individual's life in every relation," had a decisive influence on the philosopher's whole further development. Nietzsche studied from 1858 to 1864 at the princely school, which always had a great number of famous and important teachers. Among the array of famous scholars whom young Nietzsche had as educators in Pforta was also Otto Benndorf, the present director of the Vienna Archeological Institute. On Nietzsche's diploma his name is signed simply "O. Benndorf." To our collaborator's question whether the identification of this signature with his name was correct, Privy Councillor Benndorf answered:

Yes, I was in Pforta and also Nietzsche's teacher. I was employed as a teacher at the princely school from Easter 1862 to 1864, and despite the many long years that have gone by since then, just about everything from that time is still engraved in my memory, and I remember Nietzsche very well, who was then an upperclassman. I came in contact with Nietzsche because I had set up a plaster museum of reproductions of ancient statues in Schulpforta and every Sunday after church I gave explanatory lectures on the reproduced artifacts, such as the statues of Dionysus and Apollo, the Laocoön group, etc., for the most talented students, who attended voluntarily. Even then I noticed Nietzsche because of his geniality— and in Pforta that means a lot. As I said, only the most talented students attended, and the occasion often arose, through questions of individual listeners, to develop discussions of an aesthetic and philosophical nature, in which Nietzsche often engaged. His wide reading was astonishing even then, no less than the deep understanding with which he approached all things. He would therefore have remained in my memory even if his name had not later achieved publicity. I also remember very well his external appearance at that time. He was a quiet, reflective, introverted young man of not too strong a constitution, whose long hairdo, among other things, was noticeable. In Pforta, Germany's best and model institution, there were personal relationships between teachers and students, and even outside school I had the opportunity to become acquainted with young Nietzsche's geniality. Naturally I cannot judge to what extent my lectures themselves influenced him in his further intellectual development. The fact is that he had great interest in the topic of my lectures. Nietzsche had the good fortune to have as teacher in Pforta the famous Plato translator Steinhart, who, in my opinion, must have influenced him deeply. Even the whole arrangement of the princely school itself, which to the outside perhaps gave the impression of a military academy, surely played a decisive and favorable role in Nietzsche's further course in life.

Did I follow him in his further intellectual development? Originally I read nothing of his other than *The Birth of Tragedy from the Spirit of Music* and his *Untimely Meditations*. Only much later did I enjoy the magnificent language of *Zarathustra*. I don't know Nietzsche's other works. However much I learned to admire him right at the beginning of his literary activity, I often could not accept his lines of thought, especially in their philological and philosophical basis. Incidentally, I believe that despite all objections he stood close to Goethe's trend of thought. And what we need today is mainly: "More Goethe." (7)

9   A. Fritsch   *1863–1864*

In the years 1863–64 I was a freshman in Schulpforta. Friedrich Nietzsche also studied there at the same time, but he was already a few years older and in the senior class. I came to know Nietzsche through music. In the central building of the institution was a room which contained the best piano. Only a few students selected by the music professor were allowed to play this piano. It was mostly afternoons from four to five. I first came in personal contact with Nietzsche on these practice afternoons, to which I was also admitted despite my great youth. He often played for us; he also liked to improvise on the piano, which made a great impression on all of us. We all idolized him somewhat in those days, for he wrote poetry and, what especially impressed me, he also composed wonderful pieces of music. I remained in Schulpforta for a few years after he graduated and did not see Nietzsche until I met him again in Leipzig—shortly before the war broke out, during my first semester—in the house of the Rector of the University at the time, Volkmann or Versmann (the name escapes me). Nietzsche was very friendly to me then and offered me his recommendation to smooth the way for me at the beginning of my studies. That was just before Nietzsche received his position in Basel. (*19*)

UNIVERSITY
AND MILITARY TIME
(1864–1869)

The first weeks after the abitur-exam we spent in Nietzsche's house in Naumburg in the company of his lively, always cheerful and amusing mother, who reminded one of Frau Aja [Goethe's mother], and his seventeen-year-old sister, in prettiest girlish bloom, around whom I was like a butterfly fluttering past pretty flowers. She made a charming impression, but I would not have believed there was so much seriousness in her as she later developed to face great tasks in life. Frau Pastor Nietzsche did not neglect to introduce us to the circle of her friends, the wives of privy councillors, who were delighted with my candor, naturalness and naiveté, while I gladly believed my friend's assurances that this was what elegant tone and elegant society were like. There were also friendly, though brief, contacts with Nietzsche's childhood friends from Naumburg, as well as with Erwin Rohde.

After Nietzsche's outfitting for the university was completed down to the smallest details by his mother and sister, we both set out on foot on our westward journey. Our first stop was Elberfeld, where we were given a friendly reception by my relatives who lived there and belonged to the better merchant circles. My childhood friend and distant cousin Ernst Schnabel joined the two of us. He had been my closest friend every since our school comradeship as freshmen in Elberfeld (1857–59), and the person closest to me in my whole life except for Nietzsche. As early as 1857 we both loved the same girl, a remote cousin called Maria Stürmer, who lived in Elberfeld with an old bigoted aunt of ours. This rivalry only intensified our romantic friendship. One day we tore her picture from the wall and secretly and hastily had two copies made, which turned out very pale. In 1859 I took one with me to Pforta, where I hung it in a conspicuous place in my locker and worshiped it ardently as a saint. Among my comrades it was known as the "fog picture." Meanwhile Ernst Schnabel, who had always remained near her, had succeeded in winning the kindly girl's heart, and it was perhaps on or about October 17, 1863, that a long letter from him arrived in Pforta containing, among the fieriest avowals of friendship, the bitter information that dear Maria Stürmer had stated her mind, namely that I had her greatest esteem and warmest friendship but Ernst Schnabel her love. In deepest dejection I walked the corridor that day with Nietzsche. He read my letter and tried to cheer me up with reasons from philosophy and religion, with examples from history and literature. But true solace remained hidden from me and was to do so for a long time. It consisted in this: that on the very same day, if the above calculation is right, and at the same hour as Nietzsche was trying so lovingly to console me, in faraway Berlin a girl was born who has now been sharing the joy and sorrow of life with me for fourteen years as my faithful wife. Ernst Schnabel was not as fortunate. Reckless as he was, he established a business in Barmen with a partner, married his and my little Maria and lived splendidly and joyously for a few years. The business declined and had to be abolished; worry gnawed at Maria, she bore a son to her husband and died. Ernst found no rest in the homeland; he left the child with its grandparents and moved to Havana as a merchant. His letters described how yellow fever was raging there, how fires were burning in the streets to purify the air, until a letter in a different hand announced that Ernst Schnabel too had succumbed to the raging fever and was buried in faraway Havana. Soon afterwards the child too died. So the grave was closed over this entire tragedy of love.

It was ten years before this sad end that Ernst Schnabel joined Nietzsche and me in Elberfeld in 1864. Witty, intelligent, lively to excess, but also reckless down to his fingertips, Ernst Schnabel joined our little travel group and got us involved in quite a few mad escapades. We three traveled to Königswinter and, intoxicated with wine and friendship, let ourselves, despite our limited means, be persuaded to hire horses and ride up the Drachenfels. That is the only time I ever saw Nietzsche on horseback. He was in a mood in which he was interested not so much in the beautiful scenery as in his horse's ears. He measured them again and again and claimed he could not decide whether he was riding a horse or a donkey. We had an even wilder time the next evening. We three strolled through the streets of the town to pay our ovations to the girls whom we suspected of being behind the windows. Nietzsche whistled and crooned: "Fein's Liebchen, fein's Liebchen"; Schnabel recited all kinds of nonsense about a poor Rhine boy begging for shelter for the night; and I myself was standing around, not knowing how to adjust to this new situation, when a man ran out the door and chased us away with invectives and threats. As if to atone for this escapade, which incidentally was an isolated one, the next day in the piano room of the Berliner Hof we ordered a bottle of wine and purified our souls through Nietzsche's wonderful improvisations. Finally we all three reached my parents' house in Oberdreis and here for weeks we enjoyed a quiet existence in the pure mountain air of the Westerwald in the company of my parents, my brothers and sisters, and male and female friends who enlivened the hospitable country rectory with their coming and going.

On October 15, we celebrated my mother's birthday and Nietzsche's at the same time, and then we descended from the Westerwald Mountains into the Rhine Valley to Neuwied, where in a few hours a steamship took us to Bonn.

Our first concern was for an apartment. Originally we had intended to share a larger room, but we changed our mind when it turned out that such a suite would be more expensive than two single rooms. And we both had reason to watch our money. My parents could send me only twenty talers per month, while Nietzsche, who was using his inheritance from his father for his studies, was supposed to get by on twenty-five talers per month. As a rule that was probably not possible, and then he complained to his mother in letters that the money always ran out so fast, probably because it was so round.

So we rented two single rooms, "dens," as the student expression goes. Mine was located on Hospitalgasse, while Nietzsche's was at its juncture on Bonngasse. A church tower rose on the other side, and Nietzsche often discussed with me his plan to rent a room high up in the tower in order to be further from the noise of street life.

We also ate our noon meal at the turner Oldag's house, where
Nietzsche lived. A pretty relative of the house, Fräulein Mary,
served us and often joined us at meals. She had an open Rhineland
temperament, but a no less moral one, and neither of us had a more
intimate relationship with her. We matriculated in the next days,
both in the Theological Faculty at first. Nietzsche transferred to the
Philosophical Faculty after only one semester, and I after only four
semesters, to my parents' disappointment. But this depended on
external circumstances. Our real study from the first was classical
philology; Ritschl and Jahn were the celebrities who had attracted
us to Bonn. We had joint recommendations from Pforta to both
professors, as well as to Schaarschmidt. We went to see Jahn. He
read the letter and said, good-heartedly but tersely, "Just contact
me, if I can help you in any way." We went to see Ritschl, in whose
house there was a constant coming and going as he rapidly processed students. He tore the letter open hastily: "Ah, my old friend
Niese! What's he doing these days? Is he all right? So Deussen is
your name. Well, visit me again very soon." Nietzsche stood non-
plussed and could not refrain from remarking that the letter spoke
of him too. "Ah yes, that's true," cried Ritschl, "there are two
names, Deussen and Nietzsche. Good, good. Well, gentlemen, visit
me again very soon." This reception of our letters of recommendation was not very encouraging, and since Schaarschmidt was not
at home we left our letter of recommendation at his house and forgot the whole matter. But Schaarschmidt invited us to his house. We
found him to be a man lively and mercurial almost to the point of
restlessness, and as we left him we looked at each other in astonishment. So that's a philosopher!? We had pictured them quite differently. Incidently, Schaarschmidt was the only one who really did
anything for us. He drew us into his family, arranged a tutorial on
Plato for us, and always had a willing ear for all our concerns. We
attended his classes on the history of philosophy and the Platonic
question; also Ritschl's on the *miles gloriosus* and Jahn's on Plato's
Symposium, plus a few theology courses, which however we soon
neglected as too boring. [David Friedrich] Strauss's *Life of Jesus*
appeared at around this time. Nietzsche got a copy, and I followed
his example. In our conversations I could not help expressing my
agreement. Nietzsche answered: "The matter has a serious consequence: if you give up Christ, you'll also have to give up God."

Nietzsche felt attracted in this first year of university study
mainly to the Greek lyricists. While I spent a great deal of time on
Sanskrit, he always chose small subjects but was immediately pro-

ductive in them. A favorite theme was Simonides' Danaë song, the critical treatment of which occupied him for a long time. In addition he revised his Theognis for a seminar paper, and was already interested in Homer, Socrates, Diogenes Laertius, and whereas I sought to enjoy the poets and thinkers and to rest in their enjoyment, he found no pleasure where he could not be productive. Meanwhile new circumstances had come about for both of us which were to limit scientific work very much for the time being. We had both had no particular inclination to join any fraternity but we wanted to take a look at the matter, and so we had no objection when Stöckert, a former Pforta student and presently a Franconian, invited us to accompany him to that fraternity's tavern. Besides us two, they had invited five other Pforta alumni; the atmosphere was very lively, and I believe it was Haushalter, who now works in Rudolstadt, who amid the frenetic jubilation of the approximately thirty Franconians, declared that he was joining up, and soon the second and third, and finally all seven, including me and Nietzsche, followed. We went home dimly aware that we had let ourselves be drawn away from our resolutions and had taken a step with unforeseeable effects. The Franconia, which had acquired so many valuable members in one evening, was characterized at that time by a wild, free and easy life, which degenerated into eccentricities on every occasion. Neither Nietzsche nor I could take much pleasure in it. The ridiculous patriotic rituals had little attraction for us cosmopolitans; we found the mandatory drinking bouts on the tavern evenings disgusting. The pedantic instructions which the pledge master gave us in chapter and verse on the most trivial things seemed ridiculous to us, and when on almost all Sunday evenings we had to skip lectures, no matter how interesting they might be, in order to watch the Franconians and Alemanians slashing their faces in a faraway barn outside the city, we could not really enjoy that either. Of course the dueling floor was visited zealously; even Nietzsche practiced as well as he could, and he also managed to get a challenge to a duel. The way he behaved in that affair was amusing enough. The following day he told me, "Yesterday, after the tavern evening, I went to the market for a walk. An Alemanian joined me; we had a very lively discussion on all kinds of topics in art and literature, and upon parting I asked him most politely to 'hang one' on me. He agreed, and as soon as possible we'll have a go at each other." With some foreboding I saw the day approaching when our friend, who was somewhat corpulent, not like Hamlet through a printer's error ("fat" for "hot") but in reality, and moreover very myopic, would have to undergo an adventure for which his qualifications were so ill-suited. The blades were tied and the sharp rapiers flashed around their bare heads. After barely three minutes the opponent applied a cut diagonally across the bridge of Nietzsche's nose right where too hard a pinch leaves a red mark. The blood was dripping to the ground, and the experts determined it to be sufficient atonement for all past injury. I loaded my well-bandaged friend into a carriage and took him home to bed, cooled the wound diligently, denied him visitors and alcohol, and in two or three days our hero had recuperated except for a tiny diagonal scar across the bridge of his nose, which he kept all his life and which did not look bad on him. So for a time we put up with the more eccentric than imaginative activities of our fraternity brothers. The verses of the Franconian national anthem written in our honor and chanted on every occasion typify more what they thought of us than what we really were. Nietzsche's tavern-name was "Gluck," and they called me "Master." Our verses ran:

> Gluck has composed and set to music
> The tragedies and romances he delights in;
> When he comes home evenings, a red mouth kisses him;
> From sheer tea and pastry he'll go to the dogs;
>   And with a hurrah-sassah the Franconians are there!
>   The Franconians are jolly, they shout hurrah!
>
> Rubbing his nose Master sits at home.
> Studying seventy-seven langauges, puffing seventeen pipes;
> Whenever he has been drinking and someone addresses him,
> He answers in Greek, the very learned man.
>   And with a hurrah-sassah the Franconians are there!
>   The Franconians are jolly, they shout hurrah!

The remark about tea and pastry was quite accurate. Nietzsche had a great liking for sweets and often ordered them while I smoked my cigar. Jokingly, we often quarreled over which of us got off cheaper in his way. But as for the aforementioned kissing of the red mouth, I never noticed Nietzsche to be inclined in that direction. I will now tell, not altogether gladly, a story which deserves to be torn from oblivion as a contribution to Nietzsche's way of thinking. One day in February 1865, Nietzsche had traveled to Cologne by himself, and there had hired a guide to show him the sights of the city; he finally asked to be taken to a restaurant. The guide took him to a house of ill repute. "Suddenly," Nietzsche told me the next day,

"I found myself surrounded by a half-dozen creatures in tinsel and gauze, looking at me expectantly. I stood speechless for a while. Then I instinctively went to a piano as if to the only soul-endowed being in the place and struck a few chords. That dispersed my shock and I escaped to the street." According to this story and everything else I know about Nietzsche I am inclined to believe that the words which Steinhart dictated to us in a Latin biography of Plato apply to him: *mulierem nunquam attingit.* Such a fact, if determined, would have to not be overlooked in judging what Nietzsche says about women. Incidentally, it was never his intention to remain unmarried; in his view, it seems, a woman was supposed to be utterly absorbed in the service and care of her husband, and already in Pforta he used to say half in jest: "I would probably wear out three wives just for myself."

Our association with Franconia was not permanent. I myself left it at my parents' urgent wish, and as a well-liked partygoer I was nominated an associate drinking partner, a privilege I made very little use of. Nietzsche left Bonn in August 1865, without even informing the fraternity or sending back the insignias. He was therefore dismissed and bore this fate with the greatest indifference.

As far as was possible, given the disturbances that fraternity life entailed, we attended classes regularly, especially those of Ritschl and Jahn, besides which Nietzsche attended Springer's class on medieval history. We then still had no idea of establishing a closer relationship with Ritschl. We sat credulously at the celebrated master's feet, hoping that some of his arcane, much praised method would rub off on us. But I must admit that, although my soul was filled with the magnificence of classical antiquity, precisely Ritschl's way of reveling in variants, corrupt passages and conjectures and the entire hours Jahn spent enumerating book titles alienated me more and more from classical philology, however much Nietzsche tried to keep me attached to it and noted with concern my still unmastered inclinations for theology. In our love for art we saw perfectly eye to eye. We visited the Bonn and Cologne theatres regularly, and were never missing from the meetings of the Beethoven Association, and on Pentecost in 1865 we enjoyed the offerings of the Lower Rhein Music Festival in Gürzenich near Cologne, especially Schumann's composition for the ending of Goethe's *Faust.* Nietzsche himself set some poems of Petöfi and others to music and, for example, dedicated a written notebook with his own compositions to my sister.

Much is still vivid in my mind of the common experiences of the year in Bonn, the last in which I enjoyed daily association with Nietzsche, but I seek in vain in these memories for traces of the surprising turns which Nietzsche's development later underwent. We two had still not discovered Schopenhauer, or rather he was concealed by the behavior of those who would have been called to lead us to him. His name was hardly ever mentioned between us. Richard Wagner was discussed frequently and heatedly but seemed to be of very problematic significance. Of course, we were freethinkers as regards positive religion, but there was still no trace of an enmity toward Christianity and Christian morality such as Nietzsche later developed. On the contrary, one day when I wanted to characterize prayer as just a subjective means of stimulating religious convictions, he explained this to be a shallow Feuerbachian view, as if I had borrowed the idea from this thinker, with whom I still was totally unfamiliar.

In 1865 the old rivalry between Ritschl and Jahn had become aggravated into a dispute which made it impossible for the two men to continue working together. Ritschl went to Leipzig and many students followed him there, among them Nietzsche, while I vaguely intended to follow later. As I was accompanying Nietzsche to the night steamship one evening in August 1865 for his departure, a painful feeling of loneliness came over me. But I also breathed a sigh of relief like one from whom a heavy pressure is removed. Nietzsche's personality had exerted a strong influence during the six years of our life together. He had always shown a sincere interest in my situation, but also a tendency to correct, criticize, and occasionally torment me, as was shown perhaps even more clearly in our continued correspondence. Since he feared that I might revert to theology, he constantly urged me in the first letters to come to Leipzig, to strip off the theological bearskin, as he later once expressed it, and to act like a young philological lion. I finally made up my mind, and on Easter in 1866 my books were all packed and waiting for the order to be shipped to Leipzig. Among them were a few volumes of Ersch and Gruber's encyclopedia, which Ritschl had by mistake auctioned off together with many other books and which I had bought. Ritschl had then searched for them and I was happy to give him the message through Nietzsche that I would arrive in Leipzig for the summer semester and bring the books along. Meanwhile I went home for the Easter vacation, met my brother Johannes, who was studying theology in Tübingen, and he did everything he could to win me for Tübingen and theology. In a sleepless night I pondered the two possibilities: Leipzig or Tübingen; Nietzsche or my brother, plus my future father-in-law; the fertile plain of Saxony or Swabia's vineyard-covered slopes; grammar, manuscript comparison, micrology, or the Orient and Bible study with its religious and ethical problems. I made a quick decision and went along to Tübingen. The semester I spent there studying under Beck and associating with Northern German theology students completely took away my joy in theology. With a heavy heart I wrote to Nietzsche after only a few weeks and sent the books for Ritschl. All I received for this were reproaches for unreliableness, indecision, lack of punctuality, etc. In a well-meaning but harsh manner, Nietzsche had insisted that my real vocation was philology and that my recent turning to theology was a mistake I would have to pay for dearly. The events had already proven him right; nowhere did I find in Tübingen an open-minded discussion of my thoughts, as I was accustomed to with Nietzsche; everywhere I ran into narrow-mindedness, prejudice, and quarrelsomeness. (*10,* 15–28)

11   Heinrich Wilhelm Wisser   *December 1865*

To the person who knows my name, I am the compiler of East Holstein folk traditions and editor of Low German fairy-tales. But I entered this field only at the age of fifty. What I studied was classical philology and on the side I did a little German studies.

The first three years, I studied in Kiel under Professor Ribbeck, a pupil of Ritschl's, then, starting on St. Michael's Day, I did three semesters in Leipzig.

In these three semesters I belonged to the Ritschl Society and the Philology Club together with Nietzsche and Rohde, and so I frequented the same circles as they did. These circles were made up mostly of especially talented young people, without exception ambitious, who, far from student externalities but also free of philistine pedantry, lived just for their science and were incipient scholars rather than ordinary, lecture-note-taking students.

The Philology Club, which still exists today, was established by us at that time, by Nietzsche, Wilhelm Roscher, later principal of a high school in Saxony, a son of the Leipzig economist, Arnold, from Königsberg, and myself.

Ritschl gave the suggestion for this (according to my diary on

December 4, 1865) one evening at a party, to which we also were invited. Toward the end of the semester, the number of members came to ten.

The Ritschl Society numbered about as many members. They were almost exclusively non-Saxons who had come to Leipzig because of Ritschl, and probably had for the most part been recommended to Ritschl by their former professors. For Ritschl, who had had to leave Bonn shortly before because of his dispute with Otto Jahn but had immediately been given a university position by the Saxon government, had exercised such attraction on young academicians that the number of philologists in Leipzig suddenly soared from forty to one hundred and forty.

The Society met once a week in Ritschl's study, namely in the first semester on Sunday afternoons, to discuss, under Ritschl's direction, a paper written in Latin by one of the members. So it was not at all different from a philological seminar, such as exists at every university and also existed then in Leipzig, except that the members were personally closer to the old master.

Members of the Society I can name were: Kohl, later professor at Kreuznach, Wegehaupt, later director of the Hamburg Johanneum, and Clemm, later university professor in Giessen.

Rohde, the son of a Hamburg physician, joined only a few weeks later. I noticed him because at one of the very first meetings during a difference of opinion he contradicted the venerable old gentleman very brashly, I felt.

Nietzsche joined only at the beginning of the next semester (in the summer of 1866)—not, as he himself erroneously assumes, just in the following winter semester (1866–67). This is striking. For, since Ritschl had, by repeated proofs of his special favor, made it clear to him that he was very welcome, all it would have taken was a word from Nietzsche for him to be accepted into the Society. The contradiction is explained by the fact that Ritschl had practically asked him to join, but Nietzsche had rejected the invitation. For what reason? In his pride he refused to be called a Ritschlian, i.e., to be considered another man's disciple. My feeling is that he once told me this himself. If my memory is deceiving me, though I believe it is not, then we others discussed this as a suspicion and accepted it as an explanation. Certainly, the matter was discussed in this sense at that time.

If Nietzsche later did join after all, that was probably the result of Ritschl's praising his essay on Theognis during a visit about which

Nietzsche reported enthusiastically to us in Gohlis on February 24, 1866. After this open recognition of his extraordinary significance, his coyness would no longer have made any sense. Perhaps worry that Ritschl would have held a further refusal against him played a role.

Among those who joined the Philology Club and were all attracted by Roscher—for we three friends had no acquaintances among the students—there were four Saxons, including Angermann, later rector of a Saxon high school, and Windisch, later professor of Sanskrit in Leipzig, and a foreigner, Dr. Kinkel, son of Gottfried Kinkel, a German-educated, musical Englishman, interested especially in archeology. Later Romundt also joined.

Nietzsche stood in closer contact with Romundt and—as I now first see from Nietzsche's biography—to my surprise also with Kinkel. Romundt, with whom he used to discuss Schopenhauer very often, later followed him to Basel, where he was a privatdozent for a time.

Like Nietzsche, Roscher and Romundt too were later at the same time members of the Society, just as several Society members such as, for example, Kohl and Rohde, in time also joined the Philology Club. So the two associations overlapped.

In this circle I associated most often and most closely with Roscher and Romundt, in the third semester also with Kohl and Rohde. I also met Nietzsche just about every day. But the difference of our natures, inclinations, and talents was too great for a more intimate association between us to have developed.

Whereas I left Leipzig after only three semesters (Easter 1867), Nietzsche and Rohde stayed there for yet a fourth semester (summer 1867). This is the semester Rohde's letter speaks of.

At the end of this semester they too left Leipzig. Nietzsche, to serve his year in the army in his hometown, Naumburg; Rohde, to continue his studies in Kiel. . . .

All those with whom I was together in Leipzig at that time have probably passed away by now. And I, now eighty-two years of age, am probably the only one still alive from that circle. (*67*)

12   Heinrich Stürenberg   *1866*

When I introduced myself to him [F. W. Ritschl], he received me with friendliness in memory of an already deceased older brother of mine who had been his pupil in Bonn. And he told me that if I wanted to become known in his circle of pupils I should visit the by far most talented person in this circle, Friedrich Nietzsche.

His name had already been mentioned to me with admiration by my first philological acquaintances in Leipzig. Especially by Emil Jungmann, later for many years a highly respected teacher and principal of the Thomas School. He had, as a high school student in Schulpforta, already been with Nietzsche for four years and, although two years below him in age and class, he had in the close living conditions of the princely school gotten the impression of an extraordinarily talented person and then confirmed this while studying together in Leipzig, where Nietzsche had followed Ritschl from Bonn. So I went somewhat hesitantly to the young man, who was already admired at so young an age and who lived in the house of the famous historian and political scientist, university professor Karl Biedermann, and although just three years younger I immediately felt like a greenhorn in relation to a mature and superior man. Our conversation touched on Bonn, from where he had expected no further philological transfers after Ritschl's departure, on the professors Bernays and Usener, who had been appointed there to replace Ritschl, on Lucretius, for whom I had been particularly won by Bernays. On every subject he tried to elevate the conversation from the personal to the universal. His appearance even then was already dominated by a stern expression and a large mustache. In the Philology Club, in which we students gave lectures and discussed them without the presence of any professors, I then heard Nietzsche speak twice in the next semesters—as already an "old timer" he no longer came to other students' lectures—and both times, like everyone else in the audience, I came away with the impression of an almost astounding precocity and confident self-assurance of his lecture. The first dealt with Menippus the Cynic, and sought masterfully to draw a picture of the man based on the scanty information about his life and works and on the still scantier relics of his writings, a picture that made his imitation by a Roman under the term Menippean satire explainable. The second lecture was about the question of Homer; and, in contrast to the tendency prevailing at that time to substitute for the idea that one or several poets wrote the Homeric poems the so-called folk-poetry theory, he stressed most strongly that outstandingly creative individuals always must be behind such a *Volksdichtung* anyway; that it is inconceivable that literary works as magnificent as Homer's could stem from momentary inspiration. This was essentially the same train of thought on which his inaugural lecture at Basel the next year was based. (*60*)

13   Elisabeth Förster-Nietzsche   *February 2, 1869*

That February 2 always remained a very delightful memory to the three of us. Our good mother had no idea what to make of us. As a nursery rhyme says: "We ate not, we drank not" and we gave confused and mysterious answers. Fortunately the answer to the riddle arrived after two days: Fritz sent his calling card:

Friedrich Nietzsche
Professor of Classical Philology at the University of Basel
(Salary: 3000 francs)

Our dear mother's happiness and boundless surprise were beyond description. Then the marvellous news spread further and further. Everyone, even the newspapers, were astonished at this twenty-four-old professor. Praise, honor, and adulation resounded on all sides about our Fritz, so that it finally became too much for him and he once wrote with considerable annoyance: "What's so great about it? There's just one more professor on earth, that's all." From the very beginning, ever since he first got the appointment, my brother was not sheer delight and joy. (*13*, 296)

14   Paul Deussen   *1869*

In the spring of 1869 I almost lost my friend forever. I had been living for a whole year in my parents' house in the country, cut off from urban comfort and from association with young people my own age, finishing my doctoral dissertation after long tedious work and preparing for the oral examination. I was nervous, overworked, and in a dismal mood. Then I was surprised by a letter from Nietzsche in which he told me that, without first having taken his doctoral examination, he had been appointed a professor at the University of Basel. I sent him my most heartfelt congratulations, but honest as I always was, I could not omit also reporting about myself and drawing a parallel between his brilliant success and my depressing situation, and a little envy may have shone through between the lines. But who can describe my astonishment, indeed horror, when by return mail I received Nietzsche's answer in the form of a calling card containing approximately the following words: "Dear Friend, unless perhaps accidental mental disturbance was to blame for your last letter, then please consider our relations to be over. F. N."—These words burned into my soul like hellfire. I was at that time, when Schopenhauer had not yet made me free, still too caught up in the usual concepts of honor and the like, not to immediately tell myself that such a clear rejection necessarily had to result in a renunciation of any further association on my part. But my mind could not accept the thought of losing such a friend. I felt the urge to write to Nietzsche and ask him how he could have so misunderstood my letter. Nietzsche answered by sending me three written items: (1) My inculpated letter; (2) a commentary on it explaining it as a mixture of envy, crassness, and peasant pride; and finally, as an example of how the thing should be done, (3) a letter from Erwin Rohde, who knew no limits of rapture at being able to call a real professor, moreover one so young and popular, his friend. I cannot say that I was particularly ashamed of my letter, which at least sincerely expressed my attitude. In my answer, I thanked him for his conciliatory stance, without raising the issue again, and drew from it a lesson for the future. I now understood the words Nietzsche had once written to me: "Seriously, my friend, I must ask that when you speak of me, you speak with somewhat more respect." (*10*, 60–62)

PROFESSOR AT
THE UNIVERSITY OF BASEL
(1870–1878)

I met Nietzsche in Maderanertal in 1870, quite by chance and fleetingly. He gave the impression of a very introverted, somewhat ailing
man. He tended to avoid encounters and conversations; but if they
took place, then he was striking for the cordiality and earnestness
he developed and seemed to direct to his counterpart. One immediately felt challenged to tell him something that one felt to be
important. During a music session we played him Brahms' four-
handed love-waltz and Beethoven's Opus 26. He listened attentively, then replied with Wagner's "Eulogy" from *Die Meistersinger.*
He played it freely and seemed to reproduce it according to a performance he had heard rather than a studied extract of sheet music.
In later years I heard it played again by him in exactly the same
manner. He had no virtuosity, played almost hard and squarely,
seeking the tones in memory, then on the keyboard. Near Nietzsche
I had the feeling of a riddle, a mystery. He responded to something
like a girlish naturalness with a certain solemnity against a background of modest humor and high spirits. I can still see him walking
on the woodland paths, robustly but still seeking the path, which
gave his stride a trace of awkwardness and unfreedom. Yes, he was
certainly a schoolmaster, and one would have liked to learn more

about him. Already then, but much more later, I noticed Nietzsche's hands. They had artistic form, expressing a play and energy of the nerves, and he often held them in a lightly suggested round curvature without any particular intent. Nietzsche's demeanor was amiable, and could even have a trace of femininity. An accidental look at his hands revealed a new trait: Nietzsche's fingernails had a peculiar form: they were arched and sank at the points, one thought of a high-flying bird up in the blue sky. After a few days of avoiding one another, of conversations and observations, news arrived of the victory near Wörth. Then a new patriotic tone arose, and Nietzsche vanished to put himself at the fatherland's disposal. I could not forget Nietzsche; I had the feeling that with him something significant had passed by me. Later I obtained a copy of *The Birth of Tragedy,* and little by little the *Untimely Meditations.* How extraordinarily the impression I had gotten was deepened! At that time I knew very little of Wagnerian art and the analogy he made between Greek tragedy and the Master's works was completely incomprehensible to me. But his deep comprehension and delineation of the elements of Greek art and his introduction to Greek tragedy literally exhilarated me. So the schoolmaster in Maderanertal was really capable of this! I saw in two persons how deeply Nietzsche's influence affected them. First, in Theodor Kirchner, who as a self-creative artist spoke somewhat superiorly but compellingly of this young scholar who wanted to point the way for art. Later in Frau Henriette Feuerbach, who had been introduced to Nietzsche during a stay in Basel and who had immediately seen him as an important personality.

A few years later I met my husband and we were married in the summer of 1876 and moved to Basel. Little by little Nietzsche frequented our house, all the more often since he had had to give up all his other former associations. He told of an essay by Renan on medieval art which he had read and he practiced his talent as an instructor on me. He interpreted and argued so skillfully that he actually put the phrase "the baroque of Christendom" into my mouth and then broke out in exuberant, loud laughter and assured me that such a thing was actually in him: a hyperintense, self-destructive religious need. I was enormously bewildered and disappointed and did not want to accept that Nietzsche could be anything else but a Greek and a completely natural, free person. At that time Nietzsche could develop some of the mobility whose absence had struck me in Maderanertal. He had poor eyesight and could hardly recognize a person on the street. Thus I once or twice saw him striding really boldly, and certainly filled with no petty thoughts. This constant association lasted through the years 1876 to 1879. *(43, 234–235)*

16   Julius Piccard   *ca. 1870*

I first received my appointment to Basel in 1869 and moved there at the end of the same year; so I am one of the few surviving first colleagues of Nietzsche and Overbeck; moreover, in the first years I lived in three different apartments in the Schützengrabe, in the immediate vicinity of both. As a chemist I pursued other goals than the philologist and the theologian; but on at least one point Nietzsche and I felt mutual sympathy, in the real sense of the word; we both had ailments. Therefore he was less reserved with me on questions of health than with healthy friends, who were less able to understand him in this regard. Under the dateline March 25, 1871, he wrote to me from Lugano: "Dear and valued colleague, you truly surprised me with your letter: how rarely have I received such a pure sign of sympathy. The whole day put on a friendly face since it had begun by my receiving your letter. I assure you that I can never forget a trait such as this. It also happened to be the first day I spent together with the excellent Heusler in Lugano. Through him I am again informed about conditions in Basel; indeed we have the *Baseler Zeitung* sent here daily. I hope to arrive there again in the middle of next month and to recommence with the old professional activity by the beginning of May. I was very glad to hear that you yourself endured this whole long winter semester without longer disruptions, moreover in a climate that, it seems to me, is not alto-gether safe—and it gives me the best hopes for the complete res-toration of your health. Summer in Basel is very bearable and warm; I cannot write the word 'warmth' today without longing. For the beautiful lake is completely overcast with cold, dense fog, and gray displeasure spreads over the hotel and its inhabitants, who are very dependent on the weather . . ."

The most relentless of all philosophers was, as a person, most touchingly kindhearted and sensitive. One would, however, have to be blind not to see that even then this sensitivity tended somewhat toward the morbid. At about this same time we two—the only strangers—were invited to a family evening at Privy Councillor Vischer-Bilfinger's house. Nietzsche played on the piano one of his own compositions, which turned out to be quite bewildering. On the way home he asked me what people had thought of it. I answered politely but asked about the meaning of a repeated staccato that had seemed somewhat peculiar to me and probably to others. "But Piccard! You didn't understand that this was the stars in the sky during a walk in the night?" And the poor man became so sad that I felt very sorry for him. One will recall a similar event for Wagner in Klein-Tribschen.

Another time, at the rector's annual banquet, someone proposed a toast to the Academic Society and remarked incidentally that since not everyone could be a specialized scholar there necessarily had to also be some "educated philistines." This catchword, which Nietzsche had coined shortly before, was completely suitable in this sense. He got up and left. When I soon followed him home, he lay completely perplexed on his sofa; in the dark room his eyes had an eerie gleam. When I tried to calm him, he stared at me: "But Piccard, didn't you hear how they were all making fun of me?" It sounded like a touch of persecution complex.

Somewhat later, when he traveled to Montreux for a visit, I recommended very strongly to him to take a little side tour to Lausanne, especially to see the cathedral. He promised, and kept his promise, but how? From his description I reconstructed the route he followed in about two hours: from the railroad station he walked eastward around the city, past the prison to the village of Chailly, and roaming around finally returned via the Vuachère to the railroad station, barely in time to catch his train, without having seen a trace of the real city, not to mention the cathedral. "But why didn't you ask someone the way?" With childlike shame he answered: "You know, Piccard, they would have laughed at me!" This hypersensitivity only increased with time! (*44*, 168–171)

17   Jakob Wackernagel   *1870ff.*

I had Nietzsche as a teacher first in the upper high school class 1870–71, then in 1871–72 as a beginning student of philology, and finally in 1875 just before my examination. He made by far the strongest impression on me in high school. I do not know whether we acquired much positive knowledge. But any students who were at all receptive were strongly impressed. The entire instruction was on a high level and went beyond technicalities. He began one period with a question addressed to the class: "What is a philosopher?" and was very troubled to receive no answer that was at all satisfactory. He was not interested in a rote type of instruction. He assigned themes to us and encouraged us to write treatises, for example, on Euripides' *Bacchae,* or on the justification for humanistic education; he also had us do metrical translations of Aeschylus. Most impressive, however, was the man himself, the freedom and dignity of his whole behavior. Anything trivial was out of the question for him; everyone could feel this.

In my opinion, his philological teaching was not on a par with his teaching at the high school. In contrast with his high school classes, at the university the distance between him and Jakob Burckhardt, whose instruction I enjoyed at both levels along with his, was tremendous. As a first-year student I attended a class of his on Plato. A few bold statements, especially from the introductory hour, have stayed with me. But on the whole we were bored. There was a very thorough enumeration and reproduction of theories on the Platonic question, followed by a synopsis of the individual dialogues. Perhaps had I been more mature I would have seen the usefulness of such a depiction and now I respect the conscientious work Nietzsche spent on this task, but he did not thrill us. Nor was his lecture suited to do that; it was based completely on written notes.

The seminar began well. Not sufficiently aware of our total immaturity, we enjoyed dealing with broad literary-historical questions based on Nietzsche's own treatises. But I cannot at all remember the further course of the seminar exercises; I believe I obtained a concept of exegesis from other philology teachers.

In 1875 I attended Nietzsche's classes on the history of Greek literature, if I remember correctly. I was left with a few brilliant remarks, but no more than that.

As university students we were also enthusiastic about Nietzsche and proud to have him as teacher. But this applied not so much to his philological instruction as to what we otherwise got from him or knew about him. He was very accessible for visits and could then be brilliant. Of course we were all enthused about his *Birth of Tragedy* and felt deeply moved by the public lectures on education which he gave in those years.

Even today I still esteem it highly to have had Nietzsche as a teacher. Without that my life would have been a bit poorer and more trivial. I am also grateful to him for the friendly attitude he had toward me till the end, although I in part could not and in part would not follow his bold flights. But I can hardly say that I owe him anything for my technical philological training.

Perhaps my judgment is wrong. I once expressed myself similarly to Prof. Thureysen in Freiburg, who was Nietzsche's student in later years. He seemed to be of a different opinion and to value even Nietzsche's philological instruction more highly. Again I must point out that I attended Nietzsche's classes only in immature and then again in overly advanced semesters. (*64*)

18   Dr. Promitz

In Basel it was and still is the custom for humanists at the university to give instruction for their colleagues in the higher classes of high school. Like Jakob Burckhardt, Nietzsche was not a dry professional pedagogue in this secondary office, but an excellent teacher, who like an Ephorus from ancient Greece stepped with a leap across time and mores into the midst of his pupils, as if he were reporting of self-evident things he had seen with his own eyes.

Since his eyes needed protection at an early age, even with moderate sunlight the window blinds had to be kept half-shut. The beneficial twilight heightened even further the magic effect of his method of instruction, which was completely ruled by the spirit of aesthetic freedom. He was far from any rigid pedantry and unhesitatingly allowed the reasonable use of German translations, provided we read as many Greek authors as possible with pleasure. Now it happened quite often that he randomly asked: "Now tell me, what is a philosopher?" And after the astounded student's not very exhaustive reply he finished the class period with a captivating extemporization.

Once he asked the class to read the description of Achilles' shield during the summer vacation and to voluntarily report on it. When classes began again he asked at random: "Did you read the passage?" The perplexed student answered falsely in the affirmative.

"Good, then describe the shield."

An embarrassing silence followed, as the pupil's excitement increased. For ten minutes Nietzsche, apparently listening, strode through the room with pensive steps, pretending to be listening to the fictive description. Finally he said without any sharp emphasis: "Now that N. N. has explained Achilles' shield to us, let us continue." During a public examination he came upon a particularly difficult Thucydides passage. "Have you already read this?" he picked out a pupil. "No." "You find difficulties in it?" "Yes." "Others too have already found difficulties there."

From his pedagogical experiences, Nietzsche coined the moral maxim: "Whoever is a teacher at heart takes all things seriously only in relation to his pupils, even himself." (*46*)

19   Leonhard Adelt   *1870ff.*

A half century and more has gone by since then, but I still see him as if it were today. I still feel the jerk with which I spontaneously sat up straight when he looked at me sharply and piercingly through his eyeglasses. Barely twenty-five, he had become Professor of Classical Philology at the University of Basel and was teaching Greek on the side at our high school. He read the lyrical anthology and the philosophers with us freshmen. The inner freedom and superiority of his nature, his dealings with the more mature university students, and probably also his own education in Schulpforta resulted in the young professor's setting the boundaries of his school program unusually wide and expecting from us an independent treatment and mastery of the assigned work. Sometimes our juvenile, philosophically unschooled minds were no longer capable of following the train of thought of the laboriously translated text and its congenial interpreter, especially since our class had through a prior temporary arrangement remained behind in Greek instruction anyway. But the strong and pure personality of our teacher, whose outstanding intellectual significance we sensed, never let us lose courage. His strict sense of justice distinguished precisely between the limits of good will and of indolent negligence, and none of the favorite school tricks worked with him. I recall how one of us (today he holds high office as a tenured seminar director), badly prepared and called upon shortly before the end of the period, with pretended zeal prolonged the reading of the Greek text to be translated, until the bell rang. To be cautious he read one more sentence and then broke off confidently. Nietzsche did not move. Our freshman's brow sweated with fear. Stuttering, he managed to say, "Professor, perhaps you overlooked the bell?"

Nietzsche stared at him for a moment, then—without changing expression—he corrected him: "You mean overheard," and left the classroom. The next day he began the instruction by calling on the same pupil, "So, translate."

When Nietzsche was teaching, an exemplary discipline always prevailed in our class and it even carried over to the preceding and following intermission. Although we never heard a word of blame or ill-temper from our teacher, we had boundless respect for him. He had a way, in stony silence, of leaving the badly prepared pupil to his disgraceful stuttering and stammering, which was incredibly embarrassing and shameful for the person in question, and after a brief breathtaking pause, putting an ironic end to the spectacle with a curt "So," or "So much." That was the sharpest expression of his blame—just as his praise never went beyond a brief "Good." But what wouldn't many a one of us, who otherwise was not numbered among the strivers, have given for this brief praise! Difficult hours as Nietzsche prepared for us, on the other hand we felt it to be a distinction that he gave so much credit to our intelligence, and we had youth's fine sense for the violence which his high-flying spirit did itself for our sake. We shared the university students' enthusiastic respect for their professor, who was only a little older than they themselves were; we read everything of his that was published, and were caught up in the exhilaration of his enthusiasm for Wagner, as he was just then writing his *Birth of Tragedy*. With a striking nobility of appearance, a captivating amiability of conduct, and also geographic proximity to the best of men, such as Jakob Burckhardt and Richard Wagner, who lived in Tribschen, the young firebrand at this early age stood at a height of life whose full happiness would later no longer be his. (*1*)

20   Rudolf Eucken   *Spring 1871*

It was the spring of 1871 when I first heard more about Nietzsche and soon came into personal acquaintanceship with him. At that time Councillor and Professor Vischer, the famous archeologist, came, as director of the university's board of trustees, to see me in Frankfurt am Main to negotiate with me about my proposed appointment to Basel. These negotiations did not run into the slightest difficulty, and so a lively conversation developed between us two; this led also to Nietzsche and to his appointment, which had aroused no little attention in academic circles. Nietzsche was not even a Ph.D. when the important professorship was conferred upon him. Vischer told me the details of a conversation he had had with the prominent philologist Ritschl in Leipzig. Vischer came to him to get a philological faculty member for Basel. Ritschl named various names, but then he interrupted himself and said: "We have a young scholar who is far more important than all the others, but he is still very young, and does not even have his doctorate!" Vischer said that was not bad if the man really was as outstanding as Ritschl described, but Ritschl with great confidence answered this question affirmatively. So Nietzsche came to the University of Basel. The university was then externally small, it had only 156 students, but it had excellent scholars among its teachers; I will mention only Hagenbach, Heusler, Vischer himself, Steffensen, Jakob Burckhardt, and others; the university had a lively and fresh vitality, and relations between the native Swiss and professors appointed from Germany were most cordial. Thus Nietzsche entered a significant circle, in which he immediately enjoyed a high reputation. In the winter of 1871–72 he gave his lectures on the reform of education, which attracted a great deal of attention and enthusiastic support. I myself first met Nietzsche in the meetings of the senate and faculty, and we often had to hold common doctoral examinations; I still remember vividly how amiable Nietzsche was toward the doctoral candidates, how he was never unfriendly or excited, but discussed in a kind but superior manner; one got a most favorable impression. Then we often met at small parties, where he proved to be a pleasant conversationalist, without any trace of pettiness or malice; he was more reserved than obtrusive, but he could tell charming little stories and he was not without humor. We rarely discussed questions of principle, since in scholarly circles each has his own world of ideas which he does not easily relinquish. But I remember, for example, one long conversation we had on the Germans' mania for measuring all achievement by fixed stereotypes and their lack of esteem for creative individuality.

Until then Nietzsche was considered primarily a philologist; now came the *Untimely Meditations* and put the matter in a new light. That book may have made the predominantly conservative citizens of Basel uncomfortable on this or that point, but the high esteem of the man did not suffer in the least under it; everybody realized all the more that he was an outstanding faculty member. Meanwhile new writings were being published, but though they were received with enthusiasm by closer friends, they did not reach broader circles; Nietzsche was considered very talented but a strange eccentric. He could not treat this disrespect for his noble and ardent striving with indifference, he had too much concern for people and too much love of mankind for that; an unemotional mode of thought was far from his nature. I will never forget a conversation I had with him in the Basel Readers' Society. Numerous periodicals were available there, and Nietzsche showed me an article in a Berlin newspaper that mocked his striving in an unworthy fashion and tried to brand it as ridiculous—for that is a favorite weapon of little souls. I said he ought not to take such a thing too seriously, he stood too high to be affected by such attacks. He said: "Yes, logically you are right, but it does hurt to be treated this way." This little conversation enabled me to feel clearly the tragedy in his life: a fine noble nature, called to the highest goals, colliding with an alien, dull world; there can today be no doubt about the intellectual insensitivity of those times, the age disregarded the treasures that were being offered; Nietzsche, in his healthy days, never experienced a second edition of any of his books—except *The Birth of Tragedy*. Finally signs of an inner turn in art and literature came, but for Nietzsche himself it was too late, a hard fate had torn from his hands the pen that promised a rich future creativity, and he never experienced his full success with a clear consciousness.

Such a fate must move every sympathetic person painfully, but the faithful and self-sacrificing love which his family, and most especially his sister, showed him offers some consolation. Such a loving mentality is the highest thing one person can offer another, but besides the purely human aspect there is here additionally the untiring care for the great intellectual treasures, whose complete preservation and effect we owe to Frau Förster-Nietzsche; not only German literature, but all intellectual life is indebted to her; so on her anniversary we want to give her our sincere and heartfelt thanks. (*12*, 53–55)

21   Emanuel Probst   *Fall 1871*

I came with my class list to register for Professor Nietzsche's seminar and lectures. The following dialogue took place during this registration:

    Professor: So you are a philologist.
    Student: Yes, professor.

Professor: Do you know what that means, to be a philologist?

Student: I should hope so, professor; I have five semesters behind me.

Professor: No! I will tell you. Just think, a man has a beautiful painting, a real work of art. But the picture has a spot or is torn, and whenever he looks at the painting to enjoy the master's art, his look falls on the repulsive flaw and he cannot enjoy the picture.

Now the friend of art, who is not lacking in energy, tells himself: "With conscientious work and sufficient expenditure of time I have already achieved some things that at first seemed impossible to attain." So he sets right to work. He goes to school under artists like a young painting student, takes instruction in paint-mixing and brushstrokes, puts countless attempts on canvas and through his innate sense for art he is his own severest critic of his work, which he continues for years and enriches with studies. Finally he has reached the point where he believes he can start work on the painting itself. And the man's conscientiousness and his reverence for art, which he wants to make enjoyable again, are rewarded. The restoration of the work of art is marvellously successful, so that he feels the urge to invite his friends to come and share his joy with him. What complimentary and enthusiastic judgments were expressed can be imagined; the invited guests stood for a long time viewing the picture attentively, and everyone was full of praise. The quintessence of all judgments was: "No one who has not seen the picture earlier will be able to believe that it was ever disfigured by an ugly spot."

The next day his dearest friend came to the happy restorer of the picture. "Listen," he said, "I too have such a picture, a valuable one, but it has a spot; couldn't you lend me a hand and make the spot vanish?"

"Yes, of course! I'm interested," was the answer, and the correction was begun right away, with the same good success as with the first picture and again to the great joy of a circle of art-loving friends. But before the next day, another dear friend appeared with a defective painting, and soon another, and another; and because our man was financially independent, and liked to immerse himself in the particular nature of ancient art, he was always occupied with such restoration of paintings, which he performed with great dexterity.

Do you believe that such a man, when he goes to a gallery of paintings, can look for anything else but spots and torn places?

That is a philologist! (*45*)

22   Karl Heckel   *December 1871ff.*

My personal contact with Nietzsche took place in young years in December 1871. At that time Richard Wagner was in my native city of Mannheim directing a concert that was being performed as the first concert for the Bayreuth Theatre Festival by the Wagner Society established shortly before by my father. A few days before the concert, Nietzsche arrived in Mannheim from Basel together with Frau Cosima Wagner to attend not only the concert but also the rehearsals, as well as the premiere of the *Siegfried Idyll,* which took place before a circle of invited guests. He often accompanied Wagner on his visits to my father, Emil Heckel, and I heard of profound conversations between Wagner, Frau Cosima, and Nietzsche in those days, dealing mainly with the Greeks and Schopenhauer, and with cultural conditions in Germany, and this stirred my interest in the Basel professor who was such a loyal devotee of Wagner and took such a warm interest in the endeavors of the Wagner Society.

When the news spread after Wagner's departure that he had fallen critically ill with typhus in Tribschen near Lucerne, Nietzsche telegraphed to my father: "Rumor completely unfounded; best news from Tribschen. Cordial New Year's wishes to the Wagner Society. Professor Nietzsche."

And I heard of Nietzsche again when he met my father the following May at the laying of the cornerstone for the Bayreuth Festival House. After the ceremony, Nietzsche, his friend von Gersdorff, and my father drove back to the city together with Wagner. Wagner sat seriously and silently, "gazing long into himself," as Nietzsche so aptly expressed it. In his *Untimely Meditation* "Richard Wagner in Bayreuth," the first work I read of Nietzsche's, he associates with this return journey from the Festival Hill deep meditations which he closes with the words: "But we, those closest to him, can follow up to a point what Wagner saw internally in those days— how he became what he is and will be—and only from the vantage point of this Wagnerian gaze will we ourselves be able to understand his great deed, guaranteeing its fertility by this understanding."

Even in later years Nietzsche still remembered warmly the days of the laying of the cornerstone and "the small entourage that cele-brated it and had sensitive fingers for tender things." (*26*, 4–5)

23   Heinrich Gelzer-Thurneysen   *ca. 1872*

So J. Burckhardt stands in a very peculiar relationship to the two great heroes of the nineteenth century and to its dying culture. He never completely understood Bismarck, that genius of statesman-ship, or judged him congenially. And despite all his high recognition and loving attention to Nietzsche's lonely trains of thought, he always remained primarily somewhat skeptical toward him too, inso-far as this was allowed by a genuinely French courtesy toward a younger colleague who admired him boundlessly. Upon the appear-ance of *The Birth of Tragedy,* he spoke about it to me full of admi-ration, but with that rather unpleasant kind of admiration about which one immediately notices that it is really full of badly con-cealed, acrid irony. Thus it is indeed striking that Burckhardt, a gen-uine son of the nineteenth century as few men were, did not show the understanding one might well desire toward these two genial representatives and last defenders of his culture. (*22*, 38–39)

24   Jacob Mähly   *1872*

A great deal is being said about a closer association of Nietzsche with the important cultural historian Jakob Burckhardt, but I have no knowledge of it and will not believe it until documentation from their correspondence teaches me otherwise. Their two natures were altogether too different for a more than external relationship, a real intimacy and regular contact to have arisen; Nietzsche, an open and candid, affectionate and uncalculating character, relatively uncon-cerned with the judgment of the masses and not timidly weighing every word in order to avoid any misinterpretation at all costs— Burckhardt, an extremely reserved, tight-lipped nature, who never or rarely fully revealed his innermost thoughts, not even in hours when relaxed conviviality opened the hearts and loosened the tongues of others, and peered timidly, almost suspiciously, to see whether some allusion to his person were not hidden behind this or that word or some other hostile demon on the prowl.

But there was another factor: Burckhardt was an official teacher of history; he lived in and worked for this discipline, his strength and his fame lay in it. And Nietzsche? In one of his works Nietzsche declared war on history—though with youthfully exuberant rashness—but Burckhardt was not accustomed to forgetting that kind of thing and he surely would have held it against him. In student circles the legend circulated that once when Nietzsche sat in on one of Burckhardt's classes without first asking, Burckhardt took offense at it and later reprimanded him. Is this really just a legend? I am tempted to doubt it, because the facts, assuming they were true, would fit perfectly with Burckhardt's character; he could have an incredibly tender skin for certain contacts. But all this is not meant to deny that the two men had a high opinion of one another and judged one another according to their merits, as was right and proper. Both men have in common one great quality which cannot always be found even in great scholars: a masterful style. Both men use language with astonishing skill and accuracy, but Nietzsche allows more room for beauty and brilliance than does his older colleague. (*34*, 249)

25   Franz Overbeck   [*1889*]

The relationship between Jakob Burckhardt and Nietzsche was, even as portrayed by their extant correspondence, a one-sided one. Nietzsche made wrong assumptions about the feelings expressed toward him by his correspondent. In truth, Burckhardt had been following Nietzsche's writing for years with feelings that were little short of horror, and he suffered greatly from the copies of Nietzsche's writings from the time of the aforementioned correspondence, which used to reach him with infallible regularity, inviting him to share his joy. What I say here of Burckhardt I got substantially from his own mouth in statements that came not from any confidence with which he would have honored me more than others, but which I heard in the course of a longer association with Burckhardt that lasted until his death. A letter of Nietzsche's to Jakob Burckhardt made him the first witness of the outbreak of madness among the people who then stood in real contact with Nietzsche.

On the afternoon of January 6, 1889, a Sunday, my wife and I were sitting together in my study, whose windows faced the street and the adjoining front garden, when I saw Jakob Burckhardt enter the gate and walk toward our front door. Under our existing circumstances, the idea that Nietzsche was involved had to strike us like a flash. Burckhardt's appearance was, as such, puzzling to me, since there was absolutely no closer contact between Burckhardt and me at that time, although we were both silently aware of the relationship we shared with Nietzsche—Nietzsche, on the other hand, was ever present in our thoughts. For the last three months the gravest worries about him had filled my mind, superseding almost all other cares. Since the mailman had brought me the second Turin group of Nietzsche's letters, i.e., since circa mid-October, the entire nature of the letters increasingly suggested the likelihood that their writer was insane. The purpose of Burckhardt's visit was to tell me of the horrible letter he had received that very day. As soon as we had read it together and exchanged the more lively counterparts which I already had in my desk, it became perfectly clear what a state Nietzsche was in. What I had been afraid to suspect for some time was now clear as day.

I responded to Burckhardt's information by reporting without delay on the journey I had immediately undertaken to fetch my friend and accompany him here from Turin! Probably on the very first day of our association which began thus, Burckhardt made statements from which the testimony I am about to give is taken. The remarks were urgent and unmistakable, as Burckhardt spoke when he wanted to, and they were stamped indelibly in my mind, unveiling a state of affairs that confirmed my own vague suspicions till then.

On the extensive journey seeking information with which Nietzsche's sister prepared her biography in the summer of 1895, she also visited Basel in late summer and asked Jakob Burckhardt to do his part in describing her brother's Basel period. The reception she got cannot, as I know from Burckhardt's own description of this strange interview, have been much else than a polite escorting out of the room, which is self-explanatory if one reflects that the participants were a lady and Jakob Burckhardt. The version of Burckhardt's behavior on this occasion that is circulating around town seems to be that "Kobi" pretended to be a senile "moribund."— Jakob Burckhardt was a Port Royal type of person, quite inclined to a certain pusillanimity and therefore severely vulnerable to situations he had to withdraw from at all costs, even at the cost of assuming the appearance of a mentally deficient fool.

Nietzsche and Burckhardt can be said to have agreed only in their unconstrained stance toward Christianity. As disciples of Schopenhauer, they both attributed the greatest achievements of the Greeks to Greek pessimism (from an excess of suffering), but Burckhardt only "empathetically," while Nietzsche's understanding of the Greeks is based on a primordial relationship of his individual temperament. For if, as Burckhardt believes, Greek sentiments created a distinctive greatness from the fact that they grew on the soil of an egoism unrestricted by any religiously legitimated morality, then the burning ambition that animated Nietzsche was, as far as I could see, the core of his being. His pity for them was precisely not a "Christian" one.—Of the qualities of classical letters, Nietzsche's letters have at least one to a very outstanding degree: they are written "ad hominem." That is why I was so startled when I saw his letter addressed to Jakob Burckhardt in his madness. It was almost indifferent to the addressee; and to me this was almost a more cogent indication than its crazy content that Nietzsche was insane when he wrote it. How could he so lose all self-control, precisely toward this man!

Whoever is familiar with Nietzsche will not be hard-pressed to find documentation of his high views on friendship; his writings abound with them. In the "friendship temple" erected to her brother by his sister, the correspondence with Jakob Burckhardt, Gottfried Keller, and H. von Stein is of particular interest, since it relates to friendships in which Nietzsche's contribution to the lyric quality of the whole relationship, to the emotional expenditure required for its realization, is incomparably the greater, so much so that Nietzsche almost seems to be a victim of the relationship. In each case Nietzsche attaches to the friendship hopes and aspirations which the other party is hardly aware of. This is true even of his friendship with Heinrich von Stein, not to mention that with two others in whom friendship was almost only like *lux beim lucus—a non lucendo,* at least on one side. Since Nietzsche himself, even before his definitive departure from Basel (in the spring of 1879), had presented me the youthful work of his later young friend Freiherr von Stein, *The Ideals of Materialism* (I still have the little book in my library), whereas Nietzsche's personal association with Stein first began in the fall of 1882, I was in a position to follow the relations between these two men from the beginning. Nonetheless they remained, on the whole, very long concealed from me and are very seldom and incompletely mentioned even in my correspondence with Nietzsche. These relations became really transparent only through the double treatment they received for the public through Frau Dr. E. Förster in 1904, in *Friedrich Nietzsche's Collected Letters* and *The Life of Friedrich Nietzsche*. In both works, this so-called friendship with Stein seemed to me, as a friend of Nietzsche's, a depressing and most saddening memory—as grateful as I am, and as everyone who wants to learn something on the subject is, for those publications of Frau Dr. Förster's. Even this encounter, which at first seemed so extraordinarily promising, was to lead to nothing for Nietzsche, whether through the mercilessness of the sickle of death and its encroachment upon Nietzsche's life, or through the natural incompatibility of Nietzsche's temperament with that of everyone else he met.

Poor Nietzsche always felt deep affection; others liked him much less or not at all. And yet I, who stood so far below him, do not in the least intend to deny that he was, like very few other men, made for the feeling of friendship. But precisely in this sensitivity, as in others, he had a copious source of the unhappiness which was poured out over his whole life and which I had in mind in my shy attempt at a very brief but not completely accurate characterization in my *Christianity of Our Contemporary Theology*. Nietzsche's real friends (not his true ones, which don't exist at all, just as there is, according to Nietzsche, no true world other than the real one) had in him the same "hard nut to crack"; they all shared this problem and can judge and evaluate only one another, even in regard to their success in this. (*42*, 228–231)

26   Malwida von Meysenbug   *June 1872*

The numerous and really elite society that had gathered for this artistic votive festival dispersed again after a few days, and Nietzsche also left, returning to his work in Basel. I stayed with Olga for six more weeks near my dear friends in the pretty surroundings of Bayreuth, then left to attend the performances of *Tristan und Isolde* in Munich under the direction of Hans von Bülow. To my great and, I believe, mutual joy I met Nietzsche again, who together with his friend von G . . . had also come for the performances. During the intermissions the two gentlemen came up from their box seats and we walked around in the aisles of the first row in a joyful and excited mood, praising the high work of art we had seen. "I feel so happy," said Nietzsche, "not at all stormily excited, as was prophesied of this work, but internally happy and delighted that such a thing could have been created and performed so magnificently." And it was indeed a magnificent performance. We parted in cordial friendship, and there now began between us a correspondence which was for many years among the dearest of my manifold associations.

[I] immediately told him that on my return journey to Italy with Olga I would pass via Basel and there await Gabriel Monod, to whom Olga meanwhile had gotten engaged after several years of acquaintanceship in Florence, where Monod also spent a long period of time. We even wished to spend some time in Switzerland in the country as a sequel to the cure taken in Kreuznach, and I also told this to Nietzsche.

We did come to Basel, Olga and I, and there we met Gabriel Monod, who then drove with Olga to Mühlhausen in Elsass to introduce his fiancée to his numerous relatives who lived there, while I stayed with Nietzsche and his sister, whom I now met. Here I first got to know Nietzsche's amiable, friendly, kindly nature, of which the present letter gives eloquent evidence. He always wanted to help, to be useful, to do something kind and friendly for his friends, and even the sharpest excesses of his critically negative reason had a touch of mitigating humor that often led us from the deepest seriousness to merriment and laughter. With Monod he enjoyed a mutually respectful friendship, and so we spent a few perfectly beautiful days together, which unfortunately were not followed by any stay in the country, since compelling circumstances called us elsewhere. Afterwards I heard nothing from him for some time. Olga and I continued traveling for a longer time and returned to Florence only in late fall. (*36*)

27   Luise Elisabeth Bachofen   *ca. 1872*

My relations to Nietzsche are limited to only the first few years he was here; he was one year older than I, we were both very young at the time and, as you can imagine, in my eyes he was not the great professor and philosopher, but our relationship was friendly, innocent and cheerful. My first husband also liked him and I know that Nietzsche respected him very much; he had often told me so. *The*

Birth of Tragedy was published then, and my husband was delighted with it and had high expectations of Nietzsche—but then came his further works, which my husband totally rejected and according to his views had to condemn, and little by little the beautiful friendship was tarnished and broken off. But I am always glad that I knew Nietzsche in this early period when he was still enthused with Wagner—and *how* enthusiastic he was! Every Sunday he traveled to Lucerne and returned from there each time filled with his God and told me of all the splendors he had seen and heard; I believe most firmly that the break with Wagner was a deathblow for Nietzsche, at any rate he was afterwards a completely changed man. (5, 17–18)

28   Ida von Miaskowski   *Summer 1874*

Leopold von Scheffler's interesting article on his personal acquaintanceship with Friedrich Nietzsche, which was published recently in the *Neue Freie Presse,* aroused in me memories of the relations my husband and I had with Nietzsche in the years 1874 and 1875. He was still a healthy man then, whereas by 1877 the incipient sickness had alienated the formerly so amiable and sociable man from his former circle of acquaintances.

So my memories ought to form a not uninteresting counterpiece to L. von Scheffler's portrayal. My husband had been called to Basel as a professor of economics in the spring of 1874. One Sunday in June we went on an outing to Frohburg, a beautiful spot in the Jura, together with various acquaintances. There I saw the high range of the Alps for the first time.

I had been enriched by a new delightful experience, which served as a dividing line in my life. Whoever sees the Alps for the first time at a very young age can never experience such a deep impression as they made on me that sunny Sunday morning.

And that day brought me an additional gain: I met Friedrich Nietzsche, who had been working as a professor of philology in Basel for a few years. He and his two friends, the theology professor Franz Overbeck and the philologist Dr. Romundt, belonged to our party.

Nietzsche, who at first had hiked alongside my husband, later also walked for a long time chatting at my side. He had won our hearts most warmly. That Sunday laid the foundation for our later friendship. I will never forget a remark Nietzsche made to me even then. He had been listening to me telling about how well things had been for us in Jena, where my husband had finished his studies shortly before, and how easily we had become acclimated to academic circles. He interrupted my description with the question: "Yes, does your husband possibly not feel repulsed by the narrow-minded arrogance of the German professors? They allow no difference of opinion. But if one has such, then they try to silence him by saying that he is sick!"

The next winter, together with two other young professorial couples from Germany and the three gentlemen, Nietzsche, Overbeck, and Romundt, we established a little social club that met every other week on Tuesday evenings, alternately at one of the three families'. The respective hosts were always supposed to provide some special entertainment, and the unmarried men were supposed to help. I find, in a still extant letter to my mother, an extensive description of a little performance we once arranged at our house. We had set up a carefully prepared tableau vivant from Richard Wagner's *Die Meistersinger* with our five- and three-year-old sons and a little girl of the same age, especially to delight Professor Nietzsche, whose friendship with Wagner was then at its peak.

When our guests had gathered, I asked Nietzsche to play Walter's "Meisterlied." Then I opened the door to the adjacent room, in which stood the tableau vivant set up by my husband. Each of the children was quite characteristic, and doubly charming because of his youth. Little Eva, in a light-blue Gretchen costume, was having her shoe measured by three-year-old Master Hans Sachs in a leather apron and cap, and from an improvised step the little knight von Stolzing, in a splendid red jacket with white cuffs and lace and a heavy gold chain, looked down at the pretty picture. "All were delighted," I reported, "and Nietzsche was even quite moved. He took my two hands and pressed them again and again, thanking me for the delightful surprise . . . The evening ended with more music, Nietzsche improvising again very beautifully on the piano . . ."

On one of these club evenings at one of the other members' homes we had also taken along a young girlfriend, who was a guest at our house. When we returned home she said, as I in turn wrote to my mother, that "she had never before been in such an innocent and pleasant circle. The funny thing about it was that the two main jokesters among us, Overbeck and Nietzsche, are known in all Germany as horrid pessimists and Schopenhauerians." And another time I wrote: "Last Tuesday we again had a very merry time. We read, played and leaped again until 1 o'clock at night. We Baselers must unfortunately do completely without the pleasure of dancing, since there is almost never any dancing in private houses here. We lively Tuesday-clubbers all regret that very much!" Another letter says: "For this evening Professor Nietzsche is said to have once again obtained a simply magnificent book to read aloud from." It was Mark Twain's humorous short stories, which had just been published.

Another time I wrote: "This morning Professor Nietzsche visited us for a while. He brought me a book I very much wanted to read. He also lent me the text to Wagner's *Nibelungen*. . . . On Sunday the three gentlemen, Overbeck, Nietzsche, and Romundt, and J. S. were at our house. After the simple noon meal, which went very cheerily, we had coffee in the garden in the most beautiful weather. Later we played 'Room for Rent' most enjoyably for about an hour. When we had run ourselves quite tired, we went in. Later I sang a few songs to Professor Nietzsche's accompaniment, then he improvised again very beautifully."

In the winter of 1874–75 Nietzsche also came every Friday afternoon to accompany my singing. He always brought many new scores, which we studied and practiced together. At the end my husband used to join us, while Nietzsche improvised or played extracts from Wagner's operas, which he always did from memory and very masterfully. Those were pleasant hours, which we often recalled wistfully later on, after the poor philosopher was just as famous as he was sick.

In the eighties, when Nietzsche's later writings containing some of the oft-quoted sharp words against women appeared, my husband sometimes told me jokingly not to tell people of my friendly relations with Nietzsche, since this was not very flattering for me. It was just a joke. My husband, like myself, always kept friendly memories of Nietzsche, whose intellectually lofty, yet humanly gracious and cheerful demeanor always remained unforgettable to everyone who knew him. And his behavior precisely toward women was so sensitive, so natural and comradely, that even today in old age I cannot regard Nietzsche as a despiser of women. The few hostile words he wrote about women—for I do not call a just castigation of certain weaknesses of the sex hostile—can, it seems to me, be attributed to his illness which sporadically showed its traces in his works quite early. And on the other hand there are so many beautiful, indeed sublime words about woman and marriage in his works, with which the philosopher, as it were, refutes himself.

Nietzsche's external appearance at the beginning of the seventies of the past century still stands vividly in my memory. He was only of medium height, but of slender build, brisk and lively. His features seemed ordinary to me, but the wonderful eyes and impressive forehead made one forget this, and on the whole one had the impression of a personality that towered above the average, even externally.

In the year 1876 we left Basel for a year. When we returned in 1877, we found Professor Nietzsche a sick man, living in complete seclusion. The cheerful friendly home on Spalenthor Way, Nr. 48, had been dissolved. Professor Overbeck was married, Dr. Romundt had returned to Germany.

At first Nietzsche's faithful, caring sister, later Frau Förster-Nietzsche, lived with her brother, and we still associated with her. We saw Nietzsche himself only here and there on the street. Because of his eye ailment he sometimes wore a green eyeshade and greeted us from below this and a wide-brimmed felt hat in so shy, hasty a way that it was hard to recognize this as the cheerful, amiable person with whom we had associated so frequently hardly two years before. (37)

29   Kurt von Miaskowski   *ca. 1874*

Our high school was, as became clear to me later by comparison, a really outstanding humanistic educational institution of the good old style. The rector was, at that time, a member of an old Basel family, and among the teachers were two scholars of world quality. One was Friedrich Nietzsche, who was then still a young professor of ancient philology, still unrecognized by anyone in his future philosophical character and greatness, and as an artist in word and tone perhaps by just a small select circle of friends, among whom were also my parents. I must, however, say that I have no firsthand knowledge of the fact that Nietzsche also taught at the high school. I believe I read in some Nietzsche letters or memoirs that he attached very little importance to this teaching. But I do remember seeing the elegant and distinguished looking man with the large mustache and deep-seated, pensive eyes rather often at our house. He belonged to a musical and literary circle of younger university professors, mostly from Germany, that rotated among the participating families. Nietzsche played the piano very beautifully and often accompanied my mother, who often sang in the glee club, in society, or at home. In the seventies this Basel literary and musical circle ranked among the innovators—at least in Switzerland—reading and appreciating Gottfried Keller, who was then by no means universally recognized, and studying and singing Brahms' incomparable songs, which then still seemed novel and hard to understand, though today they are at the core of every concert program. As for Gottfried Keller, apart from certain Zurich circles, which however included a great number of German and Austrian scholars, oddly enough his fame was made first by the German literary world, and even more oddly not or scarcely by Jews; his great public and glorious name in broader Swiss circles are of later date. Then, of course, he became the poet of the Swiss national anthem and exponent of Swiss literature, on which more or less consciously all subsequent German-Swiss writers are based. (*38*, 86–87)

---

30   Peter Gast   *October 1875ff.*

While I was studying counterpoint and composition in 1872–74 under the chorus director of the famed St. Thomas Church in Leipzig, Professor E. F. Richter, one day my friend Widemann recommended to me a book that had moved him to the highest ecstasy. It was Nietzsche's *The Birth of Tragedy from the Spirit of Music.* The book also impressed me incomparably. No one, we felt, had ever peered into the depths of the Greek character with such perceptiveness; and since we were still filled with the study of Schopenhauer's and Wagner's writings (which latter had just appeared in a complete edition), we now believed that we had in ourselves many of the modern preconditions needed to understand the book. Leaving aside the question of how far our understanding went, at any rate we felt that here was a mind speaking with interpretative force the like of which we had never seen before. The most secret impulses of culture seemed to unveil themselves before us. When Nietzsche had the Apollonian and Dionysian forces finally destroyed by utilitarian rationalism (as expressed by Socrates), we suspected why a sprouting and blossoming of great art is almost impossible under the domination of our culture of knowledge and reason. Joyously we saw, therefore, how Nietzsche turns against this culture:—*The Birth of Tragedy* is a mighty protest of artistic and heroic man against the will-weakening, instinct-destroying consequences of our Alexandrian culture. As one sees, already in this book Nietzsche was the great revaluator. From the very first he saw types of human vital energy, measured by which modern mankind seems very philistine. Our culture destroys nature in man; but culture should intensify human nature by discipline. Only the most highly potentialized man can give highest value to the world, as Goethe and Nietzsche wish it; the debilitated person devalues it.

When Nietzsche cited David Strauss as a corresponding example, and then in *Untimely* [*Meditations*] *II* contrasted his ideal of a great historical conception with the desiccating type of historical activity, our admiration of his mind increased along with our understanding and was transmitted to others. Among these was Widemann's friend Ernst Schmeitzner. He had taken up the profession of book-dealer, intending to become a publisher. When in 1874 family circumstances put him in a position to do so, he consulted with Widemann about authors to be recruited. Widemann advised him to approach this magnificent Nietzsche immediately, as well as Franz Overbeck, whose *Christianity of Our Contemporary Theology* had likewise aroused great interest. It happened that Schmeitzner's inquiry arrived in Basel precisely when Nietzsche's publisher E. W. Fritzsch had stated that he would probably be unable to publish additional *Untimely* [*Meditations*] (mid-July 1874). Since Nietzsche in those weeks was expecting to complete his "Schopenhauer as Educator" and wished to send the book to press soon, Fritzsch's rejection must have disappointed him as much as Schmeitzner's offer gladdened him. Therefore he did not leave our friend without hope of becoming his publisher. Likewise, Overbeck, who was just then finishing volume I of his *Studies on the History of the Ancient Church.* Schmeitzner was, however, known to the two Baselers only by correspondence, and so more certainty about him was desirable. Overbeck, who spent the summer holidays in Dresden, therefore used his return journey for a meeting with Schmeitzner in his native city, Chemnitz. It took place on August 14, and Widemann was present during the second part of it. Overbeck and Schmeitzner soon came to terms on the publishing matter: Overbeck even gave the young publisher a long manuscript of his above-mentioned *Studies.* From Chemnitz, Overbeck went via Bayreuth to get Nietzsche and to travel to Basel with him. Soon afterwards a manuscript from Nietzsche too arrived in Chemnitz by mail, "Schopenhauer as Educator," for the time being just the first four sections (the book was actually finished; but Nietzsche, since he could never be satisfied, subjected the entire fifth section to a thorough revision). When the two books appeared toward the end of October, Schmeitzner also purchased from E. W. Fritzsch Nietzsche's three earlier books and Overbeck's *Christianity*. To take care of this matter, Overbeck then returned to Chemnitz on December 23, 1874, on his way to Dresden; by chance I too was passing through Chemnitz on that same day and was happy also to be introduced to Overbeck by my friends. His impression corresponded to the enthusiasm in which we young artists were then living, enthusiasm at the prospect of Bayreuth and the hopes which Wagner and, much more deeply, Nietzsche attached to it. We believed Overbeck to be in much closer contact with these things than he was, and saw him, the cheerful, scholarly historian, probably even as an emissary from the luminous land of such cultural hopes. Enough, through him we learned at least a few facts about Nietzsche, of which precisely the relations to Wagner interested us most (which the foreword to *The Birth of Tragedy* had led us to deduce); but so that our joy was not without a counterbalance we unfortunately also had to hear that Nietzsche's health had recently often left something to be desired.

What we heard refined our interest mightily and led us to a new insight and penetration into Nietzsche's problems. "Schopenhauer as Educator" had won us over completely and became our standard in the highest questions of culture. For while our contemporaries understood "culture" to mean approximately Bentham's ideal of a maximization of general comfort (the ideal of Strauss and all socialists since More), Nietzsche suddenly appeared among them like a lawgiver out of thunderclouds teaching that the goal and summit of culture was to produce genius. This was the explicit statement of something that important predecessors surely had suspected but never stated. The entire play of forces of culture would be changed if many people really accepted this doctrine. But, as quiet readers of Nietzsche, we felt especially that an extraordinary personality, a high model, must be behind these words. And so, while we were living in rapture over the *verba docent,* we were already seized by longing for the *exempla trahunt,* I mean the longing to have the man act directly upon us, to hear his voice, read his features, if possible win his confidence.

In the summer of 1875, my friend Widemann came back to Leipzig to continue his university studies; there the decision matured in us to go to Basel because of Nietzsche. Equipped with Schmeitzner's recommendations, we arrived in Basel in mid-October 1875 by way of Bayreuth. The first days, we tried to orient ourselves about the city and its spirit. Once in a bookstore we asked the salesclerk for a photograph of Nietzsche, since such pictures of Basel professors could be seen in the showcases, and we eagerly wanted one since we were still without any idea of Nietzsche's external appearance. We were astonished, however, to be asked, "Professor Nietzsche? Is there anyone here by that name?" Nor could Nietzsche's picture be purchased in other shops. From this we concluded that he must have an excellent mastery of the Epicurean "quiet life." Soon afterwards when we called on him, we were struck by his appearance. A military type! not a "scholar"! Now all the world knows his picture, though only the person who has had the pleasure of his presence will be able to picture him vividly and accurately. We had pictured the author of *Anti-Strauss* as having some degree of harshness, but were surprised precisely by his kindliness, his inner seriousness, the absence of any sarcasm. He seemed intentionally to want to soften by his words the energy that his face expressed, the fire that flamed in his eyes. He gave an impression of eminent self-mastery. Strict toward himself, strict in matters of principle, he was, however, extremely benevolent in his judgment of other people. This was to come to our advantage in a singular way. The way he received us already showed this. "Oh, I know you gentlemen already," he said with cheerful dignity. Puzzled as to when he could have met us, we learned that he had been in that bookshop at the same time as we and had immediately taken us for the friends recommended to him by Overbeck. This turn of events put an end to all bashfulness; the remainder of the conversation dealt with our study plans, our past, and the like. Since we were afraid of wasting his valuable time, we left soon although he assured us that he liked to be interrupted in his work now and then. He also met with us for walks, the first of which remains vividly in my memory; Overbeck also went. In my opinion, my friend Widemann had greater affinity with Nietzsche than I, and yet as we were walking along, the discussion between four people broke up into two separate dialogues: Overbeck had joined Widemann, and Nietzsche, me, and the two pairs were engaged in separate conversations. We walked to the new cemetery, which still had just a few graves and resembled a large garden with beautiful long paths. The first thing I, as a musician, discussed with Nietzsche was the Gluck-Puccini dispute, about which I had just read Desnoiresterres' study. Nietzsche considered a dispute between two so decisive tastes as practically unresolvable: the cuckoo, he said mischievously, will hardly admit that "hee-haw" is also an appropriate expression of soul. Then I told of my long hikes as a boy, to which I had been inspired by the good Seume; to my delight, Nietzsche professed to be a very close countryman of Seume's: their respective hometowns, Röcken and Poserna, are located close together. On the way home Nietzsche finally began to speak about Switzerland, and here for the first time he got into full swing, with that cool eloquence peculiar only to him, and from innumerable detailed observations he soared to the highest perspectives. He obviously set store on picturing before me everything valuable about Switzerland so that I might benefit from it to the full. He started with a parallel between Paul Heyse and Gottfried Keller and with the deep difference between being a Berlin child or an heir of the old Zurich urban culture. He touched upon the literary and educational innovations made by Swiss writers of the eighteenth century, the country's position as an asylum in Europe's political turmoils, the unselfishness of the larger communities, the wholesome absence of the courtly system of decorations for scholars and officials; and finally he said that it would perhaps turn out that all the valuable qualities we tended to call "German" now could perhaps be found more often and in purer form in Switzerland than in the "Reich"—a most magnificent example of which was Jakob Burckhardt.

For our main courses we registered for Nietzsche's "Antiquities of the Religious Cult of the Greeks" and "History of Greek Literature"; Overbeck's "History of Christian Literature until Eusebius"; Burckhardt's "Greek Cultural History" and "The Art of Antiquity." It was a supreme pleasure to absorb so much knowledge, judgment, insight, and general perspective, and with the help of such mature minds to advance once and for all beyond some youthfully hypothetical standpoints.

Each semester we received several invitations to Nietzsche's home, generally evenings. What a festival those were for us! Nietzsche lived very cozily in a quiet neighborhood on Spalenthor Way 48, together with his sister; his study faced toward a garden, the parlor and living room toward the street. I will never forget the impression this brother-and-sister pair made on us; my letters to friends and relatives at the time revel in delight about it: I had never before experienced such charming cordiality mixed with delightful humor. Fräulein Nietzsche's presence and care was a deep refreshment for Nietzsche after the last six years of solitude. He himself describes this in a letter of September 26, 1875, to Freiherr von Gersdorff. On such evenings we also had the good fortune to hear Nietzsche play the piano: I can still remember especially his "Hymn to Solitude," a piece full of austere unrelenting grandeur, intermingled with sirenlike, captivating *dolce* passages that were soon rejected again with spite. Nietzsche's touch was of great intensity, without being hard, his playing eloquent, polyphonic, with most manifold gradations, so that here the horn, flutes, or violins, there trumpets could be heard clearly out of its orchestral sound. —The heart-moving kindness of the Nietzsches was also shown when they invited us at Christmas and even surprised us with presents: for at no time of the year do bachelors feel their isolation so much as on this holiday: so how effusive our gratitude was for this honor and joy.

Closer relations with Nietzsche began for me, however, really only from the moment he told me that he had begun but left incomplete an *Untimely Meditation* on Richard Wagner. This was at about the end of April 1876, when my friend Widemann had left me to carry out his military obligations. Since Nietzsche saw my great eagerness to read the Wagner fragment, he lent it to me. At home I read and read it with growing enthusiasm and when I returned it I could not refrain from saying that it would be eternally regrettable if this meditation were to remain a torso. But he considered the work too personal for publication. A few days later he said to me, "Looking into the notebook, the idea came to me whether I couldn't at least present it to Wagner for his enjoyment, namely on the next May 22nd. I am going to have a copy made of it." I volunteered to do the work, and I brought him the copy. He seemed to like it, in fact it so stirred his interest in his own work that, instead of sending the copy to Bayreuth, he mailed it as a manuscript for publication to Schmeitzner, wrote the three missing final chapters in June, and had the book published as a commemorative volume for the first Bayreuth performances. —From this time on I helped Nietzsche by taking dictation (and at times also by reading aloud), at first still very rarely, but almost daily from September 1876 until he went to Sorrento, then again in the winter semester 1877–78 until my departure for Venice (April 1878). From *Untimely [Meditations] IV* until the end of 1888 I also read without exception every proof of his successive works for publication. Therefore, this volume of letters is one of the most reliable sources on the genesis and publication history of Nietzsche's works, while on the other hand it can be considered a chronological biography of the most important decade in Nietzsche's life. (*21*, xv–xxiv)

31　　Paul Heinrich Widemann　　　　　　　　*November 1875*

The lecture "From My Memories of Friedrich Nietzsche," given by Paul Widemann at the last Miscellaneous Evening of the Society for Literature and Art, aroused unusual interest among those present and also deserves to be known in wider circles. Mr. Widemann was one of the most intimate friends and enthusiastic followers of the much opposed and much celebrated great philosopher. The nature of the relations between the two men is shown by the following dedication which decorates the dedication page of a score of *Die Meistersinger* presented to Widemann by Nietzsche on New Year's Day 1878:

> This work, originally a present from Richard Wagner, which I received in Tribschen in 1869 the first time I celebrated Christmas with him there, I now present to Mr. Paul Widemann, both to give him a sign of my warm and deep esteem and to know that he will have it in his possession as a pledge to remember me by. May this excellent friend always be aware that I will remain faithful in hope of his artistic ability, faithful in belief in his great strength, inventiveness and endurance. Indeed, the day will come when all belief and hope are fulfilled. FRIEDRICH NIETZSCHE

In the year 1874 the young book-dealer Ernst Schmeitzner wrote to Mr. Widemann asking for advice on how he could assure himself of a significant future as a publisher. Widemann, whom Nietzsche's till then published works, *The Birth of Tragedy* and the *Untimely Meditations,* had sent reeling with delight, could give him no better advice than to try to become Nietzsche's publisher. At the same time he also recommended to him Overbeck, whose book on *The Christianity of Our Contemporary Theology* had aroused a lot of attention at the time. Schmeitzner followed these suggestions, and the steps he then took actually led to success both with Nietzsche and with Overbeck. Overbeck himself came to Chemnitz to have a somewhat closer look at the young publisher. Widemann was present at this meeting and learned from Overbeck some general facts about Nietzsche: that he was a pastor's son from Naumburg, was closely associated with Wagner, taught classical philology at the university, and that his health was unfortunately not the best. This evening remained vividly in Widemann's memory. The peculiar charm of Overbeck's personality was felt for a long time afterwards in his sensitive soul. His imagination interwove Overbeck's person with that of Nietzsche, whom he had not yet seen, but who in his view outshone all else.

Nine months later Widemann went to continue his studies to Leipzig, where he had already spent three and a half years and where his friend of former years, Peter Gast, was staying. He drew Gast into the Nietzschean circle of thought and found him to be an equally enthusiastic colleague. They decided to go together on a pilgrimage to Basel to see Nietzsche and to continue their studies under him.

And so it happened. The first thing they did in Basel was to inquire about Nietzsche's reputation among the local populace. On this score, however, they experienced a bad disappointment: no one knew anything of Nietzsche's existence, not to mention his importance, and when they asked for a portrait of Nietzsche in a bookstore, they got the puzzled answer: "Nietzsche? Who's that?"

Several days later Widemann and Peter Gast made their first visit to Nietzsche and were received very kindly. Widemann describes Nietzsche's external appearance as follows: He was a strong, slender man, thirty-one years of age, but looked a few years older, had a thoroughly military appearance and could have been taken for an officer in civilian clothes. His features were almost hard, although not thin, and extraordinarily energetic; his hair blond and somewhat unruly, his mouth shaded by a huge blond mustache, his ears remarkably small, and his forehead remarkably beautiful and finely vaulted. Under this forehead sparkled two large, deep, gray-blue eyes, whose strange expression is hard to describe. His speech was not at all fluent; he seemed to ponder every sentence twice before speaking. His stride too was peculiar and made him recognizable from far away. He "tapped along" as is said in Saxony, i.e., he took small but very fast steps. Perhaps this resulted from his extraordinary shortsightedness.

Right after this reception, Widemann and Gast were invited to lunch by Nietzsche and this first invitation was followed by many, many others in the course of the three and a half years Widemann spent in Basel. In this lively association, Widemann got to know the man Nietzsche and to revere him as he had previously revered the famous philosopher. Nietzsche felt out of place as a professor. Widemann attended his classes on the history of Greek literature and the antiquities of the religious cult of the Greeks; these classes not only showed an astonishing mastery of the subject, but they also contained an abundance of deep insights into the Greek mind, Greek life, and its motive forces, and they tended to highlight the sad, tragic background of the sunny Greek cheerfulness. But it was almost painful to watch him lecture. Equipped with the strongest eyeglasses, he sat with his face almost touching his notebook on the lectern. Slowly and laboriously, the words struggled through his lips and often his speech was interrupted by pauses which caused one to worry that he might be unable to continue reading. In fact, sometimes he had to stop the class because the excruciating headaches that plagued him almost daily and deprived him of sleep at night became unbearable.

Nietzsche enjoyed the greatest respect from his colleagues, but whether they understood him completely remains doubtful, in Widemann's opinion. He had no following, only individual friends, among them Franz Overbeck, Peter Gast, Widemann, and Jakob Burckhardt, the scholarly, profound and brilliant describer of the two decisive spiritual transition periods of the post-Christian era, namely the time of Constantine the Great, when Christianity replaced the moribund classical paganism, and the culture of the Renaissance. Burckhardt—himself a monumental man—was the representative of a heroic worldview and this especially endeared him to Nietzsche. What Burckhardt thought of Nietzsche can be seen from the following: Once at the end of class Burckhardt walked up to Widemann to ask about Nietzsche's health which just then was very bad. Widemann told him what he knew, and Burckhardt replied: "That is the fate of child prodigies. Because he was so precocious at Schulpforta, marvels were always expected of him; this strained him beyond measure and undermined his health."

The lecturer then gave a great number of details from his personal association with Nietzsche. Nietzsche often visited Widemann in his humble study and had him play something that he was just then composing. Nietzsche had a good knowledge of music; he missed no nuance, no pulse-beat, no gesture and no feature of the music. He had also tried his hand as a composer and once played for Widemann and Gast his meditation on Byron's *Manfred,* a harsh, bleak composition, with great passionate passages, and most peculiar.

In March 1879, Widemann returned to Basel after a stay in Graubünden and here learned to his satisfaction that Nietzsche had arrived for an unlimited leave to restore his health. Widemann advised him to go to Italy, and Nietzsche followed this advice. In Venice Nietzsche met Peter Gast, who remained his devoted friend and helper until the end of his life. Widemann returned to Chemnitz and from then on maintained only a written correspondence with this man, whom he revered ardently. He saw Nietzsche again only when the latter already lay on his deathbed. (*66*)

32   Ludwig von Scheffler   *Summer 1876*

What I present here is a simple memory. I am not afraid to be committing an indiscretion thereby. In an important man's life, even the appearance of his real personality is of interest. In Nietzsche's case, I think, very bad images have been preserved. They are not just ordinary; they distort his features and give a false idea of him.

I want to report about Nietzsche the real man, not the genial thinker living disembodied in the realm of spirits.

I first set eyes on Nietzsche exactly thirty years ago. In Basel, in his course into which I strayed as if by accident. For how could I have sought him out on my own initiative? Not that I was till then unacquainted with his name as an author. I had heard of *The Rebirth* [*sic*]*of Tragedy*. I had also paged through the *Untimely Meditations,* the first of which had already appeared. But the widespread rejection of Nietzsche's writings also determined my judgment. Youth, as Aristotle said, tends toward the affirmative. The negative will always receive only its conditional approval. I was therefore repulsed by this author, who seemed to be speaking to me from an alien world.

But even if folly and prejudice had blinded me less at that time, one man blocked my way to Nietzsche:—Jakob Burckhardt! I had come to this Swiss university, far away from my home, just to hear him. And I found my expectations fulfilled beyond all measure—something which happened to me rarely in nature and never again in men. I was too full of this magnificent man for any other personality of the Basel circle of scholars except him to have been able to fascinate me at that time.

And yet one day I found myself standing in front of the little auditorium, which, when I asked, a few students standing nearby

identified as Nietzsche's. There was a strange tone in their pro-
nunciation of the name, so full of "s" sounds. Something like bewilderment at my question, like mockery, or a slight trace of mockery.

This aroused my curiosity.

Meanwhile it was time for the course to begin.

I entered.

It was a small room rather than a lecture hall, and instead of a
classroom full of students I saw a young man leaning on the window
sill, not dressed like a regular student but rather in the dark garment
of the Leipzig conservatorist! The black robe with the long, long
lapels! . . . I was eager to see the face that went with this strange
figure, but the youth, still engrossed in the spectacle before him,
had his back turned to me.

That spring, I must add, the Rhine was raging with one of its
most terrible floods. Its waters whirled into the adjacent streets,
rolling countless pieces of debris along in the powerful current. Not
only the old picturesque bridge, then still the only one, began to
sway from the constant assault, but even the university building, rising so directly out of the river, stood in danger of collapsing.

So the young man stood completely fascinated by the exciting
spectacle from the window when I cleared my throat loudly to
awaken him out of his reverie.

"Philosophy of the future too?!" I said to him, for some reason
sensing him to be of a similar mind.

I am still ashamed to this day of that rude word, which I had not
even invented but gleaned from a journal article that parodied
Nietzsche's teaching with the label of *"Zukunftsmusik"* [music of the
future, harebrained idealism]—a music which had not yet been
accepted by the public. But greater than my astonishment at the
young man's angry expression was my surprise at his features themselves. Another Richard Wagner! But a younger, "more handsome
version," as is said. Not just the cut of his sideburns correctly imi-
tated the "master," but nose, forehead, chin were modeled after the
great musician's bust.

Young people, if they otherwise have good manners, easily find
a way to get along. I excused myself with sincere words and soon
learned that I had a very close countryman before me. A young
musician from the Erz Mountains, whom the overpowering impact
of Nietzsche's "Schopenhauer as Educator" had led to the author
himself as an enthusiastic disciple.

"How unusual!" I felt at this explanation, "and yet how moving!" And as I looked "Peter Gast" (so Nietzsche had rebaptized his

disciple Heinrich Köselitz) in the eye in a warmer mood, the door opened. A strange phenomenon was standing on the threshold: Nietzsche!!

I had not expected the professor to come into the room in the fire of thought, like Burckhardt. And I probably was already learning that a provocative tone in a writer does not always match his behavior as a private person. But such modesty, indeed humility, of deportment was surprising to me in Nietzsche.

Moreover he was of short rather than medium height. His head deep in the shoulders of his stocky yet delicate body. And the gleaming horn-rimmed glasses and the long hanging mustache deprived the face of that intellectual expression which often gives even short men an impressive air.

And yet this whole personality showed anything but indifference to personal appearance. Here one saw not Jakob Burckhardt's short haircut, not the crude linens, nor the threadbare, almost shabby suit, hanging loosely on the laughing stoic's powerful frame. No, Nietzsche had adjusted to the fashion of the day. He was wearing light-colored pants, a short jacket, and around his collar fluttered a delicately knotted necktie, also of a lighter color. Not as if there were anything particularly striking about his wardrobe. Nietzsche was probably trying less to play the dandy—when has a German professor ever succeeded at that?!—than to suggest something artistic in his appearance. The long hair framing the face not with curls but only with strands of hair also suggested this.

But how far removed from artistic casualness everything else was that characterized this man! With a heavy, almost weary stride, his little finely shod feet carried him up to the rostrum. Then, as he sat down, his form disappeared up to his head behind the balustrade. The Professor took off his glasses and I saw his eyes for the first time. Extremely myopic, dull eyes that made a strange effect only through one peculiarity. For while the overflowing dark pupil seemed extremely large, it was nonetheless exceeded by the white of the eyeball toward the eyelids. This gave his look, when seen in profile, a touch of excitement and grimness. The false expression which photos of Nietzsche show! Actually the eye of the mild, kindly man never had this trait.

The Rhine roared with the *fortissimo* of an organ tone, and I feared it could drown out the teacher's voice despite the closed window. But a new experience now captivated and confused me: Nietzsche had a voice! Not the rounded tone of an orator, nor the sharply articulated but really ineffective modulation typical of the pathos of many a university professor. Nietzsche's speech, soft and natural as it struggled through his lips, had only one thing in its favor: it came from the soul! Hence the strongly agreeable trait that was immediately communicated to the hearer, the irresistible power which led me toward ideas which, merely read, would have aroused me to the most vehement contradiction. And even today the enchantment of this voice continues to affect me! It lays a mitigating, transfiguring veil over the most heterogeneous of his pronouncements. Whoever has not experienced the interpretive melody of his spoken word only half knows Nietzsche.

Nietzsche was teaching a course on Plato! When I entered his class he had reached the discussion of the great philosopher's view of life. It was a pleasant surprise to find him discussing a favorite subject of mine. But what was I to hear about my beloved Plato!

I had for some time been busy reading Plato sufficiently not only to follow and understand the lecture but also to compare it with the sources on various points. And thanks to the skepticism of my former teacher, Karl Prantl, I had already discarded many a prejudice in this field. I had been moved on reading in *Gorgias* of the "tragedy and comedy of life." I no longer believed in the fable of the "sunny cheerful Greece." Such a reinterpretation of the Platonic doctrine, however, into the purely pessimistic, as Nietzsche now undertook, had a bewildering effect on me. It did occur to me that Köselitz had just called Nietzsche an admirer of Schopenhauer. But never, I concluded to myself, would the latter have gone so far in arbitrary treatment of another's views. Nietzsche's depiction of Plato often turned things upside down. One example has remained especially vivid in my memory. The image of the man in the cave and the philosopher.

Who can forget the marvellous simile in Plato's *Republic* of the underground dwelling of the many (Nietzsche later changes this into "far too many"!) who all their lives see all things only in shadow images which the true events cast on their cave wall high above and behind them. Only the philosopher soars out of this prison and upward. He penetrates to the region of knowledge, the light of the sun! . . . Nietzsche, quite contrary to Plato's spirit, forces the thinker back into a dungeon! I can still hear his bewildering words: "The philosopher lives as in a cave. He sees nothing and hears nothing. He sees only flight from the world as the salvation of being . . ."

"But, Professor!" an objection hovered on my lips on hearing this and similar statements. But my resistance subsided as soon as I grasped the situation rightly. No, "Plato" was certainly not being taught here. Therefore the emptiness of the classroom was only too understandable. But something unusual and fascinating was nonetheless being offered. However, the man alone and his word had to affect us.

This insight led me back to purely human interest in the speaker.

Who was the man delivering his monologues there in solitude, so completely to himself?

Yes, Nietzsche's lecture could really be called a monologue. Even Burckhardt in his portrayals did not address the hearers directly. He was carried away by his material. He literally plunged into it. Not just historical figures, the artist and his works—everything found in him speech, movement, a dialogual life. This was just one of the most artful means of shaping the ideas all the more intensely for us! Nietzsche, however, seemed to know of absolutely no relation to another being. He spoke slowly, often halting, not so much seeking an expression as checking the impression of his dicta to himself. If the thread of thought led him to something particularly extreme, then his voice also sank, as if hesitatingly, down to the softest *pianissimo*. No, this was no Storm and Stresser. A patient sufferer, rather, was calling upon philosophy to console him in the struggle against a crushing fate. Upon a philosophy that was still not his own, but was adjusted to his feeling. The warmth of his presentation, the manner in which this worldview took shape before us in his words, nonetheless gave the impression of something new and completely individual. It lay like a cloud on this man's entire being. And over and over the question came to me as I listened: "Who is he? Where is he heading for, this thinker?" Then suddenly the speaker gave his sentences a sharp epigrammatic twist. An aphorism instead of a conclusion. Was it calculation that the Rhine instead of his words brought a roaring finale? Nietzsche sank back into his chair as if listening. Then he got up slowly. And gently and silently as he had come, he walked back out the door. As if benumbed by the whole scene, with mixed feelings of interest and contradiction I sought for an explanation of the impression I had experienced. But one thing was certain to me: I would hear out this Nietzsche-Plato! I was able to give this as a kind of answer to the friendly questioning expression of my fellow listener. And really on the next day I saw Nietzsche's characteristic signature scrawled on my registration form, although due to the professor's shy, reserved attitude, my being his student did not lead immediately to a closer relationship.

Heinrich Köselitz, however, immediately took me into his full confidence. On our walks he told me that Nietzsche, although academic youth had turned away from him, was not completely alone in Basel. Jakob Burckhardt, especially, was closely associated with him. Not only Schopenhauerian philosophy had brought these two men together; Nietzsche had formerly even attended Burckhardt's lectures (a fact which, however, puzzled many), and the latter had responded with warm sympathy when his young friend sent him his first writings. Köselitz informed me in an incidental remark that both men were amateur musicians. I hoped that Nietzsche's "compositions" delighted him more than Burckhardt's "improvisations" could do for me.

Of course, this information could only increase my interest in Nietzsche. Naturally, in my conversations with Köselitz some conflicts were bound to arise. And since the amiable fellow, so benevolent by nature, could not possibly, as it seemed to me, have gotten such baroque ideas on his own, I naturally held Nietzsche responsible for them too.

What I especially disliked about Köselitz was his lack of national pride (my father had returned from the great war as a commanding officer!) and his often almost petulant hatred of everything ecclesiastical. I was young and I still had in my soul that lyrical mood which warmed at the history, at the beautiful antique buildings of "golden Basel." It felt good to let my eye glide up and down the splendid vaults, and I enjoyed the magic of the hour when in the evening in the adjacent cloisters I could gaze at the glimmering Rhine and the dark Black Forest beyond. If Köselitz ever surprised me at such daydreaming, I was sure to hear nothing but outraged scolding at this "priest-ridden art." Even the "red inquisition-color" of the cathedral (its splendid sandstone blocks often glowing in purple!) offended my companion's eye. He found the "modest" hall structure inside to be suitable for a temple for the "poor in spirit." He saw nothing at all in the Gothic character except abstraction and philistinism.

Such attacks simply amazed me. Had the slogan "Écrasez l'infame!" or "Down with the Church" really produced such fruits under Nietzsche's influence? Soon, on a joyous occasion, I was to learn that this was not so, that Nietzsche, at least in his personal relations, never used such agitation. For the professor invited me to his home. Yes, I was once at Nietzsche's home for afternoon tea!

After one of his gloomiest lectures, not without solemnity and embarrassment he invited me to come to his house the next day. However, I had a prior invitation to a garden party at Colonel P.'s and his beautiful daughters were certainly reason enough to decline an invitation from a professor. Yet I immediately accepted Nietzsche's invitation, convinced that it would be a thrilling experience. I was not disappointed. At least the domestic milieu in which he moved was a striking one, such as I had not expected.

Nietzsche's apartment at the time was on Spahlentor Way, a neat row of houses extending outside the towering, picturesque gate structure, along a boulevardlike street. One of the most attractive of these two-story buildings was identified to me as the professor's home. Inside a gate, a young lady opened the door for me. A pretty and fascinating figure! But I was to see "Nietzsche's sister" in Basel only during this fleeting encounter. To my regret she did not appear again. Only the professor, with "Peter Gast" at his side, could be seen in the parlor. I say "parlor" because I can find no better term for this room which was marvellously divided between the coolness of a reception-room and the warm intimacy of a boudoir. Above all, it was not the customary study! Nor did one first have to have seen Burckhardt's "studio" for comparison: a dilapidated old sofa as the only seating arrangement, on which the host alone sat during his "receptions" ("Burckhardt did not like formalities!"). For in Burckhardt's home books were stacked high on every side, stacked all over the floor, and unless I wanted to stand throughout my visit with that revered man I had no choice but to sit on a tottering pile of books. But in Nietzsche's apartment, soft large armchairs invited one to sit down. They had white lace coverlets with delightful flower patterns such as the famous Mülhausen lace factories have been producing since French times! Bouquets of violets and young roses! And when one was half sunk into such a gallant armchair, one's gaze fell again on fresh flowers! In glasses, in bowls, on tables, in corners, competing in their discrete mixture of colors with the watercolors on the walls! Everything airy, aromatic and delicate! Lightly curtained windows, filtering the glare of daylight, made one feel like a guest invited not to a professor's house but to a beloved girlfriend's. Nor was this impression dispersed when the harmonious tones of Nietzsche's pleasant voice broke the silence of the room.

The Professor, as I said, did the honors himself, serving the tea with a smile that glided across his blank face like a ray of sunshine.

Yet there was something constrained about his social demeanor, and the conversation would soon have lapsed, had not Köselitz taken it over with his pleasant loquacity. So Nietzsche was able to lean back in his easy chair with the tiredness I was accustomed to observe in him, and he played the role of a listener making occasional brief remarks.

And Köselitz, like all young people, spoke of the things that primarily interested him. Of music and how it was performed in Basel! Incidentally, an especially insidious theme for him! For I had already heard that "Peter Gast" had as a matriculated student received an official reprimand from the rector of the university for a newspaper music review violently criticizing Selmar Bagge, conductor of the Basel symphony concerts, for his "backward" taste! And now, as he spoke, the young Wagnerian's rage at the reprimand he had received rumbled past us again like a storm cloud. Of course, Köselitz felt confident of Nietzsche's approval. But precisely Nietzsche's attitude on this matter surprised me. A shake of the head or a soothing movement of the hand was all he used to try to calm his follower's loquacious zeal. Only when Köselitz became too personal and blamed an influential patrician for the "low level" of musical understanding in Basel, together with the hated "Bache" (that is how he consistently pronounced the name of the good man from Gotha in our dialect!), did Nietzsche interfere with longer sentences, addressing me and presenting the whole thing as a friendly explanation. The pietism of Basel society (thirty years ago!) was, he said, indeed to blame if concerts here still had a strictly conservative character. Of course, music was, on the other hand, the only artistic interest which this conventional orthodoxy had left. To allow one's daughters to go to the theater was forbidden. But just recently a concert hall had been built, more functional and magnificent than any that could be found in Germany. However, only "classical music" could be performed there. In his understanding of music, Basel's reputable new concert director had perhaps gotten as far as Mendelssohn, but certainly not as far as Robert Schumann or any even newer composers . . .

"But why are we speaking of something we cannot change?" he smiled to Köselitz. "Tell us about the fine arts . . . What is your impression of Burckhardt?"

The Professor could have struck no theme more suitable to draw me into the conversation. For this was a topic I was overflowing with! Zealously, passionately, I spoke of Burckhardt's relationship with his students, with the same enthusiastic partiality I still feel and which leads me to look back on my semesters in Basel as the happiest time of my student years.

Nietzsche had taken off his glasses while I was speaking. I felt his large lustreless eyes focused on me. A challenge for me to describe my impressions all the more graphically! But suddenly I was unable to continue, especially since a deep sigh of the Professor's had already confused me.

I had begun speaking about ourselves, about Jakob Burckhardt's youthful audience! I stressed that just as the master rejected all pedantry almost passionately and sought to stimulate only our individual interest in the subject, so we his followers tried to clarify our taste for art completely personally. And yet we, of course only the more inspired among us, saw only through his eyes. And what circuitous paths brought us together on Sunday mornings in the museum's art galleries! From Holbein to antiquity, and from the Master's "Passion" again and again back to his "Bürgermeister Meier" and to the "Lais Corinthiaca"! We knew all the smug judgments "from the outside" which tried to spoil our enjoyment of Steinhausser's "Apollo" and "Herakles." We considered the antiquities to be genuine, because we felt them to be so. No need for authentication restrained us in our free, joyous judgments. Only one impression left us completely speechless. Even the boldest remained still before Holbein's self-portrait in the hall of drawings! And I now struggled futilely in Nietzsche's presence to define the magical attraction of that wonderful portrait. It did not help that I so-to-speak traced line after line of that face. This approach was powerless to describe the expression of fully developed manhood combined with the charm of fresh youth (Holbein's self-portrait, as is known, presents him without a beard). And I failed to capture even the individual traits in their full value. I faltered when I came to the mouth. I could see the lips before me. So fully rounded yet so energetically closed! Not avid, yet as if created for pleasure!

"A mouth . . .," I stammered bewilderedly.

"A mouth to kiss!"

Disconcertedly I looked aside. Truly, it was Nietzsche who had spoken, in an attitude and a tone which seemed to contrast most strangely with the mildly sensual coloration of his words. For leaning far back in his armchair, his head bowed onto his chest and his arms hanging limply on the armrests, he seemed to have spoken out of a dream rather than as a comment on my report.

I looked inquiringly over to Köselitz. But here too my smile met his uncomprehending, unchanged face. Nor did I think much of the event at the time. Only later, much later, did the fineness of his artistic judgment dawn on me.

For such it was indeed. Not just a reminiscence of the Latin *"os ad oscula paratum"* (a mouth ready for kisses), but a deepest grasp of what is most characteristic of Holbein's painted features. His mouth contains a joyous sensual sense of power! Loved by the beautiful "girl from Offenburg," a feast for London's lice, yet sought in vain by his "wife's" dull jealousy (how terrible the truth is in her Basel portrait!).

Yet not just this exclamation from amid violet bouquets and young roses, a much more intimate meeting was to prove further to me what a tender sensitivity was behind the man Nietzsche's apparent inaccessibility.

Even to this day I cannot speak of it without shyness. Least of all, however, because I fear an uncomprehending reader. Whoever has looked so deeply into Michelangelo's heart and drawn the veil from Platen's confessions will also not stand in timid silence before Nietzsche's mysterious psyche. But what I myself then learned and suffered, weighs on my soul like a painful memory. I was to find Nietzsche only to lose him forever! And I alone was to blame for it!

It was natural that after that visit a more friendly association developed between the professor and me. We conversed not only after class, but occasionally I accompanied him part of the way home with or without "Peter Gast." We then spoke not of Plato, but of travel destinations, of a hike in autumn, and his whole being became visibly animated each time. But once I was to find myself in a most special situation with him. Alone in class with him! Yes, once he gave his lecture to me alone!!

For some reason or other Köselitz had not come to the university. And I myself had arrived late for class. The Professor was already waiting in the classroom! I was deeply moved to see him so, and expected an offended remark. Instead he received me with the greatest friendliness, indeed with a new cheerfulness I had never seen in him. He shook my hand with a smile and then swung up to the rostrum more elastically than ever.

He had suspected that today we would not be our usual trio. So he did not want to continue with his regular lecture, but wanted to offer me a philosophical intermezzo. "Something"—he drew a manuscript out of his breast-pocket and his voice hesitated some-what—"something I once read to Frau Wagner!"

Despite the free atmosphere of Basel, I was still too full of academic arrogance not to be puzzled by this explanation. A lecture that had once been read—to a lady!? And even if she had been a diva, Frau Cosima!? I took some offense and felt cast back into that refractory mood which had prevented me from enjoying Nietzsche's first lectures. But how soon the material itself would capture my interest!

Nietzsche was giving a sort of introduction to Platonic philosophy. He let the so-called pre-Platonic philosphers pass before my inner eye in a series of fascinating personalities. Since he also quoted them directly, he read slowly and let the deep thoughts in their statements penetrate all the more into my spirit. They moved along grandly and majestically, like a shining cloud (Nietzsche himself liked so much to use the image of clouds!). But one of those lofty forms detached itself with clearer profile from that dissolving flow. Here the lecturer's voice also was overcome by a gentle trembling, expressing a most intimate interest in his subject-matter: Heraclitus!! I will never forget how Nietzsche characterized him. If not that lecture, at least what he had to say about the sage of Ephesus will be found among his posthumous papers. I always feel a shudder of reverence when I think of the moving end of that lecture. Words of Heraclitus! According to Nietzsche they summed up the inner-most motive of the Ionian philosopher's thought and intention (and his own?). He drew a breath in order to pronounce the sentence. It resounded then fully in the harmonious tones of the Greek original text. More tonelessly yet understandably in German. Nietzsche folded the pages of his manuscript together as he said: "I sought myself!!"

The rushing of the Rhine was again the only audible sound as we both remained in silent rapture for a few moments. Then something strange happened. Nietzsche did not, as usual, sustain his mood by continued silence, but he said to me in a cheerful tone that he would accompany me to my apartment. He had some business with my landlord, who was his insurance agent, and he also wanted to see how life was on the Blumenrain (The Flowery Bank). For that was the name of a stretch of the Rhine bank on the left side of the bridge, where I lived. I was embarrassed by my companion's increased affability, but soon joked at that street's poetic name and even offered Nietzsche my arm when we had left the university. For his tragicomic lamenting over the bad pavement leading to the Rhine Bridge was really quite justified. I then sought to distract his attention from his sore feet to the sky. Thick round white summer clouds moved slowly along the blue background.

"As Paolo Veronese paints them!" I said, half to myself, half to him. Nietzsche looked up, stopped pensively: "and they wander!," he added also as if in a monologue. But then he suddenly dropped my arm, only to seize it then violently with both hands:

"I'm leaving soon . . . The vacation is about to begin . . . Come with me?! Do we want to go watch the clouds pass in Veronese's homeland?!"

I was so moved by this so unexpected, urgent invitation that at first I could not say a word. Then the idea flashed through my mind that I really had no right to such a distinction. "Peter Gast" would have been the most likely prospect, and I myself did not feel so closely attached to the otherwise revered man (fullest congeniality is necessary for travelling together!). I looked down dejectedly and gave a negative excuse which must have sounded cold enough. Nietzsche's hands immediately slid from my arm. I looked at him in confusion and recoiled at the change that had come over his features. This was no longer the Professor I knew, no, the man's distorted face stared at me like a lifeless mask! But understand me rightly: not the grimace as such frightened me—on the contrary. Nietzsche's features had never seemed to me so great, so attractive in their way!—the impression of tragedy before me had a shattering effect on me! And so I forgot both him and me. I was no longer standing on the bumpy ground of Basel, I saw myself transported to Rome, to the Vatican museum the "Galleria delle maschero." There they stood in a row, the antique "tragic masks"! With the hollow eye-caverns, the open mouths, with all the rigid pain in their expression, penetrating even the bristling hairs of the forehead, the tangled curls around lips and chin! Precisely so Nietzsche's wide-opened, unseeing eyes darkened, precisely so his lips, still opened to speak, froze, precisely so even the beard fit into the tragic lines of this entire impression! And I also saw Aeschylus' verses, Sophocles' choruses, flying through the hollows of this living mask as in those marble ones! . . . For moments only! For the Professor turned away from me. He quickly resumed his accustomed demeanor, and we continued the walk to my house with an indifferent but all the more awkward conversation.

What else can I report, what further happened? Nietzsche accompanied me to the door of my room, as he had promised. But he did not enter, instead saying good-bye quickly and leaving me alone with my thoughts about what had happened. I felt that I had unintentionally offended the noble man and committed a great folly. For I now began to realize, to my shame, how much I would have benefited from a journey with Nietzsche, such an interesting and, as I had now learned, such a warmly sensitive personality. But scruples were not my thing at that time. I was young and "dumb." "Dumb" like Parsifal, who failed to ask the question on which all depended, just as I had now not given the right answer. But did this experience therefore remain completely without significance for me?

I would hardly have spoken of it—especially with my own person in the foreground—if I were really of this opinion. Later on, however, that insight into Nietzsche's soul not only explained many of his apparent eccentricities, but my acquaintance with him was of great advantage to me in understanding similar psychic problems. I have already mentioned Platen! How great the similarity of the two men's temperaments was, I had been convinced of long ago. In Platen's case the evidence is in his memoirs, which say everything. In Nietzsche's case, I learned it from life, from direct experience. And as at one time I had persisted in hearing Nietzsche's lectures when everyone else passed them by with indignation at these "contradictions, these blasphemies, this self-arrogance, which found no limits in his high-sounding speech!"—his great warm heart remained for me the only explanation for these supposed incongruities, which I probably also sensed. I felt that whoever sees himself rejected from the first in his best feelings by his fellows, stands innately "beyond good and evil," as it were. He recognizes no "divine or human order of things," which has no place for him. He feels only his fate, against whose hardness even his bitterest scorn seems like an innocent child's word. For he is alone!! . . .

In this sense Platen and Nietzsche were great sufferers.

Like the poet, Nietzsche too was a hero, a great fighter! And his personal charisma was probably due less to his intellectual brilliance than to his deeply ethical nature! But his purity, indeed this "excess of purity," as Platen rightly names his own related mood of soul, was simply—a hard-won trait. In Nietzsche's presence one felt something like an invigorating aroma that warded off everything alien. I have known men who certainly were more fascinatingly lovable and intellectual. But I never saw a calmer person and yet one who moves us to the depths of our soul!

These results of my reflection on Nietzsche, of course, did not then exist as a finished product in my soul. They were dormant there as an intimation and they also helped me soon to regain my naturalness in contact with the professor. But a more intimate association with Nietzsche never again resulted. Köselitz did try several times to get me to visit him again. He apparently had no idea of the scene that had occurred—a beautiful sign of Nietzsche's delicate discretion! The vacation, moreover, brought a natural pause in our contacts. And that this pause would, unexpectedly, be a very long one, was due to my suddenly falling ill and my father's transfer to Freiburg. Like a bolt out of the blue I was struck by a long-lasting eye ailment. I came back to Basel only to see a famous ophthalmologist there. For years I had to forgo Burckhardt's and also Nietzsche's lectures. Then I regained my health only to use my eyes all the more exclusively to prepare for my doctoral examination. I moved back to Basel, but hardly left the house, and even had to make the sacrifice of speaking with or hearing Burckhardt only scantily at home or in class. (*51*)

33   Richard Reuter   *Summer 1876*

In the summer of 1876 I was in Strassburg and Mühlhausen on business, and after taking care of it I found that I had a day left over. I used it to travel to Basel with the intention of taking a tour around the city, especially the older parts of it, and of course visiting the Dance of Death and leaving the rest to chance and to the inspiration and mood of the moment. My walk led me from the station first to a high location directly overlooking the Rhine and the covered bridge that crossed it. The river, very shrunken by the long heat and drought, flowed along shallowly in its stony, half-dried bed, more like an Alpine brook than like the magnificent river on which the stately steamship had just carried me from Cologne to Mainz. The covered bridge, such as can be found only here and there in a little remote village, or in old pictures of cities, and the ancient part of the city on the opposite bank made a very romantic impression under the late afternoon twilight and involuntarily raised images of a far distant past. I also caught sight of the cathedral which contains the Dance of Death in the middle of that part of the city and I noted the direction in order later to find my way there through the maze of streets, as I am inclined to do, without inquiring, though by a few wrong ways and detours. And I did reach my destination without mishap and soon was standing in the cloisters, which are decorated with Holbein's frescoes, unfortunately so faded and damaged that for the layman their charm consists only in the satisfaction of having seen the relics of these original pictures, which can be recognized much better from a reproduction. Then the question came to me whether I should catch an evening train a few stations' distance into the mountains or continue wandering haphazardly through the city, very likely at the risk of being forced to eat at just any café or outdoor restaurant at nightfall.

Basel did, as I knew, have one further attraction, but only for a closed little circle, to which I did not belong. Friedrich Nietzsche was at that time a professor at the university, still unknown to the great world, but regarded by a group of mostly youthful comrades as their head, their great light of the future, a pioneering genius and vanguard of a new philosophy destined to render all prior views, methods, and systems obsolete. Even the most intimate circles around Richard Wagner received him as a person called to cooperate in realizing the high-flying ideas of the creator of *Tannhäuser* and *Lohengrin, Die Meistersinger,* and *Tristan,* ideas that went far beyond the area of music. I, however, had neither personal nor other relations with him. I had been at school together with him for a year, but although our mothers were friends he had as a venerable sixth-year man of course taken no notice of the "lower classmen," who were four or five years younger. Later I had met him once or twice in society without drawing closer to him. I never had much of a mind for speculative philosophy; it did not arouse my interest even in Heinrich Heine's playful, effervescent presentation. I was, rather, always inclined to join in the unflattering judgment which the great English historian makes of it in an essay on Lord Bacon of Erulam. Still, because of these points of contact, I had taken interest in Nietzsche's appointment to a university professorship at so young an age and also at the great sensation his first book, *The Birth of Tragedy from the Spirit of Music,* had made in learned circles; I had even placed it on my list of books to be read, though it still had not gotten beyond that point. Under these circumstances, I had thought of visiting him, but now it occurred to me that according to a letter recently received from home his sister was probably staying with him, and since I had had the pleasure, the real pleasure, of associ-

ating with her from earliest childhood, the idea seemed very pleasant to pay her a surprise visit far from home. So I headed for
Nietzsche's apartment. He was out, but I got the invitation to spend
the evening there and to await his return, which soon took place.
Since I was as unfamiliar with his thinking as anyone could be and
he was far from pushing his ideas on anyone, the conversation naturally at first consisted of cheerful conversation about the immediate topics of the day, events back home, common acquaintances,
advice on how I could best employ the next day, and the like. The
conversation took a higher turn only when Nietzsche mentioned a
pamphlet published shortly before, *National Liberal Party, National
Liberal Press and Higher Gentlemanliness,* as it were, the first shriek
and angry outburst of public opinion against that Party's increasingly mindless and characterless servility toward Prince Bismarck,
which pamphlet ran through five editions in rapid succession and
was for a time an outstanding topic of public discussion and heated
debate in the press of all parties.

Nietzsche was not at all a politician in the usual sense of the
word, and still less did he belong to and obey any party. The political
questions of the day and individual struggles left him indifferent,
and even major events and developments interested him only insofar as they touched upon and affected the circle of his ideals of the
future. The establishment of a new German empire and the last
struggle for it had moved him in his deepest soul; he had seen it as
the opening of a new chapter in the history of nations; greeted it as
the beginning of a new, brilliantly glorious cultural period, like so
many others but with far higher expectations and a far deeper conception than probably any other. What his ardent imagination had
conjured up before his ecstatic eyes had been nothing less than that
German genius, in the conscious delight of its freedom and in the
pride and exuberant actions of its new youthful energy, would
achieve out of itself the rebirth of ancient Greece in a transfigured
form and heightened potency, and would realize an ideal such as
the world had not yet seen, pouring out over the world an inexhaustible stream of beauty and Olympian joy. Nietzsche, who as an
eleven-year-old boy during the Crimean war had played soldier with
the characteristic zeal he displayed in everything he undertook and
with almost unyouthful earnestness, who had written a booklet
about sieges and military stratagems, and who later did his year of
military service not only with the greatest dutifulness, but with a real
devotion to the cause, a devotion which no one would have suspected of this quiet, introverted scholar, always dwelling in the high-

est regions with his thoughts—in the year 1870 Nietzsche felt the wildest desire to reach for the sword and fight in person for this rebirth and new creation of the German-Hellenic spirit. Only the incompatibility of his position as professor at the university of a neutral country—a position which he had gotten to like—with entrance into the ranks of the fighting men, kept him from doing so, and he had to settle for leading a medical convoy before the walls of Metz and enthusiastically portraying the high flight of his hopes at the end of *The Birth of Tragedy,* the first draft of which was written under the thundering cannons of Wörth and Weissenburg. But the actual course of German affairs, which had so snidely disappointed many far more modest and ordinary hopes even then, only five years after the armistice, had plunged him down from all his heavens; and the higher his expectations and claims had been, the more depressed was his mood. That pamphlet's sharp polemical tone, its relentless and provocative rebellion against that misguided and sad public opinion which had been propagated most importunately and tastelessly as the only permissible and justifiable one in the German empire, was to Nietzsche's liking, though he could hardly sympathize with its specific political principles; and since the pamphlet was written only with the soul, we soon were embroiled in a heated discussion of it and the circumstances that had evoked it.

Nietzsche stood at a turning point in his writing and thinking, though of course I did not and could not suspect this. He had just recently finished his "Richard Wagner in Bayreuth," the fourth and last of his *Untimely Meditations.* His next book, *Human, All Too Human,* already begun or at least in preparation, was the first in the new direction of denying and opposing every metaphysical principle and element in the intellectual and psychic life and activity of mankind, a thesis expressed more and more stridently and drastically, so that it gradually led to a break with all his former friends and admirers—a break described so movingly in his poem "From High Mountains," the "After-Song" to *Beyond Good and Evil*—as well as to a violent and angry rejection of Richard Wagner whom he had formerly almost, or rather actually, idolized, and to Nietzsche's own complete isolation, even driving him to renounce himself, especially his first creation, *The Birth of Tragedy,* in my opinion by far his most brilliant work, though it bears strong traces of youthfulness and is, especially in parts, dominated by a boundless fantasy.

The ultimate causes of this strange, abnormal turn are surely extraordinarily numerous and complex. A variety of factors, internal and external, innate and acquired, stemming from intellectual activity and rooted in temperament and character, converged, and even the most thorough research will be unable to give an exact picture of them. But in memory I have once again become convinced that Nietzsche's disappointment concerning the climactic point, the culmination of all his striving and hope, contributed very strongly and was indeed perhaps the primary cause. When the keystone to the temple he had built with the entire enthusiasm of his youth and of a great age dawning in his heart and thoughts, to whose realization he had wanted to dedicate his life, and at the end of his first book urged all who felt the same to sacrifice to this cause, when the keystone toppled to the ground, the pillars and buttresses and the whole wall also began to totter, indeed even the foundation was dislocated and smashed amid the general crashing of rubble. Then he lost all belief in the supernatural, perceiving only an element hostile to life and its values, glorifying the vital force and joy of life as the only justified motive and element in human existence, and acclaiming the "Dionysian principle," which if he did not discover it, he first delineated precisely, in its most extreme and one-sided form, as the new, solely true, solely real joyous gospel.

As I was leaving at a very late hour, Nietzsche lent me an essay of the Göttingen theologian Paul de Lagarde, which would interest me because on more than one point it was surprisingly and strangely similar to the pamphlet we had been discussing, although it started from different points of view and foundations, and, following a different line of thought, aimed at different, indeed opposite goals.

Early the next morning while driving to the promontory that had been recommended to me for a splendid view of the Alps, I took out Lagarde's essay, but soon noticed that it was not travel-reading in the narrow sense of the word. When I laid it down, a Catholic clergyman sitting next to me picked it up, shrugged his shoulders, and said in a somewhat disparaging tone, "Ah, Lagarde"—a circumstance which by no means made me disinclined to have a closer look at the little book. Later, as I read it through, or more accurately, plowed through it, I was greatly fascinated by its content and style. Its content was often baroque, full of intricate ideas and impractical, unpurposeful proposals, strange digressions, dwelling with solemn earnestness upon completely insignificant things, but then again hitting the nail right on the head, stating with absolute candor truths which deserve very much to be said and which no one else considers it necessary to say; its style was almost entirely affected and mannered, but always pithy and often brilliantly to the point, revealing, to a most marked degree, both independent, original thinking and feeling—the complete, refreshing opposite of the "herd-man." On rereading this and a few other essays by Paul de Lagarde not long ago, when I already knew Nietzsche's later writings, at least in part, it became clear to me that in the summer of 1876 Nietzsche had seen more in Lagarde than merely a brilliant and stimulating writer. The drastic change in Nietzsche's thinking that took place in the summer of 1876 was most obviously influenced by Lagarde. As for the new style in which the works of the second period are written, Nietzsche is practically a disciple of Lagarde, though one who has risen so far above his teacher that the latter seems more like a precursor than a master. Yet Lagarde indubitably served Nietzsche as model, once he realized that the language of Kant and Schopenhauer, in which he had first formulated his ideas, was incapable of helping them to full expression, and so he now created his own particular, brilliant language, to which his later writings essentially owe such a great readership and impact; perhaps Nietzsche first got the idea of using this language in the future and developing it further for his purpose when he read Lagarde's works. Lagarde's influence on Nietzsche's later development is unmistakable not only in form and style but also in subject-matter and content, although there is a deeper chasm between what they preach to their listeners than between heaven and earth. Lagarde's sharp critique of conditions in the German empire and the direction of its domestic policy inevitably intensified Nietzsche's deep sense of disillusionment, indeed he perhaps became clearly aware of it only then. Lagarde's devastating judgment on contemporary Christianity, on the entire ecclesiastical system and religious activity of all denominations, especially the Protestant church, apparently had a strong impact on Nietzsche's soul and brought about or at least accelerated and completed his break with the traditions of his childhood and early youth, which he had till then by no means abandoned. But while Lagarde flung his angry thunderbolt of condemnation specifically only at contemporary Christianity, at the current concept of church and religion, and, as a deeply religious or—to avoid applying this hated word to him—pious nature, held up in its stead a lofty ideal of genuine Christianity and true piety, Nietzsche moves on to attack unconditionally and irreconcilably not only the concept of the church as such, but with mounting passion the innermost nature and principle of Christianity, until at the end of his last work which we have in finished form, the *Anti-*

christ, he concentrates all his stylistic force on pronouncing a formal and solemn curse upon it.

The relation between Lagarde and Nietzsche offers us one of the most striking examples of how a person inspired by another's train of thought can come to a diametrically opposite conclusion than the one who inspired him, without either of the two falling into self-contradiction.

Whoever wants to become more closely acquainted with the course of Nietzsche's development, especially the transition to his second creative period, which seems externally so unmediated, must read, or rather study, Lagarde's *German Writings,* one of which is a treatise. Even the paternity of individual thoughts can be clearly recognized in it. Thus the passionate, indeed wild hatred of the Apostle Paul, against whom in the *Antichrist* he finally levels the probably not quite tenable reproach of having undermined, corrupted, and destroyed the most noble product of the human mind, the Roman Empire, which represented the epitome of nobility, by appealing to the basest, meanest instincts, is found in Lagarde too, though in a milder form of contemptuous displeasure.

Nietzsche can hardly have foreseen clearly where his new direction would lead him. But the decision to go there was made in those days. I, however, had no other impression than that of having chatted pleasantly for a few evening hours.

Thirteen years later, Nietzsche departed not from earthly existence but from mental, conscious life; although his works found a growing circle of readers and some people carried on practically a cult with him, to the broad public, including scholars, he was still unknown, a lonely man, seeking and loving loneliness, yet suffering deeply and painfully from it, lonelier of soul than any hermit ever was. During this time he advanced on his course to his most extreme conclusions. He was no longer able to elaborate his last sketches, but what exists of preliminary sketches and completed works suffices to cast clear light on the final results of his thinking.

It was his destiny, too, to find recognition only when he could no longer enjoy it. He now has followers and admirers, passionate, indeed fanatical, admirers, in numbers which he could not have dreamed of when he was still working and writing.

The Nietzsche Archive was established in his hometown by his sister, for the purpose of storing, besides manuscripts, everything that has anything to do with him, essays and articles written about him, letters to and from him, originals and copies, as completely as possible. An edition of his work that meets the strictest demands of criticism is being organized, and its first part, containing the finished works, has already appeared. The first part of a biography written by his sister has also been published. His name and some of his slogans are on many people's lips.

Whether that would make up for the loss of the friends of his childhood and youth and the dispersion of the dreams of the future which he used to have, who knows? But from an incredibly young age he sought his goal and happiness in the unrelenting quest for truth, in the complete certainty that its fruits could be very bitter. And he did search for truth according to his best knowledge, sincerely, with iron resolve, unselfishly. (*48*, 1275–1281)

34   Malwida von Meysenbug   *January 1, 1877*

On the morning of January 1, 1877, I took a beautiful walk along the seashore alone with Nietzsche, and we sat down on an outcropping of rock that jutted far out into the deep blue sea. The weather was beautiful as a spring morning; a warm breeze was blowing and on the shores gleamed the golden fruits of the green orange-trees. We were both in a peaceful, harmonious mood; our pleasant, meaningful conversations stood in harmony with the auspicious beginning of the year, and we finally agreed that the real goal of life had to be to strive for truth. Nietzsche said that for the real human being everything had to serve *that* purpose, including suffering, and that to this extent he also blessed the past year of his life, in which he had suffered so much. Yes, I said, for all these truths, the Bible has always had a beautiful saying that means basically the same thing: To those who love God all things work out for the best.

How mild, how conciliatory Nietzsche still was then, how much his kind, amiable nature still held the balance with his analytical intellect. How cheerful he still could be, how heartily he could laugh, for despite all seriousness, our little circle was not lacking in humor and joy. When we sat together in the evening, Nietzsche comfortably seated in his armchair behind his eye-screen, Dr. Rée, our kindly reader, at the table where the lamp was, young Brenner by the fireplace opposite me helping me peel oranges for supper, I often said jokingly: "We do really represent an ideal family; four people who once hardly knew one another, having no blood ties, no common memories, and now living an intellectually and temperamentally satisfying life together in perfect harmony and undisturbed personal freedom." Soon there was no lack of plans for expanding this so successful experiment. I had just received a great many letters from women and girls among the unknown multitude who expressed their sympathy in the aftermath of my *Memoirs of an Idealistic Woman,* which incidentally was constantly the case in the long series of subsequent years, to my innermost joy and satisfaction. This fact encouraged an idea which originated with me and which I told my companions, namely of establishing a kind of mission-house to lead young adults of both sexes to a free development of the noblest intellectual life, so that they could then go out into the world to scatter the seeds of a new, intellectualized culture. The idea found the most ardent resonance among the men: Nietzsche and Rée were immediately ready to participate as teachers. I was convinced I could attract many girl students to whom I wanted to devote my special care so that they could help preserve this so important and meaningful cultural work from misunderstanding and distortion and by a pure and noble education lead to a beneficial development. We were already looking for a suitable location in magnificent Sorrento, amid blissful nature, far from narrow urban confines. We had found several spacious grottoes, down below by the beach, like halls within the cliffs, apparently expanded by human labor, and even containing a kind of rostrum that seemed intended expressly for a lecturer. We thought them to be very suitable for us to hold our classes there on hot summer days, since in general all this studying was supposed to be more a mutual learning in the manner of the Peripatetics and generally more on a Greek model rather than on a modern one. We often discussed this plan and we considered its realization not to be impossible since I had had the finest success with something similar at the university in Hamburg. And yet this too failed, like so many other ideals, due to circumstances which intervened disruptively, especially on the part of the men.

Our common readings now assumed a different character. We left beautiful Greek antiquity, and the subject changed to a mixture of more recent but always significant matters. Rée preferred the French moralists and communicated this to Nietzsche too, who had perhaps already read them earlier but whose closer acquaintanceship with them certainly did not remain without influence on his later development and led him to express his thoughts in aphorisms, as I later had the opportunity to notice. He was apparently also influenced by Dr. Rée's strictly scientific, realistic way of seeing things which was almost something new to his previous work, which was permeated with his innately poetic and musical element and gave him an almost childishly astonished pleasure. I often noticed this and jokingly warned him of it, since I did not share Rée's views, despite my respect for his personality and my recognition of his kindly nature, which was revealed especially in his self-sacrificing friendship for Nietzsche. His book *On the Origin of Moral Feelings* aroused in me the most decisive contradiction, and I jokingly called him a "chemical combination of atoms," which he endured in a very friendly way, while we were otherwise associated in a hearty friendship.

How much his way of explaining philosophical problems impressed Nietzsche was shown to me in various conversations. Once during a stroll a philosophical quarrel arose between Nietzsche and me, in which he denied the law of causality and said that there was just a coexistence of things and conditions, but not as an action of one on the other; what we felt to be cause and effect were unexplained facts. The Greek philosophers, the Eleatics, had indeed declared being, the unchangeable, to be the only cause and the true reality, but this was contradicted at every moment by the world as an eternal becoming and change. I answered that surely unchangeable being was the true reality, the thing as such, the so-called metaphysical. We simply had not to fear to recognize this. The world, with its apparent eternal becoming, was just the appearance of being; only to us, to our limited senses, was it change. But in all change, in life and death, in becoming and perishing—being, the all-one, was revealed. The people of ancient India already knew this: *tat wam asi,* "That is you."—Another time in a conversation on Schopenhauer he stated that the error of all religions was to seek a transcendental unity behind the phenomena and that this was also the error of philosophy and of Schopenhauerian thinking on the unity of the will to life. Philosophy was as monstrous an error as was religion. The only valuable and valid discipline was science, which was gradually fitting stone to stone to construct a solid building. The first two disciplines held men back on their way to truth, merely expressing our mind's tendency to want to find the solution to the riddle of life once and for all.

I objected to him that the error seemed to me to be precisely to regard this unity as something transcendental, whereas it was really precisely what fills everything, what manifests itself in the phenomenon. Because the limitation of our capacity for knowledge needs the instruments of space and time, we do not have the right to call what lies beyond "transcendental," merely because our perception capacity does not reach it. Still it is a logical, reasonable conclusion that what lies beyond our perception contains the same intrinsic conditions and moves according to the same laws as what is within range of our knowledge, and so we cannot call it transcendental. Therefore, we have all the less basis for delegating to an untenable transcendental area the magnificent power of thought, which, casting off one narrow form after the other, progresses victoriously through the night of the ages to ever greater clarity. And this seemed to me to be only the old pride of men who, after the theory of man's descent from the apes had destroyed the theory of the blowing-in of divine breath, were now fleeing to the elegant rejection of the metaphysical or transcendental and accepting only the experimental—the often so pitiful fact!

Indeed, what had given such high rank to Nietzsche's earlier work "Schopenhauer as Educator" was precisely his statement in it that culture has a metaphysical purpose!

In early spring Rée and Brenner left, each one returning to his hometown. Nietzsche and I stayed on alone, somewhat distressed because of our evenings, since we both, with our eye ailments, were now deprived of our excellent readers. But Nietzsche said cheerfully: "Well then, let's just converse all the more." And so it happened, for there never was a lack of rich material for conversations. Thus we discussed, among other things, "The Bride of Corinth," and Nietzsche remarked that Goethe had had the old vampire legend in mind, which the Greeks had already known in antiquity, and he had wanted to use it to show graphically how the mores and myths of antiquity were darkened into spectrelike things in the Christian world and how the dark turn which Christianity took very soon distorted the beautiful free sensory world of the Greeks and changed a flourishing natural life into a moldy smell and cult of the dead. "Yes," I said, "one must always remember that *historical* Christianity was born in the catacombs."

On another occasion we were talking about Goethe's *The Natural Daughter* and I said that I found it so delightful that in the dialogues each character always grasps and defends the highest content from his own standpoint, so that each one actually is right, as for example in the conversation between the duke and the secular priest, between Eugenia and the monk, etc. Nietzsche said that Goethe had discovered this in Sophocles, whose thirty-five characters all speak with such beauty and dignity that they all convince us.

During a conversation on Goethe and Schiller, Nietzsche said that Goethe had admired in Schiller the mighty nature, higher than himself, while Schiller had admired in Goethe the mighty artist, higher than himself. I did not admit that Goethe had been less high a nature, but saw him as the more fortunate personality who had attained harmony, while we honor in Schiller the high moral power that struggles with suffering and rises victoriously out of it.

On yet another evening the conversation turned to Don Quixote. Nietzsche criticized Cervantes for having the really ideal figure, the man with ideal striving, become the mockery of the everyday world, instead of the opposite, and he said that the book probably had had just a literary purpose: to put a stop to the reading of bad novels. I, however, understood the book as meaning that man with his ideal strivings, when he presents them in an anachronistic form, quite naturally becomes a fool and a caricature in the everyday world, which does not understand ideal intentions at all. I agreed that the book stemmed from the most monstrous misanthropy, from the cynical irony with which a man who understands the world looks down upon the poor idealist who believes he can realize ideals in such a world.

At times we also managed to read together a little, for example, one day the *Śakuntalā,* which Nietzsche did not yet know. He had many criticisms of the first four acts, first of all, finding the tragic motivation too easy and the author's merits too slight, since the whole background of flowers, animal life, and penitents' groves, etc., belong to India and not to him. But would it not rather be an error for a dramatic work to lack the local background, to have no local color? Is it better for the poet to have to create out of his fantasy all that Kālidāsa knew from his own observation and portrayed quite naturally, as airy, delicate, and colorful as India itself? Secondly, Nietzsche found the guilt motif too easy. But does it not express precisely the deep, delicate soulful feeling of the Indians? Śakuntalā loves too strongly, forgetting in her ecstasy of love the most sacred of duties, that of hospitality, and so she falls under the curse of those she offends; the king's mind is struck with blindness, so that he no longer knows her and she must now in suffering purify her love from all self-seeking and perfect her sanctification. Then the curse is broken and she can enjoy the happiness of perfected souls. Did Greek tragedy grasp the guilt motif more deeply? Antigone, like Śakuntalā, also violates the law of love and must die for it. Ethically the Indian view is perhaps here the higher one, for it grants perfection through atonement.

We spoke of Schiller's saying: "Base natures pay with what they do, noble ones with what they are," and we discussed poets in general and Mazzini. Mazzini paid with what he did, as poets do, but with the difference that the poet transfers his activity to his tragic characters, feeling, acting, suffering in them, while Mazzini was himself the tragic personality who had taken upon himself the most bitter suffering just for the sake of the ideal act. Nietzsche said that of all lives he most envied Mazzini's, this complete concentration on a single idea which became, as it were, a mighty flame consuming every individual trait. The poet frees himself from the violence of deeds which is in him, by incarnating it in forms and extrapolating deeds and suffering outside himself. He is like the will itself, he must objectify himself, streaming out his urge for action into phenomena; every feeling, every passion exists in him as a capacity, thus he can depict all the variety of beings, after he too has experienced their distress, their guilt, their pain. He redeems himself like the will by objectifying himself. Mazzini objectifies himself through his life, which was an incessant act of the noblest individuality.

One day Nietzsche arrived carrying a large bundle of written pages and told me to read them sometime, they were thoughts which had occurred to him during his solitary walks; in particular he identified to me a tree under which, whenever he stood there, an idea always fell down to him. I read the pages with great interest; there were splendid thoughts among them, particularly such as related to his Greek studies; but there were also others that puzzled me, that did not at all fit Nietzsche as he had been till now and proved to me that the positivist tendency whose slight beginnings I had already observed during the past winter was starting to take root and to give his views a new form. I could not avoid telling him about it and urging him to leave these writings aside and to re-examine them after a longer passage of time before releasing them for publication. I told him that, especially in regard to women, he ought to make no final pronouncements yet, since he still really knew far too few women. The French moralists had the right to make positive, perfectly valid judgments because they knew the society in which they lived from top to bottom, and probably applied their remarks only to it; but without such long years of precise and varied observation it is not advisable for higher intelligences to make such definitive pronouncements about psychological processes. I quoted to him a saying of Rée's, from his earlier mentioned book, which I found to be very repugnant and false, that women always prefer men who have already enjoyed their life diversely. Nietzsche smiled at my indignation and said: "But do you, then, believe that there is a single young man who thinks otherwise?" I was very angry and saddened to hear this from him and also told him that, in my mind, this was a new proof that he knew women only superficially and still had no right to make a general judgment. Later we returned to our usual subject of Greece and were good friends as before. Unfortunately I found those sentences all too soon in print, in a book titled *Human, All Too Human;* but my faith in Nietzsche's high talent was too solid to regard all this as more than a passing phase in his development, from which his ideality would emerge victorious.

It was infinitely sad that his health had not improved at all, indeed the attacks of his ailment, the horrible head- and eye-aches, became even more frequent as the weather got warmer and often forced him to lie in bed day and night in endless torment. His confidence in the South was extinguished, and with the same fervent confidence with which he had looked forward to this journey, he now looked forward to his return to the icy regions of the Alpine world, and moved his departure date ahead. I was painfully moved by this failed hope, but could not hold him back, since even the most loving care had proved powerless against this mighty disease and so one had to share his hope that the change might perhaps bring some improvement. (*35*, 56–68)

35   Reinhardt von Seydlitz   *1877ff.*

It is hard; for where shall I begin? I too would perhaps not have broken silence, or at least not till today, if Frau Dr. Elisabeth Förster-Nietzsche, his revered and loyal sister, worthy of her great brother, had not for years been asking me orally and in writing, indeed literally entreating me to do so, so that at last I took up the pen for my kind friend's sake.

Whoever speaks, however, wants to be heard, to be understood. Two kinds of people are therefore excused from reading any further; for they can and should never claim Nietzsche for themselves: these are, first, the levelers, the raucous-voiced revolutionaries; and secondly, the poor types who are so fascinated by the modern era that they have forgotten antiquity in themselves—probably considering it superfluous to assimilate the past. Whoever speaks of Nietzsche, speaks to them in vain; not a word, not a fiber of his spirit belongs to them. For his innermost being's crystal-clear core was the highest nobility the spirit can achieve: true urbaneness—an almost forgotten word, a term that has become unfamiliar. Everything crude or obtrusive disgusted him almost to excess.

The way to Basel was easy to find; and, most heartily greeted by my kind friend, I was allowed to spend a few delightful hours with him. Morning turned into afternoon, and afternoon into evening, before the beautiful conversation, which, gliding lightly over the most serious problems, had to be broken off. Oh, this precious, irretrievable happiness!

With his truly unique sensitivity, which turned him, the philosopher, into a poet, just as it had made a musician of him, he had always loved everything quiet, elegant, calm, well-measured, even in external surroundings.

I remember clearly the many afternoons in Sorrento at the end of March 1877, when he came to see me in my room, because that was where the only available piano stood. What rich music filled one's ears in that room!—And once, in Rosenlaui, he waited for the salon of the hotel to be empty and sat down at the piano. Outside in front of the slightly opened glass door we listened to the great, serious polyphonic revelations which now resounded. Soon all sorts of guests arrived, and listened, involuntarily fascinated down to the last note; no one dared to open the door lest he might stop. But one man asked me in a whisper: "Who is that, playing so wonderfully?!"—From those times I find in my diary the words: "He plays with the most extreme expressiveness and a deep conviction which irresistibly penetrates the listener. He exerts himself so much that one hour of playing causes more exhaustion than refreshment."

Musically he then (1877) probably still stood completely under the spell of Richard Wagner, though he had already outgrown him in all other respects. Even this once so magnificent and harmonious friendship was nothing but a "star-friendship" for him—though the most important one, whose end may have caused him his most difficult hours. "I am very pleased," he said on June 17, 1878, when I told him of a visit to Wahnfried, "I am very pleased and glad that one of my friends is doing something good and friendly for Wagner: for I am less and less able to cause him joy (since he happens to be—an inflexible old man). This hurts me enough . . . If he knew, moreover, all that I have in my heart *against* his art and his goals, he would consider me one of his worst enemies—which of course I am not. I refer to my views on morality and art, which are the hardest thing my sense of truth has ever wrung out of me."

In Sorrento we read to each other aphorisms which we wrote competitively: some of his are in *Human, All Too Human.*—"One should be able to have five thoughts per day," he once said; in this context he used to count the nights as part of the "days"; and he kept next to his bed a slate tablet on which, in the dark, he jotted down the thoughts that came to him on sleepless nights. His headaches, which tormented him ceaselessly, disrupted both his work and his social life. As soon as the tormenting spirit relented, however, he was active again; preferably musically: in Massa (near Sorrento) he sneaked into the church and played the organ, so that the pastor shuddered,—for the good man had never heard so violent a style of music nor ever considered it possible. At that time he was having a little, teasing liaison with the Church; in a conversation about this he suddenly became very serious: "The crazy, insipid lies circulating in Protestant countries about the Catholic Church are not only absurd but very harmful to us."

From these dismal days my memory always likes to roam back to those times of Sorrento in the year 1877;—"Those were delightful days for me."

There were precisely thirty-five days in all! For seventeen of them, however, our friend was sick; only on eighteen days did we enjoy his company, and he ours and the magic world of Sorrento. "We" means, in this case, the little Sorrento community at the time, Fräulein [Malwida] von Meysenbug, Dr. [Paul] Rée, Mr. [Albert] Brenner, and my wife and I. Young Brenner, Nietzsche's pupil, author of a delightful novella, "The Flaming Heart," which appeared in the *Deutsche Rundschau* in 1877, has been lying under the cool earth for many years now; the memory of him, the quiet, serious and modest young man remains dear and precious to us all; if I am winding wreaths in memory of Sorrento, then one of the most beautiful ones is for him; may he rest in peace! Among all persons of that thirty-five-day spectacle, however, the one who stands out most predominantly is Nietzsche's—and our—dear, revered, motherly friend, Fräulein von Meysenbug. She ruled like a venerable abbess in the "monastery of free spirits," which at that time, for lack of a better place, had its domicile in the Villa Rubinacci, a boardinghouse in the town. What plans were forged under the mild sun, amid the gentle roar of the purple-blue sea, beneath the swaying tops of the pines, and on quiet, hidden, twilight walks between walls overarched by orange trees! We had already eyed the local, disestablished, and abandoned Capuchin monastery to transform it into a "school for educators" where "they educate themselves," and—that's how practical we were!—to furnish one half of it as a hotel for strangers with all the paraphernalia, so that *this* half could provide the necessary financial basis for the *other*, idealistic one.

But Nietzsche's young friends soon departed, and later he left too. In Naples we "loaded" him onto a steamship that was to take him to Genoa and he felt, as he wrote soon afterwards, like an "ideal piece of luggage." He was always grateful, so touchingly grateful, for every little, practical help; he also wrote later, reporting on his departure from Munich, "how beautifully cared for, Anglo-American style, as they would say here in Nice, I departed from your Munich! And it was truly with the fondest reminiscences that I drank every swallow and chewed every bite (incidentally to chew right, one chews each morsel thirty to seventy times, that's what I learned from the philistine Gladstone, who orders his children to count at table)." And whenever he entered our room in Sorrento, my wife hurried to prepare the Turkish coffee which he liked and which so agreed with him. Then he sat in the garden on the terrace or àt the piano, and thanked us in his way, giving his best in words or tones. If no outings to Termini, Camaldoli, or Deserto were planned, then a festive "German afternoon" was spent in the orange grove by the ravine, with coffee and pastry, and cheerful chatter. On these afternoons, in a good mood, he used to wear a bright-colored pointed silk Sorrentino cap, remarking that this was the best headgear and most suited to the place.

Then he walked with his head leaned back, like a Sorrento prophet, with half-closed eyes, through the avenues of blossoming orange trees. His pace was broad, long, but soft. And his deep, sonorous, wonderfully melodious voice never uttered an insignificant word. His manner of speaking was undramatic and matter of fact; in the simplest tone of voice he could pronounce sentences which were so seminal and significant that they seemed spoken *sub specie aeterni.* For he was immeasurably rich!

But the whole world knows this! It is nothing new. Everyone still bows where he walked and scrambles for the coins he scattered. And since he has become "fashionable" (a consolation that he does not know it!), those to whom he should remain an eternal miracle also bow: they have to follow the fashion. For to swear by Nietzsche is still something "new"; one swears by him with the same fingers used to swear by Wagner, Schopenhauer, Brahms, or Mascagni—but the empty skull remains unaffected by the oath.

For he lacked one thing which will always accompany the great man in the customary sense: he had no dark, ignoble sides to his nature; not even sensory crudity. For great men are seldom, in the noblest sense, decent men. A part of "being great"—of becoming and staying great—is a stupid belief in oneself. That is also why great men in their "decent" moments often seem so small.

Our Nietzsche was far from all this. I have never known a more genteel person than he—not one! He could be inconsiderate only toward *ideas;* not toward the persons who had the ideas. And these bearers of ideas—some with crude mentalities—soon discovered this: they knew there was nothing to fear from him. They were silent about him, for he was silent about them even from an innate inner purity.

Where is there a person living who could accuse him of a fault? He was as crystalline and radiant as the water of a mountain brook; what am I saying? Mountain brooks could be grateful, were they so pure. Clarity and chastity received a new, higher valency through him. (*54*, 617–628)

---

36   Reinhardt von Seydlitz   *Summer 1877*

In the summer of 1873 I was having a dull time in Norderney and writing "Norderney" pieces which were not so bad: a Viking song, to which was added in 1877 a companion piece, "The Vikings' Return Home," which later delighted my considerate friend, Nietzsche.

More than theories, however, my association with Nietzsche had brought about a marvellous fructification. He was, whether intentionally or not, at every moment the genuine Maieutic; like sunshine and spring rain he awakened the slumbering seeds. And truly, whoever has seen how of a thousand seeds barely a one in the intellectual world germinates and bears fruit, must bless such a phenomenon. I owe him not only inspiration, but especially critique. For he did not consider it beneath him to go through a novella I wrote in Sorrento two or three times, giving me his kind, considerate judgment about every detail, writing a long and ample commentary, and always maintaining his benevolence toward me, although in a few parts that novella is still so childish that even now I have to smile now and then on reading it. It is titled "Im toten Punkt" (Deadlocked) and was published in the *Schweitzerische Internationale Monatsschrift*, 1882, Nr. 6–12.

The manuscript now travelled in my suitcase to Switzerland, where I gave it to Nietzsche, who lived in Rosenlaui.

Nietzsche had, as mentioned, had the great kindness to go through the manuscript thoroughly. In Rosenlaui he then took me and the pages in hand and I regret only that I could not take down in shorthand what he said; how many a person could learn from it!—if learning is at all possible for a "novelist," since a novel is really "just a fabrication of the fantasy." On the contrary, just listen to Nietzsche's words insofar as I still have them in my mind: "There is supposed to be style, isn't there? It must be kept consistent throughout. For example the hero curses: 'Himmelstausenddonnerwetter!' [Heaven's thousand thunderations!] That won't do: such a person curses altogether differently than that." (I have since corrected it to read: "all accursed devils," but do not know whether that sounds more heroic.) "I would also red-pencil the many boorish incidents, great and small, which occur especially in connection with Speerfeld, but I see that they serve a systematic purpose, so that is alright the way it is," the friendly, deep-sighted critic continued; "but one thing must be changed: the description of the miraculous hall. For a narrative is not a museum guide; it is all more foreshortened looked at diagonally, you see?" I understood, I corrected, but it still is a chapter for readers with a lot of time on their hands. "And put a gag on the American Jester, even if he has to choke on it." I immediately gagged him mentally, but the fellow stayed alive. "You especially seem to have a phenomenal talent for constructing transitions; that is very good, keep that." I must admit, it has always been my special pleasure to introduce the reader to a new scene easily, softly, and cleverly; also, if possible, to set little time-pauses between the scenes.—He did not want the ending to be tragic; I believe he soon convinced me that no blood needed to flow, no grave to be dug.—To my question whether the whole thing did not show improbable preconditions, he said laughing: "I believe not; nowhere do crazier things happen than in the world." When he gave me back the manuscript he made a genuine Nietzschean joke; he felt the bundle of pages between his thumb and index-finger and said: "Hm, nice and thick." One probably has to have known him to know how much value he set on the large or small size of a book—and to judge how much humor there was in the seriously spoken words. (55, 19, 21–22, 26, 33–35)

37   Edgar Steiger   *October 1877*

It was the end of October 1877, when I saw him for the first time. We were both sitting on a bench listening to the enthusiastic speech of a philosopher who kept flinging about the words "God," "soul," and "immortality," as he shook his white prophet's mane. Karl Steffensen was the prophet's name, and pious Basel was the city where he was preaching. I was delighted. No wonder. How could a theology student, moreover in his first semester, not be delighted if he heard a "secular scholar" confirm the entire teaching of faith, though with different words than he was accustomed to in his home parish? But *he* who was sitting only three or four seats away from me, at the outermost end of the bench—what was he doing at this lecture? Why had the professor become a student?

I looked over at him out of the corner of my eye, while the other man at the rostrum celebrated the Christian rebirth of Plato in Origen and revelled in the *pochaastasix,* the eternal bringing back of all things, that boldest thought of the Greek church father. It was more than mere curiosity, it was something like fear that caused me to observe the wolf among the herd of theologians. For my neighbor on the left had whispered to me that this professor of philology, who was attending class here with Jakob Burckhardt, was a philosopher on the side, but a completely different one than this Steffensen there; he himself had heard him lecture one and a half years ago on the pre-Socratic philosophers, but how! I don't know why, but I did not like the tone in which that was whispered to me. It sounded half like admiration, half like a stealthy warning against a great danger. So involuntarily I had to keep looking over to the object of my secret fear. But not an eyelash quivered in that wax-pale face, whose half-closed eyes were hidden under the bushy eyebrows. Only a pale thin hand—it could have been taken for a woman's hand—passed over the mighty forehead from time to time as if wanting to calm something that raged behind it. There was something infinitely weary about this movement. Today, with Nietzsche's biography lying open before me, I know the source of this weariness. The disappointment which the eternally changing one had had with Richard Wagner was not yet overcome. And, moreover, for the second time in a year, he was afflicted with that malignant headache which was to put a sudden end to his academic career a year later—fortunately for the philosopher and for us. Nevertheless, twice a week the untiring thinker, then working on his provocative book *Human, All Too Human,* persisted in attending his philosophical Antipodes' class.

Why? Was he perhaps already making studies for his *Antichrist?* Quite possibly. Just imagine the striking scene: at the rostrum the magnificent patriarch's head of a Karl Steffensen, glorifying with mighty pathos the fusion of Christianity and Greek antiquity in Origen, and below on the students' bench the pale face of the skeptic who always found loud words and grandiose gestures to be in bad taste—what fine irony and at the same time what magnificent symbolism! "I wage war on this theologians' instinct; I find its traces everywhere . . . one need merely say the words 'Tübingen Monastery' to understand what German philosophy really is—a disguised theology." I can't help it but this and similar words always pass through my mind when I recall those days in Basel. At any rate they prove that the psychologist Nietzsche took home rich gains from that course.

Only the psychologist? The first time I read the words "eternal return" in Nietzsche, I immediately had to recall Origen's *pochaastasix,* mentioned above. For the Greek church father smuggled the genuinely Hellenistic idea of the eternal recurrence of things and the eternal repetition of the origin and end of the world without further ado into Christian theology and then built on it the magnificent doctrine of the bringing of men back to God—a doctrine which denied the eternity of the punishment of hell and therefore brought the enthusiastic disciple of Plato under suspicion of heresy even during his lifetime. But this divinization of the world was, for Origen, not just an end, but also a beginning. When the cycle of things had reached its beginning again, it began all over. The terrible spectacle of the fall, sin, punishment, redemption, and return to God is repeated over and over again—from eternity to eternity or, as one could better translate the word *aion* from one world-cycle to the next.

This adoration of iron necessity from the rostrum sounded like a Greek hymn. The old man up there had completely forgotten where he was and to whom he was speaking. And at his feet sat, in total rapture, the pale man whose book *The Birth of Tragedy from the Spirit of Music* was a single eulogy to the world-redeeming Dionysus, listening in amazement to Greek mystery-wisdom from the mouth of a church father. Despite myself I cannot escape the grotesque idea that "the seminal idea of the eternal recurrence, the idea in which every other way of thinking now perishes," first flashed through the Dionysus-disciple's brain like a sudden illumination at this moment, on this school bench, in old Steffensen's philosophy class.

A year later I was standing face to face before him. I had changed majors because my faith had begun to waver. I wanted to become a philologist in order to escape theology's uncomfortable questions of conscience. I did not yet have the courage to think them through to their logical consequences, not to mention critiquing them. I still had not read anything of Nietzsche's. I simply came to the philology professor to ask him the important question: which Greek dictionary should I buy. I must have played quite a pitiful role in this. For that very reason I remember the short visit most precisely and every word that was spoken and not spoken. I can still see his big dark eyes, as they looked out with such humane warmth from under the bushy brows and looked at me coldly like those of a god. I can still hear his soft gentle voice asking me various questions. And I can still see the awkward Zarathustra smile that played around his fine mouth when I admitted stutteringly that I had studied two semesters of theology but was now weary of the gods and their scholarship. He did not say a word, not even when he heard that I was a pastor's son. He only looked at me half curiously, half mockingly, half pityingly—today, after thirty years, I can easily guess his thoughts, which he well-advisedly did not tell me then—and he recommended to me the dictionary by Suhle and Schneiderin, which had just been published and, based on the comparative linguistic studies of Georg Curtius, tried to present at least the rudiments of a scientific etymology. I am still grateful to this day to the philologist Nietzsche for this advice.

From then on I never again spoke to him in private; only in the course did I hear him present his theory of the Apollonian and Dionysian elements in Greek art—he was lecturing at the time, in the winter semester of 1878–79, on the fragments of the Greek lyricists. It was the last course he taught. It remained just a fragment, but the memory of it accompanied me throughout my life. In his book on the birth of tragedy he had first brought to light the two roots of Greek poetry; here he traced them down in the rubble-heap of the elegiasts, lyricists and dithyrambists. And once again it had to be music and the musical instrument that unveiled the double life of the Greek soul. Here the *kith ipa* and Apollo, there the flute and Dionysus. It was a revelation which spread light everywhere and let a whole poem arise from two or three pitifully detruncated verses. What had Tyrtaeus, Alkman, Theognis, and Pindar been to me before? Just names to which the Alexandrian grammarians had stuck some label or other. And now all at once they became solidly defined personalities through whom the various ages of Greek culture spoke to us. Even today, for example, when I hear the name Archilochus, a kind of jubilation runs through my soul as if after the centuries-long bondage of the epic era I were personally witnessing the greatest discovery the human mind has ever made—the discovery of the self, which suddenly begins to play with things that had previously kept it subjugated. Homer and Archilochus represented two ages, like the Middle Ages and the Renaissance—those are fruits of knowledge such as only a Nietzsche could harvest.

But how this knowledge was communicated to us! He spoke softly, very softly, as if he feared to trample the delicate thoughts by too loud a voice. And from time to time, as he spoke, his slender hand stroked his mighty forehead as if it wanted to chase away a stinging pain. Whoever saw him sitting pale and tired at the rostrum had the feeling of seeing an eternally sleepless man whose brain mercilessly rolled up one bodily fiber after another. The lectures then became rarer and rarer. Whenever one came to the university the little white note was stuck to the door of the classroom with the short remark that the professor would not be reading today. And finally it was all over. Friedrich Nietzsche was pensioned off because of his eye ailment and he moved to the Engadine to shake off the school dust forever there in Sils-Maria. For us it was a hard blow, for him a relief. He had better things to do in the world than to interpret Euripides' multiply mutilated choral songs for eager future high-school teachers. He, who later so ironically blessed the scholars' hunchback, how he must have laughed diabolically-divinely when he thought back to the time when for a whole semester he exercised his philological tightrope-walker's talents on sixty verses of the Greek poet. Ten years earlier the Leipzig student whom the University of Basel wanted as professor had written to Erwin Rohde: "Just last week I wanted to write to you and suggest that we study chemistry together and throw philology where it deserves, with antique furniture. Now the devil 'fate' is tempting me with a German professorship." And now he had reached the end: "Zarathustra went back into the mountains and to the solitude of his cave and withdrew from men: waiting like a planter who had thrown out his seed." (*58*, 1349–1353)

38   H. Göring   *Summer 1878*

In the summer of 1878 I saw Nietzsche in Basel one evening walking into his apartment. He gave the impression of a lonely man, suffering severely. I observed him with compassion. He moved me deeply as he strode slowly along, bent, perhaps oppressed by physical pain. But it moved me even more deeply that a psychological suffering was weighing on him: *the loneliness of the thinker already misunderstood in his young years.* I had here and there heard about him disparaging judgments which stemmed from an ecclesiastically orthodox partisanship and offended me as an unjust condemnation. Four years before, on reading the *Untimely Meditations* "David Friedrich Strauss as a Confessor" and "Schopenhauer as Educator" in Dresden with the ingenious Frau Mathilde Wesendonck, who was not yet esteemed as an author, I had experienced an impression and influence that drastically changed my interior life. Strauss, whom I, as a young theologian, educator and doctor, had believed uncritically, was internally torn away from me by Nietzsche's powerful work of thought. And Richard Wagner's poetic woman-friend had described David Friedrich Strauss' noble artistic nature to me so convincingly that I too had to grasp him with the spirit. That beautiful image was destroyed by Nietzsche's uncommonly mature early work.

This bold warrior, whom one faction in Basel revered highly, of whom my school colleagues, especially my judicious, intelligent landlord, the mathematician Schmiedbiser, spoke with respect, while the opposite faction rejected him sharply—I simply had to ask him what he thought of Dühring. I clung with unshakable piety to Eugen Dühring, and not even the sharp critique of the universally versatile, genuinely German thinker, Eduard von Hartmann, who in April 1876 had granted me a few hours of discussion of Dühring's "philosophy of reality," had been able to cause me to break with him. Still less did Friedrich von Kirchmann's doubts concerning the rightness of the epistemological foundation of Dühring's system lead me to abandon my adherence to that author.

At the age of twenty-seven I was still completely immature compared with Nietzsche, who was only five years older but a complete master in his first profoundly insightful books, and I simply had to hear this man, who was charging ahead intellectually at such a young age, and to hear his judgment of Dühring.

My bashful reserve intensified when I saw the young professor associating closely with Jakob Burckhardt, all of whose university classes Nietzsche moreover attended. My teaching schedule in the three upper classes of the high school allowed me to attend Nietzsche's class from seven to eight a.m.

For a long time no opportunity arose to approach Nietzsche. His university class and teaching at the high school, his well-known conscientious preparation for every official activity, as well as his writing activity so dominated his time that one felt it to be tactlessly obtrusive to visit him.

Since Nietzsche meanwhile often drank a cup of coffee in the Three Kings Hotel, one day I let myself be introduced by the mathematics professor Kinkelin, the genteel, intellectual principal of the high school and great artist of the academic lecture. Nietzsche had the noble manners of an aristocrat, listened to everything politely and amiably, was glad that we fellow Thuringians met in Basel. I told him that I was completely devoted to Dühring's view of life. We agreed in our estimates of *The Course of Philosophy* and the supplementary work, *The Value of Life*.

Nietzsche spoke wearily, and seemed exhausted. His soft speech was almost a whisper. I was grateful to him that he wanted to speak to me in detail about Dühring in his apartment.

Unfortunately this never happened. He was already too ill to be able to risk postponing his health-journey to Italy any longer. The horrible experiences in the battlefields of the Franco-Prussian War had shaken him so much psychologically that his delicate nervous system was permanently damaged. Insomnia, which was not improved by repeated overwork, by chloral and potassium bromide, but made worse, excruciating headaches, and other neuralgic ailments tormented his life.

Once more, again in the evening, I saw the heart-moving image of the lonely genius, bent and walking slowly to his apartment. I was standing on a nearby street, sadly watching the noble man who would arouse such a mighty movement of minds.

I never saw him again after that.

Soon his book *Human, All Too Human* was published. A storm broke out in Basel. Nietzsche never learned of it.

Shortly before his death, one week to be exact, I wanted to see him once again. But it was too late . . . (*23*)

39   Ludwig von Scheffler   *1878*

Then one day I met Köselitz again on the street. He was as friendly as ever, in fact it seemed as if an even more cordial tone had come into his words. But he seemed depressed and worried. I asked about Nietzsche. Then I learned something that saddened me too. Recently things had been going downhill with the honored man. His nerves were so irritable that even his sister had been forced to leave him. Now it was also his, Köselitz's turn. Nietzsche absolutely wanted to be alone, indeed to leave Basel.

"And his lectures?"

"He is still giving them. But how?!"

"Let's go hear him! I now have no other opportunity to see him, or perhaps to speak to him . . ." Köselitz followed my suggestion only reluctantly. Since it was about the hour when Nietzsche held his class, he accompanied me. Lectures on Greek lyrics! Four or five little freshman were sitting on benches in front of Nietzsche. So for once he had students! Köselitz explained to me that these young theologians believed they needed the course for their examinations. They were always shaking their heads back and forth. They found it hard to understand the speaker. And Nietzsche himself? He had become an ordinary schoolmaster for these young boys! Not a trace of the prophetic sublimity and calm with which he had once addressed us on Hellenic pessimism. Restless he too just hunted for his documentary passages. The lecture was constantly interrupted, tortured, in sum, bad. Only once did his eye meet ours with a freer expression: he scolded (like Burckhardt!) at the pedantic appropriation and treatment of the poetic as a hereditary evil of our education!

The little hypocrites' heads wobbled even more dubiously on their narrow shoulders. Should they note that down too?! . . . But it cut me to the heart to see Nietzsche in such a role. Moreover, during the lectures his accustomed weariness had increased to utter exhaustion. Afterwards he greeted me absentmindedly and curtly.

"That was perhaps his last one!" Köselitz remarked after Nietzsche had left the classroom. At least it was the last lecture I ever heard from Professor Nietzsche!

For my approaching graduation took me back to Freiburg. Then I handed in my dissertation, passed my examination soon afterwards, and was now supposed to be inaugurated as a humanist in the great hall of the university amid Basel's very impressive Renaissance aura. When I held my doctoral lecture, the picture of Aeneas Sylvius Piccolomini was on the wall behind my head! And in the "corona" before me sat Jakob Burckhardt, the greatest and most genuine humanist the modern age has ever known! When with deep emotion I felt his handshake and his embrace after the ceremony, nothing more seemed to be lacking in the happiness of the hour. Or was there something else? Had I really, on this solemn occasion, not missed him, Nietzsche?

The idea of seeking him out, since he had not come, became a sudden, firm decision for me, so that I only half understood the answers to my inquiries about him, which sounded like dissuasions. He was, so they said, now living as a complete hermit far outside the city gate. He had nothing more to do with the university. Nor any other connection with the world. Even the last of his loyal followers had meanwhile left him . . .

"Peter Gast?" I asked anxiously.

A nod of the head confirmed this to me and I measured the depth of Nietzsche's unhappiness, if he dismissed even this noble friendly soul! Will it go any better with me? Nonetheless I steered my steps to him.

"Bachletten Street!" When I hear this name today, a shudder still runs through my limbs. Yes, that was where he lived, the unhappy man! As if he had sought it out—and he had perhaps done so! The ugliest, most desolate region in the vicinity of the otherwise so picturesque Basel! A lonely country road toward Arlesheim! Poor houses scattered at long intervals, overgrown ancient poplars, such as one finds in their melancholy only along the avenues of Northern Germany. Really if I had not had the Jura Mountains before my eyes, I would have felt as if transported to East Prussia or to the province of Posen. Even the sight of the mountains did not make a more cheerful impression. Their long, coffinlike profiles merely completed the very dismal impression of the landscape.

I enter the houses to inquire and only after a long search find the building where the Professor lives. Probably once a roadside tax-collector's house. Old and dilapidated, and only the lower rooms still inhabited. I pull the doorbell draw-cord outside the door. But no matter how shrilly it rings in the house, no one comes to open the door. I muster up my patience: I ring for the second time, and after a longer pause, for the third. No answer! The house is apparently empty. I turn in resignation to leave . . . Then instinctively I look inside through one of the ground-floor windows. As at an indiscretion committed I jump back in alarm! Right, he was actually sitting there!! At a kind of improvised desk! Tea cups, cooking utensils cluttered around the scanty place that was left for him to work on. And he himself with an eyeshade on his forehead, hiding half his face, while his figure which had become even more emaciated was half bent over the table. Like someone listening fearfully and trying only to hide!

I stood aghast at the sight. Was this still the same man who had once sat before me on the delicate lace furniture, whose femininely delicate sense tolerated only beauty around him, and who now had hidden himself in the brutal misery of a poorhouse? I felt I had to get through to him—even if it was through the window—to shake him out of his painful seclusion and lead him out into the sunny world, to enjoy which I now felt the wanderer's staff in my hand. Then I saw a tremor run through the unhappy man's body as he was still waiting to hear footsteps going away. No, I said to myself, you have no right to countermand this other person's will. I felt something like the nearness of destiny. Either the lonely man dies here of his self-created ailment or after an inner victory he finds new strength, a new existence. *Per aspera ad astra!* The world knows that it took him "to the stars"!

Then I turned away from there and today I still feel the sadness that filled me on my way back to Basel. The first wilted poplar leaves whirled and danced before me. They continued their play till I reached the city gate. Then I pulled myself together and belonged to life again. I never again met Nietzsche in this life.

But I was to hear of him again and in a strange way that reminded me of his Plato lectures. That was more than ten years later. In Florence! I was then writing my *Michelangelo*. It was midsummer and during the day to gather my thoughts in a cool place I often sought out the Sagrestia nuova, the newer mausoleum of the Medici in San Lorenzo. Then I often stood for a long time in front of Giuliano's gravestone and saw at his feet the allegorical figure of "night," with its dismal, death-weary face bowed over the hollow mask of death. Yes, a "mask" no longer struck me as a chance symbol of the serious impression! Not the rigid grandeur, as ancient fantasy formed the allegory of the "illusory dream," no, still full of painful life, full of reality, like everything that stems from Michelangelo's very personal conception! . . . No wonder that I too was seized by the living, painful memory of Basel!

. . . Then, to cast out the depressing idea, I reached into my pocket and pulled out a newspaper. Literary news from Germany! And the first name that my eyes fell on was . . . Nietzsche. As one greets a dear relative again after a long separation, I rejoiced at this discovery. Then I devoured what the article said about Nietzsche. A new turn in his philosophy! The doctrine of the "superman," of the happiness of the supra-morality which feels itself to be "beyond good and evil" and recognizes the value of existence only in its own freedom and strength! . . . I had to smile to myself. So that was how the "wise man in the cave" had worked his way up to the light of day, abandoning the "pessimist" Plato and going over to the camp of those who joyously affirm, the "many" whom just this Plato had attacked so bitterly. Of course, all said in Nietzschean terms and transfigured to a high, indeed the highest, ethical level. Yet I had read the basic idea of this in *Gorgias* and in the *Republic*. The magnificent apostrophes of Casticles, of Thrasymachus! That "justice [is] merely what the strong man finds advantageous!" That "those who pass laws and recognize them are the great herd and the weak"! That the "freedom and right of the more noble" begin only "beyond them"!! And as the Greek "superman" necessarily seemed to be merely the prototype of the Nietzschean one, a different image arose before my soul: the memory of how Burckhardt had once spoken to us (presumably also to Nietzsche) of the *deigos,* the Hellenistic "all-man"! This most resplendent characterization which found its counterpart only in the description of the "demonic man," the "terrible one," of the Renaissance! Was Nietzsche too thinking of this when, guided by Plato the writer, not Plato the philosopher, he found his way to a new worldview? For though he later despised Plato, he always remained a Hellene in his whole formation and temperament. Even his Zarathustra cloak, strange as it fits in places, falls in Greek folds. I at least have felt that what is most delightful in Nietzsche's wealth of imagery and in his language is always the reflection of great Hellenistic impressions. (*51*)

In the year 1878–79 Nietzsche had stated that he had no real philosophical thought on his own, but that reflecting on the events of
the intellectual revolution he had come to the conclusion that with
firm will and stubborn industriousness one could—and it was
actually always being done—achieve what one undertook as long as
a contrast to what was currently valid was maintained. All new teachings contained a reversal of one or more old ones. I remember this
conversation very precisely; it was neither a joke nor some kind of
provocation. This was his own idea of method. He wanted to know
what I pictured as the basis for my attitude toward others. I said:
"Benevolence!" I felt pity to be too arrogant a feeling, which no one
was glad to receive, and it seemed ridiculous to me for one person
to look down on another with a feeling of pity. He sighed and
seemed satisfied. Actually he had already construed pity (co-suffer-
ing) as his method, even with the addition of pride which I found to
be so absolutely necessary an ingredient. Nietzsche had been mull-
ing this over for years until he screamed out: "Only no pity, I know
that. That is decadence."

Nietzsche's introduction to morality contains personal thoughts
that give occasion to call him inconsistent and arbitrary, unless we
remain at every moment aware of his foundation of morality. The
morality of benevolence, for which Nietzsche decided, and the
morality of pity do not diverge in their result, but the feeling, the
attitude of the one who practices or receives them is different. The
individual as such remains more secure, even when he surrenders
himself materially. We find it hard to see altruistic morality somehow branded with the word "slave morality," all the more so since
Nietzsche's way of expressing himself bears the stamp of kinship
with a long altruistic past. Nor can, in Nietzsche's freest view, morality be any different, whether it stems from God or is purely human.
So we must not forget that Nietzsche's nature led him to base and
develop genuine humaneness by way of the struggle against the conceptual formation of what he calls world-historical prejudices.
Altruistic morality then finds its opposite in the third book of *Zarathustra,* where the supreme self insists jealously on its rights. With
this very serious view of morality he combined, according to his own
statement, the concept of ordinary virtue and hypocrisy which he
had seen at very close hand from impressions of his youth. He once

said that he really had it in for morality but had to force himself to always turn back to its underlying relations until he could no longer stand it and made the leap to the aesthetic. This leap gave him great relief, the feeling of having finished with morality, of having re-valued it. He then felt all forces and expressions of the human will to be of equal value in the great economy of nature as phenomena that generated life and reality and thus confirmed for him his basic philosophical concept of power, the thought toward which everything in Nietzsche strives. He felt this very intensely, exuberantly, and then always became an artist; as such and as the founder of his view and goals, he, the moralist, called himself the immoralist. There are passages in *Zarathustra* that seem to me to have such high artistic value that I feel as if they stood at the summit of all literature. These are, however, ironic passages.

Two years later Nietzsche said he was tired of psychology. Earlier already he had always sought an interaction between his way of thinking and his physical health. The problem between body and thought occupied him so much in regard to Pascal. As early as 1878–79 he spoke of the fact that Pascal's dependence on Christianity could well have destroyed him. This view of his found its highest expression in the fifth aphorism of the *Antichrist* and it no longer has any trace of its former stamp. Nietzsche's thought started with the question whether Pascal's return to Christianity after having for a time been thinking only scientifically had been the cause or the effect of his undermined health. He saw a parallel with himself and he hoped to regain his health by his way of thinking. This opinion, that he had helped himself through his philosophy which represented nature making a breakthrough within him, underlies many of his statements. Nietzsche feels dominated by his body: great and small reason, self and ego, body and spirit. He was thinking of the psychological scientificness so variously sought and striven for by doctors, for which indeed Rée had studied medicine, and Nietzsche wanted to go with him to a major university. He used to complain then that he was so ignorant of science and had wasted his time with the futile business of philology. Nietzsche often fell into anxiety and one-sided thinking; he often could not rejoice in an acquired treasure although he made use of it. He then always believed that truth and the goal to be sought lay in another, particular direction, toward which he felt stimulated anew. But the phantasmagoria of the new perspective vanished just as quickly as the old one; he was really not made for calm meditation and objective results. It is absolutely certain that a subjective, physical and spiritual feeling of life gave form to the content of what is called his art of moralizing. There was nothing comfortable in Nietzsche; there were unbearable tensions, which he felt a longing to express and for which he sought analogies in the Greek and Christian worlds. No wonder he found them much more in the Christian world. But he had studied the Greek world and lived in it. Yet he could not bear this world, though he had recognized its greatness and preferred its unconditional certainty to Christian halfheartedness and dullness. He often stated how very much the Christian way of thinking and feeling had really suited him, so much so that on hearing *Parsifal* he could believe he had made this kind of music in his youth. Nietzsche was later much more at home in the Old and New Testaments than with the Greeks, whom in the end he no longer understood at all, but always only in their relation to Christianity and their effect on his psychosomatic being—a very derivative approach which spoils the taste for what is genuinely Greek.

Nietzsche's love for Greece met its nemesis in its philosophers. He remained faithful to the mystical, artistically creative principle he discovered in them; and for its sake he annihilated the entire later world, to which he stood close. The struggle between aesthetic-artistic contemplation and moral consciousness had flared up in him, and this struggle, which for Nietzsche's way of thinking and his way of life meant defeats and happiest victories, is the key to understanding him. Nietzsche was a poet, a musician, a philosopher, an educator, a philanthropist, though by no means a socialist. Just think of the multiple claims of one's own nature on oneself. As an educator and philanthropist he was once delighted to find me reading Pestalozzi; and as a philosopher, since I told him that this entire human striving now simply had to be based on other intellectual achievements. Nietzsche was predominantly an intellectual eclectic with artistic creativity and linguistic talent.

I always believed that Nietzsche, despite all opposition to Christianity, was not an enemy of religion, however aloof from it he stood, and that he was himself even capable of producing religious effects. The superman as a substitute for God and the doctrine of return as substitute for immortality, however, seemed not to be very tenable idealistic fantasies. Self-elevation and the recurrence of the same seemed to run counter to the laws of cause and effect. Nor does Nietzsche ever demand belief; but he has such an ardent striving for a worldview. One would really like to relive his dear life, in order to be able to live it differently and to combine a higher consciousness with it. And the two ideas simply fit together so badly; there are not two complementary lines of thinking in Nietzsche but two alternative ones. As my husband says, Nietzsche never ceased reflecting on the meaning and purpose of life; thanks to his artistic talent, which by its splendor and color makes a deep impression on the senses, he may very well have replaced the sensory side of religion for some and communicated to them a very variegated and shifting storehouse of ideas of the world. Attractive as his personality was and is, I was often depressed by the thought that his knowledge was not certain and that it was therefore not advisable to want to study Nietzsche for long.

Nietzsche's need for sentimentality is certain. Unfortunately it stood in his way only too often and forced him to endure painful semi-fulfillments. It had been heightened and strengthened by antiquity's view of friendship. But friendship could not become really significant for him as a *Lebenskünstler*. The desire for friendship was not strong enough in him; he set greater store in the emotional state. He reproached Rohde for not going along with him at least personally; and later he reproached Overbeck for not going along objectively. Was there, in the latter case at least, an obligation to do so, or even just hope of an agreeable outcome among men with free intellects? Nietzsche did not see at all how he hurt others who did not have the traditional prejudices, or at least he rarely saw it. Prejudices were so important to him that he even respected and valued them in order to find a significant strategy against them. Some of his most magnificent passages arose in this way. A free person asks himself: is it worth the trouble? Nietzsche felt a wonderful power of satire in himself. But on the other hand he had an unusual need for kindness and forbearance toward others. When he was visiting us one summer in the early eighties, he told us, deeply perturbed, that he would yet end up in prison, to which I answered very cheerfully: "Ah, Professor, then we will most certainly visit you." He immediately became calm and cheerful. Nietzsche always lacked self-certainty; such was the honesty of his character and intellect. In his kindness and consideration, which practically overwhelmed him, he often became confused and cast into internal dependence rather than freedom, into despair and indignation that his noble striving— of course its weakness—was frustrated and exploited. And when this struggle had raged its course, he was ready to start all over again in the same way. Nietzsche, the condemner of pity, was continually experimenting with it. He bred it even more into himself, in order to vivisect it, to discover it like Christianity, and then to disrecommend it to mankind. Yet exemplariness was lost in the process. Nietzsche then all too often knows only how it should not be done; he is "full of his own falsehood and that of others." "My goals, my goals," he could then exclaim in despair. The result was disgust. Nietzsche had not overcome objective disgust for the world. "The world, as it is, in great and small aspects," he exclaims in the chapter "The Recuperating Patient" of *Zarathustra*, Book III, "is disgusting." And to anesthetize this disgust, he resorts, as he always did when something plagued him, to mystical artistic ecstasy, and his liberation is only apparent, just as the worlds of good and evil were for him only apparent.

Nietzsche was a severely sick man who constantly deluded himself about his dangerous condition in order to endure it. He could not easily harmonize himself; for all his work suffered the most abrupt interruptions. Any educational activity, for which he sometimes felt great longing, was therefore out of the question. He really suffered in the head. Sick or ailing persons whose head is free can still trust their own strength. But every few weeks Nietzsche's exhaustion was so complete that all activity was impossible. This suffering must be taken into account. It imposed the shortest leash on him, whereas he desired the longest. How often be believed he had to relearn, since he knew nothing, and to cleanse himself after having wriggled free of unclean hands. Finally, he lived in fantasy only with greatness. His works and letters are fascinating for the strong personal element more than for the actual elaboration of his thoughts, as many thoughts as Nietzsche did have. Among his great uncertainties was the one that he always wanted to hear his echo but at the same time was horrified of it.

What, then, was really Nietzsche's cause? He wanted to comprehend morality historically and to reshape the conscience philosophically based on the free individual who delivers his abilities and his passions to the strength of his will. He countered the triple series of concepts, history, theology, Christianity, with a trio of his own: life, philosophy, free individuality. Just think of the abundant perspectives which result and which we all owe to Nietzsche. Nietzsche hated all conceptual systematization; he wanted to eavesdrop on life's own secrets and outshine everything that such a rich past had inflicted on man of joy and pain. A gigantic plan was, indeed, present. Nietzsche's soul was a broadly expanding wishful soul which sought to embrace everything with the ardor of love and contempt and to release it transformed. Not by external contemplation and critique, but shaping it from the core of life! His struggle against Christianity, prior philosophy, and morality has a world-historical character, and this character turns against sin, original sin, the perdition of the human guts; against reason, which wants to master and restrict life; against displeasure, suffering, boredom, hardship as the condition underlying genuine morality—all these things being forms of the denial of life. A bad chapter of Schopenhauer affected Nietzsche especially strongly, the idea that man is not constituted to share joy, and can be interested in another person's misfortune or well-being only temporarily by the detour of former participation in misfortune; that well-being, on the contrary, is suited to arouse envy; wherefore he concluded also from other premises, that hardship is the positive condition of the human race, and that only pity can be the real wellspring of morality. Nietzsche's disgust rebelled against this; he was indignant. He banned from morality happiness as the result of narrow-minded virtue and praised a proud hardness in this area; he opposed reason, though there is conclusive evidence of its presence and consultation in his own life; but in him it was attacked by the sharpest, most fanatical and truly demonic understanding, which forced itself and reason into self-laceration. In the dialectics of the emotions what he ranked as the highest and ultimate basic creative drive was pleasure, the foundress of well-being and shared joy, the Dionysian drive, which is at the same time the bearer of pain and suffering. As the opponent of metaphysics he gained perspectives over the whole world. *Twilight of the Idols* and *Antichrist,* these two existing transvaluations, rise to a true hymn of cutting satire on all denial of life, based on the Dionysian life-feeling, the acceptance and approval of life and reality. We must expect the Dionysian dithyramb to resound once again fully and finally in *Ecce Homo.* (*43,* 241–247)

MIGRANT YEARS
(1879–1889)

Later (in 1880–83) Nietzsche lived with us several more times. Unfortunately I was seldom able to display my talents as a housewife to him. He preferred to eat by himself, though he visited us for hours; the only thing he accepted was a lightly brewed tea and a few English cakes. He then sat on the sofa in my husband's study or on a certain armchair in the living room, with his back to the white stove, looking at my husband, who sat opposite him, or at the dark curtain. He spoke softly, with few gestures; and so did we, avoiding all noise inside or outside the doors. Later, when he lived with us, he often was sick. Strong broths had to be prepared, and he had to stay in bed. But when he was well, we sat cheerfully together at table, and a good meal could be served. I also took part in short hikes, out to the Neubad or to Heinrich's garden on Binninger Street, where Nietzsche was housed most modestly and was a good neighbor to the simple people of the house. But he suffered so much in the two little rooms that we feared greatly for him. As trusting as Nietzsche was, he always locked his little preserve cupboard; he hated the thought that children's dirty hands, which were occasionally present, or those of adults, might touch these things. When he praised and drank our tea, he often mentioned the beautiful fresh eggs he got from Heinrich's garden. Nietzsche could praise something with heartwarming gratitude. A few years ago when the railway spur was moved from St. Ludwig to Basel, this house was demolished and the two mighty poplars in front of it were chopped down. Before its demolition, my husband and I walked past it one more time with sad memories.

In his letters to my husband Nietzsche said little about his world of thought; that had been done orally. They had had many conversations; all his moralizing was voiced on Euler Street, where we lived; his desire to reshape good and evil, based on a new evaluation of life, judgments on Christianity and on various authors—though my part in those conversations was very modest, I know a great deal of what was said. No sooner had Nietzsche entered the room than he launched off and reflected pleasurably on statement and counterstatement. He practically never spoke of the fine arts in the narrower sense—architecture, painting, sculpture—they hardly existed for him: music and language were his world; not languages, but *his language,* which he did not even always wish to be German. I can say that Nietzsche, in oral communication, gave more allusions than detailed elaborations of his thoughts, that he listened attentively and absorbed what he heard. He knew how to listen receptively, but he never revealed his own mind completely or clearly. He felt a need to remain amid the unknown; it was no real distrust of other persons, but rather distrust of himself and the reception he would find. He was very sensitive in this; afterwards something could irritate him to the point of anger. The passage in *Zarathustra* is so true: "If you have offended the hermit, then kill him!" Nietzsche was so easy to crush. He was preoccupied at the time with the problem of a new morality. My husband read essays of Sainte-Beuve aloud, translating extemporaneously; then Nietzsche started speaking of his French authors. La Bruyère, whom he did not like because he was a man of subordinate social position and consequent dejection. La Rochefoucauld, whom he loved for his strict principles and as a man of passion and elegance who lived a full and rich life. He disliked Vauvenargues. What he heard about his early sickness and death moved him, but his good-natured stoicism was repugnant to him. In Fontenelle he felt the charm of pure, cool intellect, at home in every latitude and at every elevation, combined with the man-of-the-world's security in social relations. He loved the Age of Louis XIV, and hated the Revolution. He resented the fact that Chamfort had associated with the men of the Revolution, and did not want his own name to be mentioned together with Chamfort's. Nietzsche at the time counted himself among those aristocratic moralists, and suffered very much, already in those years when he was visiting us, because he was so little known and read. After every publication he hoped to receive enthusiastic approbation, to be greeted by the public as a new star in the heavens, and to find followers and disciples.

He really was not lacking in enthusiastic recognition but his ambition aimed for a much more general and greater influence. The nature of his ambition could become quite clear only after his own goals had been clarified in his own mind. He was often very tormented, and I was a witness to these torments of his, about which he complained to us. We tried to console him in every way, pointing to the future, and it did him at least some good to see that we sympathized in his sufferings. Once I succeeded especially well at this, and I will never forget the grateful emotion which therefore came over him. I read aloud, as applying to him, a passage from *Truth and Poetry,* in which Goethe, on the subject of *Werther,* speaks of author and public as follows: "Thus oppressed, he became all too conscious that authors and public are separated by a tremendous gap, of which happily neither has any idea. So he had realized long ago how futile all prefaces are: for the more one tries to make one's intention clear, the more confusion one causes. Furthermore, an author may write whatever preface he will, the public will always continue to make on him demands which he has already tried to reject. I likewise at an early age got to know a related trait of readers, which strikes me as very strange, especially in those who publish their judgment. For they live under the illusion that when one achieves something one becomes their creditor and always falls short of what they actually wanted and wished, although shortly before seeing our work they had absolutely no idea that such a thing existed or could even be possible."

He never once came without telling us what he was then doing— and he came several times a week. I remember especially Byron's diaries, which he brought to us; he told of Shelley, his poetic nature, the freethinking of these poets and the pious hypocrisy that persecuted them. He told of the English philosophers, Hobbes, Berkeley, Hume. Once when my husband was out he conversed with me for a while and named especially two odd fellows he was then studying and in whose works he detected a relationship with himself. He was very elated and happy as always whenever he became conscious of inner relations. Some time afterwards he saw a volume of Klinger in our apartment. My husband had not found Stirner in the library. "Ach," he said, "I was very disappointed in Klinger. He was a philistine, I feel no affinity with him; but Stirner, yes, with him!" And a solemn expression passed over his face. While I was watching his features intently, his expression changed again, and he made something like a gesture of dismissal or defense: "Now I've told you, and I did not want to mention it at all. Forget it. They will be talking about plagiarism, but you will not do that, I know." Nietzsche had before the fall of 1874 characterized Stirner's work to his student Baumgartner as the boldest and most consistent since Hobbes. It thoroughly accords with Nietzsche's nature that he could have studied Stirner sympathetically at so early a time. His nature may have rebelled against Schopenhauer already while he was writing the *Untimely Meditations,* just as he had already rejected Wagner when he published "Richard Wagner in Bayreuth." Nietzsche never subscribed to the content of Schopenhauer's teaching, although he was very involved with a few of his theses. What impressed him about the men he revered was always their strong personality, which he hoped to counterbalance with something similar from his innermost being. But this inner core was leading him on quite other paths. That Nietzsche and Stirner seem to us so diametrically different, and actually are, is obvious! But we are not thereby doing justice to Nietzsche and are not giving him the attention and respect he wishes and may demand. Nietzsche paid innermost attention to Stirner. He neither proceeded from him nor stayed with him; yet he did not underestimate him, but considered him an unprejudiced thinker, which he could so very well be, and felt affinity with him. It was the simplest sense of reality that moved my husband to note that Nietzsche had known Stirner. Stirner represents a very specific element in Nietzsche, though a small one if you wish, but for Nietzsche great and significant because of the scantiness of this element which he happened to be pursuing.

Nietzsche at that time also quoted ideas of Ludwig Feuerbach's. He criticized Wagner for having turned from Feuerbach to Schopenhauer. Not as if he himself had undergone the opposite process; for Feuerbach had influenced him long ago, perhaps even before Schopenhauer. If "The Concept of God as Man's Generic Nature" and other essays written by Feuerbach are read in Nietzsche's spirit, one will understand what their way of thinking contributed to his superman. This Nietzschean central idea drew its nourishment here, more than from all natural-scientific argumentation; returning the superhuman out of the concept of God back to man, to the generic concept, the individual, and hence achieving the simple positing of the superman, attaching his own thoughts to him, free of any merely receptive borrowing. He told me that on reading an author he was always struck only by short sentences, to which he attached his own thoughts and built a new structure on these pre-existing pillars. Thus he several times mentioned the moralist Dr. Samuel Johnson, Voltaire's English contemporary, and when I was reading his poetic satire *The Vanity of Human Wishes*, I remember how Nietzsche once had stressed the inner contradiction of the genre in Johnson: the deep energetic bitterness in the judgment, indeed the condemnation, of moral conditions, which does not escape from itself to belief in the possibility of ennobling these relations or in calmer comprehension of them, but to a quietistic religious confession.

The Kantian and Schopenhauerian foundations of ethics were discussed in their entire material without the names of the philosophers being mentioned very much. The idea of revaluation was alive in him. First he tried it via psychology. He sought the causes of morality, the desirability or necessity of this drive in himself or in past generations. He checked German, English, and French philosophers for this. They are always talking about good and evil, said Nietzsche, but all that is relative. Good can become evil, when it is old and worn out; we always have to create it anew. Good is nothing; what we must strive for is nobility, which also does justice to evil. Good can come from evil, and vice versa. Evil is the real creative principle. Everything is of equal value, if only there are strong men who impose their will. No revaluation is involved here, since Nietzsche still has the good be good and evil, evil, but only shows their interrelations. No philosopher, no thinker is ignorant of the power of passion. But in Nietzsche that is something special. Nietzsche disliked an ethic that counts on happiness, a eudaimonism that counts on success and failure. All this seemed dishonest to Nietzsche and far off the path of morality, which has nothing to do with happiness and unhappiness, and must not divide into good and evil. He tried the route of characterizing the good as weakness, evil as strength, portraying their one-sidedness, as of things that fall apart. Moreover, whereas Christianity and philosophy had always depicted the good as the highest value, he had an innate dislike for altruism, which contrary to prior custom he loved to identify in abuses and degeneracies, while he to some extent blunted intensifications of mere wrong into despicable evil, which he tended to deny. He called upon precisely the good for these intensifications, demanding of them magnanimity and nobility as equivalencies of evil which has its good and necessary side. (*43*, 236–241)

42   Lou Andreas-Salomé   *Spring 1882*

First something happened in Rome, whereby we got the upper hand: it was the arrival of Friedrich Nietzsche, whom his friends, Malwida and Paul Rée, had told that we were there and who had come unexpectedly from Messina to share our company. Something else unexpectedly happened, that Nietzsche, having scarcely heard of Paul Rée's and my plan, decided to make a trio of it. Even the place of our future stay was soon determined: that was to be Paris (originally, for a while, Vienna), where Nietzsche wanted to attend certain courses, and where both Paul Rée, from before, and I, through St. Petersburg, had connections with Ivan Turgenev. Malwida was even reassured somewhat because she saw us sheltered there by her foster daughters, Olga Monod and Natalia Herzen. The latter, moreover, ran a little salon where young girls read beautiful books with her. But Malwida would have preferred to have Frau Rée accompany her son, and Fräulein Nietzsche her brother. —Our jokes were joyful and innocent, for we all loved Malwida so much, and Nietzsche often was in such an elated mood that his otherwise somewhat moderate, or more accurately, slightly solemn temperament receded before it. I can still remember this trace of solemnity from our very first meeting, which took place in St. Peter's, where Paul Rée, in a confessional that stood under especially favorable lighting, wrote down his work-notes with fiery devotion and where Nietzsche therefore had been told to meet us. His first greeting to me was with the words: "From which stars did we fall to meet each other here?" But what began so well, soon underwent a change which brought Paul Rée and me new concern about *our* plan, since this plan was incalculably complicated by a third party. Nietzsche, however, thought it simplified the situation: he had Rée act as his spokesman to me for a proposal of marriage. Worriedly, we reflected on how this problem could best be settled without breaking up our trio. We decided to inform Nietzsche of my basic disinclination to any marriage at all; and moreover of the circumstance that I was living only on my mother's pension as a general's widow and that by marrying I would forfeit my own future small pension which was paid to unmarried daughters of the Russian nobility. When we left Rome this matter seemed settled for the moment; Nietzsche was, moreover, suffering increasingly from his "attacks" of the sickness which had once caused him to resign from his Basel professorship and which began as a terribly exacerbated migraine headache; Paul Rée therefore stayed in Rome with him, while my mother—as far as I can remember—considered it more appropriate to ride ahead with me, so that we ran into each other again only on the way. We then made stops together now and then, for instance in Orta on the lakes of Northern Italy, where the Monte Sacro, located nearby, seems to have fascinated us; at least my mother was unintentionally offended because Nietzsche and I stayed too long on the Monte Sacro to go meet her on time, which Paul Rée also took very badly since he had to entertain her in the meantime. After we had left Italy, Nietzsche made a stop at the Overbecks' in Basel, but from there he accompanied us again to Lucerne, because after the fact he considered Paul Rée's intercession for him in Rome to have been insufficient and he wanted to take up the matter personally with me, which then happened in the Lucerne Lion Zoo. At the same time Nietzsche also was busy having a picture made of us three, despite stiff resistance from Paul Rée, who all his life never lost a morbid repugnance for any portrayal of his face. Nietzsche, in an exuberant mood, insisted not only on that, but also occupied himself personally and zealously with the arrangement of details—like the little ladder-wagon (which turned out to be too small) and even the kitsch of the lilac branch on the whip, etc.

Nietzsche then drove back to Basel, while Paul Rée went with us to Zurich . . .

From Bayreuth, Nietzsche and I planned to be together for several weeks in Thüringen—Tautenburg by Dornburg—where by chance I happened to live in a house whose owner, the village preacher, turned out to be a former student of my main professor in Zurich, Alois Biedermann. At first, quarrels seem to have taken place between Nietzsche and me, caused by all sorts of gossip, which I still cannot understand to this day, because it did not at all coincide with reality, and which we also soon got rid of, in order to experience a rich time together, with the greatest possible exclusion of any third parties. Here I got a far deeper insight into Nietzsche's thinking than in Rome or on the journey: I still knew none of his works except *The Joyful Science,* which he was still revising and from which he had read to us in Rome: in such conversations Nietzsche and Rée took the words out of each other's mouth and had long since belonged to the same school of thought, at least since Nietzsche's fall from Wagner. The preference for the aphoristic mode of work—forced upon Nietzsche by his illness and by his way of life—was Paul Rée's own from the first; for many years he had been walking around with a La Rochefoucauld or a La Bruyère in his pocket and he had retained this same mentality ever since his first little book, *On Vanity.* About Nietzsche, however, one already could feel what was to lead him beyond his collections of aphorisms and toward his *Zarathustra:* the deep movement of the God-seeker Nietzsche who came from religion and was heading toward religious prophecy.

In one of my letters from Tautenburg to Paul Rée, dated August 18th, one reads: "At the very beginning of my acquaintanceship with Nietzsche I wrote to Malwida of him that he was of a religious nature, and aroused her strongest doubts. Today I would want to underscore this expression doubly." "We will experience it yet that he will step forth as the proclaimer of a new religion, and then it will be such a one as recruits heroes to be its disciples." "How very alike we think and feel about this, and we literally take the words and thoughts from one another's lips. We have been literally talking ourselves to death in these three weeks, and strangely he can now endure chatting about ten hours daily." "Strange how we involuntarily end up on precipices with our conversations, on those dizzy heights where one has once climbed to look down into the depths. We have always chosen to climb like the chamois, and if someone had heard us he would have believed that two devils were conversing."

Inevitably, something fascinated me in Nietzsche's nature and conversations that came less to the fore in conversations between him and Paul Rée, since for me this also revived memories or unconscious feelings which came from my most innocent and yet most personal and indestructible childhood. Yet at the same time it was just this that would never have allowed me to become his disciple or follower: it would at all times have made me distrustful of following in that direction, from which I had to escape to find clarity. Fascination with and at the same time an inner turning away from it went together.

After I had journeyed back to Stibbe for the fall, we came back together again for three weeks in Leipzig in October. None of us suspected that it was the last time. But it was no longer quite like the first, although our wishes for our common future as a trio still held. When I ask myself what most began to hamper my inner attitude toward Nietzsche, it was bewilderment at the increasing frequency of remarks from him which were supposed to besmirch Paul Rée in my sight—and yet also astonishment that he could consider this method effective. Only after our departure from Leipzig did enmities also break out against me, hateful reproaches, of which however only a premonitory letter became known to me. What later followed seemed so contradictory to Nietzsche's nature and dignity that it can only be ascribed to the influence of others. For example, when he exposed Rée and me to precisely those suspicions whose untenableness he best knew. But the most fateful incidents of this time were probably simply kept secret from me through Paul Rée's care—I understood this only many years later; it even seems that letters from Nietzsche to me containing incomprehensible defamations were never given to me. And not only this: Paul Rée also hid from me the fact of what strong provocations, including hatred, even *his* family was circulating against me, though especially the mortally jealous disposition of his mother, who wanted to keep this son just for herself, had a voice in this.

Much later Nietzsche probably was himself displeased by the rumors he had spread; for we learned through Heinrich von Stein, who was close to us, of the following episode from Sils-Maria, where Nietzsche once visited us (not without first having obtained our permission). He pleaded with Nietzsche for the possibility of removing the misunderstandings which had arisen between us; but Nietzsche, shaking his head, answered: "What I have done cannot be forgiven."

In the following period I myself observed Paul Rée's method of removing all that from my sight, for I read nothing more about it; he discussed neither the hostility of the Nietzsche family nor Nietzsche literature after his death. I wrote my book *Friedrich Nietzsche in his Works* still full of naiveté, only because once he had become really famous too many literary fledglings who misunderstood him were writing about the subject; I myself had understood Nietzsche's image correctly in his works only *after* our personal association; my only interest was to promote an understanding of the figure of Nietzsche by those objective impressions. And just as his image became understandable to me—in the pure commemoration of the personal—so it would remain in my mind's eye. (2, 98–107)

43   Ida Overbeck

Frau Andreas has described her experience with Nietzsche in a book which, despite its defects, is very valuable; she has also published a part of her letters from him. I have always most deeply regretted that a completely one-sided and unworthy judgment of this woman and her relation to Nietzsche has dared to show itself despite these publications. Nietzsche himself gave occasion for it in some ways. Without will and weakened as he often was, even in the wish to be just to everyone, and believing that he would after all retain the notebook in his own possession, he let himself go in subsequent excitements which lay far from his own original views. When he told my husband of the new relationship in the summer of 1882, he was extremely excited and very hopeful and confident in the fulfillment of his plans and his life. An extramarital, spiritually passionate relationship was an ideal he always liked. Passion was present, but also the wish to let himself be carried away by it. It gave him reassurance that Rée was the third party in the association, and he expected much from his helpful, selfless nature, while he asked me to talk with Lou about the fact that he always pursued only his spiritual goals and in everything thought only of himself. At the same time he said that he had told her in Rome, "I would consider myself obligated to protect you from people's gossip, to offer to marry you otherwise, etc." He feared that Fräulein Salomé could have considered this to be a proposal.

The few months that he knew Fräulein Salomé brought Nietzsche the highest psychic delights.

He had formulated his Zarathustra idea before this time. The excitement which caused him to create his "son Zarathustra" did not come originally from Lou. That a man of his age struggles with passion is self-evident. The pain and renunciation of not having a son, of never having one, had come alive in him. He stated in the summer of 1882 that he therefore had gotten the idea of creating the figure of a son artistically. The value of such confidences ought not to be exaggerated. To revaluate Zarathustra, who was for him a representative of the value-standard "good" and "evil" in the oldest history of mankind, was the real idea. Despite different, converging occasions for Zarathustra, Lou did have a direct part in bringing Nietzsche to the philosophico-religious and moral-prophetic expression of a substitute for religion and morality. Her own book *The Struggle for God* and the later *From an Unknown Soul* are signs of this. Lou's understanding and probably also her womanhood raised Nietzsche to the greatest heights. They shared values and stood in *rapport* with the Christian experience. He said later to my husband that the only experience Fräulein Salomé had known was the religious one of her confirmation, and this had been the theme, really the only theme between them. There is at any rate some truth at the basis of this statement, though it must not be understood as if it had been an exclusively religious experience even in its consequences for Lou, including the main consequence: that she shared it with Nietzsche and was then "educated" by him.

I do not know which book or manuscript he had given Rée and Fräulein Salomé in early summer 1882. He was unhappy that they both ridiculed him. He said at that time to my husband and me in a whisper something like: he simply had to have something different again and again, pure Enlightenment was not enough for him, and the two did not understand this at all. I was astonished that already such distrust, such knowledge of not belonging together, was present. I am by no means certain whether the two really ridiculed him. Nietzsche was often hypersensitive, and his imagination easily played tricks on him. I have no information about the cause of their separation in November 1882. He did not say anything about it. During a third visit with us that year he said only that it was probably all over between them. He was still expecting letters and attached expectations to them, asking whether I had not received any mail for him, even fearing I might withhold some from him. He was deeply hurt and unable to help himself by telling someone about his pain and receiving their consolation. I advised him not to give up people just because they hurt one another but to expect peace and assuagement from time and insight.

I do not want to go more than necessary into Fräulein Nietzsche's viewpoint on this matter. Her brother felt her defects and knew that they had turned not only against Fräulein Salomé but also against himself. I spoke with Fräulein Nietzsche for a moment in Bayreuth, in the summer of 1882, and was startled by her assertions. She expressed a strong aversion for Fräulein Salomé, whom she believed to be interested in her brother's enemies. At the same time she accused her of not being capable of enthusiasm, while always comparing herself with her as more excellent. She had a low opinion of Fräulein Salomé's talent and wanted to look down on her because of her greater youth and to relegate her to all possible school-benches, but in any case out of her brother's company. I had the impression that she had nothing with which to oppose this talent. She complained bitterly against her brother, as she had done earlier, because of his manner, because of his lack of consideration for herself. I had to admit to myself that she was not the person to assume an understanding and sympathetic role in the relationship. Nietzsche, with whom I had never spoken about his sister on my own initiative, had himself feared that his family would not be able to be just about the nature of this relationship. So it was certainly a mistake for him nonetheless to impose it on his family.

Later he suffered very much under all the disagreements, including with his family. I advised him not to forget that he himself had known that he was asking too much of his sister, and that after all he could tell himself that her entire aversion to him was based on foolish fantasies, which he could overcome. This did him good and built a bridge toward conciliatoriness for him. The reconciliation then also came about, but in a harmful way for Nietzsche. He abjured himself and his own experience and thus hurt himself and probably others too.

Nietzsche had in the summer of 1882 given himself over to the hope of having found his alter ego in Fräulein Salomé, of working toward his goal with her and through her help. Fräulein Salomé was not willing to be dissolved in Nietzsche. His longing for the most intimate togetherness shows the passionate nature of his psychic condition. How sublimely and heart-movingly error and disappointment resound in him! How was it possible to introduce here a truly blatant burlesque that abruptly tore apart all the threads of his feeling, a burlesque for which Nietzsche had neither the talent nor the crudity? Of what sort is the womanhood which undertook this with an air of importance and, despite all objections, carried it out with a kind of virtuosity?

The poor, splendid friend, if only he had been more self-reliant and had really represented himself. That was what I would have wished of him but he could no longer understand me. I had not spoken of false pity applied to the deepest pain of his life, but of false pity for petty machinations on which he had, after all, declared war. I was deeply miserable, after I had received these letters. How could a person like Nietzsche fall so short of himself? He was indignant at the announcements. How was it possible for him to surrender to such announcements without a trace of critique, to find someone to make them for him who had been so unjust toward himself, and herself needed the greatest consideration that Nietzsche had granted in complete conciliatoriness? How was it possible that he did not say to himself: where you have been judged so unjustly, do others have any chance of receiving a juster judgment?

He ended in the barbarity of a hateful epilogue which had no inner model in his heart. It ate at his vital roots and he did not reject it but willingly looked upon himself as its victim. He who with his doctrine of the eternal return had hoped really to encompass the woman-disciple and this time finally to be a ruler! But we too failed from a lack of any idea how important this doctrine of return was to him. In *The Joyful Science* it is still described as one among many and had a rather sobering effect on us. That was the great loneliness which came over him; it was really terrible. In 1882 I did not understand his whole gruesome pain when he said farewell with the words "So then I am really going into complete solitude." He hoped to the last for a confession, for an understanding, which did not exist. Even in 1883 Nietzsche was waiting for us, and we did not satisfy him. In 1884 he finally himself spoke in the way described by my husband. But he was ill and stayed far from me and later himself felt that he had rejected me, which naturally resulted in a cooling off. I never saw him again.

Many a woman may not be willing to hear that the man is the victim, and especially not that Zarathustra the Mighty, whose strength stands above everything human, in this case wanted to be the victim. My heart shared in his ideals.

Nietzsche later found peace. Some statements from him to this effect are on record. In memory he clung firmly to his friends and to what they had been to him. (*43*, 336–346)

44   Elisabeth Förster-Nietzsche   *May 1882ff.*

How did it come about that my brother is generally considered a misogynist? I believe it is due to a little remark from *Zarathustra:* "You are going to women? Do not forget the whip!" For that is the only thing which a hundred thousand women know about Nietzsche. They do not even bother to check up in *Zarathustra* as to who makes this statement, namely a little old woman, and even those who read it do not understand the mischievous humor of the whole chapter. I will recapitulate its meaning briefly. Zarathustra is walking alone and is asked by a friend why he is sneaking so alone in the twilight. He answers that he is carrying in his coat a little truth given to him by an old woman. She had said to him: "Zarathustra spoke much to us women, but he never spoke to us about women." Zarathustra answers: "One should speak about women only to men." But since the old woman urges him, he says various things, both good and bad, on this theme. (In fact he glorifies only the loving, obedient woman who is held in rather low esteem by the emancipated women of today and perhaps also by weak men who themselves do not quite know what they want.) "Let woman be a plaything, pure and fine, like a precious gem, radiant with the virtues of a world which does not yet exist . . . A man's happiness is: *I will;* a woman's happiness: *he wills.* Behold, just now the world became perfect, thus thinks every woman when she obeys out of complete love." The chapter ends: "Then the old woman answered me: 'Zarathustra said many nice things, and particularly for those who are young enough for those sayings . . . and now accept with gratitude a little truth! For I am old enough for it.' 'Give me, woman, your little truth!' says Zarathustra. And thus spoke the old woman: 'You go to women, forget not the whip.'"—Everyone who has a sense for nuance and humorous irony, will delight in this poetic formulation of a somewhat crude truth, with which all women who have lived in the great world, where woman generally dares to show herself more naturally than in simple bourgeois conditions, certainly will agree. There are some women who are unrestrained in their drives and character and who need a master—for of course the whip is here just a symbol for mastery—indeed a strong master, to keep them under control.

Incidentally, the origin of this remark is a quite harmless humorous story. When Fritz was visiting us in Naumburg in the spring of 1882, I read Turgenev's novella *First Love* aloud to him. A charming young thing, probably of somewhat dubious nature, is loved simultaneously by father and son. The father is a powerful, brutal man forty years of age, the son an ideal eighteen-year-old youth. The beautiful girl prefers the father. Later the youthful lover eavesdrops on a scene in which the charming creature on her knees asks the preferred lover for something, but he lashes at her with his riding whip, so that red stripes become visible on her white arms—but she loves him nonetheless. My brother accompanied the reading with all kinds of humorous remarks; but at this scene he expressed his disapproval of the lover's behavior. So I could not avoid reminding him by a few examples we knew that there simply happen to be female natures who are held in check only by a brutal stressing of power on the man's part, and who, as soon as they do not feel that symbolic whip over them, become impertinent and shameless and play games with the over-kindly man who adores them, indeed even trample him underfoot. My brother knew the examples very well and had often discussed them with indignation. At this mention, however, he leaned back on the sofa, and cried out with well-feigned astonishment: "Thus the Lama advises the man to use the whip!" "No," I answered laughingly, "of course the whip is not for Lamas and for all reasonable, virtuous women; they should be treated with consideration and love. But for the others!" We glossed over the affair with a good many jokes. A year later my brother met with me in Rome and there gave me the first part of *Zarathustra*. There I also came to the chapter where the old woman gives Zarathustra the advice: "You go to women? Forget not the whip!"—"O Fritz," I exclaimed in alarm, "I am the old woman!" My brother laughed and said he would not betray that to anyone. Meanwhile, Fritz might have changed his view of women somewhat or learned something new since reading that novella, so that now in the whip story he felt the need to stress it especially strongly. (*14*, 559–561)

45   Arthur Egidi   *July 1882ff.*

It was the last summer in the life of Richard Wagner, which still was to be crowned with the performance of his most sublime work, *Parsifal*. I too had been preparing myself for the great event by studying the piano music, but had not penetrated completely to an understanding of that sublimely spiritual creation. For quiet concentration I therefore spent July and a part of August 1882 in Tautenburg, which had just blossomed to an official summer freshness. The pastor, St., concerned for the welfare of his parish, invited me to a meeting of the Beautification Committee, which, among other things, made the following proposal: "There is presently living in our village one of the most outstanding writers on the fine arts, Friedrich Nietzsche. Here he is finishing his new work, *The Joyful Science,* and likes to spend his time in the part of the forest which we call the 'Dead Man.' However he has no bench to rest on, and so I move that one be erected to him with the name 'The Joyful Science.'"

The next day I was sitting in the shadowy woods waiting for two friends who were hiking to Bayreuth. A man approaching on foot immediately drew my attention: he was a slender figure of a man, with a delicate narrow head—narrow from my perspective—and dark hair; his slightly reddened face had an air of happiness, the victory prize of a hard struggle, for the dark eyebrows strove upward ready for battle. The eyes themselves, however, had no part in this. Broken and helpless, the figure looked out from under an umbrella, for despite the darkness in the woods the stranger was holding an open umbrella. Hat in hand, the stranger approached and offered me a friendly greeting. "That can only be Nietzsche," was my thought.

The friends kept me waiting far too long, and so I set out for Dorndorf. Instead of them I again met the stranger, who was now hiking back to Tautenburg and surprised me again with a greeting, even before my hand touched my hat.

After a few days my Bayreuth pilgrims arrived; but they had already left Tautenburg again when a happy chance brought me into contact with the interesting man. A rainstorm drove the summer strollers into the pavilion on the Alexander Parapets, and that stranger soon also entered. He sat down next to me and listened attentively to the conversations of the other people who had gathered there, interjecting himself into the conversaton now and then. When one of the speakers talked about the harmfulness of the new school of theology and mentioned the name of Stoecker with praise, Nietzsche, whom I had meanwhile recognized as the neighbor on my left, asked me: "Who is Stoecker?" Soon, however, he sank into a deep silence which I believed I could use as a welcome opportunity to introduce myself to him. With the words, "Since you are a musician I must speak to you," he took me by the arm and pulled me out of the group. Meanwhile it had stopped raining, our matter could be discussed while walking. "I am expecting," he began, "one of these days to receive the piano score of a new opera, and since my eye ailment prevents me from playing it myself, I would like to ask you to do me this favor. The work would, moreover, interest you. It is a new composition to the text of Cimarosa's *Secret Marriage.* I consider the composer to be one of the most important contemporary musicians; he is living in complete seclusion in Venice under the assumed name Peter Gast[1] and is one of the most consci-

---

1. But the piano selection never arrived. The opera first appeared in 1901 under the title *The Lion of Venice.*

entious persons toward himself. In my opinion the creative musician must not rest before he is satisfied with every note of his work, any more than the writer before he feels full satisfaction with every sentence, every word, otherwise he ought to give up writing completely. My friend, however, is filled with this striving for perfection of form to the fullest extent." I willingly declared myself ready to fulfill his wish, since I was especially interested in the development of dramatic music, and I considered the highest perfection to have already been reached in other branches of music.

"So Wagner does not seem to you to be the summit in the development of dramatic art?" Nietzsche asked. "No," was my youthfully brash answer. I then sought to explain my views: a greater independence of the music could perhaps be expected in the future than can be found in Wagner; even according to the principle of entropy, the retrogressive, opposite strivings cannot remain without influence on the future. Gluck found his Mozart. "I don't know, Professor, whether I can immediately frame my thoughts in intelligible language." Thus ended my youthful argument; but he laid his arm around my shoulder and said: "Oh, one understands one another very well, when one thinks the same!" Enthusiasm completely loosened my tongue, and thoughts and words seemed to have become one. Fortunately this led him to speak of his personal association with Wagner. He recalled the days in Tribschen, when Wagner had withdrawn there with his wife, Cosima: "His work—it was the *Ring*—was still unconcerned with the world, it was an emanation of the subject in contrast with today when it is determined more by the will. Cosima, a thoroughly catholic nature, and as such filled with a deep need for opera, had probably recognized that this need could not be separated from Wagner's mission in life and from his person. So these hours seem to me like a faraway paradise, to which I cannot think back when I look at the independence I have acquired and Wagner's enmity, which I thereby incurred."

Nietzsche then began to speak of his own work, and asked, "What reception did the Berlin press give to *The Birth of Tragedy*?" This question embarrassed me a little, for the Berlin reviews I knew were negative; moreover, when he left Basel, the false report of his death had circulated in Berlin, and Gustav Engel had made the gentle obituary: "He died of Wagner." I admitted to Nietzsche that I had not yet read *The Birth of Tragedy*, since I had till then found it necessary to limit myself to my more special studies. "Please, don't waste words on apologizing; you are doing right to

stick to your tasks," he helped me assuringly over the first embarrassment. But I had to respond to the heart of his question and tell
him that the statements of the Berlin press which I knew were unre-
peatable. He laughed loudly.

The sun had meanwhile dispersed the clouds, it was noontime.
The professor said good-bye to me in such a friendly way that it
never occurred to me to worry about having hurt his feelings.

Arriving home I found waiting for me a postcard with the fol-
lowing content: "I have come across a fabulous philosopher; since
I have known him, the snow of old age is melting from my head. He
is Friedrich Nietzsche; more about him soon. Till we meet again in
Bayreuth!" Of course I immediately wrote back: "You came across
Nietzsche's works, I just went for a walk with him!"

In the afternoon I met Nietzsche at the post office in Dorndorf
and told him about this amusing coincidence. He shook with laughter. "No, the most inventive thing of all is chance!" he concluded.
"My ideas had as rejuvenating an effect on me as they did on your
friend."

"Like a mood!" the words came from me. "Shall we go back
together!" he asked; I thanked him but explained that I wanted to
carry out a plan I had long had, namely to climb the Dornburg.

"I too love this region," he answered, "for it bears the stamp of
Goethe's loneliness; he withdrew to the Dornburg when people had
hurt his feelings. But the gestation of all really great creation lies in
loneliness."

Soon afterwards Nietzsche traveled for a few days to Naumburg
in order, as he said, to fetch from there his sister, who had just
returned from Bayreuth. He let me know the day of his return, but
I did not go to him that day; a newly discovered path with its constantly changing images enticed me further and further until I
finally arrived in Jena. On my return late in the evening I found
Nietzsche's card, which he had left. Early the next morning, it was
August 5th, I immediately called on him. He came in the company
of his sister across the yard of the farmhouse where he lived, and
soon we were on our way to Dorndorf, while his sister stayed in the
inn at Tautenburg. In our conversation I had a lot of my own opinions and views to offer; thus I discussed Hieronymus Lorm, my
favorite philosopher till then, because his 'unfounded' optimism
seemed to me a way out of pessimism, though not a particularly
happy one. Nietzsche had never even heard of the name "Lorm,"
but my statements led him to speak of his own liberation from the

bonds of Schopenhauer and to explain to me how his views had changed, based on a list of his previous writings. About the aphoristic formulation of his thoughts he gave the following explanation: "I felt close to death and therefore pressed to say some things which I had been carrying around with me for years. Illness compelled me to use the briefest mode of expression; the individual sentences were dictated directly to a friend; systematic realization was out of the question. That is how the book *Human, All Too Human* was written. Thus the choice of the aphorism will be understandable only from the accompanying circumstances."[2]

Now our conversation turned back to musical matters. I had a lot to say about Brahms' personality and its connection with his works; they led him to tell me an anecdote about him. "I had," so he began, "heard the *Triumphal Song* in Munich and been singularly impressed; it seemed to me like a revival of Handel's choral spirit. So I brought it along to Bayreuth and wanted to play it for Wagner, but he evaded my repeated requests; but I did not give in until one day he said half reluctantly; 'Klindworth, play the red score; Nietzsche is not leaving me in peace!' But after a few octaves Wagner stormily left the room, leaving behind his loyal followers in bewildered depression. I laughed and for a long time could not explain the matter, until I learned the context. The King of Bavaria had offered Wagner a high medal, which he at first wanted to refuse, but finally accepted due to the urgent arguments of his wife and friends. He hardly had it in his hands when he heard that Brahms had received the same medal, at the very same time as he did. I considered it unnecessary to explore this matter of the medal, for no external reasons are necessary to explain the internal divergencies of the two masters. On the other hand, Wagner was very good at flattery," Nietzsche continued, "Saint-Saëns played a piece of his own at Wahnfried and Wagner rewarded him with the words: 'When someone plays as well as you do, he ought not at all to play his own things.'"

Would the French master also have regarded this as flattery?

Meanwhile we had reached the Dorndorf station; the train which was to bring Nietzsche's proofs and letters was late. Although it could be seen in the distance, Nietzsche turned around energetically

2. In *The Twilight of the Idols,* however, we find yet another explanation: "I distrust all systematic thinkers and try to avoid them. The road to the system is a lack of honesty." Those who know and honor Nietzsche will hardly be astonished by the contradiction.

and explained: "I promised my sister to be at the inn by twelve o'clock, so I must not be a minute late. An official's life is regulated automatically by his office hours, but whoever is his own boss must bind himself to the minute." And this was said by the man to whom the railroad train was supposed to be bringing the galley proofs of *The Joyful Science* in which one can read:

> All nature goes silent on me,
> At the tick-tock of law and clock.

Of his earlier works, Nietzsche still recommended "The Utility and Value of History for Life," and "Schopenhauer as Educator." About "Richard Wagner in Bayreuth" Frau Wagner had said that it was the most accurate picture anyone had ever made of him and would probably retain its validity as long as his works were performed. "But," Nietzsche concluded, "it is really an idealized picture." Wagner was nonetheless his favorite theme and so he continued: "Frau Wagner had read *Parsifal* to me as a sketch, but in performance it seemed to me significantly weakened. The libretto bearing the inscription, 'Richard Wagner, High Church Councillor,' arrived at the same time as *Human, All Too Human* had been sent to Wagner, which then led to the break." But his sister, filled with the impression of the first Bayreuth performances, had caught his interest, and so he was struggling with the longing to go to Bayreuth, and was counting on my accompanying him. "There is just one bad thing about it," he continued, "that I cannot go there unnoticed and must not fail to make a visit to Wahnfried; but that is ruinous for me after what has happened." The memory of *The Birth of Tragedy* seemed to cheer him up; he hastily took one step forward and began: "Hans von Bülow had already visited me in Basel on the occasion of its appearance to express his 'admiration' of it, as he put it." Nietzsche said this almost shyly, as a charming blush passed over his face; but very soon, as he spoke of his former spiritual offspring, his elastic figure became rigid and his look of self-conscious pride sank. "On that visit," he continued, "Bülow dedicated to me a volume of Italian poems he had translated. There followed further relations which finally made me the mediator between him and his children, who were living in Wagner's house. Of course, musical matters repeatedly occasioned an exchange of ideas. He had arranged a morning concert in my honor, and on that occasion I described to him Schumann's *Manfred* music to the effect that I considered it to be *Faust* music rather than an adequate expression of the *Manfred* mood. I had tried to express this in a prelude of my own, which I presented to Bülow. His judgment, however, was: 'I've never yet heard such a thing; that is absolutely the rape of Euterpe!'"—Since then I have learned that Bülow even corroborated this in writing, but it was probably typical of Nietzsche's character that he spoke of it at all. Without wanting to take sides with Nietzsche on the *Manfred* prelude, I must mention that Nietzsche had expressed a negative opinion of Bülow's *Nirvana* long before he had any prospect of getting to know him personally. Our further conversations on musical subjects showed that the names of Beethoven and Bach evoked no resonance in our sage's soul. He fell into dull indifference. This must not be regarded as incidental! Certainly Beethoven's genius had once appealed to the heroism of his soul, but he saw in those days mainly the rough exterior of the German genius; and that Nietzsche in the times of his "independence" no longer was receptive to the resonance of Bach's art can be seen from his interpretation of a Goethean saying. Goethe, as is known, said to Mendelssohn on hearing Bach's music: "This sounds as if before the beginning of creation the eternal harmony in God's bosom were conversing with itself." Nietzsche, however, concluded: "So Bach is still not a world."

My youthful ideas on the influence of Bach and Beethoven on dramatic music beyond Wagner awakened in him the spirits of Chopin and Bizet. Everything in him came alive when he spoke of them; "esprit" and "elegance" seemed to be the only elements for which there was no echo in him. I was a bit alarmed: the dear man who shone with his words into my soul like a light was to have clouds too?

Our short rest in the shadowy woods was soon to end and also our walk. The brother and sister met again in front of the inn. The descriptions of the Bayreuth presentations with which the sister tried to persuade her brother visibly affected him. Thus the plan for his journey to Bayreuth was being reconsidered; I was to receive a definite answer by the next day, for I had to set out on August 7. "I hope soon to be a faithful adherent of yours," was my last word; and his: "I hope this will not be the last time we meet." On August 6th, however, the answer came that the professor felt too ill to travel with me to Bayreuth.[3]

---

3. No one will be surprised that after being so deeply moved I immediately took notes of the described meetings and so am still able to quote Nietzsche almost word for word. The notes speak clearly of some things that have vanished from memory, but generally they confirm what I remember accurately.

The powerful impression of *Parsifal* completely disproved both Nietzsche's critique and my own theories and it has lost none of its power in the past twenty years. Nietzsche's separation from Wagner and his final open break seemed to me like an inescapable, blameless fate, so that I was able to keep the memory of the magnificent man unsullied.

I recall again his friendly greeting in the Tautenburg forest, his helpless look on the day we first met; and the deep, deep pity which this look aroused comes to life again.

I came to this familiar place once again in the company of Friedrich Kiel in the spring of 1884. Assuming that Nietzsche's former apartment might be suited for him—I had never before entered it—we went there; but for Kiel the mere sight of the little room, scantily illuminated by a single small window, was enough. Nietzsche had told me: "One should accustom oneself to the greatest abstemiousness in order to be able to endure all un expected events." This little room was the best commentary on this statement.

In the summer of 1890 I came to a country rectory located close to the Brandenburg-Silesian border. A conversation was going on about Nietzsche. "You know my cousin?" the woman of the house asked me. "Whom do you mean?" "Well, Friedrich Nietzsche," she continued. "We recently received the news that Fritz is playing with pennies, and his mother has to lead him like a little child to church, the only place where he feels calm." A strange fate for the prophet of the Anti-Christ!

Today attitudes are cooler about the regrettable *Wagner Case* than at the time of its appearance. On the one hand the contradiction between mood and attitude which took place in Nietzsche's soul is understood as a prelude to his paralysis, on the other it is seen that Nietzsche's later ideal of beauty could at most assert itself against Wagner, but could not overcome him. Wagner's victorious campaign throughout the non-Germanic world seems already to be a verdict of history, and this gives Wagner—though he wanted to be just German—the significance of a European event, which Nietzsche had eccentrically denied. Whether an operatic style—if this term can also be applied to Wagner's artistic work—does not perhaps have more chance of survival than the views of a philosopher, however significant—is a question which will be answered by the Wagner-Nietzsche example in not too remote a future. (*11*, 1892–1899)

46   Sebastian Hausmann

In the mid-eighties, despite my youth at the time I felt a strong need for a complete rest. Throughout the winter I had been working rather too hard writing a prize essay for a competition which had been announced by the Law and Political Science Faculty at the University of Strasbourg. Since I was at the same time earning my livelihood by writing, it is understandable that I also had to work late at night, never going to bed before one o'clock, and being back at work by eight in the morning. On a marvellously beautiful summer day I therefore drove over to neighboring Switzerland and after delightful long hikes I one day ended up in the Engadine, in Sils-Maria, where I liked everything so much that I decided to stay for one or two weeks.

Not going on any longer excursions, every morning after breakfast I took a walk toward Silvaplana, on a path that was practically overrich in wonderful landscapes and vistas. The very first day, I noticed a man whom I believed I had seen somewhere before, though I could not remember when and where. He was a commanding personality with a rather unusual appearance, whom one would therefore well remember: a large bushy mustache gave the face a martial air, a striking profile; involuntarily one would have thought, a Prussian officer in civilian clothes, except that the head also showed signs of very extraordinary intellectual significance.

The next morning, when I was strolling along the same path, the striking man whose appearance had involuntarily attracted my closer attention was again walking along a little ahead of me. Suddenly I saw a letter lying on the ground, I picked it up, and hurried to catch up with the solitary walker, who in all probability had dropped the letter. I politely removed my hat and stepped up to the gentleman with the question: "I've just found this letter on the path. I assume you lost it?" After glancing at the letter, the noteworthy man's eyes flashed sharply at me: "Yes, of course, I lost this letter. Thank you very much." Then he kept on walking, but after a few paces he stopped again, and when I had caught up with him he offered me his hand with a friendly smile, and said to me: "You have done me a very real service, I would very much have hated to lose that letter. Thank you again for your friendliness."

And he made a gesture of the hand which I understood to mean that he was inviting me to continue the walk together with him. As a well-brought-up young man I considered it my duty to give him my so thoroughly insignificant name, whereupon he reached fleetingly for his hat and mumbled a name that sounded to me very similar to Nietzsche. Now all of a sudden I knew why the man's face had so struck me; it had a certain unmistakable similarity with the pictures of the famous philosopher which I vaguely remembered. I was not one of that philosopher's admirers and had never read his works to the end, because I ran into too many difficulties I could not easily solve with my simple common sense. Somewhat suspiciously I therefore asked the gentleman: "Are you perhaps a relative of the famous philosopher Nietzsche?" He looked at me sharply for a moment then answered: "No, I'm not related to him." Involuntarily I remarked: "Well, thank God!" I immediately regretted this remark, I had merely been thinking somewhat too loudly. Again he flashed a look at me from the side and asked: "So you don't like the philosopher?" To which I answered candidly: "No." He then asked further: "What has the man done to you?" I looked pensively for a few moments, then I said: "Well, of course the man has done me no harm. But it annoys me that he always writes as if the whole world consisted of professors of philosophy. Why can't a philosophy professor also write so that an average person with no special philosophical schooling can understand too?"

After a few paces the man suddenly stopped and turned toward me with a good-humored, gentle smile: "Let us not play hide-and-seek. You were quite right to think of the philosopher Nietzsche at sight of me. I am really not related to your Nietzsche, for I am the man himself, whom you chose to call a famous philosopher." When I stopped, full of surprise, and greeted him with clearly visible reverence, I had very much the feeling that this involuntary praise from so insignificant a young man touched him, let us say, not unpleasantly. From which I concluded that even great minds are not completely free of the general ingredient of human vanity.

Immediately afterwards, before I could make any serious remark he continued: "But you must tell me frankly exactly what you disliked about my style of writing. However I cannot allow to stand unremarked the general comment you just made. When one writes a book and thus steps into the public light, that is always a significant act deserving of a certain solemnity, so that one has to put aside everyday language. You have a good example in Catholicism, toward which, as you perhaps know, I am not exactly friendly, but this does not prevent me from recognizing the great worldly wisdom with which Rome has been conducting its business over the ages. Why does Rome still have the Mass read in Latin? To give the solemn act, veiled in mystery, a special solemnity even externally. But that must not be at the expense of clarity or intelligibility. If thoughts were thereby hidden, if the real meaning became hard to understand, that would of course be false, that would no longer be solemn, that would be foolish. So give me a particular example that caused you difficulty. Perhaps you have one in mind?"

So Nietzsche caused me very great embarrassment. For, as I mentioned, I had not gotten very far in reading, or rather, studying his writings. Frantically I searched my memory and at first could think of nothing, till suddenly I thought of a statement that my circle of friends had discussed in detail: "Don't forget the whip, when you go to a woman!" or something similar. When I cited this example, he looked at me in astonishment: "But, I beg you, surely that cannot cause you any difficulty! I mean, it is clear and understandable that this is only a joke, an exaggerated, symbolic mode of expression. If you go to woman do not let yourself be subjugated by her sensuality, do not forget that you are the master, that it is a woman's truly not slight task to serve the man as a friendly companion who beautifies his life." He also told me, moreover, that the much discussed and much misunderstood phrase had its origin in a personal memory.

In an equally amiable manner he discussed the various other points which came to my mind little by little, and I noticed with great delight how simple, how very clear and easily understandable all his oral remarks were. Yet his conversation had something erratic about it; I constantly had the feeling that his thoughts spouted forth in an astonishing excess, literally crowding one another out.

In the course of the conversation we also spoke about his activity at the University of Basel. I mentioned that it was the first and only case since universities had existed that a student was immediately appointed to a professorship without having received his degree, to which Nietzsche replied pensively that this was probably true, that it had been a great exception for him to have been appointed a professor without the doctorate merely on the basis of his essays published in the *Rheinisches Museum,* but that this premature appointment had also had a shadowy side for him: a good part of the Basel university professors had been against his appointment merely because of his youth, and this disgruntlement against him had even grown considerably when he had turned away from philology, for which he had been appointed, and turned to pure philosophy. He had been made to feel this especially strongly when, after the appearance of his first longer work, *The Birth of Tragedy,* he was excommunicated and declared a dead man by one of the then Popes of German philology (he also gave his name but I cannot recall it). Even the great cultural historian, the incomparable historian Jakob Burckhardt, had been hostile to him at first. However, when he, Nietzsche, had given his inaugural address in Basel on Homer and classical philology, Burckhardt had come up to him, shaken his hand, and said curtly that under the impression of this speech he was abandoning all reservations he had had against the appointment of a twenty-five-year-old and was sincerely happy to be able to greet Nietzsche as a colleague. Thereafter Burckhardt had stood by him courageously at all times. Yet Nietzsche told me in an amusing and vivid manner of the peculiar hermit's life that Burckhardt led in Basel, but everything Nietzsche said about Burckhardt radiated clearly the extraordinary respect he had for the great cultural historian. Nietzsche also stressed that he owed a great deal of his inspirations and information to his colleague Burckhardt; it was especially through him that he, Nietzsche, had acquired a deeper understanding of Romance art and culture relatively quickly. Incidentally, Nietzsche expressly remarked that if there had been certain difficulties between him and the Basel educational administration, the fault had been essentially on his side; for he had soon lost all pleasure in philology, which he had been appointed to represent; in addition, he had soon been afflicted with physical ailments which very much hampered his teaching career. Both the university and the school administration in Basel had acted most decently toward him; indeed, in Basel he had generally become acquainted with a very pleasant, proud bourgeoisie, a truly aristocratic society, a real self-governing people, which despite some individual little annoyances he always recalled with the greatest respect. In this context, he repeatedly mentioned Jakob Burckhardt, with whom he obviously felt spiritually very close, and whose aristocratically fine nature and spiritual independence in all directions he could not praise highly enough. Burckhardt had recognized him immediately and had always remained a true friend, because their two natures were closely related on the most important points. When I answered that Burckhardt, however, as far as I knew, stood on positive Christian ground, Nietzsche only made a rejecting movement of the hand and said: "Ah, let it be, Burckhardt is just more prudent and less reckless than I, but internally he surely thinks not one iota differently than I do of Christianity's relation to human culture."

On our second walk the conversation turned by chance to Richard Wagner, who, as is known, played such a very important role in the course of Nietzsche's life. For years Nietzsche had stood completely under the composer's influence, until he then broke away completely from him. I told Nietzsche that in mid-February 1883 at the Munich railroad station I had stood by the coffin of the great composer, whose body had been shipped from Venice to Bayreuth. Afterwards I told him what I had learned of Richard Wagner's relations to King Ludwig II from two of the king's former Cabinet secretaries, whom I happened to know personally quite closely. Nodding his head several times pensively, Nietzsche stopped, and said to me, pausing a few times: "I find it very interesting to hear this from you; incidentally it agrees completely with the impression of Wagner I have acquired over the years." And then, in a long, broad depiction, he told me, with an astonishing abundance of interesting details, of the development of the closer personal relations between him and Wagner; if I had not forgotten a good part of them in the thirty-five years that have meanwhile passed, I could, of course, still not state them here since he obviously gave me the information in strictest confidence without thinking that I would ever publish it. I still remember vividly how astonished I was that Nietzsche told such intimate details to me, a person whom he had just met; he may have had the same feeling himself, for he finally remarked that of course I had to treat this conversation in strict confidence. I can here suggest only this much: all the statements showed me one thing very clearly, namely that the external occasion for the break between the two great men was Wagner's *Parsifal,* its "knee-bending before Romantic Catholicism," as Nietzsche once expressed it. The real internal cause of the alienation between them, however, was obviously the circumstance that Nietzsche became more and more strongly convinced that the man Wagner did not stand on the same level as the artist. Then Nietzsche, stopping in the middle of the path, held a veritable lecture on a misunderstanding which I had actually often encountered in judgments of Richard Wagner's character. One had to be very much on guard not to consider Wagner a petty, egoistic person in the ordinary sense of the word; Wagner had, rather, been so absolutely convinced of the extraordinary importance of his great cultural mission to produce the dramatic work of art of the future that he had subordinated all relations in life to this point of view; in his innermost soul he had been convinced that he could fulfill his great mission only surrounded by glory and wealth, and he had considered it to be the damned duty and obligation of all mankind to create these extraordinary conditions which were necessary for his artistic activity; this also explained his occasional disastrous interference in important political matters; intrinsically Wagner had been a completely unpolitical nature; compared with his mighty artistic interests, politics in the real sense had had no place in his life; he had had no understanding at all of politics as such, although he had, insofar as the opportunity presented itself, unscrupulously used it as means to the end of helping him achieve his great artistic goals; so it was quite understandable that Wagner strode ruthlessly over all personal relations if they did not seem useful for promoting his artistic ideas, but that he must not therefore be considered an egoist of the ordinary kind; on the contrary, he had been by nature a very noble and benevolent character, of which Nietzsche told me a whole series of characteristic details. On the whole I got the strong impression, as already suggested, that these personal relations and personal qualities of Wagner's, much more than great questions of worldview, had actually been decisive for the alienation between the two great men; Nietzsche was far too proud and far too conscious of his own intellectual importance to submit to being used as a mere instrument in the hands of a supposedly greater genius. In later years I studied Wagner's personality a great deal, of course not from the musical side, which unfortunately is completely remote from me, and I can only say that I increasingly pictured the great composer's character precisely as Nietzsche had described it to me.

Nietzsche was much amused by my description of my personal relations with the famous Munich philosopher Jakob Froschammer. In our conversation I had stressed several times that I disliked and abhorred all philosophy, especially the philosophical mode of expression, but at the same time I had alluded several times to my personal relations with Froschammer and occasionally quoted him in individual lines of argument. This happened again on the second morning of our acquaintanceship and Nietzsche interrupted me: "But now explain to me what led you precisely to Froschammer, who quite particularly is one of the kind of philosophers whom you dislike so much." Then I told him good-humoredly that once at the beginning of the summer semester in 1880 I had gone to Froschammer's class just out of curiosity, after having heard and read so much about him, especially about his conflict with Rome; I wanted to meet the man personally just once, of course without the slightest intention of registering for the course. Counting the teacher, we were just three persons in the classroom. At the end of the class, Froschammer spoke to me and asked me to accompany him for a few steps. Outside the classroom he asked me whether I was thinking of attending his class regularly. As a young freshman I was of course too cowardly to admit openly that I had wanted to come just once out of curiosity, and I lied to him that I did have the greatest desire to attend his classes, but that surely the course would be cancelled with so few students. But he answered that he had a personal interest in offering precisely this new course once, even if there were only one student, for the other person had an unreliable face and would probably not come to class often. So I was caught, and for better or worse had to attend this course, which bored me to death, since I was totally unable to follow the philosopher's otherwise fine-sounding statements, and his entire subjective and objective fantasy. The one advantage was that I came into very pleasant personal relations with the old gentleman. Nietzsche laughed loudly and said that this was philosophy's revenge for my not believing in her, and that incidentally if it was any consolation he, Nietzsche, did not understand Froschammer's philosophy either, and he doubted whether Froschammer understood it himself. If I ever saw Froschammer again I might tell him that; anyway he had the impression that Froschammer was not exactly one of his friends. When I saw Froschammer again some time later, I told him of this meeting with Nietzsche and also hinted that Nietzsche did not have a very high opinion of Froschammer's philosophy. Froschammer answered that Nietzsche had always been a sick man and that his whole philosophy, with all its countless contradictions, was just a product of disease; Nietzsche could not at all be taken seriously.

This was absolutely not the impression I had gotten on meeting Nietzsche; on the contrary, I found him extraordinarily fresh and lively, which can perhaps be explained by the slight knowledge of human character I had at that time. It was for me practically a delight to hear him speak in broad intellectual contexts, for example of his superman or master-man, and, in that connection, of Christianity educating men to servitude. He spouted his thoughts forth, more in the form of aphorisms, always leaping from one to the other. Once when under this direct impression I remarked that I was particularly attracted by the aphoristic element in his writings, he said that the view had been systematically spread by his critics that he could not write other than in aphorisms, but that in reality this was far from so. His previous writings had all been simply pre-paratory studies, just material for thought, but now, after all these individual sketches, he hoped to begin his real, systematic works. Yet I sensed a certain melancholy as if he were thinking inside that he might never get to write these final great works. In general during these delightful conversations I could never shake off the impres-sion that he was suffering under a certain psychological pressure. The judgments he occasionally made of men who held high a position in the intellectual world were very sharp, sometimes almost snide. But I noticed with great pleasure that as a rule he was able to characterize the person in question most accurately with a single word, with such unusual graphicness that one seemed to see the characterized man almost in flesh and blood before one's eyes. And this witty conversation was carried on in brilliant language. As I said, I found it a unique delight to listen to him. However I also noticed that he occasionally fell into strange contradictions. When on one occasion I took the liberty to call such a contradiction to his attention, I noticed very clearly that this made him nervous, so I did not do so again. During the whole conversation I did not know what I should admire more, the tremendous scope of his positive knowl-edge, the high flight of his lines of thought, or the brilliant, almost poetically beautiful language. That he bothered with me, a green, insignificant young man, who of course had absolutely nothing to offer him, and spoke with me in such an amiable, friendly manner, gave me the impression that at the bottom of his soul he must have been an unusually kind and loving person, and I was filled with deep gratitude toward him. During our conversation the idea would never have occurred to me that this highly intelligent man could fall into an incurable mental illness just a few years later. When I received the news of the outbreak of that terrible catastrophe, I was astonished and deeply shaken.

As I was saying farewell to him and remarked that on the way home to Strasbourg I would be spending one or two days with an old friend in Basel, he said to me: "I really wish I could go with you. Say hello to the dear old proud city where I spent the most signifi-cant years of my life and which despite some small annoyances is for me the source of my most beautiful memories. I would like to send you with a greeting to my old friend Burckhardt, if I did not know how much he dislikes such new acquaintanceships." So he said fare-well to me in a kind and friendly way. I never saw him again. When occasionally I sent him little essays, no answer from him ever came. (25)

One summer twenty-five years ago (in 1885) the philosopher Fi
rich Nietzsche last stayed with us in Leipzig for a short time. Once
again the scholar had sought out our home just as he had in preceding years (1882 and 1883). What led him to my father's house
was certainly not luxurious internal and external furnishings, for
the room he lived in was plain and simple, but he wished only to live
quietly. What especially appealed to him was that from his room he
could enjoy an open view over the garden and meadows toward the
Rosental, which, as it were, formed a beautiful scenic background.
At that time the house was still surrounded with gardens. Unfortunately today it stands in Auen Street, Nr. 32, just as surrounded
with buildings as any other.

We children always greeted Nietzsche's arrival with mixed feelings, for the "professor" needed quiet! But when on Sundays he
went off in spotless white trousers, we found it very amusing
because in our eyes this article of clothing dated back to the time of
the 1870–71 war.

Nietzsche was then at the very height of his activities as a writer.
Thoughts of Zarathustra hovered around his head. His demeanor
was very amiable and he was grateful for every attention. A gentle
man even in the smallest things, a lion at the writing desk! Every
afternoon he strolled pensively, his hands behind his back, through
the Waldstrasse to Kintzschy's, not far from the zoological garden.
There he generally met with academic friends (Heinze, among others) and drank his afternoon coffee. In the morning he boiled his
own tea. Nietzsche lived very secludedly in our house—really only
in front of his desk, which today still stands unchanged in the same
place. The same desk which served the "Anti-Christ" has since not
refused its service to many a theology student. Where the Zarathustra manuscripts once lay, many a literature student has prepared for
the "Zarathustra course" or studied the book *Zarathustra*. Probably
none, however, has suffered psychically as severely as Nietzsche did
then. His headache at this time was often extremely painful. Immediately on arriving Nietzsche requested our "grandfather chair"
with a high back. He usually sat at his desk, working, suffering,
struggling with himself . . . and his look swept over the soothing
green of the nearby Rosental. Huge oak trees and tall poplars at the
edge of the meadow nodded to him. They were cut down in their
best years—as he was.

Sometimes, however, Nietzsche came over to our apartment and played the piano. He often revealed his inner feelings by his peculiar playing. Sometimes musical friends of my father's found the playing "bizarre!" To my father he always spoke just as a philologist wanting to use the University of Leipzig Library, but he never claimed to be a philosopher and author. So none of us suspected that he was preparing important works in our house.

Nietzsche's writings have had many enemies. We children were surely the first enemies of his writing activity. For while he was writing his books in the "back room" we were busily making noise next door. We had disturbed "the professor"! He never said anything to us children. Nonetheless we lived in a sort of state of war with him.

But that would change! Nietzsche had a great liking for the fruit of the vine! Not in bottles, however, but in its natural state. So in season his mother sent him a crate of grapes. That put Nietzsche in a very happy mood. But unfortunately the crate was nailed tight. Nietzsche first put in a good effort to get at the contents of the crate, but in vain. Then the crate was handed to my mother and brought to the living room, where it was opened in the presence of "the professor" and all members of the family. I no longer know which of us craned his neck the furthest, "the professor" or we children. In any case, the "good professor" now distributed a few grapes to us with his own hands. We celebrated a reconciliation, i.e., he said nothing and we also said nothing. He had achieved more by this donation than by all looks out the door when we were making noise, for now we left him in peace. The next crate of grapes was brought by his mother personally when she came to visit him so that he was spared the task of opening it. This time his mother distributed the grapes, and was therefore given the title "the good pastor's wife."

On his second stay in our house (1883) he gave my father a copy of Luther's *Table Talks*. This is not completely unimportant biographically. For if he had not himself needed this book at the time, he would not have brought it along to Leipzig, since he stayed here barely two months at a time. He gave my mother Montesquieu's *Persian Letters*. This was also a sign that he had finished his Persian studies for his *Zarathustra*. But the extremely free views and the often embarrassingly sentimental style of the *Persian Letters* stood in remarkable contrast to Luther's *Table Talks*.

From Leipzig Nietzsche generally went to the Engadine. His mother then always came over from Naumburg to pack his things.

His last stay (1885) was broken off suddenly by a migraine attack, nor could we offer him the rooms which had drawn him back to us each time, and so he traveled to his mother's in Naumburg—so much about Nietzsche's Leipzig house. (*29*)

48　　Ida Overbeck　　　　　　　　　　　　　　　*1883*

I remember how Nietzsche already at the beginning of the eighties, probably 1883, expressed to us his deep joy on realizing that he could combine his "yes" and his "no." He did not notice the violence with which, seeking "one line, one goal," he pressed everything into satire and disparaged almost everything that had ever before been thought, felt, and lived. Nothing is so confusing in Nietzsche as his own conflict in the treatment of history and life. He exalts reality and life, yet condemns history as life and reality; he demands historical meaning where beginnings of reality seem to him to exist, yet declares war on intellect and reason. Nietzsche is very logical in all this, but we feel pressed into unbearable formulations. Finally, this most life-affirming of all thinkers condemns and strangles life, after all. He claims to be standing at the dividing line between two ages, where real life in general is just beginning and historical miseducation sinking to its grave. And this is the same person who, not wanting to hear anything about "true" things, attaches all importance to reality and then disparages the real life of real men because they are struggling with the most varied conceptualizations and ideas of morality. He makes exceptions especially in favor of individuals. Kant is not one of them; his caricature of him is very striking. He certainly did not draw from Kant's introduction to morality everything that could be drawn from it. Kant did not base his categorical imperative on one-sided duty, as Nietzsche accuses him of doing, yet himself cannot avoid. Rather, he leads us gradually through the series of wanting-ability-duty, of the formation of the species, which is not unfamiliar to Nietzsche.

Once Nietzsche said to us with a bitter corpse-like expression— we had been talking about Napoleon—that it is a miserable situation that the world is divided into a few strong men and many weak ones who serve as prey to the strong. I said that we ought not to picture it in this way, although undeniably many people are denied their personal rights through war, disease, oppression. But even the oppressed person has the ability through psychic and material will to rise to a mastery which a firsthand ruler neither has nor suspects, and can in his own way enjoy the greatest sense of happiness. Nietzsche agreed, but of course he ranked and arranged everything differently. Another time he was deeply depressed by the consciousness that as a sick man he was not one of the strong, and could not say the last word to mankind; he was excluded from too much; to a certain extent he was already dead. This was really heart-rending. We rejected the idea that these two things are mutually exclusive. Later, however, he assured me of what a great feeling of happiness he was capable. These conversations took place before he moved away from Basel. Nietzsche was determined to draw the distinction between masters and slaves, a tragic theme toward which he really always gravitated.

Nietzsche held firmly to the tragedy of all life-will. He says he has overcome pessimism; but death and destruction remain. He was deeply filled with the tragedy of everything that has become or is becoming; he denied every concept of guilt, he looked beyond the individual to the great ring of the eternally creative, but in this ring the worm had to dare the *return of the same.* The individualistic principle relied on the god Dionysus, on deepest pleasure in eternity; death, which is life itself, could not mean the end of existence; but Nietzsche failed to reduce his individualistic principle to the stream of eternal change. Disgust, Nietzsche's disgust with himself as a particular individual, arose again and again. A tragic coercion speaks out of Nietzsche's decision to have everything return, a highest and ultimate self-overcoming. He cast himself as victim into its arms. Tragedy without guilt, that is, "fate" in the Dionysian mystery. I remember that Nietzsche several times asked what I thought of St. Januarius and finally got me to say: there is asceticism even there. Probably he asked this for the sake of the idea of return, which is developed in the second-to-the-last aphorism. Here he found his central focus and remained faithful to the meaning of the earth, as he later says in *Zarathustra.* This mechanistic equalization seemed to me cold and lifeless. I could not understand how the author of self-intensification, of the philosophy of the superman, which is based on the theory of evolution and natural selection, arrived at this thesis. I thought the mystery of the world lay revealed rather in the unequal, which is not at all pessimistic. Humanly speaking, all possibilities may and should become realities; everything that is present in the human constitution longs to appear in life; indeed in motley variety and incessant mixture and division, so that not even the slightest thing can be repeated; everything is at once friend and foe, near and far; there is no end to astonishment and curiosity, pleasure and displeasure. No two humans, no two thoughts are ever the same, no blade of grass is like the other. Earth and men came and they will go. Why should time be eternal and power limited?

I had told Nietzsche earlier that the Christian religion could not give me solace and fulfillment and that I had in me the thought and feeling of carrying in everything the fate of all mankind. I dared to say it: the idea of God contained too little reality for me. Deeply moved, he answered: "You are saying this only to come to my aid; never give up this idea! You have it unconsciously; for as I know you and find you, including now, one great thought dominates your life. This great thought is the idea of God." He swallowed painfully. His features were completely contorted with emotion, until they then took on a stony calm. "I have given him up, I want to make something new, I will not and must not go back. I will perish from my passions, they will cast me back and forth; I am constantly falling apart, but I do not care." These are his own words from the fall of 1882! Nietzsche gave us such candid insights! It can be imagined how heavily this weighed on him, and what respect I had for him. The richness and unhappiness of this so talented man—I feel almost guilty to be speaking of him, to whom I owe so much of my independence, from my own point of view. Nietzsche was a mighty education for me, although I never really was his disciple. As a woman of twenty-eight to thirty-four years of age I was too old for that. But it was a struggle in which booty could be taken. He stamped himself deep into my soul, and each of his sayings has a meaning for me. As it says in *Zarathustra:* I gave to each one what is mine.

The normal person, however highly talented he is, always finds the proximity of others. Nietzsche hated the normal person because he could not be one; he was condemned to absolute uniqueness and rose above the normal person in the feeling of the hard work which his uniqueness cost him, and probably also in the feeling of its rarity-value. He was a distinct character by nature and he trained himself in that direction. Nietzsche's happiness and his wish to set values for eternity lay, for him, unattainably far; but his destiny was near and was the *conditioned* uniqueness of his nature. How could Nietzsche's work ever seem other than that of a heroically tragic person! In theory, absolute exemplariness was his burning ambition; at any rate, he is a very personally developed individual; and as such he does not forbid anyone to be greater or happier. It is no reproach against anyone if he has rejected Nietzsche on the basis of the Nietzschean cause itself. To praise with vague expressions—greatness, positiveness, genial tendency—is lifeless. Praise is nothing at all; one must speak. What would Nietzsche have gained from another Nietzsche, but one inspired by him and his problems? That is reserved for a certain future. What would Nietzsche have done if he had found himself in another? Killed himself or the other, he could not have borne it! But it is not true that Overbeck did not believe in Nietzsche's cause, and that he would have rejected him completely if he had not known him personally. But he saw in Nietzsche a *part* of the work, not an absolute summit, however highly he thought of him. He wanted to leave the cassette of letters unopened for twenty-five years, without fearing that the contents would become obsolete. My husband had much more positive things to say about Nietzsche than many a professed "Nietzschean." Such petty, narrow people always seek the positive in a foolish place and would be capable of insinuating clericalism. They should spare themselves all those bitter feelings, though the comedy ends differently than they expect and than their staid mentality would like to prescribe. Whoever has gone through Nietzsche's world, knows at least from there, though he does not know it otherwise, that such cheap moralizing is just as foolish as the classification of people on a hierarchical ladder. My husband understood Nietzsche from his own work of soul and was very capable of respecting every imprint of Nietzsche's being. It is superfluous to ask whether he loved and respected him. He did everything in his power for him, and that was infinitely more than fanatics and even clever people can readily understand. (*43*, 248–251)

49   Resa von Schirnhofer   *April 3–13, 1884*

During the Easter vacation in 1884, at the end of my first semester at the University of Zurich, I went to Genoa, intending to meet my revered motherly friend Malwida von Meysenbug on the French Riviera. To my inquiry whether she was coming to Cannes, she informed me that she was staying in Rome that spring and advised me to go to Nice, where I would meet Nietzsche, with whom I was not totally unacquainted through her, and who needed some refreshment from his intensive work in brooding solitude.

At that time I knew of Nietzsche's writings only the *Untimely Meditations* and *The Birth of Tragedy from the Spirit of Music*, a book which had greatly aroused my youthful enthusiasm. I knew of the change in Nietzsche's attitude toward Wagner, combined with a break in his line of development—as it then seemed—but I did not know his new writings. Even in his human traits, through Malwida's stories in Rome and occasional remarks of her sisters, of Donna Laura Minghetti, and of others from her circle, who all knew him personally, Nietzsche had not remained unknown to me. Also, from conversations with Lou Salomé in Bayreuth, where I had joined Malwida von Meysenbug at the 1882 *Parsifal* performances, I had heard some things about the problems in moral philosophy that were on Nietzsche's mind. Lou Salomé's astonishing dialectical virtuosity, her mental acuity carried to the point of sophistic hair-splitting, had fascinated me. I soon heard all sorts of things about the "misunderstandings" which were then already beginning and which occupy undue space in the literature on Nietzsche. Soon afterwards Lou Salomé showed me the often discussed posed photograph in which she, sitting in a handcart with a whip in her hand (if I remember correctly), steers the two harnessed friends, Dr. Rée and Nietzsche. The team is pulling in two different directions, as if it were trying to break apart. Rée, harnessed on the left in the background of the picture with his head turned away cannot be seen very well. Nietzsche, in the very foreground, is standing crudely and coarsely in an awkward position, which instinctively reminded me of a recalcitrant plow-horse. It was not a snapshot taken outdoors, where grotesque pictures often show up unintentionally, but a picture posed in a studio. Almost puritanically I disliked both the idea of the joke itself, and its portrayal.[1] I never met a Nietzsche such as that photograph portrayed him externally and as it suggested his nature to be.

So I knew Nietzsche from the "reflex images" of other persons, and now I was looking forward to forming my own image of him and I gladly followed Fräulein von Meysenbug's suggestion. On first meeting with Nietzsche, I felt a certain embarrassment. But his dignified friendliness, his serious professorial appearance, and our common motherly friend, who was invisibly present as a mediatory link, soon enabled me to regain my fresh naturalness. During the ten days of my stay on the delightful Côte d'Azure, Nietzsche

1. E. Förster-Nietzsche in *Der einsame Nietzsche,* p. 309, sees it differently, for she says: "it was an immodest but very comical picture," whereas in a conversation with me the mild Malwida von Meysenbug, who saw the picture only later, called it "a hideous photograph."

devoted a great deal of his valuable time to me. He led me along his favorite paths; we took walks, little excursions, and enjoyed the enchanting nature and climate; he brought me books to look through, others from which I read aloud to him at times; and however great the intellectual distance was from the thinker and writer to the girl student, it was lost in our simple human relations. So unrestrained as a thinker, Nietzsche as a person was of exquisite sensitivity, tenderness, and refined courtesy in attitude and manners toward the female sex, as others who knew him personally have often emphasized. Nothing in his nature could have made a disturbing impression on me. Neither in his external appearance and behavior, nor in his spiritual nature did Nietzsche strike me as typically German. Indeed, he told me with obvious pleasure how he was frequently addressed by Poles as their countryman and that according to a family tradition the Polish descent of the Nietzsches from a Niezki was certain. This was news to me at the time and interested me, since I had in a historical painting of Jan Matjeko's in Vienna seen typically shaped heads with a far greater similarity than the merely superficial one of the mustache, and he seemed delighted to hear this. For he was very proud of his Polish background.

I could speak with the "dear, half-blind professor"—as a few acquaintances from the Pension de Genève then called him—about everything I had, with naive enthusiasm, drawn into my sphere of interests, a vast miscellany: about my favorite Latin writers, about strange dreams with transcendental content, childhood experiences, etc. This resulted in all sorts of discussions and interesting remarks on his part from his great wealth of thought. In a longer conversation about prejudices he stressed very sharply that one probably discards prejudices, only to fall into a new prejudice: *one is never free of prejudices.* And what about the famous lack of presuppositions, is it not a prejudice in disguise? I asked something of the sort. With a smile Nietzsche answered only: not so fast.

Only much later did I recognize my folly and regret my carelessness in having saved in the storehouse of memory none of the intellectual wealth of the present such as had fallen gratuitously to me in my association with Nietzsche and other important personalities. Except for a few things, I lack precise sketches and word-for-word notes. So, unfortunately, except for a text which is hardly legible any longer, some memories which I thought engraved deeply for all my life have disappeared from my memory!

Nietzsche once gave me the good advice to keep paper and pen-

cil on hand at night, as he himself did, since at night we are often
visited by rare thoughts, which we should record immediately on
awakening in the night, for by morning we can usually not find them
again, they have fluttered away with the nocturnal darkness.

Of our little excursions and walks I remember especially a morning walk up Mount Boron. It was a splendid day, and when after a
short tram ride we were climbing up the mountain, the mistral was
blowing and whipping everything up. Nietzsche, in a dithyrambic
mood, praised the wind as redeemer from earthly gravity; he felt a
beneficial relief in the vibrant blowing of the wind. When we
reached a certain elevation, French sentries blocked our steps, since
the path to the fortified top of the mountain was off limits from that
point on. A simple *osteria* was located on this level spot; wooden
tables and benches stood under an arbor. We sat down amid the
splendid mountain nature with our gaze directed, in picturesque
variety, up at the rounded heights or down at the charming coast
with its delightful bays, bordered by a luxuriant green wreath, out
of which groups of houses gleamed forth like bright blossoms.
There I tasted for the first time "vermouth de Torino," poured by
Nietzsche, whom the mistral had stirred up into a most excited
mood, full of humorous ideas. The "guarded mountain" was the
starting point for a series of verses which bubbled out in great abundance. I was surprised, but then I began to contribute my own two-
cents' worth. It was no improvisation of a higher kind, just amusing,
witty couplets, which showed me an unexpected Nietzsche.[2]

Another time Nietzsche invited me to accompany him to a bullfight in Nice, where an official regulation prohibited the use of
horses or killing of bulls, which agreed with my animal-loving views.
Soon however this tame skirmish seemed like a caricature of a bullfight and began intensely to stimulate our desire to laugh. The similar behavior of the six bulls which succeeded one another in the
same arena seemed to betray knowledge of the regulations on their
part, and it had an especially comical effect when at the end the bull
ran as fast as he could out the large gates that opened in the
background.

We applauded and hoped he would come back out and bow
gratefully like an actor. The music of *Carmen* at prelude and inter-

2. Only many years later, through reading *Der einsame Nietzsche,* did I learn that
accompanied by his sister during a long train ride from home to Como he had made
the most comical rhymed couplets the whole time, "something which he liked to
do when in a good mood."

mezzo was absolutely out of place at this bullfight in the "Happy Laughter" arena, like sounding battle-trumpets at a rural dance. And suddenly, provoked by the contrast between this ridiculous spectacle and the stimulating rhythms and exciting melodies, I felt, out of unconscious depths, a strong desire to see a genuine Spanish *corrida de toros* with all its breathtaking splendor and *grandezza,* with its stylized wildness and bulls that defended themselves heroically. To my statement about this newly discovered vein of cruelty in my nature, Nietzsche appended all kinds of interesting remarks from general and individual psychology, which due to a lack of notes I unfortunately cannot repeat in his exact words and do not wish to falsify by my own formulation.

This music had an electrifying effect on Nietzsche, who listened ecstatically, calling my attention to its pulsating rhythm, its elemental vigor and picturesqueness. I had not yet seen *Carmen,* only heard fragments from it, knew nothing about Bizet, and so I listened with interest to what Nietzsche told about the composer, who had died at the age of thirty-seven without achieving recognition. Later, when I read somewhere that Nietzsche's enthusiasm for Bizet's music had been contrived, artificial, a pose, a reaction against Wagner, it conflicted with my memory of him from Nice. It seems to me, rather, that Nietzsche may have felt the nerve-stimulating element in this music as a vivifying current, which, penetrating into the depths of his inherently psychopathic nature, confused it and filled his whole interior, producing a feeling of happiness similar to the effect of the rushing mistral. I believe his love for his music was genuine, but how he subsequently transformed it into a musical value-judgment and used it against Wagner belongs to the area of the will and stems from the recesses of his being.

Nietzsche also invited me on an outing to Monte Carlo to the casino, but I immediately explained that I would suffocate in that atmosphere and preferred to watch a Nice bullfight again rather than degraded human beings. Nietzsche laughed heartily at my naive moral indignation and said it would be interesting to study this casino-public: men of various nationalities and various classes, most of them "ruined, whether in honor, health or purse." But I clung to my refusal, explaining that gambling halls and gambler-types had no attraction for me, though I would have liked to see, in all its breathtaking beauty, the picturesque landscape which I could admire only in small segments from the passing train.

Sometimes we spoke about our common acquaintances, and

Nietzsche always found tones of high admiration for Malwida von Meysenbug, though he occasionally laughed humorously at her optimistic estimation of man and her superlative mode of expression. He spoke with high admiration of Lou Salomé's extraordinary intellect and her "Hymn to Life," which he quoted completely to me. Once he said that I should not take offense at the—later so notorious—whip-passage in *Zarathustra*. This had not occurred to me, since I did not read it as a general indictment of women, but only as a poetic generalization of individual cases. He did not explain to me the original source of this "advice" as extensively as I later read it in Elisabeth's book, but he did tell me in so many words whom he had meant by it when he was writing *Zarathustra*.

After a long morning stroll on the beach, which I remember clearly, and a conversation about Sallust's *Jugurtha*, occasioned by my preference for this writer at that time, and in which my judgment received some corrections through Nietzsche's objections, as we were nearing the city again my companion began speaking of Napoleon, the only historical personality which seemed to fascinate him and whom he characterized with the greatest admiration as a transition-type to the superman. He later also mentioned to me that his own pulse had the same slow rate as Napoleon's, just sixty beats per minute. What Nietzsche did not state then and became clear to me only later after reading his works, is his affinity with the great Corsican in *strength of will*, despite the difference of their two personalities over the entire scope of their psyches. So while standing on the jetty at the railing we came into lively conversations, and he pointed across the shining surface of the sea to the place where Corsica can at times be seen as a faint stripe. He then mentioned his plan to visit Corsica and to cross the island, starting from Bastia over the mountains in the direction of Ajaccio, the final destination. He now studied this Romantic travel-plan. Imaginative and lively as I am, I exclaimed without thinking, "That is an adventurous and delightful plan!" Then Nietzsche asked me if I did not want to come along and said that he had thought it over precisely and knew exactly "how that could best" be done. We were just then turning from the jetty back toward the Promenade des Anglais; the bustling street scene fascinated my attention intensely—and the theme of Corsica was never mentioned again.

Nietzsche told me that Malwida had given him some of my poems to read. He judged them favorably, but added: "You have not yet found your background." I was very perplexed and did not want to continue the conversation, although I would have liked to know whether Nietzsche meant that I was completely lacking in background or in a "common" background for the three poems or whether his judgment related to the last poem, on Wagner's death, which Malwida had called "a very beautiful poem" in a letter to me. His statement made me think, but I asked no question. I was so ignorant of backgrounds and caverns at that time, and yet the living Zarathustra could have instructed me about many a fateful labyrinth.

Both in Nice and later in Sils-Maria Nietzsche spoke to me often and much about Wagner. At first cautiously, later more sharply and with increasing fervor. Analyzing Wagner's nature and his music relentlessly and stressing its ungenuineness and theatricality with devastating critique. Through him I learned for the first time that Wagner's stepfather [Ludwig] Geyer had been his real father and that he therefore had Jewish blood. Although Nietzsche had other-wise *never* spoken to me disparagingly of the Jews, he did so in this case, at least with a pejorative nuance. The theme of Wagner had a mysterious attraction for him and without any encouragement on my part he returned to it again and again by the most varied lines of thought. Begun with hard-struck major chords, it always ended in moving minor tones, especially when it recalled the time in Tribschen, when there still was no "hermit in his cave." Then a suf-fering from the depths exuded from his words and his eyes filled with tears. Those happy times must have been interwoven with the most intimate emotional fibers of his heart! The more often he spoke of this to me in Nice and Sils-Maria, the clearer became the tragedy of that experience and the loss of this lofty—perhaps immoderate—friendship and the more visible the bleeding of a wound that refused to heal.

Apart from his spiritual alienation over events that had occurred, Nietzsche told me nothing, neither positively nor allu-sively about any other condition or necessity for breaking this friendship, about any discoveries in his own soul or the other man's of such a kind as necessarily open an unbridgeable chasm between friends.[3]

One of the first books Nietzsche brought me to leaf through was *Inquiries into Human Faculty and Its Development,* which had recently

3. His "love" for Cosima Wagner, if this means any more than admiration for this highly talented woman, is, in my view, one of those constructions of the fantasy that is carried along by tidal waves of secondary literature about Nietzsche.

been published by Francis Galton, the founder of eugenics. While I paged through it, reading the chapter headings and looking at the list of photographs with great interest, Nietzsche outlined to me the problems it dealt with and the results achieved in the field of heredity and development, based on Darwin and yet in partial refutation of his theories. After this fascinating private lecture on the work of this English scientist whom he admired so very much, he took back the book.

I heard a lot from him about Henri Beyle, who came to many countries with Napoleon's armies and empathized with the foreign cultures, especially Italy, spiritually, artistically, and emotionally. This writer, esteemed highly under the pseudonym of Stendhal, and much admired for his sharp analyses of psychological processes, and founding a school in France at that time, caught Nietzsche's interest to a high degree. When Bourget calls him "a philosopher, a man-of-the-world, and a soldier" and speaks of his "power of, and, if you wish, mania for intimate dissection,"[4] this characterizes Stendhal's sphere of life and spirit. Nietzsche stressed especially how Stendhal had with astounding certainty announced that he would become famous forty years later. And in this context he remarked about his own later fame, "when the time is ripe." To introduce me to the psychologist he esteemed so highly, he gave me *The Red and the Black,* one of Stendhal's most famous works. He asked me to read aloud from Emile Montegut's *Poets and Artists of Italy,* and he lent me Père Didon's book *Les Allemands,*[5] whose characterization of the traits in the spiritual face of the Germans and the French he found to be accurate, and what Didon says about the institutions of higher learning and their historical development in the two nations to be worth reading. I read it during my stay in Nice and I find a few antitheses noted down in my notebook from that time; e.g. "The German sees broadly and confusedly, we see clearly and precisely; his danger is vagueness and obscurity; we must fear to be superficial. Our defect, as Frenchmen, is excessive candor; the Germans' defect is excessive reserve. We speak too much, they speak too little; we are eloquent, they are taciturn. Duplicity is an exception among us, cand is the exception among them" . . . etc.

Books Nietzsche recommended for me to read were: the memoirs of the Count de Maurepas and those of Madame de Rémusat,

...ssais de Psychologie contemporaine (Paris, 1885).

...(Paris, Calman Lévy, 1884).

Galton

the brothers de Goncourt, Saint-Simon on history, as well as the *Mémorial de Sainte-Hélène* by Las Cases, "the most studied of the contemporary French writers," etc. Except for Grimm's book on Emerson, whom he liked very much, the only German books Nietzsche named were the work by the great Catholic historian Johannes Janssen, which he characterized as "the most important work on the Reformation, with a tremendous wealth of materials," and *Indian Summer* by the Austrian writer Adalbert Stifter, which he called a book of rose-fragrance. On later meetings he spoke often and with high esteem of Georg Brandes' literary history of the nineteenth century, especially the volume on French writers. He was very busy with contemporary French writers and he liked to draw parallels between French and English authors. Drawing sharp nuances with delightful zest and a shifting distribution of light and shadow, often cascading into precise images, he gave priority to French authors, "who reach the utmost perfection, artistically and intellectually." He had only words of admiration for French drama of the classical period as well as for French acting. He characterized the French culture of the seventeenth and eighteenth centuries to me as perfection in form, stylistic attitude, and distinction of manners, which radiated from courtly circles and found expression in social life. And he cited many examples of historical personalities to illustrate the preservation of this beautiful form even in difficult moments. And there were always side-jabs at German lack of culture, form, and posture; for nothing seemed to repel him more than bad manners and slovenliness. He found words of disgust for the drinking bouts of German students.

Nietzsche spoke to me a lot about Taine, with whom he was corresponding, and whose *Origins of Contemporary France* he advised me to read. From that source he related with dramatic vividness the moving scene, taken from La Harpe's papers, which Taine describes. I was especially impressed by the mounting intensification in Nietzsche's mode of depiction, when toward the end of the narrative he came to Cazotte's conversation with the Duchess of Gramont and presented it and the following scene slowly and hesitantly. On reading Taine's work soon afterwards during the summer semester in Zurich, I saw how precisely Nietzsche had narrated all the details of that strange event. To this day an echo of the *narrated* not the *read* scene still is vibrant in me whenever I think back to that time. Nietzsche added neither mocking nor frankly critical remarks and expressed no doubt as to the truth of the scene described in La

Harpe's papers, and he made no attempt to explain this true prophecy. When I think of how Nietzsche manifested himself in his later writings, which often have a fatal similarity in tone and accent to the statements of members of "that academic society," though they stand high above them in the degree of genial spirituality, and when I remember that retelling of the story from Taine, his impressive manner of doing so, and the emphasis on the passage where Cazotte, amid the laughter of all those present, prophesies La Harpe's change of attitude, a peculiar light and pathos falls on it.

Nietzsche also told me what I had formerly heard from Malwida about his meeting with Mazzini, whom he had by chance had as neighbor in the post-coach on a journey over the Alps, as he learned in conversation. Malwida had spoken of Goethe with deep admiration and quoted the following verse, which Nietzsche did not know, from the poems to the Masonic lodges:

> To wean oneself from the half-hearted
> And to live resolutely
> In the whole, in full beauty.

Nietzsche gave me as a present the three parts of *Thus Spoke Zarathustra,* which had just recently appeared in print, handing the book to me with amiable solemnity, inscribed above "With warm affection" and below "In nova fert animus" (The spirit carries one to new things). Before I had even paged through it he opened it to the "Night Song" in Part II and asked me to read it aloud. Its very beginning, "It is night: now all the leaping fountains speak more loudly. And my soul too is a leaping fountain," which I had begun to read hesitantly, in a soft voice, in its lyrical beauty aroused sympathetic tones in my soul, and I surrendered completely to the romantic mood, and soon the initial disturbance of hearing myself read vanished. This song, with its bewildering magic from the boundary-land of abysmal loneliness, filled the atmosphere with its radiations of deep melancholy. Nietzsche long remained silent, probably remembering that night in his lodgings high above the Piazza Barberini in Rome, where he had written this song to the splashing of the fountain.

Another time he asked me to read the "Dance Song" from Part II of *Zarathustra.* That song, which Zarathustra sings at the end, while Cupid and the girl are dancing in the meadow, is heart-moving. Like a transparent web woven from threads of melancholy it hovers tremblingly over the dark abyss of the longing for death.

The sun has long since set, he finally said;
the meadow is damp, coolness comes from the woods.
A pensive stranger looks at me.
"What, you are still alive, Zarathustra?
Why? What for? Where to? Where? How?
Is it not fruitless to still be alive?"
"Ah, my friends, it is evening that asks this
Of me. Forgive me my sadness."

Motionless, slumped wearily, Nietzsche sat there as if rapt in renewed experience of his poetry, completely forgetting my presence in his own most private world in that "unknown," "unquenched," "unquenchable" realm of which Zarathustra sings in these two songs that it *is around him, and in him.*

Any word would have been a disturbance. I was silent for a long time and let Nietzsche's inner echo and my poetic mood gradually fade. Later Nietzsche told me it did him a world of good that with me one could speak, laugh, and also be silent, which was rare with women.

Another time Nietzsche asked me to read aloud "The Other Dance Song," from Part III of *Zarathustra.*

I had probably not intoned the end of it mysteriously enough to suit him, for Nietzsche repeated with a solemnly altered voice the midnight tollings of the "old heavy booming-bell":

One!

Oh man, pay heed!

Two!

What says the deep midnight?

Three!

"I slept! I slept—

Four!

"Out of deep dream I have awakened!—

Five!

"The world is deep,

Six!

"And deeper than the day 'tis thought,

Seven!

"Deep is its woe—,

Eight!

"Pleasure—deeper yet than heart's grief;

Nine!

> "Woe speaks: Perish!
> Ten!
> "But all pleasure wants eternity—
> Eleven!
> "Wants deep, deep eternity!
> Twelve!

Then he got up to leave, and as we were standing by the door his features suddenly changed. With a stolid look on his face, casting shy looks around him as if a horrible danger threatened if a listener should hear his words, muting the sound with his hand over his mouth he announced to me in a whisper the "secret" which Zarathustra whispered into life's ear, to which life had answered:

"You *know* that, oh Zarathustra? *No one* knows that."

There was something bizarre, indeed eerie in what Nietzsche told me of the "eternal return of the same," and the tremendous scope of this idea. I was bewildered far more by the way it was told than by its content. A different Nietzsche was suddenly standing before me and had frightened me.

But since he returned to his natural way of speaking and his usual demeanor without developing the idea further and added calmly that I would understand the great significance of the revelation in its full scope only later, I was left with the impression that Nietzsche had intentionally played on the instrument of my impressionability to make the enormity of this discovery unforgettable to me. In Sils-Maria this scene was brought back to my memory in a different light by a new experience.

Nietzsche also selected for reading aloud the "Grave-Song" and the "Seven-Seal Song" of Part III of *Zarathustra,* nor did he fail to comment on the owl-monster passage. But in contrast with the three other songs, my memory of the reading of these two others has faded markedly. It is impossible for me to conjure up their effect on me out of the dark realm of oblivion, nor the memory of Nietzsche's behavior on hearing his seven-fold confession, which sounds like a mystical love oath:

> For I love you, O eternity!

The fact that I read him the two songs is clearest in my memory, but as to any further circumstances, my memory is a *tabula rasa.*

I had seen and heard many new and interesting things in Nice, received an abundance of intellectual inspirations, and so I returned to my studies enriched and satisfied.

Toward the middle of July of the same year, Nietzsche showed up in Zurich for a short time. I remember a beautiful walk in the shade of tall and huge old trees on that picturesquely located cape called "Limmat Point," where the Sihl and the Limmat rivers join. His thoughts roamed in past times of Swiss history, of which he let a few gleaming pictures shine forth for me in clear, vivid strokes. (52, 251–260)

50   Johannes Volkelt   *June 1884*

I came in contact with Nietzsche four times, though of course always briefly. In the summer of 1884 he visited me in Basel. (He had given up his Basel professorship long before because of his undermined health.) It was a strange feeling for me to have the author of *Zarathustra* sitting opposite me as a simple, natural person inquiring with lively interest concerning my position in Basel. Soon the conversation turned to the moral-philosophical phenomena of recent times. When I underscored among these Eduard von Hartmann's book *The Phenomenology of Moral Consciousness,* an expression of intellectual displeasure passed over his features and he changed the subject. Not long afterward we met on the cathedral square and walked for a long time back and forth in the cloisters of the cathedral in lively conversation. We were immediately right in the middle of the question of whether we have knowledge of our own consciousness processes. While I represented the standpoint that there is no more certain knowledge than that of our consciousness, Nietzsche represented the most extreme skepticism, trying from various angles to prove the superficiality, subjective coloration, and perspectivality of our knowledge of ourselves. (*62, 67*)

51   Meta von Salis-Marschlins   *July 14, 1884*

In one of my scrapbooks from my university days is the entry: "Zurich, July 14, 1884, 8:30–10:30 a.m., a visit from Friedrich Nietzsche." The day before I had followed the invitation of acquaintances to a country property on the edge of the canton. Returning to the city with the early evening train, I found the few lines at home: "My dear Fräulein, assuming that you know who I am, you must also not be surprised if I wish to make your acquaintance. I will be staying in Zurich for a few days, Hotel Habis: please

give me a message informing me when and where we can meet.—
Your devoted servant, Prof. Dr. Nietzsche.—Piora near Airolo, on
departure."

Nietzsche's card lay next to the letter. By his calculation I should
have received his letter in the morning, and so he had wanted to
visit me during the day. Not knowing how long his stay in Zurich
would last and not willing to forfeit his personal acquaintanceship I
immediately took a carriage and rode to his hotel. On the Bahnhof
Bridge I saw Fräulein von Schirnhofer in conversation with a friend
slowly coming in my direction. Because she had associated with
Nietzsche a great deal the summer before, I could surely assume
that he was the one she was walking with. I got out; we were introduced and agreed that he should come to me the following morning, since there were no classes that day.

We were having extremely hot weather: air and sky glistened and
shone from morning to evening and the lake reflected sparkling little lights. My apartment up in Fluntern, with its windows facing the
green front garden on the north and west side, enjoyed some coolness and muted brightness, at least in the morning. Nietzsche,
whose sensitive eye- and head-nerves suffered intensely under heat
and bright light felt this to be beneficial. We remained in conversation together for about two hours.

What impression did Nietzsche make on me on July 14, 1884?

He himself used to say of places that there must be an optimal
place for everyone, and that for him Sils-Maria was this. I think
everyone also has his optimal experiences with people. For me
Nietzsche embodied this optimism in one direction, which is saying
a lot, since I have been spoiled in my association with men and
women of different nations. Halcyon and tranquil as he character-
istically called himself, the times we were together were halcyon for
me, suited to spreading a golden glimmer over the rest of my life.

Even the first impression was comparable with no other. The
strangeness and un-Germanness of his face matched his unassuming
behavior, which gave no clue to his being a German professor. A
strong self-confidence made any posturing superfluous. The man
who recognized vanity as a residue of slavery had nothing to do with
the familiar pedantic petit-bourgeois scholarly airs. "There is a slave
in the blood of the vain, a remnant of the wiliness of slaves, which
seeks to seduce others to a good opinion of oneself; it is also the
slave who later on himself kneels before these opinions, as if he were

not the one who had evoked them. Vanity is an atavism," he says in *Beyond Good and Evil.*[1] A soft voice full of gentleness and melody and his very calm way of speaking caused a pause in the first moment, approximately like Gladstone's fine organ, when one first heard him in the lower house. When a smile lit up his face, bronzed by so many sojourns outdoors in the south, it took on a touchingly childlike expression that called for sympathy. His look generally seemed to be turned inward, like the one we see on statues of Greek gods, or seeking out of the depths something he had almost ceased to hope for; but his eyes were always those of a man who has suffered much and, although he has remained a victor, stands sadly over the abysses of life. Unforgettable eyes, shining with the freedom of the victor, accusing and grieving because the meaning and beauty of the earth had turned into nonsense and ugliness.

What did we talk about? About heat and storm clouds, common friends, and places we both knew well, in short about things usually discussed at a first meeting of two people who know of one another. Nietzsche asked why I intended to get a doctorate, and I explained that I set little importance on the title for myself, but in the interest of women's rights I did not want to leave the university without having gotten the degree.

Later we deviated from the traditional subjects, i.e., Nietzsche spoke of his intellectual interests and I listened. A note from those days reminds me that he touched upon two of his favorite thoughts. The first was that man knows only the smallest part of his possibilities, in accord with Aphorism 335 in *The Dawn of Day*, with the final sentence: "What do we know about what circumstances could drive us to!" Aphorism 9 in *The Joyful Science:* "We all have hidden gardens and plantations in us; and, with another analogy, we are all growing volcanoes which will have their hour of eruption—but how soon or how late this eruption is, no one knows." And Aphorism 274 in *Beyond Good and Evil:* "Fortunate coincidences and much that is incalculable are necessary for a higher man in whom the solution of a problem sleeps too still to manage to act at the right time— 'to erupt,' as one could say. It does not happen on the average, and in all corners of the earth sit waiters who hardly know it, since they are waiting, nor even less that they are waiting in vain."—The second dealt with music, which in his view is just as much determined by the character of a cultural period as are the other arts and sci-

1. Aphorism 261. Cf. also *Leben Friedrich Nietzsches* II, 1, p. 188: "The pathos of posing is *not* a part of greatness; whoever needs to pose is ungenuine."

ences. A whole series of aphorisms proves how extensively Nietzsche tried to prove this.

I subsequently found confirmation that in conversations Nietzsche liked to dwell on themes he was currently working at. He was a better and more fascinating speaker than anyone I knew, but he by no means avoided common things, but gave them meaning through his completely individual perspective and did not use affected expressions for higher trains of thought or slip into careless jargon when talking about everyday matters. He disliked to speak in dialect (just as I do) and gave the most brilliant proof that a thinning and blurring of language is more certainly avoided by the power of thoughts and the fineness of feelings than by dialect. How many of our journalists and editorial writers came from a social environment where only a dialect is spoken and throughout their life used no dialect-free language without therefore showing a trace of greater wealth and eloquence in their written statements!

In farewell Nietzsche took my two hands in his and expressed the wish that we might see each other again. As far as I know he left Zurich the next day. (*50*, 5–6, 12–16)

52   Resa von Schirnhofer   *mid-August 1884*

The second meeting with Nietzsche took place in Sils-Maria, where I had come at the end of the summer semester 1884 on the way back to my Austrian homeland, which began with journeys on foot with the medical student Clara Willdenow. In Nice I had met a Nietzsche who, apart from his sick eyes, was apparently healthy, but this image changed during my short stay in the Engadine, where he spoke a lot about himself and his ailment and also suffered a severe attack of it which kept him in bed for a day and a half. During the rest of the time of my stay he again acted as my guide on walks and showed me various of his favorite resting-places. He led me also, as he led others of his visitors before and after, to the waterwashed boulder on the shore of Lake Silvaplana, the Zarathustra stone, that wonderful place of serious natural beauty, where the dark green lake, the nearby forest, the high mountains, the solemn silence join in weaving their magic. After I had, at his request, sat down on his "sacred stone," Zarathustra began to speak out of the world of his intellectual and emotional high-tension and poured out an abundance of ideas and images in dithyrambic pronouncements. Then he told me of the astonishing rapidity of the origin of each individual part of this work, stressing the phenomenalness of this production, an inspiration with which the writing process could hardly keep up. There was not a trace of pathological megalomania, nor even of quasi-normal boastfulness, in the way he spoke about that, neither in the choice of words nor in the tone of his discourse, which revealed rather a naive, boundless astonishment, as at something puzzling to him, and set his entire being in vibrant unrest. This visit to the Zarathustra stone is today still a vivid reality in my memory. Nietzsche's poetic mode of creation seemed to me to stem from potentiated geniality; it never occurred to me to regard it critically or to interpret it symptomatically.

As we walked further along the lakeshore, leaving behind us the zone of Zarathustra magic, the mysterious vibrations in Nietzsche's being were also lost, a natural relaxation began, favored by the delightful coolness and purity of the air and the clear summer day, unthreatened on the horizon by any "little lightning cloud," which Nietzsche so feared.

According to the proverb, "It is just one step from the sublime to the ridiculous," we soon left the ideal regions of philosophical literature for the lowlands of crude reality and the mood of solemn earnestness for the light play of everyday comedy. As we were entering the woods, a herd of cows came charging merrily down the mountainside toward us in playful bounds. I tried to get away and Nietzsche, who saw my involuntary alarm, although very much amused by it, gallantly raised his famous constant companion, the gray umbrella, and leaped back and forth, waving it defensively, while the herdsman drove the scattered herd together and soon disappeared with it. These defensive gestures stood in such striking contrast to his external appearance, his otherwise so sedate and calm demeanor, that the comedy of the situation became apparent even to me and I joined in his laughter. This little scene reminded us of the sleepy, good-natured bulls of the arena in Nice which we had fun goading on, and we ended in joking conversation. Then to motivate my shameful retreat before the exuberant herd, I told him how, when I was a five-year-old child in the country, my mother and I, pursued by an enraged bull, had barely escaped to the first house of the village. An interesting conversation followed about the wave-effect, often through an entire life, of a nervous shock received in childhood. I still remember a morning walk along the shore of Lake Sils up to a place from which one could see in the distance, picturesquely located, the large, newly built Maloja Hotel, destined "for Catholic aristocracy," as Nietzsche said. Then we walked back, climbed a small promontory, where on a luxuriantly green lawn with scattered moss-covered boulders surrounded completely by dense bushes Nietzsche had his hidden resting-place, where the poet and thinker could hold dialogues with himself undisturbed. Here he again touched upon his favorite theme, this time grieving deeply, with tears in his eyes, lamenting the irreplaceable loss of his former friendship with Wagner. He also spoke again of Taine, since I had meanwhile read the *Origins of Contemporary France,* the work he had recommended in Nice, and again he dwelled on the famous true prophecy of Cazotte's. He also mentioned that Taine had recently written to him that he kept *Zarathustra* on his nightstand and read from it as the last thing in the evening. On a visit to Weimar, Frau Förster-Nietzsche told me that no letter with this statement had been found among Taine's letters.

In Sils-Maria Nietzsche told me about his bouts of raging head-aches and the various medications he had tried against them. In Rapallo and in other places of the Riviera di Levante, where he had spent his times of worst health, he had written for himself all kinds of prescriptions signed Dr. Nietzsche, which had been prepared and filled without question or hesitation. Unfortunately I took no notes and the only one I remember is chloral hydrate. But since Nietzsche, as he expressly told me, had been surprised never to be asked whether he was a medical doctor authorized to prescribe this kind of medication, I conclude that some dubious medicines must have been among them. At any rate, he claimed to know his own sickness better than any doctor and to understand better which medications were to be used. Nietzsche never spoke of having used hashish, nor can I remember ever hearing the word hashish from his lips, but no doubt in his intensive reading of contemporary French authors— among them Baudelaire—he was already familiar with hashish in the summer of 1884 as a new drug that had recently appeared in Europe. Hashish smoking is mentioned as early as 1882 in *The Joyful Science,*[1] though only as an Oriental habit of self-intoxication. When I came to Paris at the end of October 1884 all kinds of things were told to me about hashish use; I read an article about the physiolog-ical and psychological differences between opium intoxication and hashish intoxication and I heard celebrities from the ranks of high society mentioned as having tried to dream the hashish dream, etc. In my notebook from that time can be read: "Hashish, or *dawamesk,*

---

1. Cf. p. 109. "Theatre and Music: the hashish-smoking and betel-chewing of Europeans." [Footnotes have been renumbered.]

is a distillate of *cannabis indica,* mixed with a fatty substance, with honey and pistachios to give it the consistency of a paste or jelly."[2] I was also told that there were very tasty hashish candies. I felt a desire to try its effect myself—just once, out of psychological curiosity—but I resisted the attraction of this sweet poison.

As Nietzsche used all sorts of medications against his unbearably painful attacks, so he made all kinds of dietary attempts. During a conversation on dieting he recommended for my study the physiology textbook by the English physiologist Foster, from which he had learned a great deal. At that time I first heard mention of "stout" and "pale ale." Whether Nietzsche praised the "good effects of the alternate use" of these English types of beer from his own experience I do not know, but I believe that these two belonged to the series of his often changing dietary experiments. On this occasion Nietzsche also spoke of physiological anomalies and idiosyncrasies. Then changing the subject to intellectual matters, he began to apply the expression "idiosyncrasy" lavishly to conceptual constructions and moral justifications, in a witty and interesting play with analogies.

After Nietzsche had remained invisible for one and a half days because of illness, Fräulein Willdenow and I went one morning to inquire about his health. We were told that he felt much better and wanted to speak with me. While my companion waited for me by the entrance of the little house built against the cliff, I was led over through a gate up into a modest little dining room. As I stood waiting by the table, the door to the adjacent room on the right opened, and Nietzsche appeared. With a distraught expression on his pale face, he leaned wearily against the post of the half-opened door and immediately began to speak about the unbearableness of his ailment. He described to me how, when he closed his eyes, he saw an abundance of fantastic flowers, winding and intertwining, constantly growing and changing forms and colors in exotic luxuriance, sprouting one out of the other. "I never get any rest," he complained, words which were implanted in my mind. Then, with his large, dark eyes looking straight at me he asked in his weak voice with disquieting urgency: "Don't you believe that this condition is a symptom of incipient madness? My father died of a brain disease." Deeply saddened by this completely unexpected question, I saw all kinds of thoughts pass through my mind, and I suddenly remembered a lady suffering from a persecution complex who had sur-

2. *Les Fleurs du Mal* by Charles Baudelaire. Introduction by Théophile Gautier.

prised me with a similar question. I did not answer right away, and for a second time Nietzsche asked me this heart-rending question, which seemed to me to reveal a great, almost uncontrollable state of anxiety. I was bewildered, but felt that I had to say something reassuring, though against my intuitive grasp of the situation, and I declared in a definite tone that these excitation phenomena of the optical nerves of his weak eyes were certainly not presages of mental illness, etc.; and on parting I wished him a quick recovery from this seizure. This scene left a deep impression on me, especially the rampant anxiety expressed more strongly in his attitude and looks than in his words. Still deeply moved, I told of this conversation to Clara Willdenow, who as a first-semester student of medicine knew no more about the start of mental illnesses than I did. We needed a long time to calm ourselves about these dark fears and severe states of anxiety revealed in Nietzsche's statements.[3] Like the sudden illumination of a lightning bolt, I had looked into the fateful depths of his personality for the second time; once again for a moment I had caught a glimpse of a different Nietzsche.

It is impossible for me to believe that Nietzsche told *only me* of this fear of insanity, even though it—perhaps—befell him only fleetingly and rarely. I myself know only little of the very copious Nietzsche literature, but in the Nietzsche issue of the *Süddeutsche Monatshefte*, November 1931, in which Josef Hofmiller, drawing on and selecting from many sources, presented interesting quotations about Nietzsche's state of health, I found no passage containing a direct statement of Nietzsche's similar to the one made to me in August 1884. When at the end of October 1897, on my return from Russia to Switzerland, following a repeated invitation from Frau Förster-Nietzsche, who wanted to know me personally, I visited her in Weimar, she wanted to hear a lot about the time of my meetings with her brother and asked me about this or that one of our conversations. Naturally, I also told her, among other things, about that fateful question of Nietzsche's in Sils-Maria, which had remained in my memory as a devastating revelation of the most obsessive fear and premonition. But she immediately rejected my report with alarm and stressed that I must have misunderstood the meaning of this statement of her brother's, who was still under the effect of a terrible attack, but he could absolutely not have said that his father had died of a brain disease, for he died as the result of a severe

---

3. Dr. Med. Willdenow, who later set up medical practice in Zurich, died there several years ago. Regrettably, therefore, she cannot confirm the accuracy of the content of that conversation as I have just described it.

accident. Then I noticed that the conversation excited her extremely, so I did not answer and we let the matter drop. But a denial, no matter of what kind it may be, cannot nullify or cancel a personal experience which by its very nature had to leave so deep an impression. In 1914, [Elisabeth Förster-Nietzsche's biography] *Young Nietzsche* was published.[4] It confirms that Nietzsche's father died of a "brain ailment." In Nietzsche's question to me, his father's brain disease is brought in connection with his own eye ailments, his severe headache attacks, and his tormenting states of anxiety, etc., and thereby interpreted by him as a hereditary disease, while Frau Förster-Nietzsche, according to the description in her book, seems to regard the fall, which had taken place a few weeks before, backwards down seven stone steps onto the outside pavement as the cause of her father's brain disease, from which he died eleven months later. In April 1936 the Nietzsche Archive published an autobiographical sketch of the nineteen-year-old Nietzsche.[5] In it one reads, among other things: "The first incident which affected me as my consciousness was growing was my father's sickness. It was a softening of the brain. His increasing sufferings, his blindness, his emaciated form, my mother's tears, the doctor's worried expressions, finally the incautious statements of the farmers, let me sense imminent misfortune. And this misfortune did occur. My father died. I was not yet four years old." *The fall down the steps is not even mentioned.*

As soon as Nietzsche then appeared again ready for walks and conversations, nothing reminded one of this scene from his illness. The time of our stay went by fast, and when Fräulein Willdenow and I were waiting for the post-carriage of Maloja and Nietzsche said good-bye to us, he said to me with tears in his eyes: "I hoped you would stay here longer. When will I hear your refreshing laughter again?" (*52*, 441–445)

53   Helen Zimmern   *1884*

" . . . Only later in Sils-Maria was I to get to know him more closely. I was then living in the Hôtel des Alpes, to which Nietzsche always

4. Elisabeth Förster-Nietzsche, *Der junge Nietzsche* (1914), p. 18ff.
5. Titled "My Life," written by Nietzsche as a pupil in the provincial school of Pforta on September 18, 1863, it was found among Elisabeth Förster-Nietzsche's posthumous papers in a chest filled with old letters and other documents from Nietzsche's ancestors.

came for lunch, when the *table d'hôte*, which he hated because of its noise, was finished. Afterwards he always went for a walk with me along Lake Silvaplana, to a boulder which protruded into this lake, a boulder which he loved very much. He then often told me of what he had written that morning. I understood very little of it; but I felt that it was an alleviation for him to be able to express himself to a human being. The man seemed so lonely, so terribly lonely! If, which happened seldom enough, I made any objection, then he used to answer: 'Yes indeed, but as Zarathustra says'—and then came a passage from his main work, the greatest part of which he had already written."

"And what impression of Nietzsche did you have at that time?"

"Nietzsche was reserved and almost awkwardly shy, when he came together with people with whom he had nothing in common. But once the ice was broken, then one immediately became aware of being in the presence of a man who was completely conscious of his value—'who was thoroughly conscious of his merits.' Once he even told me that someday professorships would be established dedicated exclusively to his philosophy, its explanation, and its dissemination."

"Did you, Miss, ever detect traces of megalomania in Nietzsche? You know that especially in Anglo-Saxon countries his philosophy has often been, and still is, considered that of an insane man. And precisely the mental disease into which Nietzsche later fell seemed to confirm his opponents' opinion of him. And the literary critics were supported in this view by medical authorities: thus for example, a German doctor, a certain Dr. Möbius, once wrote a book about the Nietzsche case, in which he tries to demonstrate a progressive paralysis—which, as is known, accompanies megalomania—even in *Zarathustra*, a book written in his healthy years, and in its strange word formations."

"Yes—I've heard of this. But I myself never noticed in Nietzsche a sign of the coming misfortune. Not only was no sign of insanity detectable in him, but he was not even eccentric, as are so many artists and authors. He did, however, as I have already told you, avoid coming to the *table d'hôte*. He also had the habit of eating an apple each day, but, as the English proverb says, 'An apple a day keeps the doctor away.' No, no: I deny emphatically that Nietzsche was already sick then. Quite the contrary, he gave the impression of a very healthy man in his best years."

"Were you, who knew Nietzsche's book, you, who as an Englishwoman were accustomed to English customs in regard to women, not especially favorable toward him because of his views on women?"

"I know what your question is aiming at; it has been asked of me often enough. I also know what Nietzsche wrote about women. But according to my experiences I can only say that Nietzsche always was of the most perfect 'gentilezza.' There are apparently men who have theories about women which they never put into practice. There are apparently others who can combine brutal practice with the most beautiful theories. Nietzsche certainly belonged to the first category. Once, up in Sils-Maria, I witnessed one of his acts which has still remained vividly in my memory and to my knowledge never became known to a broader circle. In the Hôtel des Alpes there lived at the same time as I an old Russian woman, Madame de Mansuroff, a former lady-in-waiting at the Russian court, who had had a nervous breakdown and was suffering from severe obsessions. It was already September and had gotten cold, and the patient's friends had a coach waiting in front of the hotel every day to take her to Italy and a warmer climate. But every day this coach had to return home without the patient, who always refused to leave her room. One day, Nietzsche, who had heard of the strange case, said to the lady's worried friends: 'Leave her to me just once!' And one noon, when the coach had driven up again, Nietzsche suddenly appeared at the front door of the hotel with the sick lady, who followed him obediently like a little dog, whereas she otherwise used to fly into a rage at the very mention of the journey. But none of us ever learned how Nietzsche had done that. Certainly he did not use the famous whip . . ."

Here Miss Zimmern broke off and began to interview the interviewer, who would have liked to hear more.

"But what is the situation with Nietzsche in England and America? You know, I live in Italy, and I hear but little there about the companion of my youthful walks around Sils-Maria and Silvaplana. Can you give me any information?"

"The English Nietzsche edition was reprinted in 1924—a good sign! And your translation of *Beyond Good and Evil* has even fallen victim to businesslike publishers: it has been reprinted in America and is circulating there in tens of thousands of copies. You know, the Americans like to do that with English books, and there is no legal protection for the victims of such piracy."

"Bad for us poor translators," answered Miss Zimmern, "but

good for the publishers! And especially good for Nietzsche! If only he had experienced this! But he was, as he himself said, born too early. Maybe he was even right about the professorships."

"Well, we have not reached that point yet . . . Thank God, not yet. Professorships, professorships! As Nietzsche himself once said, what good can come out of a paid mouth?"

Miss Helen Zimmern looked at me and nodded with a smile.

It was a very youthful smile that came from her face, a face which age could affect but little, for it was illuminated and translucent with intellect. It was not at all the face of an old woman. Miss Zimmern was an old woman only in years: for she had turned eighty recently.

She then spoke to me also of Liszt, Robert Browning, Karl Hillebrand, of the Italian marshal Cadorna, all of whom she knows or knew. Full of wit and vitality and sometimes even interjecting a story that went against her. "To tell a story against oneself"—what woman has ever been able to do this? And what man?

My final question to the remarkable lady—a question which an author likes to ask his colleagues—was thus fully justified:

"And what are you working on now, Miss Zimmern?"

"Oh, nothing at all, or rather: only at my garden, at my beautiful rose garden in Florence . . . 'Cultivez votre jardin'—the last conclusion of wisdom which Voltaire proclaimed. In literature I have become a mere back number."

"You a back number, Miss Zimmern? Never! The woman who introduced Schopenhauer into the English language; the woman who knew Richard Wagner at the height of his fame; the woman whom Nietzsche deemed worthy of his personal companionship and confidence, the woman who took walks with Nietzsche and was allowed to listen to his conversations for nine weeks—she can never really become a back number!

"And then don't forget what Nietzsche said of you in one of his letters: 'A very intelligent woman, very vivacious, an Englishwoman, of course, a Jew!' This statement alone would suffice to guarantee you a permanent niche in the temple of world-literature!" (*68*)

54 Eugenie Galli   *June 1884ff.*

I told the lady next to me at table in the Christian hospice in Zurich how I hoped soon to see Nietzsche's apartment in the Engadine at

Sils-Maria. But who knows, I said, "whether in view of my so short a stay there it will be accessible to me immediately?" "Let us hope his trail has long since been wiped out," answered the lady maliciously; she was, incidently, a recent doctoral candidate.

So I had spoken to the wrong person! And later in Sils-Maria, I also did not immediately succeed in speaking to the right persons. The trail which I found was very modest. First, I looked haphazardly for Nietzsche's name in the visitor's book of the oldest inn, the Alpine Rose. In June 1884, he had registered as "Professor from Basel." I asked the peasantlike innkeeper whether he would sell me the page from the book. "Not for the world," he answered. But to conclude from this refusal that he had even an inkling of the writer's spiritual significance would be too bold. Only his business acuity dictated this reserve to him. Of course, he remembered very well the professor who had, as he said, always given him so much trouble with the food!! "You know," he began his report, standing astraddle before me. "By the food I noticed right away what the professor was after. My *table d'hôte* is certainly quite good, but the professor could not stand it. It was too hot for him in the large, magnificent hall, and he could not endure the many people, he said, so he generally ate a beefsteak by himself and otherwise only fruit all day, a dreadful lot of fruit! Some days almost three kilos. Naturally, no stomach can stand that! Then he was sick and did not come for days. I often said to him, 'Professor, the fruit is what is making you sick.' 'No,' he then said, 'the meat; I can't stand your beefsteak'; and he laughed. He could not be won over from this standpoint." Involuntarily my gaze fell on the fruit bowls which decorated the inn-table with stone-hard plums and grass-green apples. "Three kilos of this fruit, that is really a lot," I thought. The innkeeper seemed to guess my thoughts. "Professor Nietzsche," he continued, "bought his fruit from the wandering Italians. And he also had friends who sent him some because they knew his passion for it; *that* is what ruined the man."

Since it did not seem like I would learn anything else from him, I asked him to show me Nietzsche's house.

"He lived over there in the rear of the village in the little dry goods store next to the new Edelweiss Hotel," he said. The "dry goods store" was perhaps the smallest house in the whole magnificent Sils. I found the shopkeeper in his store selling blue veiling to two Englishwomen. I waited until they had left, and only then spoke to him about his former tenant. The elderly shopkeeper was of a finer sort than the fat innkeeper. He fully understood that for seven years he had had one of the most unusual minds working under his roof. When I asked him about the Professor, he first answered hesitantly, as if he did not like to talk about such solemn recollections amid the odds and ends of his shop. Then he asked me over to his beautiful paneled living room, aromatic with pinewood, and there he became more communicative. "Yes," he said, "who would not have loved him! He was so good, so pure, and so excessively modest! I don't believe he had even one defect, except that he worked too hard. No one should, no one can work the way he worked in our house those four summers without harming his health. In the morning he got up who knows how early. From dawn he wrote behind locked doors, so that no one could disturb him. At eleven o'clock he came out of his little room. Yes, is it not so, you find it small? Of course, it looks particularly bad now—we have since had to turn it into a storage room. (Involuntarily I thought of the Zurich doctoral candidate and her pious wishes!) The Professor wanted everything very, very modest; he chose precisely this room because it was so remote and had only the pair of cembra pines in front of the window. He could not work where it was bright and blinding. A whitewashed house opposite his writing place would have been unbearable to him. His eye bore the light very badly.

"At eleven o'clock he then went walking, ate in the Alpine Rose, walked around a little more—preferably into the Fex Valley toward the glacier. At four or five o'clock he went back into his room, wrote till eleven o'clock, boiled some tea, and worked, and worked!! Many books were written by him right in this house. He left his things with us over the winter, and when he came in June, he said: 'How happy I am to be back *home* again!' For he did belong completely to us. Often when he lay so sick, with his raging headaches for days on end, and vomiting constantly, I sometimes sat by his bedside. He bore everything with angelic patience. But he could not stop working, which was really the cause of it all.

" 'I did far too much when I was young,' he sometimes said to me. 'As a student I sometimes studied all night, I always had a bucket of cold water under the table; if I noticed that I wanted to fall asleep, I put my feet in it, then I felt fresh again . . .' Of course he was then a professor at twenty years of age but—such a thing avenges itself later. I don't have a single line from him anymore, absolutely *nothing* from him; his sister came and got everything from us, even every letter. She lived with us for two additional summers when he was sick and could not come. She is also an unusually intelligent woman.

"The seven previous years the Professor always came alone. He did not like to be with people, and he received only the scholars who sought him out from all countries of the world, but he could not stand even their company for long. Rest, solitude, work—otherwise he wanted nothing. I believe it when you say that he wrote his name in the visitor's book only once *at most,* he was modest, reclusive, I would almost say timid; he probably found the single time that he registered possibly already obtrusive, at any rate unnecessary." Then the shopkeeper showed me Nietzsche's picture. About the familiar stern look, he explained: "Because the Professor could hardly see, he strained himself in photographing, to focus on an object, and so the kindly but almost extinguished eye suddenly peeps forth hard and intently from under the arched forehead."

It was touching to hear what a deep, childlike respect this man had for the man Nietzsche, only the man, for what must his simple soul have thought of "Zarathustra thoughts," "whose first lightning," in Nietzsche's own words, "flashed for him near a mighty pyramidally towering block not far from Surlei," which he wrote down on the same day and set below it the words: "Beginning of August 1881 in Sils-Maria, 6000 feet above sea level and much higher above all human affairs." (*20*)

55   Robert Freund   *Zurich, September 30, 1884*

Nietzsche, who revered [Gottfried] Keller very highly but still did not know him personally, once said to me that he would be visiting Keller the next morning. After the visit had taken place, I went for a walk with Nietzsche in the afternoon and asked him how it had been with Keller. He had been very nice, Nietzsche answered, but he abhorred the horrid (sic) German which Keller spoke, and the laboriousness with which the great author expressed himself orally. The next Sunday I asked Keller whether Nietzsche had visited him. Keller said yes, and added: "I believe the fellow is mad." (*18, 25–26*)

56   Paul Lanzky   *1884ff.*

It was in the spring of 1880, in the study of the now deceased astronomer Wilhelm Tempel—world-famous just then for his observations of the nebulae—at the observatory in Arcetri near Florence, that Friedrich Nietzsche's book *Human, All Too Human* fell into my hands. Five years later in the same study at the observatory I introduced the heaven-storming thinker to the almost child-like astronomer and it was touching, not only how the two really so very different persons liked each other but also how afterwards each separately judged the other. For each of them had a store of goodness and uprightness which left no room for doubt when one enjoyed their confidence to some extent; but Wilhelm Tempel was not "a worldly-wise man in a paradise," and Friedrich Nietzsche acquired "no reason" for a further five years, so that he "went blind not in his eyesight, but in his mental light."

After *Human, All Too Human* I read the *Miscellaneous Opinions and Sayings,* then the *Dawn of Day,* and *The Joyful Science,* which latter I reviewed in the *Magazin für die Literatur des In- und Auslandes* and in the *Revista Europea.* In 1883 the first two parts of *Thus Spoke Zarathustra* led me to begin a correspondence with the thinker, who was then in the process of moving from Genoa to Villefranche, which he soon exchanged for Nice, where he invited me to visit him. I was able to accept his invitation only the next year. Meanwhile I read *The Wanderer and His Shadow,* the four parts of *Untimely Meditations,* and *The Birth of Tragedy,* and published an overall evaluation of the thinker in the *Westeuropäischer Courier.*

All these works, like Nietzsche's photograph, had given me the impression of dealing with a thinker who was firmly anchored in himself, self-conceited, and equal to any struggle. The letters were more human, less secure, complained about many everyday ills, but could also be harsh and arrogant beyond all measure. I was careful not to send the author my favorable but not at all flattering reviews of his works; but he was informed by his publisher, for in April 1884 I had to read a hard tirade for failing to see the goal of his *Thus Spoke Zarathustra,* "this most significant book of all times and peoples that ever existed." Only six years later he said this publicly in almost the same words.

How much more human this same man was in personal association! To whoever had no inkling of the tremendous problems which he was carrying around in his head, he seemed like a naive scholar who chats for a few hours about everyday matters then withdraws politely because he "has to work." He revealed himself only to the initiated; and then not only the problems were discussed, but also his hesitation before the tremendous responsibility which their mere asking involved: the struggle constantly engaged in between insight and feeling, which had long since been decided in favor of the former; the temporary laming of his moral and intellectual as well as physical forces, and the consequence of this: the feeling of a boundless abandonment and of hovering over an abyss.

[In 1879] Nietzsche, his eyesight and his stomach ruined, left the University of Basel, like a walking skeleton, with a provisory pension of three thousand francs that flowed from three different funds, the longest of which was approved for ten years; he became a wandering philosopher. Thus he wrote his next works in Genoa, in Sils-Maria, in Venice—venturing as far as Messina. But who took him seriously! The philosophers knew that he was an outstanding philologist and a fanatical Wagnerian; the Wagnerians criticized him or shrugged their shoulders with pity. Moreover, no one knew where he was staying. His publisher complained to him that none of his friends was doing anything critically for him and named me as the only one who bought and critiqued his works.

Was that enticing after his position in Basel and as a favorite guest of Richard Wagner's in Tribschen, near Lucerne? Was he not finished, while the master of Bayreuth ruled supreme, interpreted by Wolzogen and Hagen and applauded by the whole world? Was it not a hard fate, to have lost him now, or to have once found him or once believed in him? These questions crop up again and again in the dark rooms and on the sunny streets along which he crept, not knowing the local language, unknown, perhaps considered to be a morose scholar, although he was carrying a bright new world inside his head.

Yes, it had to be bright and shining to be affirmed. For all negation is over from now on! But where is it sunniest? "Come with me to Murcia or Barcelona: 220 cloudless days per year!" he invited me in 1885. But, like himself that winter, we remained stuck in Nice together in 1884–85. It was already for him the "big city," but the Spanish ones were even bigger; he also often closed his eyes, and he lived in rooms that faced north to avoid the abundance of light; but the dryness of the air and the moral impression of tension did him such infinite good, that he could not be moved to leave.

Yet over and over again he sought for a change, for a "semi-definitive" home, i.e., a place to spend his forties. It had to be *quiet:* Nice was not; it had to have dry air: Ajaccio, which he examined for seventeen days, did not; it had to be not too far from all scholarly aids: and the Oasis Biskra on the edge of the Sahara was. Cannes was rejected as a small Nice; St. Raphael because of its strong mistral winds; Monaco as the mother of the gambling hell of Monte Carlo. So we spent a long time researching the peninsula of St. Jean, between Beaulieu and Villefranche, busily seeking a permanent residence. On the one side lay Nice with the most necessary library resources, and nearer in Villefranche an aquarium to study lower sea animals; on the other side one could now and then attend the classical concerts of Pasdeloup in Monte Carlo. And in the middle, as if belonging to our apartment, the entire peninsula of St. Jean, washed by the southern sea, covered with olives and grapes and crisscrossed by many comfortable and tranquil footpaths.

It was idyllically beautiful, but—the idyll did not suit Zarathustra! A few days of weariness, a longing for rest and silence could feel divine; but then the demon of the superhuman task came forth and found itself in gruesome contrast to this rural peace. The reason was: Zarathustra needed disciples, adherents, assistants, work-material—all this was not offered to him by solitude, which he really could not bear.

From that moment on I sought to convince him, since his health was much strengthened, to return to his teaching position and deal with philosophical questions at a German university. He had often thought of that himself, except that he wanted to lecture on *his own philosophy,* instead of discussing general or specific themes. His plan was doomed to failure from the first, or rather it could not be considered again, due to this precondition and to his exceptional position compared with the rest of the faculty. But he did not give up hope that the years were no longer far off when he could interpret his Zarathustra "to a circle of high-minded and brave people" in a "lonesome castle" for this purpose.

I left Nietzsche sadly at that time, in the spring of 1885.

At the end of September 1886 I met with him once again and spent the last month with him. Our rendezvous was at Ruta Ligure, a truly Attic landscape, between Rapallo and Recco on a high plateau on the slope of Montefino, overlooking Genoa. Here his heart opened up while in the mornings he worked on the prefaces with which he intended to introduce the second edition, not printing, of his earlier philosophical works, and in the course of the day he visited, together with Professor Altmann of Genoa and me, the well-known favorite places from the winter of 1882–83, part of which he had spent in Rapallo. He again felt a voice calling him, like a siren, to set up camp here; but I knew what was up and did not agree.

October came to an end. Horrid, rainy days began, with creeping mists. Then the old longing returned for the cloudless sky and dry air of Nice: every physically dismal hour seemed doubly dismal to the thinker's mood and spirit.

I should have gone with him and it became hard for me not to do so; but I had already parted with him intellectually and not kept it secret from him, when I had given him Chapter Two of my *Nightfall* in manuscript to read in contrast with his *Dawn of Day*. He did not approve, but he understood and wished for us to remain friends. He also knew that I wished him well, that I myself saw how much I meant to him. So we both understood our parting and both suffered from it.

The hour came. It had rained all night and the morning was not yet dawning. But I had gotten up and dressed slowly by candlelight. Then there was a knock at my door and Nietzsche entered. "Do not come with me: I must walk alone through night and fog . . . the ring of all rings . . ." Something like sobbing sounded through the broken voice. The friend embraced me and rushed out. I heard him feel his way down the stairs, and slam the door shut, as the clock was striking five, and I stood near the table as if entranced. After a while, which seemed like an eternity to me, I heard the conductor's horn, the bus stop briefly and drive on. Then I grabbed my hat and umbrella and rushed down. In three-quarters of an hour I was in Recco; the train to Genoa had of course left, but the conductor answered my anxious question: "The Professor got aboard safe and sound," a remark which referred to his myopia, but provided me some relief. (*31*, 333–340)

57   Paul Lanzky

Among the most influential events in my life, which I would not give up for any price, is my rather long life together with Friedrich Nietzsche in the years 1881–86. Having barely escaped a nervous breakdown, which severely incapacitated me physically, I became more than ever a pessimist. I had actually grown up under the pessimistic influence of Schopenhauer, Hartmann, Mainländer, Bahnsen, Leopardi, and under various unfavorable conditions. As such I then also was convinced that "suffering is life and living is dying," and thus I had sought to create a subjectively theoretical anchor against all future occurrences, which could no longer hurt me in my deepest soul.

But it would not work out that way. As if by chance Nietzsche's *Human, All Too Human* fell into my hands at the critical moment at the observatory of Arcetri—with an astronomer who was anything but a philosopher and in this case had merely forgotten to return the examination copy to the book-dealer on time. Informed by Karl Hillebrand only about a few earlier writings of the Basel university professor, I cast a few curious glances into the book, which however led me to take it home and a few weeks later order *Miscellaneous Opinions* and *The Wanderer and His Shadow*.

A new horizon opened up for me; but at first my interest was directed at the thinker and the person who showed it to me. But it was strange: the three "staid Baselers" (including one lady) whom I succeeded in locating in Florence could tell me nothing about the thinker, and only absurdities about the person. He had studied too much; he had really helped Richard Wagner get his start, but had now fallen away from him out of envy; he was half crazy if not completely so, for "stomach and eye ailments" are just pretexts to be received in the sanatoria; otherwise, he had been the youngest, most talented, most eligible professor, who could carry on interesting conversations even with ladies, who always went out elegantly and wearing gloves, and more of such silly nonsense!

All this did not keep me from reading also the earlier writings, and ordering *Dawn of Day* and *The Joyful Science* when they were published, which last work I reviewed in *Magazin für die Literatur des In- und Auslandes,* and I was the first to point out the rising significance of Nietzsche's writings. But I was interested not just in the thinker but also in the man who had apparently, under the most unfavorable conditions, dared to reject pessimism and to profess theoretical optimism and no longer to expect a palliative from art but a cure from science.

So the appearance of the first two parts of *Thus Spoke Zarathustra* gave me a new incentive to seek out the philosopher, about whom even his publisher had answered me very mysteriously, that "he was living in complete isolation in Italy"! which, however, seemed to corroborate this last genial creation. The graciousness of the then Rector Magnificus of Basel finally gave me the long-sought address: "General delivery, Genoa." Then in September 1883 I addressed my first letter to Nietzsche, which after general human remarks, asked for an explanation of the hidden cause for the diametrically opposite view of life which I found between the last of the *Untimely Meditations* (1876) and the first of the really philosophical works,

Human, All Too Human (1878), since this gap was filled by no work, nor even an allusion. A few days later I received a crowdedly written postcard, which circumvented the main question but otherwise was written in a very amiable tone, invited a new reply, and gave me his next mailing address: Villefranche sur mer. Now a lively correspondence began between us, and it soon contained Nietzsche's invitation to come to him to Nice, where he had moved—an invitation which I accepted only many months later, when I believed I had armed myself more strongly against life and its new eulogist, Zarathustra.

Finally I ventured out almost lightheartedly although many a letter had already spoken of physical sufferings and temporary moral depressions, while Zarathustra's first demand of his disciples: "Become hard," and the second one: "Learn how to laugh," had till then found an unfavorable field in me. What therefore first struck me about Nietzsche was his humaneness, his amiability, I would almost say his spirituality. The thinker who seemed to be conjuring up a new century in apocalyptic pronouncements, and proclaimed in his teaching to be interested only in strong-willed people and unusual life-tasks, seemed in personal association to be just a harmless scholar who was extremely glad to personally meet his true disciple and friend who had been the first to accord him the title of master long ago. Only when the joy of meeting had subsided and the security of a first direct discussion had been overcome, when we had looked each other in the eye, and our words had penetrated through the ear into the innermost depths of the soul, did the "former professor, now a wandering fugitive" make way for Zarathustra, and his voice became more alive, louder, shriller, his brown eyes flashed, the folded umbrella was swung through the air like a sword, and the meaning of his discourse could become harder than the coldest of his written thoughts.

Then followed the other side: Zarathustra was silent, strode along sunken introvertedly, and groaned. What he had seen lay so far in the future; what he had described as attained, remained beyond his strength; what he had believed overcome, drew him to itself with fibers of the heart. Into this dichotomy, the eastern evening sky perhaps gleamed through palm and aloe, the Mediterranean waves murmured, or a melody from *Carmen* sounded: they were the drops of nectar on the melancholy beverage. Returning home between four cold walls, the loneliness of evening awaited him, which he found doubly hard to bear because he could not read due to his eyes, and in this dark dungeon his own bold daylight thoughts turned against him and threatened to crush him. Is it a wonder that he spoke for an hour longer about everyday matters with simple boardinghouse-table neighbors who had no idea of the "five-hundred problems" which he "constantly carried in his head" and that to get over these sleepless nights he took chloral, thus numbing that feverish brain for a few hours?

At the first cock's crowing he awakened again, and before daybreak he sat by the table lamp on his desk, selecting from his notebooks only the thoughts of his sunniest hours, forgetting his suffering and his fate. It was the formal recapitulation of what had already been thought through and actually fixed; it was followed, in the late afternoon hours, on walks in the open, by new work whose improvisations were immediately written down in pencil in handy notebooks. Nothing disturbed the very shortsighted thinker in this: not the crowd, nor the individual being; not the landscape, nor the sea; at most an all too loud noise of cargo-wagons, and a very dismal sky. He was so wrapped in his thoughts that his eye, when he looked up, not only saw nothing of his surroundings, but to any passerby seemed alien to the world.

In such concentration of a few hours, and not of all days, Nietzsche's works came into being, at least in improvised form. That is, for example, how half of his "Poems" from September and October 1884, published in Volume 8 of his complete works, came to be; and so I was present when in January 1885 the fourth part of *Thus Spoke Zarathustra* received its first form in fourteen days. Nietzsche also assured me then that the three earlier parts had each been written down in exactly the same short span of time. During this time no particular reserve or absentmindedness could be noted in the man; with the last chapter, however, or a few days later, his strength collapsed and he declared himself "pregnant." But strangely it was physical sufferings, especially disturbances of the digestion, and not a direct mental tension that harassed him; but that too is evidence of excessively great exertion of the psychic and intellectual forces, the price of which had to be paid by his physical health, which the thinker did not know how to spare.

This was one of the main reasons for his premature insanity. Nietzsche did not at all understand how to live materially, and often leaped from one way of life to another without first trying either one. About nutrition he therefore stated the most contradictory theoretical views, which had been followed in practice. So in his last healthy years he loved almost exclusively meat-meals, egg-yolks, and rice, while he had earlier led a more vegetarian way of life, which he believed had not agreed with him. Meat and eggs supposedly supplied the most substance from as little material as possible, though he had "trouble digesting them"; but instead of taking more vegetables and chewing better, to be eating at all, he complained afterwards about his stomach and low pulse, which beat only sixty times per minute. Cognac and grog on the one hand, rhubarb and tea on the other—he used wine only exceptionally and moderately—were supposed to help him get over the complaints which developed; but after 1882 the most dangerous medicine, only a palliative that brought oblivion, became, with brief interruptions: chloral, which he used to help him endure the moral and physical suffering.

Such a life was conditioned by an overpowering thought, just as this thought again suffered enormous influences from such a way of life. On a mild February evening in 1885 we once talked about it for a long time while walking back and forth in the public gardens of Nice, and went more deeply into our mutual life, prognosticating our futures. I first asked the master to predict my supposed fate: he shook his head and kept walking. So I asked him again with words suggesting that the verdict did not concern myself but a stranger. He stopped, looked at me silently for a few seconds, laid his left arm on my shoulder and spoke with an almost trembling voice: "It cannot be, I do not want to believe it, but . . ., but . . . I fear you will go crazy . . . if you do not take your own life." I stumbled and must have looked horror-stricken, for Nietzsche sought to erase the impression of his verdict with the most amiable words, so that shame and fear let me gasp barely audibly: "That's not so! But you, you, you!" "You are right," he answered with a smile, "so it will be I?" But I could not and would not speak. "Say it, dear friend, speak!" I was still silent and disconcerted; Nietzsche practically started laughing, and joked: "Now, dear friend, if you believe in fortune-telling, which I did not yet know, I—don't believe in it; but since I told my impression about you, you can say yours about me, as we promised one another." "Well then . . . I thought the same of you, as you believe of me, and this coincidence saddens me!" We walked on in silence; after a minute I heard my friend draw a deep breath, then he stopped and said with a solemn seriousness, but calmly: "I . . . will die by my own hand . . . when my hour will have come." Again we walked on in silence; at the end of the park we turned into the Massena Quay and started the walk home, by mutual agreement, without exchanging one word more. Only a threefold firm hand-shake by the door to his room told us more clearly than the broken-voiced "Good-Night" that each one wanted the evil omen to be warded off from his friend. *My* wish however remained unfulfilled: less than four years later Nietzsche was to be irredeemably lost in an insane asylum in Jena.

We never reminded each other of that evening; indeed at times I thought that precisely the intensity of Nietzsche's brain could get over the tragic heritage, the false and meandering way of life, and the terrible anesthetic. Every afternoon and sometimes in the morning, we took long walks, or at times went by rail to Beaulieu and Monte Carlo; we explored especially the peninsula St. Jean for a longer residence there. Yet Nietzsche's being displayed so much naiveté and idyllic observation of nature, so much wise devotion to the most modest and world-remote life, that to me the catastrophe seemed avoidable.

But this longing for stillness, indeed this temporary reveling in the idyllic, suddenly seemed to him like a "weariness" of soul, and a new cycle began, on which the goal was to be found or a penulti-mate and last stage to it. Meanwhile for years he went from Nice in spring to Venice, then to Zurich and Sils-Maria; in the fall at times to central Germany, then to Northern Italy and again to the Medi-terranean. The aphorisms of *Dawn of Day, The Joyful Science,* and *Beyond Good and Evil* had probably been written in Sils-Maria, but they had first received their definitive form in Italy, just as the four parts of *Thus Spoke Zarathustra* had been written by the bays of Rapallo, Genoa, and Nice. Thus the scientific resources of a Ger-man university library seemed necessary to the thinker, but he believed that he could as little get along without the stimulating air of the high mountains, the clear sky and dry climate of Nice. He gave objective reasons as pretext, when what really was at stake were subjective impressions and feelings which I pleaded with my friend *no longer* to follow, showing him the possibility of finding the resources he needed in or near Florence.

Fate was to make my effort fruitless in the fall of 1885, when from the observatory of Arcetri I showed Nietzsche the hills of the flowery city with bright field-paths and the nearby Apennines with shadowy summer squares. I tried to fascinate him once again, a year later in the truly Attic Ruta Ligure, halfway up the Montefino; but I was already distrustful, as he himself seemed more dismal, almost ill-tempered, despite sunny-bright looks, which swiftly fled. A few months before, he had published *Beyond Good and Evil* at his own expense and had retrieved his earlier works from Schmeitzner's press in order to find a new publisher who would bring out a second edition, not just a printing, and from here he was providing them with prefaces. When everything was done and we had once again visited Rapallo, Santa Margherita, San Fruttuoso, and the Montefino with its "Philosopher's Stairs," then on a rainy, foggy late-October evening had drunk a half bottle of Barbera, our last day together was over. Before dawn the next day he embraced me sobbingly and rode out into the early twilight; I hurried after him to Recco in vain: he himself was fleeing toward the "ring of rings," which was to seize him two years later in Turin. (*32*, 19–25)

58   Adolf Ruthardt   *June to September 1885*

My meeting with Nietzsche was arranged by a Fräulein von Mansuroff, a lady who belonged to the highest Russian nobility, and was the aunt of Prince Orlow, ambassador in Paris, then in Berlin. Living in Geneva (in which city I worked as a pianist and music teacher in the years 1868 until the end of 1885) she dedicated herself, at the same time as Friedrich Klose (now in Thun), and Houston Steward Chamberlain (son-in-law of Richard Wagner, now in Bayreuth) to contrapuntal studies with the success that she wrote a whole notebook of fugues for two, three, four, and five voices that can bear scrutiny and that Nietzsche also later got to see and to hear. With a command of German, French, English, and Italian as well as her mother tongue, she was also studying Spanish in addition to counterpoint. And this remarkable lady must, according to my calculation, have been about sixty years old, for in her youth she had had the good fortune to still enjoy Chopin's instruction. Despite her advanced years, her eagerness to learn was so intense that she continued her study with me by correspondence during her summer stay in Sils-Maria in the Engadine. But because we both saw the inadequacy of such a procedure, I gladly accepted her invitation to resume oral instruction again in Sils-Maria personally and under pleasant conditions.

Already on the first day after my arrival on August 1, 1885, I came into contact with Nietzsche through her. Walking with me along the secluded forest path which leads along Lake Sils to Silvaplana, Fräulein von Mansuroff said: "I led you to this path not unintentionally, for Professor Nietzsche usually takes his morning walk here, and I want you to meet him, for he is very musical. He is considered unsociable in Sils-Maria, but you will find him extremely friendly, if you do not let him escape. Don't you believe that, if necessary, he tries to escape only from young and pretty ladies, but also from us old and ugly ones." And she smiled quite peculiarly. Well, she was old; pretty she was not, and could not have been so even in Chopin's times. But what did she mean by that? Did she want to put me in the embarrassing position of having to pay her a silly compliment? I knew that at times she liked to play such tricks, to a certain extent rather obviously, so I repeated good-humoredly and without losing my composure: "Miss, whoever has command of five languages as you do, and on top of that is learning a sixth, is never old. I have known persons who reached almost their ninetieth year with one single language and gradually became not only more youthful, i.e., more childlike, but finally completely childish. And whoever throws himself ardently into the arms of the fugue and loses himself in its impasses and complexities, beautifies . . . beautifies his existence, although other people flee from such activity— Hence the name fugue is derived from the Latin 'fuga' (flight)."—"There he is," Fräulein von Mansuroff cried out with relief, for she felt that I was about to deliver a long discourse, and at a small turn of the forest path Nietzsche suddenly was standing before us.

Nietzsche's external appearance made an extremely agreeable impression on me. Above middle height, slender, well-formed, with erect but not stiff stance, his gestures harmonious, calm and sparing; the almost black hair, the thick Vercingetorix mustache, his light-colored, but distinguished-looking suit of the best cut and fit, allowed him so little to resemble the type of a German scholar that he called to mind rather a Southern French nobleman or an Italian or Spanish higher officer in civilian clothes. Deep seriousness, but by no means the somber, angular, demonic expression that has been attributed to him in pictures and busts, spoke out of his noble features, with a healthy tan from going out a great deal in the open air and sun, and out of his large dark eyes. After exchanging a few polite phrases, gallantly trying to entertain Fräulein von Mansuroff, he accompanied us as far as the doorstep of the Alpine Rose, the hotel where we were staying. He had already shaken my hand and said a most pleasant farewell, when Fräulein von Mansuroff held him back with the words: "You are cordially invited, dear Professor, to honor us with your visit this evening here in Nr. 4, the first room to the left on the ground level, which I have reserved as my music room and provided with a good piano shipped from Chur. Mr. Ruthardt will play us Bach, Chopin, Schumann, and we'll be just a pleasant little group." Not without a certain embarrassment and with almost a pained expression, Nietzsche passed his hand over his magnificently vaulted forehead, complaining: "Ah, music! . . . Music is no good for my condition!" That seemed to me a clear rejection, for which I had complete understanding; for who suffers most under the obtrusiveness of music? Is it not the musician? Fräulein von Mansuroff then whispered to me: "He just imagines he's sick."

On the evening in question I had just begun with the Prelude to Bach's organ Fugue in A Minor, transposed by Liszt, when completely against my expectation Nietzsche appeared after all and listened attentively. I also played Chopin's *Little Nocturne in F-sharp Major* and finally Schumann's *Kreisleriana.* Between the music pieces, interesting conversations developed, in which I listened avidly to Fräulein von Mansuroff's recollections of Chopin and admired Nietzsche's pertinent remarks. About the *Kreisleriana,* however, he remained completely silent and let that lady's enthusiasm run its course.

The following afternoon Nietzsche came to get me for a brisk walk into the Fex Valley. In quiet and pensive admiration he pointed out to me the Piz Lagren and the Piz Palaschin, as we were passing the houses of Platta and Cresta, toward Curtins, one of the highest constantly inhabited places in Europe. In the course of a few hours I saw the eternal gigantic mountains shining in the sun, glowing reddish and melting away in fading bluish haze. Nietzsche was delighted to see me so ecstatic and he began to speak to me of the evening before. "Explain to me the highly noticeable preference which Fräulein von Mansuroff has for Schumann, especially for his *Kreisleriana.* For my part I can only ascribe it to an unclear sensibility, especially since, in contrast with her surprisingly great talent for languages and music, she seems to have no interest in literature and perhaps has not read E. T. A. Hoffman at all, and so cannot know what this unsuccessful untitled program music is really about." I answered: "This Russian woman's sense of music is thoroughly German . . ." "German," Nietzsche interrupted me, "German, that she is, in the sense of an introverted sentimentality and immersion in a personal, petit-bourgeois sugary sentimentality, which leaves humanity quite indifferent. Schumann was certainly an honest nature and a great talent, but not a boon to music in general, not to mention German music in particular. This tendency to hide inside oneself is even dangerous, no less dangerous than Richard Wagner's theatrical extroversion." Then I answered vigorously, and not without sharpness: "Schumann, due to his thoroughly unique nature, which was based on a poetic background, had an extraordinarily positive and wholesome effect, since he, who was otherwise so peaceable and so benevolent to true young talents, declared a merciless war on pedantic philistinism, stereotypes, shallow virtuosity, and brought it to a victorious finish. As a productive critic he is unequalled. Of course, whoever puts himself into the mind of the composer, to a certain extent devoting himself to him without reservation, as did Theodor Kirchner, must pay dearly as a consequence." —"Theodor Kirchner? Wasn't a collection taken up for his benefit recently?" asked Nietzsche. "Yes," I could report to him in more detail, "A committee was formed, consisting of Kirchner's friends from Zurich and Winterthur and famous musicians such as Brahms, Gade, Gevaert, Grieg, Joachim, Reinecke, etc., together with a few publishers, to obtain the means to protect the old Kirchner from starvation and to provide him with a carefree old age. In a short time, no less than 36,000 marks were collected."—"Now, you see," said Nietzsche, "doesn't this occasion speak in favor of my statement?"—"Certainly," I replied; "but, as I believe, only insofar as it speaks against an excess of epigonalness, to which Schumann tends to mislead pensive fools, but he seduced none more than precisely his most faithful and talented disciple, Theodor Kirchner. Incidentally I know that despite Kirchner's efforts to win Richard Wagner for Schumann—it was in Zurich—he came up against an insurmountable dislike, which was then inherited by all Wagnerians: that is how the lord and master wanted it, otherwise a defamatory essay by Joseph Rubinstein in the *Bayreuth Blätter* (1878) would have been impossible."—"Do you still consider me a Wagnerian?" Nietzsche answered not without surprise. But without waiting for an answer he again began attacking Schumann—this time as a dramatic composer. Even with more eloquence than I had at my command, a convincing defense in this direction would hardly have succeeded. For I had to admit that I had never seen a flatter effect from the stage than the, as such, noble and beautiful music of *Genoveva.* But I defended the music of *Manfred,* which Nietzsche seemed quite especially to resist. But he disarmed me completely by enticing a loud laugh from me by asking me with complete seriousness, whether I could picture the chamois-hunter Astarte, the Alpine fairy, transposed to the Saxon Switzerland? I believe the agreement of Nietzsche's thought and speech with his writing could not be illustrated more graphically than by showing the patient reader, for a change, how this sharp thinker, this soul-searcher who lights up the darkest corners—apparently shortly before or after our conversation—stated about Robert Schumann in his writings: "But as far as Schumann is concerned, who took things hard and from the beginning, and was also taken hard—he was the last composer who founded a school—is it not considered among us as a good fortune, a breath of relief, a liberation, that precisely this Schumann-romanticism has been overcome? Schumann, fleeing to the 'Saxon Switzerland' of his soul, half like Werther, half like Jean Paul, certainly not like Beethoven, certainly not like Byron!—his *Manfred* music is a misunderstanding and an injustice—Schumann, with his taste, which was basically a small taste (namely a dangerous, for Germans doubly dangerous, penchant for the quiet lyricism and the wild drunkenness of feeling), constantly going aside, retreating shyly and withdrawing, is a noble weakling who reveled in sheer anonymous happiness and sorrow, in a girlish *noli me tangere* from the first: this Schumann was already just a German event in music, no longer a European one, as Beethoven was, and as, even more comprehensively, Mozart has been—with him German music suffered its greatest danger, namely to lose its voice for the soul of Europe and to sink to a mere chatter about the fatherland."[1]

My great naiveté and candor, which I showed on almost daily walks with Nietzsche into the Fex Valley, required a clarifying explanation, and also my astonishment at the expressions "theatrical" and the question "still?" in reference to Richard Wagner. To recall it once again, I had been living in Geneva since 1868 and now (1885) was about to move back to Germany for good. I knew nothing more about Nietzsche than that he was or had been a professor at the University of Basel and that he was one of the gifted and enthusiastic men around Wagner, such as von Stein, von Wolzogen, Peter Cornelius, Felix Dräseke, etc. His book *The Birth of Tragedy from the Spirit of Music* had, however, attracted so much attention that it had even reached all the way to me in Geneva. The clearly and energetically delineated contrasts and concepts "Apollonian"/"Dionysian" were understandable to me without effort, and the mystical deification of Wagner did not disturb me in the least: for I

1. *Beyond Good and Evil*, Nr. 245.

too succumbed to the magic of this magnificent, marvellous phenomenon, which outshone everything in the artistic sky then and now. Thus Nietzsche's break with Wagner had remained unknown to me. Ah! I was not spared to hear quite enough about that defection from the man himself, and to feel truly moved. For if Nietzsche's attacks on Wagner had till now remained within moderate bounds, from now on they intensified day by day, and my last conversations with him put me, as I said, in a very sad mood. No matter what I might present in plausible contradiction, conclusiveness, rhetorical skill: I tried it with full loyalty to conviction and warmheartedness! In vain! The gleaming and harmonious image of his splendid personality would have experienced in my memory an inextinguishable darkening and distortion, if shortly before our departure, scales had not, so to speak, fallen from my eyes. But this belongs to another chapter which will be saved for later. (*49*, 489–491)

59   A. Fritsch   *June to September 1885*

I saw Nietzsche for the last and longest time in the year 1885. I then had a severe neuralgia, which forced me to stay in Sils-Maria for several weeks. I lived in a Palazzo P . . .; a shoemaker was housed in the cellar. My sister, Julie Fritsch, had accompanied me on this journey. Since I was very ill, I slept late in the mornings, often till eleven. During this time my sister Julie often went across the street to the hotel where we ate, sat down at the piano and played. (My sister was a personal, very musical friend of Johannes Brahms.) Sometimes Nietzsche sat down with her; they conversed for a long time and also played four-handedly. When Nietzsche learned of my presence from Julie, he immediately came over to visit me. We went walking together regularly for about three weeks. Nietzsche spoke a lot about his thoughts, about Wagner, his break with him, and difficulties with publishers (Schmeitzner), which were then especially tormenting to him. It is a crying shame that I did not write down any of these conversations. Now I have, as a rather unphilosophical person, unfortunately forgotten the essential. I still remember precisely that one day Nietzsche did not come for the usual walk. When the next day I asked him why, he grasped his forehead and said only: "Yesterday I had a terrible headache again." I never saw Nietzsche again later. (*19*)

60　　Johannes Volkelt　　　　　　　　*Summer 1885*

The next year I met him twice in the Engadine. From St. Moritz, where I was staying with my wife, we visited him in Sils-Maria, where he used to spend the summer months in those years. He was not home, but on the way back we saw him coming toward us across the road. We stopped, got out, greeted one another, and agreed in praising the splendor of the Engadine. Nietzsche emphatically characterized it as a "heroic landscape." The sight of the wanderer striding with a rapid step and upright head in the evening sun will always remain unforgettable to me. A few days later we saw him again by the little lake between St. Moritz and Pontresina. (*62, 67*)

61　　Marie von Bradke　　　　*June 30 to September 25, 1886*

To see a great man from close by during one's developing years is a gift of grace of immeasurable and indestructible value.

In the year 1886 I received such a gift.

I was making my first independent journey in still very young years. The doctor had prescribed high mountain air to me, and Switzerland attracted me mightily.

The journey led across the Albula to Samedan and from there in a coach through the wonderfully beautiful Engadine to Sils-Maria.

It was the end of June and the little village was still quite free of strangers. In the Alpine Rose there were plenty of rooms available, and I chose one overlooking the peninsula.

Days of rain made all the splendor of this God-blessed nature unrecognizable. Then suddenly the sky cleared. I rushed out into the wetness, beyond Sils onto the great street to Maloja, and could not contain my excitement. What now became visible—how beautiful it was!

Sublime beauty had been at work to make something great and unique here. And now blissful days began for me under the deep-blue sky, in the shining sun.

The hotel began to fill up. There was joyous, high-spirited company at meals. But the time between meals was devoted to a pensive, solitary contemplation of nature. I will never forget the quiet hours on the peninsula, which at that time was still wild and natural, with its enchanting vistas, the hikes on the little paths illuminated by alpine roses across Lake Sils, the tours to the magnificent Fex Valley and to the peaks where edelweiss grows.

One was as if lifted to another world, beyond the dull, petty everyday affairs.

Once when I had returned for dinner a little late from the black Lake Cavloccio and found the dinner table already abandoned by the guests, a newly arrived gentleman sat down opposite me—it was Nietzsche. I did not observe him, being still completely rapt in the landscape I had just seen. Then he, who had been sitting facing the window, suddenly got up and sat down next to me; and when I looked at him with some surprise, he apologized that the bright window had blinded him. Something in his voice, his look, attracted me. We soon got into a lively conversation, whose content I have forgotten, but I do remember that it was unusual.

Now he always appeared at noon-meals but sat at a separate table.

I had once surprised a singer from Munich with a beautiful, strong, well-schooled voice, as she, alone, to her own accompaniment, was singing in the salon, and music-hungry as I was, I listened to her performance of the Brahms' song "O versenk."

Since then it was the custom for us two to meet shortly before noon in the empty salon. She had a huge repertory and could accompany almost everything herself, and I could choose. Those were delightful half-hours. Once when I was listening to Grieg's "Du mein Gedanke," which had just become known in Germany, the door was opened very softly and Nietzsche joined us without a word. To the song he added a commentary on the new harmonization.

After that he managed to arrange to join us at those times devoted to music.

And he added to them many a good word which my soul sought to process on my lonesome afternoon walks.

Unfortunately I did not write any down. But some became my flesh and blood and gave direction to my life.

Weeks passed without my even having learned his name. It did not mean anything to me. His writings were still completely unknown to the German public. Only a small clientele read and, for the most part, rejected them. It was not through his name that I became aware of his greatness.

I often watched him as he directed his quick steps to the peninsula mornings before six o'clock, as he did every day, with his yellow umbrella open to protect his sick eyes. The man walking there, I noted clearly, had an artist's eyes and bore high, lonesome, unique thoughts into his experience of nature's beauty. When one saw the great, strong, well-dressed figure with the full, rosy face and the mustache, hastening along so, one would have taken him for a *Junker* [landed nobility] rather than a scholar or an artist. Only the large, brown, velvety eyes revealed a deep, kind, spirit-filled artistic soul. Never would I have wanted to disturb these, his creative hours, with a meeting, great as my desire for one sometimes was, as to follow him stealthily in the morning freshness to study the attractions of the peninsula.

Afternoons I sometimes met Nietzsche on my walks. And always he stopped and made some significant statement. Often French, or perhaps also Russian literature provided the material for conversation. He knew both very well and esteemed them highly. At the time he was very busy with Stendhal.

I especially enjoyed it when he discussed the beauties of nature and pointed them out. Never again in all my life have I had the joy of finding as fine an eye for them.

Once, it was on the narrow path across Lake Sils, he whispered to me as if in secret: I ought to go with him, he wanted to show me a point which only he knew and which he liked above all others.

We passed through the bushes and emerged from a sea of blooming alpine roses. Lake Sils suddenly looked forth from its magnificent framework. "Here is where one must sit," I said, and sat down under the red-glowing shrubs. This delighted him extremely. "You recognized right away that only so is the picture perfect."

I have only rarely dared to enter this place and have never betrayed it to anyone. It should belong to him alone.

Before my journey home, I wanted to hear *Parsifal* in Bayreuth and spoke quite candidly to him about it. He did not advise me against it. But a shadow passed over his face at mention of Wagner.

But he was too great and independent to be able to be totally absorbed in a subordinate role. He wanted to stand next to the artist as a creator, and the latter did not want to accept that. So their ways parted. Nietzsche probably never recovered in all his days. One could tell this from every word on the theme of Wagner.

Generally Wagner's step to the mystical is given as the reason for their estrangement. But given Nietzsche's disposition, which delicately spared the opinions and feelings of others, that might have led to disagreements, but never to a parting.

He never spoke of his works, and I dared not ask. Once however—it was when my departure was drawing nearer—I resolved to ask him for the title of the work which he considered his best.

For a long time he did not want to come out with it—finally he named *Thus Spoke Zarathustra* and wrote the title and publisher for me on a scrap of paper.

But I should not read the book, he said; it would only frighten and repel me. And then, lost in memory, he described how the book came into being on a hill above Rapallo—almost without any action of his own. It had seemed to him as if someone were dictating and he needed only to write. In a few days it was completed. I ordered the book immediately. But at that time I understood very little of it, and did not fully recognize its value, indeed I directly rejected much that was in it. He knew that I had the book and was reading it. The mail was given out at noon, and those sitting next to me had read the title.

Shortly before my departure he asked me what impression it had made on me. It still hurts me now that I was able to apply only immature criticism to the book. I especially recall speaking of its incompletion and he answered in a friendly tone, that his sister had made the same criticism.

Our last meeting revealed to me the pain of his loneliness and of not being understood.

He felt abandoned by his friends, misunderstood, not supported in Germany by any sympathy for his work.

The pain that burned in him probably contributed to his destruction.

Good-bye, we said on parting. He had me give him my home address in order to describe to me, as he said with a smile, what Sils-Maria looked like without me.

And he indeed wrote me a nice letter from there, though unfortunately I received it too late, for traveling in a coach from Maloja to Bergell I suffered an accident that kept me in Lugano for weeks.

Meanwhile he had left Sils-Maria, and I did not know how to reach him with my letter.

I did not return to Sils-Maria in the next years, and I heard about Nietzsche again only when insanity had unmistakably seized him.

Many years have passed since my meeting. I have become old, and countless memories have faded away. But Nietzsche's image and nature have remained ineradicably engraved in my memory.

I have read in his works and learned to understand and value

them better. And I have also had some association with his followers. And this has caused me to revive my memories of Nietzsche,
though they are certainly as such of no great relevance.

When I saw how they behaved, vaunting their power, mimicking
power-figures such as Nietzsche glorified; when they impiously
trampled on what others honored, and could not outdo themselves
in international bravado, then I, who had known their reverential,
sensitive leader, had to say to myself: those who call themselves his
followers would have rejected him! He would have sent them far
from him and again have felt painfully how misunderstood he was.

The inner struggle with his pathologically delicate soul, overflowing with pity, was what had led him to preach, "Be hard!," and
to look up with admiration at those Renaissance men of violence
who had walked stolidly over corpses to their goal.

He would have offered no teachings to relentless men who are
poor in love and pity and who drape a philosophical cloak around
their innate monstrousness.

He thundered a great deal against Germany, but only the way a
loving, ethically high-standing father deals more strictly with the
child whom he loves best of all. It burned like a hot coal in him that
it was not as he wished it.

He would have turned away, like from repulsive vermin, from
Germans who scorn their fatherland as lackeys of foreign powers.

Be hard! At no time did we need this word more than today:
hard against our own mistakes, hard in fulfilling our duties, hard in
insisting on what is our country's right, and yet not loveless toward
its neighbors.

That would let us develop into true followers of the noble man
Nietzsche, as he lives in the memory of those who had the good
fortune to see him from close up with discerning eyes. (9, 394–395)

62   Resa von Schirnhofer   *Zurich, April 28 to May 6, 1887*

Little has remained in my memory of a few later meetings with
Nietzsche in Zurich, which were of only a fleeting nature. On one
occasion I met in his company Professor Freund, the musician, with
whom he had been discussing Gast's *The Lion of Venice*. Even earlier,
but especially on this occasion, Nietzsche poured out the enthusiastic eloquence of his musically attuned temperament over his friend's
creation, which he could not praise enough in its grace and melodic
richness. He did not, however, succeed in arousing my interest,

because he let the points against Wagner be too clearly felt. But what he then told me about Hugo Wolf—"your countryman," as he emphasized—fascinated me very much, because he was the first one to speak admiringly about this musical genius to me, who was unsuspecting of the future and of how the personal fate of both these men would be similar!

This last time I spoke with Nietzsche was on May 6, 1887, when, to my joy, he showed up at my apartment one morning. Returning from Paris the evening before, I had found Nietzsche's calling card and to my great regret heard that he had come several times to inquire whether I was back yet; and he was about to depart. After the first words of greeting I immediately began to speak about interesting books I had recently read in Paris. One that had left a deeper impression than the others was still spooking around in my head: *The House of the Dead.* Nietzsche interrupted me vehemently and exclaimed with astonishment that he had been about to tell me about his discovery of Dostoevsky, and now I had beat him to it. He advised me to read *The Underground Man,* an "extraordinarily fascinating" book, and added that the German translation was defective. He had compared the German with the French translation and found that in the German precisely the finest summaries and also longer psychological analyses had simply been left out. One of his acquaintances whom he had asked to do so had compared the Russian text with the two translations and confirmed that the German one mutilated the original text. Then I came to speak of a visit to Natalia Herzen, an outstanding personality in character and spirit, a very close friend of Turgenev's who was also personally acquainted with Nietzsche. At her place I had met Prince M., who, if I was not mistaken, knew Dostoevsky well in person, and told me so much about him that was still completely unknown to the general public and that also was of interest to Nietzsche. So on the Rue d'Assas in Paris Nietzsche continued the conversation on Turgenev and Dostoevsky in his characteristic way of illuminating every theme intellectually and causing it to sparkle, so that though I do not remember all the details of the conversation, it has left its reflection in the twilight of remote memory.

In retrospect I would like to mention a few things that are part of my image of Nietzsche, as it was then formed directly under the aura of his personality, uninfluenced yet by any reading about him. That image has a tendency to fluctuate, as did also his being and his conversations. In answer to objections or questions on my part, he often stressed that I should not consider him a destroyer of old val-

hmmm?

ues, he wanted to build them on a solid foundation. At times he said, "that he was still in transition, and was aware of some surprises himself." His allusions could be variously interpreted; in his psychological confession, "Short Habits,"[1] which includes everything changeable and variable in human needs and relations, one reads among other things: " . . . my nature is completely oriented to short-term habits, even in the needs for its physical health, and in general, as far as I can see: from the lowest to the highest. I always believe that *this* particular thing will give me permanent satisfaction . . . And one day its time is over . . . That is how it goes for me with foods, thoughts, people, cities, poems, music, teachings, daily schedules, ways of life. On the other hand, I hate permanent habits." He told me several times that no fixed limits are set to the world of his teachings, of his problems of knowledge, no limits which could prevent a transition to another world of thought. He did not formulate it as unambiguously as I am doing here—I do not have any word-for-word notes—but he pointed out this possibility on various occasions in varying forms of expression.[2]

In the emotional field of his complex nature, the thinker and poet seemed to be very sensitive to the temperature-fluctuations in human relations; he seemed to be easily irritable, easily offended and vulnerable to positive or negative influences, "a shifting sphere of opinions and moods."[3]

Even then, the emotivity in his temperament struck me as strange. Especially his monologues on Wagner, which began calmly with rationally founded judgments, but soon accelerated into an avalanche of words that stirred up psychic depths and ended in tears. His emotional hyperaesthesia could easily be proven by many passages from [his sister's biography] *The Lonesome Nietzsche*.

Proofs of friendship, interest in his human personality, or a milieu he found agreeable struck a response in his particular nature, his amiability in dealing with others, his kindheartedness and tender feelings, and acted as a tonic to the soul of this homeless, volatile man—though only temporarily. Thus he enjoyed the stay in his Sils-

1. *Die fröhliche Wissenschaft* (1882), p. 213. [Footnotes have been renumbered.]
2. In *Quelques Souvenirs sur Frederic Nietzsche* by Silex (Bibliothèque universelle et Revue Suisse, 1908) one reads, among other things: "Did he not write to a woman-friend in 1882 in mysterious terms: 'Look through the phase in which I have been living during the last few years. Look beyond it. Do not let yourself be deceived about me. Surely you cannot believe that to be a freethinker is my ideal! I am . . . excuse me!'"
3. *Menschlich, Allzumenschliches* I. "Aphorismus: Von den Freunden."

Maria under the "sappy, broad-shadowed, quiet trees"[4] in full draughts of a grateful heart, prepared for him as if by a kindly fate, when he returned tired and freezing "from the vicinity of the tall mountains where the mightiest rivers have their source."[5] The center of this circle was an old, sickly, intelligent Englishwoman, Mrs. Fynn, a believing Catholic, for whom Nietzsche had a sincere respect. When I later got to know her personally in Geneva, she told me how Nietzsche had, with tears in his eyes, asked her not to read his books, since "there was so much in them that was bound to hurt her feelings." His statements about pity as his "inner enemy" are by no means empty phrases but the expression of his contradictory nature. His rationalistic frame of mind struggled with his feelings, which had grown out of and were still connected with Christian ethics. His will, however, rising mightily out of the dark abyss of the drives at a very early age, preached to him heroism against his emotional nature, even in regard to pity, and it always sovereignly dominated his world of knowledge,[6] this mighty will of which he says:

"Yes, an uninjurable, unburiable force is in me, a cliff-leaping stream: it is called *my* will. Silently and unchangingly it strides through the years."[7]

Surely Nietzsche suffered from these conflicts, until the pathological intensification of his intellectual hatred under a frenzied work-drive caused his thoughts, which stood in the sharpest mental focus, to fall into immoderation of expression in image and word, so that the Nietzsche I knew in Nice and Sils-Maria became the Nietzsche of *Ecce Homo.* (52, 445–448)

63 Meta von Salis-Marschlins *May 1887ff.*

From New Year's until the spring of 1887 I did not hear from Nietzsche again. On May 1, in the midst of all kinds of purchases

---

4. *Menschlich, Allzumenschliches* II. "Natureindruck der Frommen und Unfrommen."

5. *Ibid.*

6. According to Nietzsche, as he expresses it in the aphorism, "What is the Meaning of Knowledge?" (*Fröhliche Wissenschaft*, p. 240), "intelligere" is not something in principle contrary to the drives, but only a certain behavior of the drives toward one another. He opposes Spinoza's philosophical maxim, "Non ridere, non lugere, neque detestari, sed intelligere," and he declares this distinction to have arisen from an error concerning the nature of conscious thought.

7. *Also sprach Zarathustra* II, "Das Grablied."

for my sister and her children, who had lost even the most basic necessities in a fire, a postcard announced his arrival in Zurich. On his first visit the similarity of our experiences led us to exchange similar observations—the great earthquake of Nice, remember, had just taken place. My sister, physically delicate, indecisive and timid in ordinary life, had for the second time acted prudently and resolutely during a fire. In Nice, patients in advanced stages of their ailment had worked with greater presence of mind than crude servants and healthy guests. The higher achievement-capacity of the more delicate species in moments of aggravated danger had been brilliantly proven.

Nietzsche also came to see me two days later to apologize for having turned down an invitation for a trip to Sils Forest. A Zurich musician whom he knew had promised to play some things for him on the piano, but had not shown up, and so left him high and dry. The arrival of an acquaintance to invite me to a party revealed to him that my doctoral examination was fast approaching. I told him my recipe for attaining a certain degree of security: alternation between the strictest memory-work and the most frivolous distraction.

I left the university shortly after Nietzsche had departed from Zurich again. He intended, until moving to Sils-Maria, to stay in Amden, high above Wallen Lake, charmingly portrayed by the "European Travel Pictures," but because of the heat and lack of shade he could not stand it and fled to Chur, whose magnificent evergreen forests appealed to him. Toward the end of July, I too went to Sils with a woman friend.

The summer was extraordinarily hot. Even up there so close to the boundary of the eternal snows, one preferably stayed in the house at noon. The wild flora were more luxuriant than ever: the large, white chrysanthemums lined the meadow path on the peninsula; between Isola and Sils the underbrush shone with alpine roses; further up on the swampy mountain meadows the aromatic brown nigritellas gleamed between the silver-haired and wool-grasses, and dryads and saxifrages mocked the life-hostile stones.

The two hotels were full of guests, and almost every family in the village had rented rooms. We were housed in a stately house in the Engadine this side of the bridge over the Fex Brook and right next to the Fex Valley road. The front stairs and windows were full of flowerpots, cared for by the landladies with undaunted diligence through the harsh winter. Here too the splendid sun brought superabundant rewards, every pot was filled with blossoms. A rosebush especially bore two roses of a perfection in form, color, and aroma, such as is not found among its more favored brothers in the valley. Nietzsche sometimes stopped to look at these super-roses, these children of the heights, of the pure air and proximity to the sun.

Nietzsche lived in the same house as before, across the bridge, and came over to see us almost every morning, and sometimes also in the afternoons, when the weather was beautiful and the heat moderate, to take us for a walk; otherwise, for an intimate conversation in our room. If he stayed away for a whole day, it meant that he was ill. That was not often the case, and the weather, with a few short interruptions during my seven-week stay, remained gloriously beautiful.

Until mid-August the village and its closer vicinity were swarming with adults and children, but Sils is embedded in such an abundance of beautiful points, near and far, that even in the highest season one had a selection of lonely destinations for walks. In the Alpine Rose, arriving friends and a few strangers who were looking for companionship gradually formed around myself and my girlfriend a small circle to which we devoted ourselves at meals—Nietzsche ate at the hotel only at noon, alone and before the others. Otherwise we were considered exclusive, which indeed we were, for we preferred to take our excursions alone. Nor did I want to be hampered in Nietzsche's visits by a motley crowd, nor still less to permit, for example, American women journalists, who had no idea of his importance, to satisfy their curiosity through me and exploit the result for their bank account.

I once put Nietzsche's innate courtesy severely to the test by indifferently dismissing a lady of this sort who had come all the way to my door. I was able to reconcile the offended lady later by a greater show of amiability—but I would never have forgiven myself if I had made a crude spectacle of Nietzsche or wasted his precious time. For I knew that he was embarrassed by the bad manners of modern ladies, who sit on a bench with dangling feet and at the age of thirty still proclaim their friendships with noisy high-school allurements, making themselves conspicuous by loud talking and laughter! My sense of distance is too great for me not to have tried to protect the elite of my friends from unpleasantness at the price of a few so-called lacks of consideration.

Revenge did not delay, but I had seen it coming and was prepared. When a few months later an acquaintance, under the pretext that others were gossiping, expressed surprise that Nietzsche and I did not marry, I answered coldly: "Indeed, why shouldn't we marry, if we wanted to marry?" and I told Nietzsche nothing of it. I was so certain that a mistake on this point could not arise between us; I found it so unworthy that women still see a friendship between a man and a woman always only from this perspective.

Nietzsche loved to "recreate" himself with me as a reprieve from his loneliness, from his work, and sometimes from demanding visitors. We sat for many hours in my flower-decorated room, I with some work in hand, he speaking about what he was thinking, reading, experiencing. He liked a good listener. An older lady had shortly before taken away his pleasure in personal confessions by hastening to document everything he said by citing personal experiences in bad taste and base surroundings, robbing him of his aura. The man of the world puts on a thicker epidermis for such events, but the soul-searcher and mental struggler cannot. Nietzsche never despised the simple things that came across his path: he spoke with compassion of his landlord's worry that his ox might also catch the hoof-and-mouth disease that was going around, just before hay-harvest—the main agricultural event in the Engadine!—and little Adrienne's fear of thunderstorms; but he never learned to endure baseness and bad taste. And still less, intellectual pedantry! Perhaps women fall more frequently into the error that important men like to speak and hear only about important things, and so they become shallow or betray how common they are.

Nietzsche remembered with special joy a visit he received in Sils. It was that of Heinrich von Stein (who died young) in the summer of 1884. In lively conversation, the two men had wandered about for three days in the region, which consecrates thoughts by its earnest beauty. Nietzsche led me to the place where the road to Fex bends up past the church and down into the valley properly-so-called and one's look ahead falls on the gleaming glacier, and backwards on the bald, dark wall of the mountain. Here Stein had cried out in rapture: "That is heroic!" Nietzsche liked very much the way he spoke about his teacher Dühring, who had strongly influenced him in his young years. He reflected for a while before making a statement, for "Stein was a very serious person," blinded neither by love nor by hatred. Nietzsche also to a very high degree had this quality of thinking a matter over before announcing his view. I recall this especially clearly when I see men and women of mature age take sides pro or con at the drop of a hat. Once, when I was speaking about Ribot's theory, in his *Heredity,* that women in old families display the strong type longer than men he said: "I haven't thought about that." Likewise on Leopardi's assertion that it was only the lack of an opportunity to act that caused a man to write what he would in a more favorable case do.

Shortly before the first conversation on Stein he brought over a letter from the deceased, in which their common friend in Rome, Fräulein von Meysenbug, is mentioned cordially. Stein wrote that he could understand that near her Nietzsche felt better even physically. He had been in Rome the winter before I had been introduced to the idealistic lady by Wagner, and later he had been tutor in Wahnfried and deeply devoted to Frau Cosima. Nietzsche was delighted by the tenderness with which he expressed his respect for the intelligent woman. If I combine with this the fact that Fräulein von Schirnhofer, after meeting Stein, though full of praise for him, said to me: "He would suit you better than me," and a few breaths later: "He is brusque," then I understood how much this man's *delicatezza* for Nietzsche was worth. The shock of his death was still felt.

It was Nietzsche's way to refresh himself with excellent people like Stein. But the warm spring of affection for all his friends, despite fallings out that took place, also bubbled forth afresh. Nietzsche knew how to "share joy" as few people do, and how to show it tactfully. Right after my arrival he had congratulated me on receiving my degree and expressed interest in reading the published dissertation, which, when it came out, seemed to please him, although the paper and type did not seem to meet his expectations in quality and clarity. As I learned the following summer through acquaintances, he also expectantly welcomed my plan, expressed in 1886, to write a history of my family.

With a meaningful smile Nietzsche communicated to me, in the course of those weeks, best wishes from his mother, who had a much higher opinion of me since I had the title of doctor. The son guessed very well that the excellent woman rated much more highly a respected public position and scholarly fame than his intellectual world, which was alien to her, and he felt painfully her lack of understanding for his personality, although he understood this lack and managed to shape their relationship in the most considerate fashion. He sought to make his mother's stance toward him easy and joyous by keeping from her his peculiar knowledge and conclusions, advising her not to read his books and initiating her in a friendly manner and in detail into his other experiences.

He rejoiced with his friends when they received the recognition of the world, which he personally renounced. For instance, when Dr. Deussen received the professorship in Kiel, thus becoming the first Schopenhauerian to be called to a professorship by the state. Nietzsche had been the one who introduced his childhood friend to Schopenhauer; and since then he had grown so far beyond his teacher! The professor from Kiel and his wife—he had recently married—came to Sils for a few days while on a trip to Greece. Nietzsche showed the liveliest interest in his Indian studies and spoke much in those days about the unique brotherly people on the Ganges. The story of how Buddha, to provide food for a hungry lion, changed himself into a rabbit; the fakir, sitting still and radiating benevolence, with his glass button; the theosophic movement's link to the Eastern religions—all this and much more was the topic of discussion in those days. And the transferral of these alien things into modern life was very fascinating.

How well aware he remained of what was of special interest to others, Nietzsche proved to me in one of his last letters from Turin, in which he reported in a postscript: "Have you heard that Madame Kowalewski in Stockholm (she is descended from the old Hungarian king, Matthias Corvinus) received from the Paris Academy the very highest prize in mathematics that it can award. She is now considered the only genius in mathematics." He often told me of women who had somehow distinguished themselves. One winter in Nice he had, for example, been the neighbor of a woman from Württemberg who had emigrated to America and had acquired a fortune by introducing a hair-treatment still unknown there.

The good Swabian woman from America also took us to a completely different theme. As a faithful child of her old fatherland she ranked Schiller above Goethe and based the priority on the casual cant of higher moral value. Nietzsche had to smile at the grotesque appearance of this prejudice in the present case, but otherwise he could not bear the juxtaposition of these two authors. Nor did he like to hear talk of Gottfried Keller and Konrad Ferdinand Meyer jointly, because he recognized far more content and originality in Keller than in the language-artist Meyer. The shallow way of thinking that sees no distances depressed him most when it practiced its leveling urge on literature.

I saw how much Nietzsche loved Goethe, when one day he found the *Goethe Yearbooks* lying in our apartment, took them home, and later brought them back with the words: "One always feels good in the company of this great man" (despite laundry-list additions, he believed). One of the *Yearbooks* was the 1885 issue, with the beautiful picture by Darbes and Victor Hehn's essay on Goethe's verse. In the case of Hehn we both learned that Dr. Förster had "discovered" him and called him to our attention. Nietzsche used every opportunity to do justice to his brother-in-law, precisely because he opposed him relentlessly on the issue of anti-Semitism. He recognized his noble nature and gallant qualities, which qualified him to be leader of a new people. He also esteemed Hehn's intelligent book on cultivated plants and domestic animals.

During his stay in Zurich, Nietzsche had also become personally acquainted with Gottfried Keller. Keller, he told me, had liked to be compared with Stifter. Last winter when I saw the passages about Nietzsche in the Keller-Kuh correspondence,[1] I asked myself how Keller might have later thought about Nietzsche. I am aware of nothing on that subject, but it can be presumed that Nietzsche was able to evaluate Keller more accurately than Keller Nietzsche, despite their striking agreement on one point.[2]

Nietzsche's preference for Adalbert Stifter is a clue to a peculiarity of his temperament. As a consequence of harnessing all his intellectual forces to trace the roots of morality to their ultimate

---

1. J. Baechtold, *Gottfried Kellers Leben*, III, pp. 121, 122.

2. Here I cannot refrain from pointing out the remarkable coincidence in the emphasis on race of Nietzsche, who had always been aristocratic, and of the archetypal democrat, Gottfried Keller. This view already begins to show itself in *Frau Regula Anrein*. In *Martin Salamander* it is so clearly present that no cry of rage from the Zurich democrats would have been needed to confirm that the master was right on target. An aristocratic tendency also is shown in Keller's tendency to have women be the respective carriers of his main idea. A foreigner could even draw the conclusion that woman is the more important factor of culture than man. Nietzsche did not overlook this trait.

Since publication of the last volume of the Keller bibliography we no longer need to first interpret his literary characters. We have direct documentation in the materials on *Martin Salamander*, e.g.:

> The principle of race. The goodness and badness, the nobility and baseness of persons is a question of the finer or cruder breeding. Excelsior (Martin Salamander) and his family have good breeding. The woman with the hat (the mama) and her twins have none . . .
>
> Pestalozzi. Folk-book. Vogt Hummel. What progress have we made after a hundred years? What has been achieved by the forty-year influence of the school, enlightenment, prosperity? Questions of education. How can people provide social and moral education if they are themselves uneducated? . . . (Natural) aristocracy of the educated. (*Leben* III, pp. 639, 643, 646).

depth and not to shy back from any conclusion, as a consequence of a gruesome internal tension and discoverer's unrest, which made all his feelings quiver painfully, Nietzsche at times needed to rest in a friendlier surrounding. He himself was delicate, easily offended, yet conciliatory and fearful of offending others; but his mission required hardness, forbade compromises, brought himself and others pain and bitterness. Then he read books like Stifter's *Indian Summer,* Dostoevsky's *The Insulted and the Injured.* For the moment, the long chapters of Stifter's novel, in which the wise autumnal mood of resignation extends through four volumes, had a soothing effect; but this did not preclude subsequent critique. *The Insulted and the Injured* is a whole scale deeper, more resigned, almost unbearable and humiliating for proud persons, because of the faceless despondency of the heroes. Nietzsche had read it, as he told me on an evening walk along Lake Silvaplana, with tears in his eyes. He—that is the salient point—had condemned a whole series of intense feelings not because he did *not* have them, but on the contrary because he *had* them and *knew* their danger.

Of course, we talked a great deal about books and writers. Nietzsche had a flair for books and read a lot despite his suffering eyes. When he was struck by a sentence's significance or beauty, he liked to repeat it to his friends. He once quoted from a French correspondence the phrase "avenues for the most roving fantasy." Like almost all good readers he marked certain passages in the text or in the margin. Thus a part of his intellectual life is preserved, as it were, in the books he owned.

The modern Scandinavians fascinated him with their literary achievement far less than the Russians and their detailed development of psychological analysis. But, for him, the first place was held by the French, both of the classical period and of the eighteenth and nineteenth centuries, especially the moralists, psychologists and novella-writers. At his suggestion I read Fromentin, Doudan, the Goncourts' descriptions of culture and mores, and I occupied myself even more with Stendhal, Mérimée, Taine, and Bourget. Modern authors who interested him were Vigny, de Lisle, and Sully Prudhomme.

Stendhal impressed Nietzsche certainly mainly because with an iron will he controlled a sensitive temperament capable of strong emotions. Nietzsche saw the real reason for the apparent foppery that on the Russian campaign on days of the most imminent danger Stendhal alone among the comrades trimmed his beard—that real reason being the attainment of self-mastery, and so he rightly admired it. Likewise, the introduction to his daily work, the reading of a page of the *Code Napoléon* for its clarity, sharpness, and brevity of expression. His book *On Love* best corresponded to love in Nietzsche's view, and probably served him as a kind of touchstone for men. He was very pleased to find it in the library of his friend R., since in general the books a person gathered around him served him as a guide to his soul.

Nietzsche repeatedly stressed how much more convincingly Stendhal solves the problem of beauty than Kant does by contrasting the "promise of happiness" with "disinterested pleasure." The analogy between Stendhal's posthumous valuation—predicted by him in 1880 with the words "I will be read"—and the absence of any echo for his own assertions did not escape him. Stendhal's sudden, lonely death in Civitavecchia left a painful ache in his soul.[3]

As an opponent and detester of the French Revolution and all the falsifications of concepts and of history that followed in its wake, Nietzsche greeted Taine's great work on that event with a light and joyous heart. He was most powerfully moved by the volume on Napoleon. He told me that he had written to Taine summing up the overall impression in the formula: Napoleon is the synthesis of superman and monster; but it seemed to him that the French historian had found the term too strong. Like Taine, Nietzsche saw Napoleon as the last great man whom history has presented, a wielder of power without a conscience, like the Italian *condottieri* of the fifteenth and sixteenth centuries intrinsically an immoralist. Nietzsche had a prenatal physio-psychological reason for his fascination with Napoleon. His grandmother, a woman of thoroughly Napoleonic sympathies, as was frequent in Saxony at the time, had been expecting the birth of a son, who later became Nietzsche's father, in the days of the battle of nations near Leipzig, in the immediate vicinity of the battlefield. Nietzsche was quite impressed by this connection with the hero.

This same grandmother, so he said, on the occasion of the *Goethe Yearbooks* and Froude's publications on Mrs. Carlyle, owned valuable letters from the Goethe circle. Her nickname "Muthchen" (for Erdmuthe) occurs in the correspondence of the time, and was the occasion for research. But an aunt of Nietzsche's had destroyed these

3. Why does Professor Ludwig Stein, then, speak so disparagingly of Stendhal, whom he moreover seems to know only by repute? When I recall his lecture on Keppler, I cannot understand this prudishness.

letters out of an exaggerated love of order; her brother believed it was done out of discretion and found the motive to be in accord with his own feelings. The brutal revelation of private relations, as in Froude, upset him deeply. He did not grant the public any right to them as a national property; indeed, rightly so, in my opinion. The ideological philistines quibble shamelessly and shortsightedly enough over the well-reflected statements of the few great men of a century; why allow them to take a look into the intimate sphere, which evokes misunderstandings from the very first?

Daudet's *Immortal* both delighted and repelled Nietzsche. It delighted him for relentlessly exposing the drive-wheels of the venerable French Academy although Daudet cannot completely hide his own ardent longing for one of the forty seats; it repelled him by the unloving, ungrateful satire on Corsica and its people. He read with satisfaction the answer which the islanders, who had been mocked for their poverty, gave to the man who had enjoyed their warm-hearted hospitality and eaten their despised chestnuts. 'Poor' as a synonym for 'contemptible,' this valuation was alien to Nietzsche and worthy of the rich mob. He intended to go to Corsica someday. The island which had given Europe a Napoleon proved that it contained innate reserves of strength and possibilities which poverty and moderation only promoted.

Nietzsche disliked Rénan: he called him a faun—we had been speaking of *The Abbess of Jouarre*—and he took him as little seriously among the French writers as he did Eduard von Hartmann among the German ones. Of Hartmann, he believed that he was mocking his readers. It was delightful to hear him retelling Ebers, who regaled his readers with the daughters of Leipzig professors in Egyptian dress.

On the whole, English and American writers left him cold. He denied them philosophical talent (nor do they have it in the German sense). Darwin's struggle for existence, Spencer's explanation of ethical and biological phenomena were not nearly enough to suit him. He envisaged Carlyle in the image of a stamping aurochs and cited him as an eloquent example of the importance of nutrition all the way up to the spiritual activities of man. For Carlyle's philosophy stood under the martyr-sign of a constant dyspepsia. On the other hand, he liked the sunny, delicate, yet manly Emerson. His judgments on this subject can be seen in *The Twilight of the Idols*.[4]

4. *Götzendämmerung*, pp. 126–127.

The presence in Sils of many people from Basel and association with those among them whom he knew took Nietzsche back vividly to the time of his professorship. He had, on the whole, gotten and kept a good impression of Basel, just as everywhere he preferred excessive constraints rather than a crude, formless existence. We repeatedly discussed the phenomenon that strict Christians and political conservatives are often more just to the outsider than so-called liberals of all types. Whether because the feeling of reverence is better developed in them, or whatever, the fact is that the more intelligent among them discover what is most worthy of respect in the opponent, while the "leveler" in religious and other matters transfers his lack of respect for everything and everyone, to a stronger degree, to the non-party-member and always attributes a divergent view to malice. The others have stronger convictions, and so they conclude: "Shouldn't we be able to win this noble person over?" and they hope for his conversion because they recognize his value. The worthy attitude of the Basel Orthodoxy toward Nietzsche was not denied even at the most difficult moment. Whereas radical newspaper writers in Switzerland claimed, after his illness had begun, to have prophesied it long before from his works, the high-church *Allgemeine Schweizer Zeitung* had only words of reverential sadness for his mental illness.

Unfortunately, there is no question that a number of persons had declared Nietzsche to be abnormal, years before the worst happened. Chamberlain writes[5] that his understanding had been deranged shortly after he wrote "Richard Wagner in Bayreuth" and one of his former acquaintances asked me at the beginning of 1888 whether I had not seen any signs of mental disturbance in him the summer before, and smiled superciliously when I said no.

Normal or abnormal, those are easy slogans, if one reflects that, as Nietzsche loved to emphasize, there are no normal persons at all. Even less than there are perfect lines, circles, ellipses! For the mob, every not completely ordinary person is crazy; Lombroso characterizes the genius as abnormal[6]—I can still recall the reference to Goethe's youthful memory, so vivid that it created the illusion of physical presence—though he cannot with any degree of accuracy designate the dividing line between the genial and the non-genial

5. *Richard Wagner* (1876), p. 14. Thus the works of Nietzsche which stem from his deepest characteristics appear in a dubious light, because published later!

6. This view was reflected earlier and better by the English expression: "There is a crack, but the crack lets in light."

person. As a lay person I do not venture a judgment on such a delicate question, but I unhesitatingly assert that whoever wants to declare Nietzsche mentally ill before the end of 1888 must draw the same conclusions as Lombroso and consider the outstanding minds of all times to be suspect.

In the summer of 1887 Nietzsche was at times very cheerful and disposed to harmless jokes. He enjoyed accompanying me and my girlfriend onto the lake, allowing himself to be initiated into the skills of rowing and enjoying the slight shimmer of danger which the journey took on. "You are a real adventuress," he called to me one morning when the sky was filled with storm clouds and he had not shown up at the agreed time, so that after having sent for him I was sitting waiting impatiently in the boat. And to my girlfriend who had told him that she had overcome her virtuous ladylike reservations to riding with us in the boat without doing her share with the assurance that she was useful to us as ballast, he promised as she was disembarking "to remember her as a welcome ballast."

In return for my invitation to the boatride to Pontresina, Nietzsche invited us one afternoon on an excursion to Fedoz. At one of the most beautiful places we sat for a long time on a flat boulder and let our looks and thoughts rove in the distance. He began to tell about his school years in Pforta. In Schulpforta, he said ambiguously, he had on the average been third in the class, according to the natural situation that in an institution operated according to the customary moral principles the most industrious student should rank first, the model of virtue second, and the "exceptional being" third. If he suffered under school discipline and from his fellow students that was because he was "such a peculiar human being," and he did not at all blame the institute for this. The mostly comical memories finally ended in a melancholy mood, which was expressed on the little footway down from Laret, as he recited softly to himself from the familiar song "Auf den Bergen die Burgen—Im Thale die Saale" the words "Verdorben, gestorben—-Ach alle zerstreut" (Ruined, dead—alas, all dispersed). His greatest art of living was the compulsion to be joyful; it kept him, "the man of deep sadness," alive, and it matured him for his task.

About at the halfway point of my stay I was called home by important events. Meanwhile my girlfriend fell sick. When on the morning of the third day I got out of the post-carriage in Silvaplana and began walking quickly to Sils, I heard someone running behind me and, turning, I recognized Nietzsche. He had obtained information about the time of my arrival and was considerate enough to come and meet me, although this delayed his mealtime.

I will never forget our parting in September. The last day before my departure was a Sunday. We were walking along on the shore of Lake Silvaplana, at the foot of Corvatsch. The air had that silvery autumnal tone which Nietzsche liked to call "otherworldly." The lake was slightly agitated and the little waves, in which the rosy evening clouds were painted, ran murmuring onto the sandy shore and back again. "As if they too wanted to shake your hand in farewell," said our companion in his melodious voice. Then, as we were walking home across a desolate stretch of field between the lake and the slope of Sils facing it, he remarked with a small sigh: "Now I am widowed and orphaned again."

My memory plays me the trick of preserving yet another circumstance from that time, which shows very clearly how alien Nietzsche was in the fall of 1887 to the official great intellectuals of Germany. Among a varied sequence of visitors whom I received after my return home was also a famous married couple. The man is an authority as a writer and a privy councillor, his wife, now deceased, was distinguished for the intellectual traditions in her family and for books of her own. As urbanites generally are, in a country castle surrounded by the aura of variegated romanticism, the two were curious. On a small table in my study lay Nietzsche's works in the new editions with the prefaces, which they occasionally looked at. "Who is that?" asked my literary colleague, and when my girlfriend and I informed him somewhat enthusiastically he said with an indulgent smile: "So, so, this is a little Nietzsche community!" "Remember?" (*50*, 40–59)

64   Meta von Salis-Marschlins   *August 1888*

From the end of January to the middle of May 1888 I stayed in Rome and on the Riviera. The following summer began desolate and rainy in Switzerland; one did not have to flee to the high mountains to get away from the heat. Nonetheless I thought of spending a few weeks in Sils-Maria and was strengthened in this resolve by a letter from Nietzsche, who had returned from Turin to the Engadine in June.

I had not written to Nietzsche any more since September of the previous year, always worried about pestering him with letters. Now something like a reproach about my silence sounded from his lines, and I decided to go to Sils anyway. It is now a solacing thought that no doubts held me back. One should not be stingy with one's personality and time in regard to an elite person, because each time you see one another again may be the last.

It was the end of July by the time I set out. The stormy weather had not changed for the better and it stayed the same both in Sils and down in the valley. I requested and got my former room in the house before the bridge. Unfortunately this time I did not escape a lively hubbub of visits—I allow myself this remark although the relationships in question were very pleasant. One day when Nietzsche, having missed me and moreover been sick, said, "I don't have any chance with you anymore," I detached myself more from acquaintances who lived elsewhere and cheered him up with the remark: "They ought to court me a little, that is very healthy for them," which I applied to the most obliging among them.

The musical talent of two guests of the Alpine Rose, a professional musician from northern Germany and a lady from Zurich who was a very capable amateur, offered a slight substitute for missing the sunshine and the frequent outdoor walks. Nietzsche, for instance, heard them in the morning in the conversation room; we others by special request after supper. Nietzsche often associated with the gentleman, acquainted him with his hymn to life and discussed Wagner and his influences. Herr von H. was not a follower of the Bayreuth master and once at table he expressed his astonishment at having learned that Nietzsche had "suffered over him." The good conversationalist had not the remotest idea of how much love had preceded this suffering.

The time of the publication of *The Wagner Case* led the author to deal more than ever with his relationship to the Bayreuth work and its creator. Whoever suspects Nietzsche of any ugly motive for turning against his formerly revered friend has utterly misunderstood him. In that case a poisonous word about the master would sooner or later have had to betray the rancor, the hurt vanity, or whatever, stored up in his soul; but these things were completely missing; and if he could not break free of the need to account for his change of heart it was his conscientiousness not to be silent after recognizing a danger that forced him to speak out by word and pen.

On a beautiful morning in August I rowed Nietzsche to the little island between Chastè and Isola, of which the entomologist Dr. J. had told him in the fall of 1886 that it was especially rich in insects. We compared it with a miniscule Capri and Anacapri. Once, later, we rowed under a dismal sky and rough sea around Chastè and toward the bridge of Baselgia. My companion told of Messina and a swim he had taken in the straits. If a dog had not swum around him like crazy he would infallibly have been swallowed up by a whirlpool under the surface of the water. "Others would have recognized the finger of God and a special calling in that incident," he concluded, laughing. He also spoke of the little fishes and the unusual life under the thick ice-crust of the lake.

Despite the disconsoling weather conditions, which depressed Nietzsche's state of health and his mood, we managed to go on an outing to Lake Cavloccio. We rode in a one-horse carriage to Maloja and went from there on foot. For the first—and last—time Nietzsche saw this water surface which in its darkness is the exception in this region. On the way he was enthusiastic and full of memories of his childhood days in Naumburg and of his mother. "She had very beautiful eyes," he remarked, and he was very grateful to the young widow, who had plenty of suitors, for not having given him a second father, who might have interfered with a rough hand in the education of the "strange child." Once there he remained sitting on the bench in the foreground of the lake in melancholy silence until I told him softly that it was time to go. The next day he walked, as so often, to Silvaplana to the post office, and he told me that he had given the mailman an enthusiastic description of the lake. He lived so little for his own pleasure that every interruption of his work-filled days became an event for him.

The next few weeks provided few opportunities for walks in the vicinity of Sils. By chance the three which Nietzsche took with me always had the sawmill as destination. On the second—it was in the hilly forest before the ravine, strongly aromatic with resin and herbs—we suddenly met all my closer acquaintances from the Alpine Rose, all young, cheerful girls who had slipped into bright dresses. The contrast between their carefree affability and the deeply significant subject which the thinker had just been discussing could not have been greater: Dostoevsky's idiot and the figure of Jesus according to the four Gospels!

Strangely enough, nothing ever took me back to that circle of thought—not even the *Antichrist*—as much as did Murillo's "Feeding of the Five Thousand" in the Caridad in Seville. The physiological type of Christ as portrayed by the strongly Catholic painter of the Counter-Reformation period coincides with Nietzsche's appearance!

My stay in Rome at the time of Kaiser Wilhelm's death, the moving interlude of the reign of his mortally ill son, and the succession, soon afterwards, of his youthful, strong grandson aroused expectations based on the character of this monarch. I repeated the superficial reports of some of our newspapers, tailored according to the republican stereotype. With a deprecatory gesture, Nietzsche, as it were, shoved these aside and emphasized conscientiousness as a trait probably perceivable in the ruler's profile till then. Nor did he fail to notice the Kaiser's relations with Frau Cosima Wagner. Nietzsche was favorably impressed by the strong personal streak in Wilhelm II.

A few of our last conversations have left painful impressions in me. It was not Nietzsche's way to want to arouse pity or to complain. Charmingly grateful as he was in accepting the daily little courtesies in human contact, he unmistakably rejected every intervention concerning his well-being. The previous summer he had occasionally said that he disliked to slice away at a ham and that he could not obtain any cold cuts in the village. A lady informed him of a shop in Basel, from which he ordered several small deliveries, which revealed a new defect in the form of a quantity of added fat. I succeeded in giving him the address of an institute for people with stomach ailments, where he could get it to the required quality. So far, so good. But those were unimportant matters; the only thing that would have really helped would have been the assumption of all concerns for his physical needs—if he were not thereby forced into a feeling of dependence on the person who assumed this responsibility. He preferred to suffer from his needs rather than from a caretaker. My own fanatical love for independence enabled me to understand him perfectly in this. I therefore never offered him anything that he had to refuse. But I felt sorry for him.

He laughed at the Italian boy who in Turin gradually spooned out his cocoa-boxes; he was amused by the scene when late one evening in Sils he put an empty sugarbag before the door of his room and the next morning his landlord checked it with his finger to taste what its content might have been in order to fill it before he got up and prepared his breakfast; he was ironical about the loss of a few laundry items, the ruin of others—but at times the little miseries did hurt him.

I was more deeply worried about his increasing lack of hope to publish his works other than as self-publications, which he had spoken of to me before our last parting. Worry that his capital could run out before the mission he had set for himself was fulfilled, had,

I fear, begun to cause even greater strictness and increased renunciation toward himself. "I have no fortune," he said, probably because he set his goals further than he could expect to pay for. At that time it became clear to me that the highest concept of friendship would lead one simply to ask the friend: "Can you help me?" because the friend would feel the distinction of such trust.

For his stay that winter, Nietzsche spoke of Turin, "the elegant city" with its wide streets, and of Corsica. One of the ladies in the Alpine Rose had fled to Ajaccio to escape the effects of a bronchial catarrh. He turned to her for information on accommodations for strangers in that place. For the coming spring I was planning a long visit to friends and relatives in Ireland and England. So we would not be seeing one another again soon.

On the last afternoon before my departure Nietzsche came over to chat for a longer time. A visit by a lady-acquaintance soon chased him away. So he came once more toward evening with better success.

I will not say that particular feelings moved me, because I am not certain whether such intimations are not added to memory after the fact. Each farewell to Nietzsche had made me sad. One thing I know for certain: after he had gone, I stepped to the window and watched him leaving in the twilight of the declining day. He walked with his head bowed slightly to the left, as was his way, across the bridge toward his "cave."(*50, 59–67*)

65   Elisabeth Förster-Nietzsche   *June 6 to September 20, 1888*

Among the narrators who, though well-intentioned, disseminate false information is my brother's landlord in Sils-Maria. I will give an example. My brother was accustomed to washing with cold water from head to toe, as soon as he got up in the morning. So he had a little tub of water brought to his room. Now in the summer of 1888 the weather in the Engadine was especially bad (incidentally all the landlord's stories refer to that year; he seems to have completely forgotten the six earlier summers with their very different conditions). From this bad weather my brother caught a strong influenza and was forced to give up his six- to eight-hour walks and to stay in the musty little room. As a result of the influenza and the lack of movement he was tortured by an "absurd insomnia," as he expressed it, so that sometimes he could no longer sleep at three o'clock in the morning, but got up and worked. In order not to bother the landlord so early in the morning, he had the little tub of water brought into the room the evening before. What does the landlord conclude from this fact? In good faith he tells that my brother, to keep awake and be able to work, put his feet in cold water at night! Perhaps a reminiscence of Schiller is at work here.

But the excellent man seems to misconstrue in the strangest way even comical episodes, such as the story of the frog which my brother had sought and found for an English woman-painter for a still life, but which to the general delight absolutely refused to be treated as a living model and leaped out of the still life. The landlord now tells this event, which he did not witness (all he did was provide a box for the frog) as his own experience. But in his memory it appears in a completely false context and the story now sounds as if Nietzsche had eagerly collected frogs to frighten timid ladies with and then to make fun of them. For one newspaper reporter this is not piquant enough so he changes the frogs into toads. That is how anecdotes originate and are presented as history. (*16,* 178–179)

66   Carl Albrecht Bernoulli   *June 6 to September 20, 1888*

This toad-story from Sils-Maria deserves to be examined more closely and more deeply for more than one reason. In her article "Nietzsche Legends," published in the journal *Zukunft,* dated January 28, 1905 (as a supplement to the final volume of the biography), Frau Förster takes the good landlord Durisch to task:

> But the excellent man seems to misconstrue in the strangest way even comical episodes, such as the story of the frog which my brother had sought and found for an English woman-painter for a still life, but which to the general delight absolutely refused to be treated as a living model and leaped out of the still life. The landlord now tells this event, which he did not witness (all he did was provide a box for the frog) as his own experience. But in his memory it appears in a completely false context and the story now sounds as if Nietzsche had eagerly collected frogs to frighten timid ladies with and then to make fun of them. For one newspaper reporter this is not piquant enough so he changes the frogs into toads. That is how anecdotes originate and are presented as history.

This verdict, presented allegedly as a contribution to the truth, all of a sudden gives an apparently insignificant note among Overbeck's posthumous papers the value of a document. For Nietzsche's mother, in the first period after the Turin catastrophe, expressed her eternal gratitude for Overbeck's services as a friend through numerous letters, but also by occasionally giving him articles she received (e.g. on the Förster colony, New Germany) or letters from friends. She then copied these out for Overbeck in her own hand. Now, among these original copies there is a long letter from Mrs. E. Fynn, the Irish woman who was Nietzsche's friend, to his mother, written in very good German and dated: Geneva, March 31, 1880; I have already made its content the basis of my text describing this Sils spa-acquaintanceship, and will here quote the decisive passage word for word:

> He also was very graciously interested in my daughter's paintings, and always said that she ought to paint something ugly in addition, in order to heighten even more the beauty of her flowers, and then one morning he also brought her as a model a live, hopping toad, which he himself had caught; and he greatly enjoyed his successful prank! In return we sent him after a few days an apparent preserve-jar, but as he was carefully opening it, grasshoppers sprang at him!

As can be seen, the description of the closest active participant coincides completely with the Durisch tradition formulated by Diederichs in his *Berliner Tageblatt* sketch of August 8, 1906. Without any justification Durisch's reliability as a witness is questioned and dismissed; and yet Frau Förster has at her disposal her mother's entire correspondence—and according to assurances of the Archives precisely the storehouse of letters is preserved, studied, and used most precisely and faithfully! including this written testimony which says in black and white that it was not at all a frog, but "a living hopping toad, which he himself had caught," and unmistakably in connection with the expressed intention of providing the painter a model for "something ugly." Perhaps just this insignificant little example is suited to open the eyes of many over-indulgent people as to which industrial district is responsible for manufacturing "Nietzsche legends"! (*8*, 469–470)

67　Wanda von Bartels　　　　　　　　　　*undated*

But I want to tell you of him as he was so that you will believe me when I scold you.

We were in Venice, my husband and I. And we were both young and full of enthusiasm. And we wanted to get to know the country we were staying in and its people. So we lived with the Italians in the places where we saw them praying, and where they sang and laughed, far from those places which foreigners know. And there was an *osteria* in a narrow alley (so narrow that the peddlers with a basket-yoke on their shoulders had to push through sideways). It was dark in there because of the houses which stood in the sun's way and cast a pleasant shadow all around; in the windows lay fishes and lobsters wrapped in thick cabbage leaves, and chickens, and narrow light-colored heads of Roman lettuce; and over everything hovered the aroma of boiled artichokes and white wine.

There we met Nietzsche and honored him. Ah, so differently than you do today. I see you setting his name on white pages in large letters which readily strike the eye and under it you set a little folly (for instance, about a dancing girl's leg), then you stick out your chest and believe that no matter how narrow your spirit, it is related with his, because you use his name as a shield.

But he kept silent the name he bore. He spread out the treasures of his mind and the gleaming sparks of his thoughts after he knew us, but we did not know his name, nor he ours, but he loved us both, and we loved him.

That was the beginning of our friendship, and we often laughed about it when we thought about it later. Every day we sat in the dining hall of the *osteria* (which actually was a little piece of roofed-over courtyard with a skylight) a man came to us and greeted us in Venetian dialect, also ordered his food in the same dialect, then was silent. He came when we came and left when we left, and heard us speaking but did not speak.

We believed him to be an Italian like everyone else around us, and so we exchanged our thoughts unrestrainedly about everything beautiful we saw and about everything great we discovered. And we laughed at the eccentric man at our table, who sought our company and yet did not speak with us, and who was strange-looking: in short white linen trousers and a black jacket, he had a thick mustache and sad brown eyes behind thick polished eyeglasses. But our laughter was not malicious, for we liked him and we missed him when he was late. We laughed most about his hair. He wore it over his forehead in a thick tuft and it had grown at a somewhat sharp angle over his brow; and in a strange mood he had shaved off its endmost corner. But the next day it had grown back with a bluish shimmer; the day after that it was shaved again.

We were so childish that we burst out laughing. And one day he joined in our laughter and talked to us in our language, and that was the beginning of our friendship.

And he told us all the lofty things which he has Zarathustra say to his disciples, and we could question him when the lightning bolts of his mind had blinded us. And he took care that we understood his opinion correctly.

We were with him daily and everything around us gave him an occasion to develop the bright blossoms of his thoughts. But although the days turned to weeks, we still did not know his name, nor he ours. We had not thought of asking him, nor had he; but we looked forward each day to one another's presence. That was enough for us.

But one day this changed.

A scholar in the arts (one of the clever ones who divide the laughing arts into schools and systems) had found the way into the sunny courtyard of the *osteria*, and he heard our talk as the sparks flew like from steel and flint. And he liked that, so it seemed; for he joined us and wanted to share in our thoughts.

But he was a man of order, and before he began he wanted to know who he was dealing with. And he gave my husband a card (with his name printed on it, and the government-certified degree of his wisdom), and an identical one to Friedrich Nietzsche.

And do you know how Nietzsche answered him?

"With me you'll have to be satisfied that I am a European like yourself."

That is what he said to him. And then he was silent and ill-tempered. And outside the door he asked for the first time where we lived, and then the next day he came to us in our modest little hotel room, and we three ate together what we had bought, and he gave us *Zarathustra* and we laughed together at the wisdom that wants to make systems out of the laughing arts.

And we first saw his name on the book.

Thus Nietzsche protected himself against the uninvited person who wanted to share his thoughts. He avoided him. And in order not to see this man who waited for us noon and evening in our *osteria*, what clever ruses Nietzsche, though otherwise so inexperienced in life, invented so that we three could sit alone and say whatever came to our mind!

Those were beautiful times and we used them and got to know his high thoughts. And when parting came, it was hard enough for him and us.

After a time he wrote to us that he had decided to settle in Munich, and we should look for an apartment for him, close to the English Garden, on a quiet sunny street. And we did so and found everything he wanted, and looked forward to seeing him.

And then he came to us quite unexpectedly and sat with us in my husband's large studio. And we had the window half-shut so that a semi-twilight kept out the blinding summer sun which hurt his poor eyes and he sat in an old-fashioned rocking chair and spoke to us, as in Venice. But a sadness and weariness lay over him as before the beginning of a great illness, and this mood also fascinated us and lay like a burden on our thoughts.

From Sils-Maria in the Engadine he then wrote us a long letter saying that he had given up the plan to live in Munich. And the ending of this last letter to us touched a note of bitterness against those who read into his works what he had not thought. (6)

68   Karl Strecker   *undated*

As editor of the correspondence between Friedrich Nietzsche and August Strindberg (Munich 1921, Verlag Georg Muller)—which, as is known, was written in Nietzsche's last healthy days and ended with his being declared insane—I went to Turin to study his conditions at the time when he had lived there during this correspondence and where his mental breakdown had taken place.

During these last days of his mental health, Nietzsche resembled a man who must suddenly begin a great journey and now hastens through the house hiding all valuables, locking old locks, taking care of old duties.

The unparalleled tempo of his production in the last ten years was increased in these few months to a breathless haste. Just the listing of his writings in this short time takes up about twenty-five lines of print. No wonder such tremendous exertions most dangerously undermined Nietzsche's physical and mental health, which became noticeable externally also in the strong overexertion of his head- and eye-nerves, in the aftermath of a very violent influenza, and finally led to an unbearable insomnia, which Nietzsche tried to fight with strong doses of chloral hydrate.

All the people who during my visit in Turin still remembered Nietzsche reported their impressions of a lonesome, introverted, deeply melancholic man. The cheerfulness displayed here and there in his letters of that time and his emphatic praise of the city speak for rather than against this fact. He was too proud to show his deep psychic pressure, and he did not want to cause grief to his loved ones. Moreover, doctors are familiar with temporary excitements of this kind in patients like Nietzsche; they are usually followed by an even greater depression.

Carlo Alberto Street, on which Nietzsche lived, extends from the Corso Vittorio Emanuele—near the railroad station—to the Piazza Carlo Alberto, it is long but not wide, and darkened by very tall identically shaped houses. In dismal weather, and Turin has 107 rainy days per year on the average, it is a melancholy, disconsolingly long ravine. However, the house Nr. 6, where Nietzsche lived on the fourth floor, is located on the corner of Carlo Alberto Square, of which Nietzsche's room had a view. But the road leading there was as monotonous as the inside of an automobile tire, and no one will claim that Nietzsche, so very sensitive to external impressions, and to whom the fresh breeze, brightness, and broad vistas were vital needs, did well to live here in his darkest hour.

His landlord at the time, the newspaper-seller Davide Fino, had moved away. I found him in the large building of the main post office where he had a shop right at the entrance, selling picture postcards, magazines, newspapers, stationery. The little, oldish man made a pleasant impression; one could read the honesty in his face. He was very glad when I told him I was following the trail of "Professor Dr. Nitzky." And although customers, whom he served by himself, were constantly coming and going, he found time enough to tell me what he knew. What I learned here was confirmed and completed in the German bookstore of Rosenberg and Sellier in the Via Maria Vittoria, where I found a German gentleman who had been clerk here already in Nietzsche's time, and now apparently was the business manager.

The core of these reports was each time: Nietzsche's lonely life, his sadness. Even in his last days he had often been in the bookshop, and since everyone had been very considerate toward him—something of this is reflected in Nietzsche's letters from Turin—he had often sat here for a long time, reading in the new books, but in his great thrift rarely buying anything. Always alone, he had walked about, wrapped in thought; every day one could see him buying fruits from the fruit-stand women. In his letter to Gast, dated December 16, 1888, he praises the "friendly highland woman," who "seeks out" for him "splendid grapes, they are all perfectly lovely people." In the evening, as Davide Fino tells, he often improvised on the piano for hours; and Fino's daughter, who was musical, claimed that it was mostly—Wagnerian music. A few days before his breakdown, he had in a nervous attack already caused a crowd to gather. A tired old cabbie-nag standing at its place in front of its carriage so aroused the great pity-destroyer's pity that he embraced it by the neck and wept violently . . . The misery of the creature, of which he speaks somewhere, had overpowered him . . . Was it not always so with Nietzsche that his philosophy stemmed from most violent struggles against what was most deeply rooted in his self?

We recognize his true mood at that time in the poem which originated then, "Amid Birds of Prey" *(Dionysos-Dithyramben 2),* whose ending reads as follows:

> They surely will "dissolve" you,
> They already hunger for your "dissolution,"
> They already flutter around you, their riddle,
> Around you, hanged man!
> Oh Zarathustra!
> Self-knower!
> Self-knower!

The complete breakdown then occurred around the turn of the year 1888–89, marking the start of the unilluminable mental night of this great thinker and poet, who had more reason to lose than others. For more than twelve years he then lived on physically in Weimar under the faithful care of his mother and especially of his brave sister, Frau Dr. Elisabeth Förster-Nietzsche, until on August 25, 1900, a gentle death released him. *(59)*

69   Viktor Helling   *undated*

"A noble mentality is shown in the will not to be favored at the expense of others," wrote Friedrich Nietzsche. In recent weeks one often had to think of this saying of the great hermit of Sils-Maria.

I sought out his residence in Turin, where for almost two years he had the deepest loneliness in the seclusion of a bachelor's quarters. To find his lodging is very time-consuming. No inscription betrays to the stranger in Turin the house where Nietzsche set up his quarters a generation ago. Even Baedeker, who has made so many travellers happy with his *From the Alps to Naples,* revised since the prewar period, knows nothing of Nietzsche. I did not shirk from the long way to the Corso Francia, where the German consulate has moved—which Baedeker also did not know—and I inquired. A young lady asked me the counter-question: "Who is Herr Nietzsche?" Finally an old lady from Southern Germany living in Turin directed me to a woman writer, down on the Via Balbo. Frau Dr. Barbare Allason said to me: "You can learn all you want about Nietzsche's apartment if you consult Signor Fino at the post office!"

So I went to Signor Fino, whom one cannot miss when one walks into the Posta Centrale on the Via Alisieri. For the way into the post office goes right past the Sala di Scrittura, Signor Fino's stationery store. Here picture postcards and stamps are sold, and one can write one's letters at clean tables.

Signor Fino hustles about with youthful agility in the middle of his stationery shop. Only when he takes off his cap do you notice that the years have robbed him of his curls. He is in his late sixties and was in his early thirties when he went every day in and out of the room which the philosopher Friedrich Nietzsche had rented from his parents on the Via Carlo Alberto.

"Did I know Herr Nietzsche?" says Signor Fino. "Oh, very well! I can still see him as if it were today. For Nietzsche was our guest. He played on our piano. It was a fine piano. I offered it to the Nietzsche Museum, the piano on which Nietzsche played every day. They declined." And Mr. Fino pulls out an old letter which he shows me. The Nietzsche Museum thanks Signor Fino, but it has no need for the piano on which the philosopher played. It has already purchased two pianos on which Nietzsche played somewhere. It cannot buy just pianos, Signor Fino must see that. So it was no deal with the sale of the piano. With a sigh Signor Fino puts away the letter of reply. He still does not understand how they could be so impious as to reject precisely the Turin piano. One had the best intentions. One wanted to help the people out with a piano.

But Herr Nietzsche had not foreseen this. He had always been satisfied with the piano—as with the whole apartment. He had been well taken care of among the Fino family. But only Signor Fino is still left of this family, and the large apartment on the Via Carlo Alberto has long since been given up. I have been in the shop-building that bears the number 6; it is the corner building on the piazza where stands the bronze equestrian statue of Carlo Alberto di Marochetti. A silk store is in it and a large shoe-shop, the Talzaturificio di Borese. Through eerily dark lobbies, which must be illuminated by electric lights even in the daytime, the way leads over 116 steep, cut-stone steps, to the fourth floor, where Nietzsche lived for two long years . . . he, who recommends the better housing for which socialism is fighting. Here was his modest dwelling, the dwelling among modest little people who could offer him room and board—and a piano.

But something delightful must be added: the wonderful view over the green chain of hills on the other side of the Po. For that might well have been the real point of attraction and the advantage of this apartment, which one could reach only after surmounting the pitch-dark staircase—that the gaze could roam to immeasurable space, far, far into the countryside, over to the shining Monte del Cappucini, which rises fifty meters over the river and today has an aerial tramway, and toward the proud white dome of the almost seven-hundred-meters tall Superga, the magnificent crypt-church of Victor Amadeus, the first king of Sardinia. (27)

AT THE JENA
SANATORIUM
(1889–1890)

*On January 3, 1889, Nietzsche suffered a final, complete breakdown on
the Piazza Carlo Alberto in Turin. Franz Overbeck, Nietzsche's friend,
perturbed by letters which he and other colleagues in Basel received during
the first week in January, traveled on January 7 to Turin and brought the
ill Nietzsche back to Basel two days later. Nietzsche was admitted to the
neurological clinic of the university at Basel, where he was diagnosed as
suffering from "paralysis progressive," i.e., the final stage of syphilis (also
called, in contemporary medical terminology, "dementia paralytica,"
"general paralysis of the insane," or "terminal lues"). On January 17 he
was taken by his mother (and two male nurses) to the psychiatric clinic at
the University of Jena, to be closer to his mother's home in Naumburg.
There he was again diagnosed as being in the terminal stages of syphilis.*

70   Anonymous   *January 1889ff.*

It was in the year 1888–89, when I was under treatment in the
nerve-clinic in Jena. What interested me most was a patient who was
always quiet and secluded and held in his hand printed notes on
which stood: "Professor Friedrich Nietzsche." He said this name
often every day. He had no keeper at his personal disposal. He was
in the general supervision hall; at night he was usually isolated. He
got up at six in the morning and washed in the general washroom.
Here he had to be watched so that he would not steal an institute
comb. He was most interested in an institutional hat, a so-called
"progress-hat," which he wore from morning to evening and which
no one could take away from him. If Professor Otto Binswanger
made his rounds and Herr Nietzsche was in a good mood then he
got up and took his hat off; if he was in a bad mood, then he
remained sitting. He was most annoyed when he was inspected after
a walk, since stones and all kinds of things were found in his coat-
pockets. He liked very much to bathe; when he was missed, one

221

needed only to look in the bathroom, where he could always be found, although we bathed twice a week. I had sketched him once when he was sitting quietly there. When he noticed this, he straightened his hat and made a friendly face. When I was finished, I gave him the picture. He stood up, shook my hand and said to himself, "Professor Nietzsche." The professor must also have been a lively dancer in his young years, for when Baron X. played on his zither, Herr Nietzsche could not get on his legs fast enough to begin a marathon dance until the head warden led him off to calm him down. (4)

71   S. Simchowitz   *1889–1890*

A quarter of a century has now passed since Nietzsche's death and more than a generation has gone by since an incurable disease excluded him, who thought of himself as the returning Dionysus, from the ranks of living and active men. His figure has meanwhile become mythical, was in part already so when his body remained on earth for almost a dozen years while darkness already held the godlike spirit prisoner. Having become mythical through necessity: for everything great in events and persons becomes *mythology* for posterity. But that does not exempt one from the duty to obtain clarity about how things and persons "really" were (to use one of Ranke's terms). That is not an easy task in Nietzsche's case. For besides a person's own testimonies, those of his contemporaries are also necessary, and the number of Nietzsche companions was few even from his youth on, and the older he became, the more he withdrew into his self-chosen solitude. Only a few, however, had an opportunity to see him after his mental breakdown. So a personal memory precisely of this time may have its modest value.

In the winter semester 1888–89 I was a medical student in Jena and attended the lecture and clinic of the famous psychiatrist Professor Otto Binswanger. One day—it must have been in January 1889—a patient who had recently been brought in was led into the classroom. Binswanger presented him to us as ... Professor Nietzsche! Now one thinks that this would have caused a mighty uproar! Not a trace. Although as early as 1888 Georg Brandes had given lectures on him in Copenhagen, the name Nietzsche was practically unknown in Germany, not only to us clinicians in Jena but also to quite different people. There is a classical witness to this fact:

Nietzsche is not to be found in the fourth edition of *Meyers grosses Konversationslexikon* from the year 1889. And how many small feathered creatures can be found there—and in the year 1889 Nietzsche's literary activity was finished forever. So Professor Binswanger should not be blamed if all he could tell us about Nietzsche's writing activity was that Nietzsche had formerly been active as a zealous Wagner-apostle but that he had in recent years become just as fanatical a Wagner-enemy, and that this change had perplexed his friends. I, for myself, when I heard the name Nietzsche, recalled having read it once in the writings of the outstanding Viennese music critic Eduard Hanslick, namely in an essay written in the year of the first Bayreuth *Nibelungen* festivals (1876), in which the Wagner literature of that time was examined critically. Two books which Nietzsche had in print at that time, belonging to this circle were: *The Birth of Tragedy from the Spirit of Music* and "Richard Wagner in Bayreuth." Hanslick dismissed them with a gesture of contempt and characterized the writer as a crazy philologist who really had no idea of music. At the time when he was brought into the Jena psychiatric clinic, Nietzsche was unknown to the German public, and it must well be the greatest irony of literary history that people were beginning to read his works precisely when he stopped writing: one or two years later Nietzsche was the great literary fashion.

But let us return to that Jena classroom. The man sitting before us did not at first sight have the external appearance of a sick man. He kept his figure, of middle height, in a stiff position; his face was haggard, but not exactly emaciated—his face, which a short time later the whole world knew from countless pictures: the magnificent forehead bordered by thick, plain, dark brown hair, the spirit-filled eyes under strong brows, the nose short as Bismarck's, and under it, also suggestive of Bismarck, the mustache that covered the beautifully matched lips, and to top the whole thing off, an unspeakably beautiful chin. The clothing simple, but clean and neat. However, the patient seemed to be having one of his good days: he was of clear consciousness and good memory-capacity. Professor Binswanger began a conversation with him about his former life. We learned to our astonishment that he had been a professor in Basel at just twenty-four years of age, even before receiving his doctorate, and that later persistent headaches had forced him to resign from his office. He did not say a word about his activities as a writer. Finally, as he reported, he had lived in Turin, and he began to praise this place, which had particularly suited him since it combined the advantages of the big city and the small town. This discussion made us all listen attentively, for we had never heard a man speak this way. And in Jena we were very spoiled on this point, for teaching there at the same time were people like Ernst Haeckel, Rudolf Eucken, Otto Liebmann, Wilhelm Preyer, all not only famous scientists but also brilliant speakers. But this Basel professor emeritus was quite something else! Later, when I read Nietzsche's works it became clear to me what had startled me. I had just felt the magic power of the Nietzsche style for the first time. For he spoke as he wrote: short sentences full of peculiar word combinations and elaborate antitheses: even the scattered French and Italian expressions which he so loved, especially in his last writings, were not missing. His way of speaking had nothing of the lecturing professor about it. It was "conversation," and by the soft tone of the pleasant voice one recognized the man of best education. Unfortunately he did not finish his discussion. His thread broke off in the middle of a sentence and he sank into silence. Professor Binswanger then wanted to demonstrate a few disturbances in the patient's gait. He asked Nietzsche to walk back and forth in the room. But the patient did this so slowly and lazily that one could not perceive the phenomenon in question. "Now, professor," Binswanger said to him, "an old soldier like you will surely be able to march correctly!" This memory of his military time seemed to have a stimulating effect on him. His eyes lit up, his form straightened up, and he began to pace the room with a firm stride.

I subsequently saw Nietzsche quite often during visits to the patients' wards which our teacher used to make with us. His health varied: sometimes one saw him quiet and friendly, sometimes he had his bad days. When I saw him for the last time, he presented a different picture than the first time: he was in a highly excited state, and his consciousness was apparently troubled. He sat there with a strongly reddened face and eyes that flared up wildly and painfully, guarded by a keeper. On the whole, however, institutional treatment had a favorable effect on him. He calmed down and could for a time be left in the care of his mother and sister, who took him to their home in Naumburg.

And Nietzsche's disease? Someone will ask what really was wrong with him? In Jena the diagnosis had been made: "Progressive paralysis on a syphilitic basis." For as Nietzsche himself very clearly indicated in Jena, he had during the 1870–71 campaign, which he took

part in as a medical corpsman, contracted syphilis, which soon afterwards, still during his days in Basel, had manifested itself in a syphilitic infection of the retina of his eyes; Professor Schiess, ophthalmologist in Basel at the time, had treated this disease. Nietzsche's
own data were that precise and exact. After the diagnosis made in
Jena no long duration of his life could be predicted for Nietzsche.
But he did live on for almost a dozen years in a tolerable physical
condition. Was he really syphilitic? I began to doubt it more and
more as time went on, but in the course of the years I was too far
removed from these fields of thought to venture a judgment, or
indeed even just an opinion. Soon after Nietzsche's death I had the
occasion to consult an important neurosurgeon, Dr. Erlenmeyer-
Benndorf. We soon got into a conversation about the great
deceased person: I told him of my experiences and also expressed
my doubts as to the diagnosis of paralysis. He agreed with me completely on this and came to the conclusion that Nietzsche's case must
have been not a progressive paralysis but a luetic infection of the
brain. The rest must be left to medical science.

A generation has now gone by since I had the privilege of seeing
Zarathustra face to face. But these images have remained fresh and
vivid in my memory: the image of the calm man sitting before us in
the gray classroom on that dismal January afternoon surrounded by
an almost Apollonian charm, and the image of the man in his room
cruelly tormented by disease, whom one could observe only with the
deepest pity. And although I have seen his suffering with my bodily
eyes and the analytical mind asks for reason and cause, in the mind's
eye, in inner contemplation he does again become mythical: the
incomparable face contorted with Laocoöntic pain, his gaze glowing
with affliction—yes, he himself is the god of life, so ardently honored, wound about by the serpent of the mortal disease: the sick
Dionysus. (56)

72   Paul Deussen   *April 1889*

Regrettable as it is that Nietzsche no longer could see the sun of his
fame rise, still it was a providential blessing that he had no clear
awareness of his condition. He no longer recognized the persons
around him, perhaps with the exception of those who stood the very
closest. I first saw him again in 1889, soon after he had fallen ill.
His mother "the little fool," as he used to call her affectionately,

who used to take him for a daily walk, had accompanied him to the railroad station to meet my wife and me. On the way home I took his arm in a friendly fashion and he did not resist, but he did not recognize me. I turned the conversation to Schopenhauer, and all he could say, as if he were speaking the most important truth, was: "Arthur Schopenhauer was born in Danzig." I told of Spain where I had travelled the year before with my wife. "Spain!" he cried and became lively. "Deussen was there too!"—"But I am Deussen," I answered. Then he stared at me and could not gather his thoughts. So he still had the concept of me, and mentally he recognized his friend, but the power to subsume this image under the proper concept was no longer present. His interests were again those of a child; he watched a drummer-boy for a long time, and the locomotives coming and going especially fascinated him. At home he mostly sat brooding quietly on a sunny veranda entwined with grapevines, at times holding conversations with himself, often about persons and events in Schulpforta, in a tangled confusion.

I last saw him on his fiftieth birthday, October 15, 1894. I showed up early in the morning since I had to leave soon. His mother led him in; I wished him happiness, told him that he was turning fifty that day, and handed him a bouquet. He understood nothing of all this. Only the flowers seemed for a moment to arouse his interest, then they too lay there ignored. Nietzsche's mother died in 1897, and his sister took over from her the care of the sick man as a precious inheritance. She moved with him to Weimar, where he continued to live till August 25, 1900, in the house of the Nietzsche Archives, surrounded by witnesses and documents of his budding fame, without himself having an inkling of it.

No one can say to what extent the seeds of insanity were already present as a disposition in this highly talented mind. But if Nietzsche had not diligently separated himself from human society, in which he occupied such an honorable position, if he had kept his position, established a family, and allowed the fruits of his mind to mature slowly, instead of pursuing his thoughts in solitude with ascetic over-exertion of his energies on tiring walks during the day and at night compelling elusive sleep by stronger and stronger narcotics—who knows whether he might not still be living with us in full health and be able to offer us, instead of the torso of his posthumous works, the perfected divine image of an eccentric but highly noteworthy worldview. (*10*, 96–98)

UNDER HIS MOTHER'S CARE
IN NAUMBURG
(1890–1897)

73   Franziska Nietzsche*   *February 1891*

Milan is in Northern Italy. It has the largest bookshop. It has a very beautiful cathedral. Fritz came from Lugano to Milan. La Scala is the main theatre in Milan. A hotel Zinkwe Emperio, 2½ francs per night. There is a very beautiful art gallery where a painter Perudjine especially excels in caricatures of Jews.

It has a very beautiful location. Every year it has a carnival time just like in Southern German cities. A lot of comfort is discarded, but even when one is wearing a top hat, for example, plaster is dumped down on him from the windows. [Good old] Turin.

The most famous speaker of Turin was Patre Agostino, whose oratorical talent was almost inexhaustible; he was the most popular speaker and criticized mainly Protestantism and the Annunciation to Mary.

Prof. Dr. Adolf Bastian lived till now in Siberia and is the best expert in ethnology. He stood in correspondence with Prof. Bachofen in Basel; as the former is for ethnology, so Bachofen is the greatest expert on matriarchy. Explanation of matriarchy described by an Englishman which sets special value on ancestral law.

With Herr Köselitz first in Vinzenza [. . .] him a very good [. . .] to you [. . .] There is a race track [. . .] where famous [. . .] are. In the vicinity of [. . .] is the famous [. . .] which is a bit too dusty [. . .] most beautiful pine forests.

Around Lake Garda are many nations hostile to one another

---

*For an analysis (in English) of the difficult and only marginally grammatical notes made by Nietzsche's mother of the conversations with her son during the course of his illness (selections 73, 74, 77), see Sander L. Gilman, "Friedrich Nietzsche's 'Niederschriften aus der spätesten Zeit' (1890–1897) and the Conversation Notebooks (1889–1895)," in Bernd Urban and Winfried Kudszus, eds., *Psychoanalytische und psychopathologische Literaturinterpretation* (Darmstadt: Wissenschaftliche Buchgesellschaft, 1981), pp. 321–346. This also details, with extensive contemporary documentation, the nature and course of Nietzsche's final illness.

Austrians and Italians and is surrounded with fortifications which one is however not allowed to enter.

Between Sils-Maria and the Maloja Hotel there is a post transportation. *(39)*

74   Franziska Nietzsche   *February 24, 1891*

How much the good Fritz spoke today 1891, February 24, for which I thank our good God.

I was reading to him, then Zola was mentioned and I asked him who that was? then he said: isn't his name Emile? he lived in Paris. I ask, he was probably a songwriter? No, a novelist. Where did he come from? From Northern Italy, he is from Bergamo.

This evening he was in a mood for talking as never before. I asked him what he remembered about his hometown Röcken he said: wasn't there a garden-house and many fruits and he named all, there were quince too, weren't there? Then we spoke about Mother Nietzsche and his aunts and he said Aunt Augusta was a good cook? then of the large parlor (in the house of the Otto's where they played, where he remembered the library at the end of the hallway and the "apartment" and whether there wasn't at that time a powder-explosion and all windows had been broken and had old Fr. Otto not stopped a man who had been driving straw through Priester Alley believing that he had injured the windows through the too widely loaded wagon. Wasn't there a fire once in the little Priester Alley? And he laughed very much after having seriously asserted, "Well little Lisa, your bathing boy, your darling, is saved I have him in my pants-pocket." *(41)*

75   Heinrich Lee   *1893*

"Frau Widow Pastor Nietzsche, Weingarten 18"—so I read the city directory in Naumburg. "Nietzsche? Oh, that is the crazy professor," said my innkeeper, "I saw him once on the street. He was going for a walk with his mother. A philologist pointed him out to me. Otherwise I would have known nothing of him. The people around here don't know him."

A little street on the market with small, low, plain houses. "The pastor's?" "Down there to the left, the house on the corner," said a little boy. A white-washed two-story building with a red-tiled roof.

Opposite it, closing off the street, an old vine-covered wall, partly crumbled down, the old city wall. To the right of the house, the yard, next to the windows on the second floor a wooden veranda, also covered with wild grapes and with flowers in front. From these windows, behind white curtains, suddenly a noise is heard . . . loud, violent words. The house door is closed, I pull the bronze bell-ringer . . . one, two, three. Finally an old woman looks down from above. After a while she, Nietzsche's mother, opens the door for me. "If you please," she says, leading me to a room on the ground floor, "I have to go see to my son again, he is so restless today." Then we sit facing each other and she narrates . . . mildly, amiably, plainly and modestly, full of motherly love and motherly pain, but solid, only sometimes with a moist shining in her eyes.

"There is no more hope. If only he at least stays alive. He has not taken a drop of medicine for four years, and that does him good. But I make him stick to a diet. Early in the morning, milk with honey, he likes to eat that; for the second breakfast blueberries for digestion. At noon a soup and meat, afternoons a large glass of lemonade, and evenings sour milk. The doctor sometimes still comes, but he prescribes nothing. He has no attendants. My servant-girl Alwine, faithful soul, does what is necessary, she has been with me for fifteen years, she does what she can for my son. She also always consoles me. Last night he was so loud and I became very afraid. 'Ah, Frau Pastor,' she said, 'that is not so bad, I can stay up with him tonight.'—I hope to God it will pass. I didn't leave him in the clinic in Jena. I visited him there at that time and experimentally took him for a walk. We stayed together for nine hours the first day, he went with us to eat in the hotel, and the others did not notice anything wrong. 'Keep him for good if you want to risk it,' said the professor peevishly. Well, I took him with me.

"The house was rented for a time, but now we are staying in it for good. It lies off the beaten track, and the air is good; unfortunately he sees nothing of the green outdoors, he's too shortsighted for that. A noblewoman wrote to me from Constance, offering me a place to stay in her villa on Lake Constance; I don't know her, she wrote only that she was a devoted admirer of my son. Such love does one good, but I declined. Formerly, I took many walks with him in the vicinity and also in the city, mornings and afternoons always for three or four hours. But gradually his legs became heavy. I then rented a carriage. Now he doesn't like to come down the stairs; I always tell him a poem aloud as we come down; he listens to it and does not notice the stairs. Of course, he doesn't understand it. I had the veranda added so that he could always enjoy the fresh air. He's out there a lot; in the evenings he falls asleep there until toward eleven o'clock I bring him to bed. His consciousness is almost completely extinguished. He still knows me and Alwine, otherwise no one, I admit no one to see him, no one should see him. Now he constantly speaks of Hannibal and Moltke and the former Prussian generals—and all of a sudden also of Schopenhauer. He never speaks of his own books. 'My mother,' he said to me, 'I am not stupid.' 'No, my dear son,' I say to him,'you are not stupid, your books are now world-shaking.' 'No, my mother, I am stupid.' Alwine tells me that when he is without me he mumbles continuously, 'My mother, my mother!' Even as I am leading him to the veranda, he says: 'Where is the veranda?' I have to lead him because of his shortsightedness.

"When he is awake, he generally sits quietly by himself on the chair, then I read something aloud to him, and meanwhile he falls asleep. Any occupations, God knows, are over for him; we have to help him even with dressing and undressing. Last night we dressed him up already at one thirty, because he was loud; then in the morning we put him back to bed. I sleep in the room next to his and with open doors so that I can be right at hand. A Swedish writer, called Ola Hanson, has written that his sickness was hereditary. It is not true, and in response to my objection he revoked his statement. His book also contains other errors, which have to hurt me. I can imagine the source from which he got it. There are some people who find pleasure in such things. However, my dear husband did die of a softening of the brain. But the cause was that he fell down a stone stairway onto his head, long after my son was already born. Today everything is supposed to be heredity. He worked too hard. That is how he was even as a child. When he came home on vacations from Schulpforta, he read all day long. 'My dear son,' I said to him, 'the holidays are there for you to rest.' Then he said: 'My dear mother, people rest and enjoy themselves, each one in his own way, so I in mine.' And later. He gave six long lectures per week, always from memory; he could not read from manuscript; his eyes were not good enough for that. The six lectures are as long as twelve sermons, I believe. He only laughed at that and said I was the typical pastor's wife, I always came back with sermons. So he fell into insomnia, and started taking medicines. He used all the sleeping medications that have ever been invented, said the professors. His worst one was chloral. That one practically killed him.

"Already in Rome he said to my daughter: 'You know, for some time now things seem to me completely different than they really are. I also believe I know the answer. I will tell you, I need chloral.'—'My dear, dear Fritz,' said my daughter, 'ah, don't do that, I beg you.' It was no use. Otherwise he was so moderate. He lived like a saint. In everything. And he was good. In Basel the family where he lived told me: 'No, such a good man as your son can't be found anymore.' I remember a story from Basel myself. There he made the acquaintanceship of a future missionary who still had one examination to pass. He had to learn Hebrew for it, but he was too poor to hire a teacher. My son taught him for free. In summer there was terrible heat, often 40° centigrade. 'My dear son,' I said to him when it was so hot, 'don't teach today.' 'My mother,' he answered, 'I've promised.' He gave what he could. Everyone flocked to him. He got that from my dear husband. He was that way too. When he left the parish, the parishioners said to me: 'Ah, Frau Pastor, we don't care who comes now, we'll never get another one like your husband.' 'My mother,' my dear son sometimes said, 'How do the poor people really live? Tell me that! That is how I want to live.'— 'My dear son,' I replied, 'that is no life for you, they drink a lot of coffee.' For he did not like coffee.

"I would never have believed that he would become anything else but a theologian. Recently I spoke with a furniture-dealer who had him as a teacher in the public school—his guardian said that he had learned the most and the things most useful in his life at the public school. The furniture-dealer now told how Fritz had once read aloud the poem, 'Whoever lets the dear God rule,' with such expression that he still thought of it today. A barber then told me the same thing. It's a joy to me that all his acquaintances are still fond of him today. Recently, the preacher from the cathedral came to see me. No one folded his hands like Fritz, he said, so sincerely and piously and devoutly. All our friends called him: the little pastor.

"Later when a new book of his came out, he said to me: 'My mother, don't read it, that can't give you any joy.' And he also told his little jokes to me. With a smile he said a little poem that began: 'The pastor widow looks at me . . . ' He was then still joyful and happy. He got along very well with his sister. That is an intelligent woman. She is married to Bernhard Förster, founder of New Germany, if you know the name. She is coming back to me. 'Dear mother,' she writes to me, 'I can no longer live abroad. I must return to my homeland.' Then she will see him again. He has hardly changed. His best picture is in the new edition of *Zarathustra.* I always kiss his splendid forehead in the picture. If only he remains alive, at least his flesh and blood. It is perhaps presumptuous on my part, but I think he is best taken care of by me, his mother. I hope to God. I am sixty-eight, and he was a good son to me . . . "

Once again the path leads me past the house. On the veranda sits a man stooped, his head bent, probably dozing. Pale, with unparted hair, the forehead of Socrates, glasses on the sharply pro-truding nose, a mighty, shaggy mustache, the chin, as far as I can see, sharp and massive, the cheeks sunken in, with engraved fea-tures. Peace is on his face. He is asleep. A wagon rolls by. May it not awaken him. (*33*)

76   Sophus   *1894*

The little two-story house Nr. 18 with the vineyard in Naumburg on the Saale, owned by the widowed Frau Pastor Nietzsche, is where the philosopher lives together with his mother and sister. It is painted a light color and provided with white shutters on the first floor. The main front of the house, with six windows, faces the vine-yard; another side with five windows in a row faces the wall of St. Jacob's Church. Often one sees German and foreign admirers of Nietzsche standing in front of this house and looking up at the upstairs windows, but the gate remains closed, for his mother, who together with her daughter is nursing the unfortunate man with unspeakable tenderness, admits only the most necessary persons to him.

In 1892 Nietzsche's condition was still such that his mother could take him out walking. If an acquaintance met the two on such a walk and addressed the mother, then the patient usually stopped, took off his hat only when his mother told him to, and looked uncomprehendingly at the stranger. He answered questions only with a stupid smile. Now these walks have long since stopped, since the patient's sudden states of excitement began to arouse attention that pained and saddened his mother, who accompanied him. The former regular visit to a swimming pool also had to be given up for the same reason.

Thus the man whose mind had encompassed the whole world is restricted physically to two rooms on the second floor of this little house. In one of them Nietzsche sleeps, if restless turning-about in bed can be called that. Of course, the patient is not very refreshed by morning and so he lies in bed for a good part of the morning and until noon. His faithful mother helps him get up; then he goes to the other room and stays there until evening if the weather is not suitable for a short stay on the wooden balcony attached in front of the room. The balcony is overgrown with green foliage and allows one to look outward from it, but not inward from the outside. Both the room and the balcony overlook the low city wall and the city moat toward the park that extends around the inner city. But the sick philosopher can no longer appreciate the beauty of this place, which his mother has arranged for him. He is unreceptive to his surroundings. When he is not brooding dully to himself, he plays with dolls and other toys. When states of excitement come over him, his mother best knows how to calm him down. She caresses him, speaks to him in a friendly tone, and when he wants to scream she fills his mouth with small slices of apple or easily digestible delicacies, which he then chews and swallows while growling dully to himself. Under this treatment he gradually calms down. Similarly his meals must be brought to him. Apple wine is the usual beverage. There are also times when he repeats the same sentence over and over again almost for hours without interruption. His memory has remained undestroyed for individual poems learned in childhood, and the mother also uses this circumstance to subdue the patient. The sight of strangers always arouses his displeasure, and yet some company cannot be avoided completely. His large full beard grows out strongly and shaggily and needs a barber. When he enters, the mother usually says "This is Herr Robert . . . " and the patient adds: " . . . Hartung." But he immediately continues: "But I don't like you, Herr Robert Hartung, I don't like barbers, I don't like them," and now he tries to get away from the barber. Once he is with great effort compelled to remain sitting, his mother must always speak assuringly to him and fill his mouth so that the job can be done. Something similar happens with the masseur, whose activity is essential as a substitute for the lacking physical movement. The mother generally keeps the patient quiet during the massage by reciting to him a poem which he knows quite well and whose rhyme-word he always adds. For example, Chamisso's "Gigantic Toy":

Mother: Castle Riedeck is in Elsass well . . .
Nietzsche: . . . known,
Mother: The hill where once the giant's castle . . .
Nietzsche: . . . stood

and so on until the end.

The patient is not receiving any medical treatment in the strict sense. His mother has had every conceivable cure be tried, but without success. About a year ago the nature-cure specialist and inventor of the massage-sitting-baths, Kuhne from Leipzig, had his technique tried on Nietzsche, but the procedures carried out by his assistants increased his states of excitement, and the treatment was given up. The mother's greatest fear is that the patient's excitement could take a form that would necessitate his being committed to an institution. Now only one friend of the family and follower of Nietzsche's teaching, the Naumburg physician Dr. Gutjahr, comes to the house now and then to see the patient. Since a cure is out of the question, it is only a matter of following the prescribed diet, and the mother is fearfully concerned that the patient always receive the strongest and most nourishing foods that are appropriate for his condition, in the best preparation. She does not have any material worries about this because the University of Basel, when he was pensioned, allowed him the enjoyment of his full salary, in recognition of his merits.

Thus Nietzsche stays physically at about the same level, despite all the fluctuations of his condition, indeed he is probably gaining weight, but it cannot be ignored that his condition is generally worsening. The portrait of the philosopher presented a few months ago in the *Illustrierte Zeitung* is too favorable, for especially the expression and look of the eyes is much wilder, duller, and more stupid than they appear in the picture.

And while the unfortunate man, thus mentally dead, vegetates, several scholars hired by the publisher are busily at work examining his manuscript-legacy under his sister's direction and preparing for publication whatever is sufficiently finished and processed. The guardianship, which is in the hands of a relative of his mother's, is said recently to have withdrawn its initial ban on the publication of some items. (57)

77   Franziska Nietzsche   *January 1895 to July 1896*

Sayings of my good sick son in January 1895:

> I have translated much, I am accustomed. I lived in a good place in Naumburg and in a completely different place not Naumburg. I went up to the attic and awakened my sister. I lived in Naumburg a lot, because I was good. I swam in the Saale like a whale I was

very fine and I played vocally in the cathedral. I was very fine because I live in a house. I write letters everyday to very good people and to His Majesty. I was very fine and give a housekey to my mother every day.

On another day:

But I was excellent my mother was very fine because she loves me very much, *pour le mérite*. I drank Hungarian wine. Counted a thousand people. Drew [animals]. Liked whales. No one left over. Alumni good people. Liked adjuncts very much. I was very fine to draw a thousand people. Opium, Alwine from Droyzen.

On another day, February 13, 1895:

I loved him [when we were speaking of Dr. Gutjahr, who was his doctor] very much. Health. I am no longer a child. I loved someone very much, myself. I have lived in many places in the world. [. . .] where. I did not love Friedrich Nietzsche at all. I lived in many good places. I liked very much to be in one place, née Oehler. I read very much. I liked to live in a house it was really a good house. I liked to go out of house. I didn't love anyone not even one person.

On October 13 he spoke.
To the question do you want the meal he said:

Do I have a mouth for it Should I eat that? my mouth I say, I want to eat, What is that? Nice milk I always liked. What do we want to eat now. Precisely the thing. Will that taste good? That is tasty. What else do we want to eat? Nice things. Who will eat this? eat it yourself. What does Frau Pastor have? beautiful eyes. What is that here? a spoon. What is his designation? Friedrich Nietzsche.

What is that here? an ear
What is that here? a nose
What is that here? hands I do not love
He also said the stanzas from the poem "Billeting." With a note in his hand. Went in to him in his room.
On 22 December 1895 he spoke much.
"I am proper because I am fine. To the son [. . .] I gave two reichstaler." To Alwine's question he said "Franziska Oehler" and when I pointed to Alwine and asked him who that is he said "Alwine from Droyzen lives in the kitchen where the clock stands."
What do we light on Christmas? "A Christmas tree, I don't want to light the Christmas tree. I have dreamed of all the good people

who live in the house." What do we want to give our professor? "We want to give nothing at all." What do we want to drink now? Nice milk, good milk?

On April 21 he spoke: "Food, for example good milk" " I love my mother very much, elegant very loved." "I don't like Napoleon Bonaparte" When I had gone to the veranda and taken a little walk there he had apparently missed me and said to Alwine "Where does my mother actually live." Meanwhile he spoke all possible words "Philax" "Mademoiselle" "spoon" "dreamed nothing" To the question what is your sister's name "Lisbeth Lama" " To the house a key." To the question where we were going now "to bed" Whom did you love "mother" "Susanne Wenkel" "I believe there is no music" "I never loved the bath-master." "I have every day where the clock stands" "The mother elegant I love very much" "Good eyes." "What should I underestimate."

On July 22, 1896 he said

"I am quite elegant in that I love good people"

"I loved people very much Bismarck"

"I loved my mother very much because she is good"

"I wrote letters every day to all good people"

"I am elegant because I am fine in that"

"I was very excellent because I was elegant"

"I love mother very much because I love mother very much"

"I loved my sister very much"

"I underestimated many things very much"

"Franziska Fränzchen née Oehler"

When I then asked him when my birthday is

"February 2?"

When I then asked your birthday

"October 15?"

"I was dreaming"

When something seems to him especially beautiful, probably, he calls it "a good book." (*40*)

ON DISPLAY
IN WEIMAR
(1897–1900)

As already mentioned, I came to Weimar for a visit in the fall of 1897. It was my first meeting with Nietzsche's sister, who tried to make my stay in Nietzsche's house as pleasant as possible in every way by her cordial, amiable manner. Located on a hill above the city in elegant seclusion and presenting an open view in all directions, this villa stands in a suitable location for the purpose it is supposed to serve. I saw Nietzsche for the last time in this house, which was prepared for him and his works. His own rooms were located on the top story, separated from the others and from the Archives. There, most cleverly, all conceivable arrangements were made for his physical well-being; there he was nursed unselfishly for years by faithful sisterly love.

It was natural for Elisabeth Förster-Nietzsche to suggest to me that I should visit her brother, although I had not myself expressed this desire since I feared that the friendly memory-image from the time of our earlier meetings could be blurred by the impression of an external appearance altered by disease. But this fear did not materialize, for the image that presented itself when I entered the sick man's day room was apparently an idyll. In a bright room the brother-and-sister pair sat in comfortable calm at a corner of the table. Nietzsche, much heavier than formerly, had the typical appearance of an older, quietly satisfied man, fixed in a state of rest. I stood at the door while Frau Elisabeth, nodding to her brother, said: "Look, Fritz, the person coming in the door is Resa Schirnhofer." But the peacefully sitting heavy figure did not raise his somewhat bowed head, did not look over, and gave no sign that Nietzsche had even heard his sister's remark. Immobile, apathetic, sealed off in a world of his own, he sat there like a robot where someone else's will had set him. I do not remember saying a word of greeting and overcoming the anxious stiffness that seized me at

237

the sight of this personality whom I had once known and who was now so unknown and silent. I only know that his sister said he was not having a good day that day. So I left sadly, pondering what thoughts and feelings might still be alive behind that impenetrable external mask in this form of life which bore the seal of human help-lessness and in which every spark of mental life seemed extinguished.

Frau Elisabeth wanted to hear some things about my meetings and conversations with Nietzsche and asked me, among other things, whether he had discussed with me Stirner and his book *The Individual and His Property.* After a little reflection, I answered that I did not remember him ever having mentioned this name. She seemed very satisfied with this answer and, reformulating the ques-tion, she insisted: whether I could state with certainty from memory that he had *not* named him. I felt like a criminal under interrogation by a prosecuting attorney and said I could only state that this name occurred neither in my notebook, nor in my memory as having been named by Nietzsche. She, however, came back to this question sev-eral times and always received the same answer. But this did not answer the key question as to whether Nietzsche knew Stirner, because not mentioning him to me is not the same thing as his not knowing him. But that Frau Elisabeth asked me this question is very explainable, since R. Schellwien and Henri Lichtenberger had, in their studies on Max Stirner, drawn a few parallels with Nietzsche's theories.

Henri Lichtenberger—if I am not mistaken—visited the Nietzsche Archives shortly before I did and the question of whether Nietzsche had known Stirner's book must have been discussed intensely. Lichtenberger's book on Nietzsche, which appeared soon afterwards, states about this:

> It is certain that despite his claims to complete originality he sub-mitted, consciously or not, to the influence of his contemporaries, and that his thinking, once stripped of its paradoxical and aggres-sive style, is often much less new than it seems on first encounter. Uncompromising individualism, the cult of the self, hostility to the state, protest against the dogma of equality and against the cult of humanity are found stamped almost as strongly as in Nietzsche, in an author who is quite forgotten, Max Stirner, whose main work *The Individual and His Property* (1845) is, from this point of view, very interesting to compare with Nietzsche's writings.

Frau Förster-Nietzsche had then told me much about Paraguay, about her life there, about a few German elements which had not proven good and had harmed the colony, about her husband's death under heart-rending circumstances, about the burden of her position, etc. To me, a foreign woman completely aloof from this enterprise, her descriptions of conditions in "New Germany" seemed like accurate pictures of the difficulties of such a foundation. I urged her to record in writing the important, partly dramatic episode of her life; she, however, said that she had no time now, since her first duty was to devote herself exclusively to her brother, to preserving his work and portraying his life. I don't know whether she did it later.

Both on my first and on my later visit she spoke a great deal about the great amount of work required for sifting and arranging the existing, confused manuscript material, about the activity of co-workers in the Archives, etc. She also talked about the disappearance of various documents out of the Archives and about breaches of confidence. I cannot remember any more specific data precisely, but I was left with the general impression that special interests were at work in a disloyal manner.

She told me several times that her brother had stressed in conversations and letters what a beneficial effect my fresh and cheerful laughter had had on him. I was glad to hear that. Perhaps it had during our meetings alleviated the pressure of fate somewhat for the "profound affirmer of life" in hours of dismal premonition.

My last visit to Weimar took place in October 1900, again on the occasion of a journey from North to South through Germany. I did not live at Frau Förster-Nietzsche's house but spent a great deal of time with her and in the Archives, whose arrangement had been changed considerably and improved. Frau Elisabeth was consistently amiable and on October 15th, the first birthday anniversary of her brother, who had passed away in August, she invited me cordially to drive with her to Röcken. It was a dark, cold, rainy day; I had a cold, and the short carriage-ride from the railroad station to Röcken seemed endless. I was glad when finally we could leave the carriage and I was able to warm my shivering limbs through movement. A moist gray veil of fog hangs over the flat landscape far and wide, harmonizing with our mood and accompanying my thoughts.

The rectory where Nietzsche's cradle had stood and the cemetery where his grave is located are not far apart. Places of birth and death—beginning and end—spatially near; and temporally interposed, a human life animated by the creative urge of a highly talented mind driven by the demon of a will whose power and work Nietzsche himself expressed under the striking image of a wave. This prose-poem of fascinating beauty is a meaningful picture of the action of will and wave. Toward the end it says:

"So live the waves—so live we who will! I say no more!—For you and I, we are of the same race!—You and I, we have a secret!"

The elementary natural process of the ocean wave greedily licking at the edge of the solid land becomes the symbol of the conscious activity of the conscious Nietzsche: the "secret" is easy to guess.

Frau Elisabeth led me through the little modest rooms of her former parental home, where brother and sister had spent the first part of their childhood. We stayed in there for quite a while and, returning to past times, my companion recalled lively memories of long-forgotten things. She seemed to be having a hard time parting with the past.

Nietzsche rests in the grave by the wall of the church where his father had preached the gospel, Nietzsche, a descendant of preachers, who fought against their faith—*cum ira et odio*—with the malignantly intensified passion of intellectual hatred. At this grave I became fully conscious of the entire tragedy of this life in its externally unstable change and end, and in its severe internal conflicts.

The aphorism "On the last hour" reads: "Storms are my danger: Will I have any storm by which I perish as Oliver Cromwell perished? Or will I go out like a light that got sick and tired of itself—a burned out light? Or finally will I blow myself out in order not to burn out?"

He lived in storms and died weary, and slowly extinguishing—a light that burned out. (52, 448–451)

79 Gabriele Reuter

"The bust of Nietzsche is now going to Vienna to the *Secession,*" the sculptor Kruse recently said. "I am curious as to what the Viennese will say about that," I thought to myself. So much is now being written about "the Viennese" and "the North German," and that the two simply cannot understand one another, so very possibly this work, in which Nietzsche appeared to be of so sour, brooding and solemn a North-German nature and is portrayed by such a nature, must have seemed very strange to the Viennese. But perhaps they are delighted precisely by the alien and the strange: to find a man of our time portrayed as a seer of mighty eternal thoughts . . . The view of the artist who sees the quintessence of Nietzsche's being as embodied in *Zarathustra* and recognizes the immoralist and Anti-Christ as the priest of new strong religious feelings, whose eyes look out of deep caves under the roof of mightily protruding brows with a spectral gaze into the depths of things—down into regions where torment and pleasure are still one—who loves the hard and relentless truth-seeker as a pain-contorted idealist whose thought-furrowed forehead, crowned by flamboyant hair, rises like a cliff.

It is now three years ago since I met Max Kruse in Munich in the house of Ernst von Wolzogen. I was walking in cool, early fall twilight past his garden fence, was invited in by a friendly call, and there followed one of those evenings that are governed by a happy chance that brings together strange contrasts and gives us impressions and incentives to some thoughts that have long-lasting effects. Besides the great, broad-shouldered, red-bearded, somewhat awkward Kruse, also there was a fine delicate Austrian, Franz Adamus, the author of the often banned *Wawroch Family,* then in the happiest time of a young writer who has just finished his book and sees thousands of hopes blossoming forth out of it, which no hoarfrost has yet wilted, no merciless criticism smashed to pieces. He said amiable, tender things, and it seemed strange to me Wolzogen, who with his varied intellectual experience feels at home everywhere, when and was the connecting link between two such different types of men, revealed to us that Adamus had written a bloody, realistic tragedy. I would have tended more to read from Kruse's face the sense for the relentless and hidden tragedies of life. He came from Weimar, had sculpted the sick philosopher there. Had sat there for weeks, the wet clay between his fingers, alone and silent, sunken in dreams of life opposite the silent man, heart-sunken into a dream of death.

I saw all that before me, saw how the solemn silence was interrupted now and then and the patient's sister fluttered in with her
youthful mobility, her excess of feeling and enthusiasm, always busy
with a thousand matters, very worldly and very sublime, with mixed
feelings, her eyes overflowing with tears, and yet again a little communicative smile around her mouth, a golden fishing rod in her
hand—ah, no, it was Zarathustra who saw the fishing rod in the
hand of life before evening fell over him.

And while his sister, in loving industriousness and intelligence,
saw to the spread of his fame on earth, Zarathustra sat in his chair
or lay on his bed, silent and indifferent, hour by hour, week by week,
year by year—his beautiful, slender, white hands crossed over his
chest, occasionally muttering indistinct sounds under his mustache,
which grew to fabulous size.

I had the privilege of seeing him once, for just a few minutes!
And when I entered and stood facing him, deeply moved by the
greatness of the fallen giant, a look fell on me from the deep eye-
caverns—this look lasted hardly a second, as it took in the alien phenomenon, then the pupils slid wearily under the eyelids, only a strip
of white remaining visible—the spark had gone out again . . . But
the power and the horrible mystery of this look from the deep eye-
caverns had taken my breath away.

When I later saw Max Kruse's bust of Nietzsche, I was shaken
by the same look. (*47*)

80   Philo vom Walde   *1898*

My heart urged me to see Zarathustra's dreamy, sunny eyes again.
I arrived in Weimar late in the evening. The night sky was covered
with quickly moving clouds through which the half moon sailed
quickly along like a silver boat on rapid, curly waves. The hotel "To
the Elephant" on the marketplace was still filled with bustling activity, for Weimar is always visited by many tourists. The next morning
I visited the cemetery by the old castle-church with the burial places
of Lucas Cranach, Musäus, Christiane Vulpius, and Euphrosyne,
then I strolled to the grave vault of the princes and into the wonderful court library until finally noon had arrived.

The house has three floors and a mansard-apartment. The style
is simple, plain, but noble: an unstuccoed red-brick building with

white trim, a gently sloping slate roof, lobby and balcony, a large garden with young olive trees and clusters of other trees all around. An old Dutch windmill is nearby. When I rang the doorbell, Alwine, whom I already knew from Naumburg, answered. She has now been serving in the Nietzsche household for nineteen years, has a slender, well-shaped figure, a genteel, very pleasant, somewhat pale face, and is dressed simply but tastefully. On seeing my card she is filled with joyful surprise, and says: "Frau Doktor is already expecting you, Herr Doktor!"

The Kaiserin Augusta Street, into which Louisen Street abuts right at the beginning, curves down from Wieland Square. I knew I would find Nietzsche again at Nr. 30 Louisen Street. So I walked further and further and finally reached the open field; on the left I passed the "Felsenkeller" Inn; then there it was before me, the villa "Silver View," which dominates the whole region like a queen over the common people. Peaceful solitude, distant horizons, laughing sky all around, and golden sunshine in all windows. Various conditions made it seem necessary that Frau Dr. Förster-Nietzsche move the Nietzsche Archives from Naumburg to Weimar. For this purpose she rented this villa, which belongs to the well-known Nietzsche-admirer, Fräulein von Salis (author of *Philosopher and Nobleman,* C. G. Naumann Verlag, Leipzig) in order to be able to live here completely undisturbed.

The reception room which I enter is richly furnished and makes a very moving impression. Here stands the piano on which Nietzsche, who incidentally was an outstanding musician, so often played; there out of luxuriant greenery and from between aromatic flowers, the bust of Dr. Bernhard Förster, who perished at the noble work of colonization in Paraguay. Now I hear steps behind me, coming down the stairs—it is Frau Dr. Förster-Nietzsche who enters to meet me. The mourning clothing stands out sharply against her lively, ruddy face. She does not seem as vivacious this time as she did on my previous visit.

We talk about many things: about her brother's physical condition, about his life's work, about his sickness and her mother's death. Often her eyes become sad with tears, but her lively, cheerful nature wins out again and again, so that a hearty laugh like out of a child's temperament beautifully transfigures all pain and suffering. Then Alwine comes with an announcement, and I say a few hearty words about the selfless care which she has given the great sick man.

Frau Dr. Förster tells me that Alwine, who comes from the vicinity of Naumburg, did feel somewhat homesick after the move, but she was otherwise cheerful and undiscouraged. She did every task willingly, and in every service for the patient she never lacked the proper respect. Even at night she was always available at the slightest call. Other service personnel in the house are a cook and a servant who is also bath-servant and masseur.

Frau Pastor Nietzsche and her daughter have always been convinced adherents of the hygienic dietary method of treatment (natural medicine) and felt great pain that their dear Fritz had used all kinds of medications against his insomnia and neuralgic pains, thus ruining his nervous system more and more until finally he was destroyed by using chloral. It was determined scientifically that the large doses of chloral attacked certain parts of the brain so that he got a stroke in Turin in 1889. The process has continued since that time.

Nietzsche is suffering from *dementia paralytica* and all improvement and help is absolutely out of the question. Only a miracle could save Zarathustra, the godless one. But who could ever hope for such a miracle at the end of the nineteenth century? In the first years his condition was quite satisfactory. The patient was calm, participated in conversations, went on walks arm in arm with his mother, and enjoyed tolerable health. Little by little the individual systems of nerves were affected. His consciousness vanished more and more, his limbs failed, his language became unclear.

To get him enough fresh air he was pushed around in a wheelchair on the promenade or taken to the city forest in a carriage. When these excursions had to be given up because of the public's importunity, his mother had a grapevine-covered veranda built for him, where he could spend the most part of the summer days and nights. In winter so-called "long tours" were undertaken every day inside the room, as his mother told me jokingly. His sleep was almost always quiet; only three times in four years was his mother forced to awaken Alwine in the night; otherwise she always took care of everything "for my beloved son" by herself. His care was truly ideal. The patient never lacked the cleanest air and sunshine in his room. His diet was nutritious, but unexciting, mostly vegetarian. Twice a week the patient was bathed and he also was massaged to replace active movement. He was never given any more medication. This treatment could not undo the past damage but the process of deterioration was slowed down almost uniquely in the history of this disease. When I saw Nietzsche for the first time I was surprised at his good appearance, and in a letter dated February 13, 1897, Frau Pastor Nietzsche writes to me: "We spent the afternoon with our good patient. On the whole, things are going quite tolerably with him; of course, one becomes more and more modest. Thank God, however, that he is not suffering, as our family doctor always repeats and as I was assured during an occasional visit by his former doctor, Privy Councillor Binswanger from Jena, who was almost astounded at his good appearance and told me many nice things about the care we have been giving him."

The newspapers reported everything possible about Nietzsche's move from Naumburg to Weimar last summer. Dr. Förster told me the following about this: A private parlor car was rented from Berlin, a special wheelchair had been constructed, the railroad conductors had received special instructions. The trip was made during the night, and by the first light of dawn the patient had arrived in his new home. Between Naumburg and Weimar everything went swiftly and secretly. The separate entrances and exits, which are otherwise used only by the Grand-Duke, flew open and shut, so that the public noticed nothing further. When the patient saw himself in a new room he looked up at the ceiling and smiled. He never felt the loss of his mother. He had always seen only two females around him. When his mother died, she was replaced by his sister, his beloved Lama. At night he lay in bed, in the daytime usually clothed on the sofa. A light-shade on the window dulls the entering sunrays, the table is pushed right next to the bed to stop him from falling out of bed. Sometimes he begins talking (unclearly): "I have a sister. My sister is a good woman. Only good people live in this house . . . " At times he also tries to sing. The first days after the move the Weimarans virtually besieged the villa and crept between the surrounding grainfields just to catch a glimpse. No one saw Zarathustra!

The rainy summer unfortunately did not often permit him to come outdoors. For this year an iron staircase was constructed by which he can easily be carried down into the sunny garden.

We had chatted for a long time downstairs in the Archives when Alwine, toward four o'clock, gave a sign that the Professor had awakened from his midday nap and was looking around for Frau Doktor. We now went upstairs to the high-ceilinged, spacious, well-lighted and pleasantly furnished sickroom, where one of the greatest intellectual fighters whom the world has ever seen is dreaming away the rest of his existence. There in that corner he rests in a half-sitting position. A white pillow serves him as backrest, his upper torso wears a blue jacket, his legs are covered with a light blanket. Yes, those are Zarathustra's eyes which now rest on me. They have seen into the deepest abysses of life, and into the sunniest heights of creative happiness—that is why they are so lost in dreams. . . A martial mustache, such as can be found nowhere else, overgrows the mouth down to the energetic chin. The gray-blond, abundant hair on his head falls simply backward. His sister tells him amiably that a gentleman is here to see him. Then he holds out his hand in greeting. Ah, whoever has ever felt Zarathustra's hand in his—will never forget it! It is extremely fine and delicate and cool. I stroked his hair and said to him: "You weary fighter, now you are resting!" Then the bushy eyebrows were raised, I felt as if I were looking into the eyes of the Sphinx . . . Finally we both said good-bye to him and went back down to the Archives. (*65*, 578–580)

81   Fritz Schumacher   *1898*

The first page which unexpectedly coalesced effectively in my attempts at charcoal drawings was a monument to Nietzsche: a quiet round temple on a lonely high plateau; on top a genius of mankind spreads his arms longingly to the heights; below dark giants twist in their fetters. This sketch had drawn some attention among the circle of Nietzsche's intimate friends, and one day Nietzsche's sister invited me to visit her in Weimar. They were thinking of building the monument based on the drawing. It was at the time when Ernst Horneffer was processing the Nietzsche manuscripts—as it seems to me, one of the most harmonious periods in the stormy history of the Nietzsche Archives, at least the life I saw in that house gave a rounded impression. The lively lady of the house who always tried to remind one that she represented the realm of a prince of the intellect, received me with charming civility; Horneffer, with priestly dignity, read aloud from the manuscripts; for the noon-meal a cheerful little circle gathered, and never did one forget that upstairs, separated only by a layer of beams, the eyes which had looked deeper into the abysses of the human heart and higher up to the icy peaks of his longing than those of any other living person lay awake.

When the guests had left and Frau Förster-Nietzsche wanted to go up to her brother, she asked me whether I wished to see him. I declined most definitely since I did not want the effect of his works to blend in me with the impression of his pain. But when I had been sitting in the library alone for some time, a servant suddenly stood before me and asked me to come up. His sister had asked the patient: "Do you want to see a young friend?" and unexpectedly he had said yes. So I had to go after all. Nietzsche lay half-erect on his bed. When I appeared at the door, his eyes first encompassed me with a searching, uneasy look; then he seemed to be satisfied, and his expression became very quiet and calm; so serene and peaceful as I have seen only in a very pious person.

His eyes were not extinguished; dark and velvety in the depths of the fine and richly arched brows, they seemed to be looking inward, far into a harmonious silence. His features were as if chiseled, except that the mustache grew beyond the line of the mouth, destroying the unity of expression. The pale, noble hands lay on the blanket as if listening. No one who saw this picture could have believed that he was looking at a body from which the mind had fled. One had to believe one was looking at a man who had risen above little everyday things and withdrawn into himself.

We sat down on the bed and his sister adroitly began a conversation with me, always directing to her brother a part of it that called only for affirmation or negation, for those were apparently the only two forms in which the patient still participated in life, and it seemed to please him to be drawn into the flow of the present event in this way. Perhaps it was the intonation of the voices that pleased him, or perhaps merely the closeness of loving persons to whom he belonged. Who can say! The loneliness which now surrounded this mind in a different sense, was penetrated only by the simplest forms of human expression—the mysterious waves of human sympathy and the mysterious waves of rhythm, the simplest forms, and at the same time the mightiest ones that life knows.

As I was leaving he shook my hand and I took with me the feeling of a deep inner calm. What I had seen was, in its strange way, peace.

Real peace came a year later. A circle of about twenty persons whom his sister had called together from all around the world gathered at Nietzsche's coffin for this last solemnity.

In the little library room—the house still had not been rebuilt by Van de Velde—the open coffin, covered with a veil, stood amid

wreaths and flowers. It could not be avoided to step right close to
it, and with a mixed feeling of reverence and shame one thus stood
in closest proximity to the deceased. And now the Berlin cultural
historian Kurt Breisig, leaning into the open window, began to give
a eulogy. An obvious feeling commanded that the mood of the hour
be captured in a few solemn, deeply felt words, in terms of both the
internal and external situation of the moment. Instead the speaker
pulled out a thick manuscript and began to read. Since he had trouble holding his manuscript, a lecturing stand was improvised for him
out of Frau Förster's sewing box, and now he mercilessly read to us
a cultural-historical analysis of the phenomenon of Nietzsche. Seldom have I experienced grimmer moments. Scholarship pursued
this man all the way to the grave under the guise of the culture
against which he fought like no other. If he had revived he would
long since have thrown the speaker out the window and chased us
out of the temple—even us who were innocent of this outrage.

Fortunately the torment of this speech was followed by the
soothing song of female voices from the next room:

> When a weary body is buried
> Bells accompany it to rest,
> And the earth, it heals the wound
> With flowers, most beautiful.

Now Horneffer spoke brief, monumental words, such as could
be said only here; and then, after an ancient Palestrina melody had
been sung, a faithful friend of the house, Count [Harry] Kessler,
lifted the veil from the dead man's head for a moment and we saw
the marble-like face unveiled for a moment. It lay there great and
solemn, not marked by death but by life, and ennobled in death. For
a few moments one forgot oneself and the surrounding world, then
one hurried out into the rain which lashed at the tall house on the
hill. That was the final act of a great intellectual tragedy. Alas, how
differently I had pictured its style when I was designing my
Nietzsche monument. (*53,* 199–201)

82   Walter Jesinghaus   *Summer 1899*

Whenever I come to the public library of my native city of Barmen
to get any book by the much-discussed, sick philosopher who is now
living in Weimar, I am told to my disappointment that Nietzsche's

books are always out on loan, and only rarely available. This fact proves that even in Wupperthal there is interest in the peculiar thoughts which this teacher of wisdom in Weimar, so severely stricken by fate, has bequeathed to this generation and to posterity. But if such interest is already prevalent even here, it is probably much greater elsewhere. So someone or another may be interested in learning a little about the present abode and life of Friedrich Nietzsche, who excited and moved the minds of the present cultural world probably more than any other man. Since I myself was in his house for several days and with him personally for brief moments, I may well be permitted to communicate briefly to broader circles my experiences in Weimar and at the Nietzsche Archives.

But first a few words about how I had the good fortune and honor to be allowed to stay as a guest in the philosopher's house.— When I was in Italy last winter and in the high mountains of Genoa, I studied Gallwitz's book on Nietzsche; in the course of my meditations I was seized by the desire to discover where the solitary thinker had lived during his stay in that same city in 1882. So I wrote about this matter to his sister, Frau Dr. Elisabeth Förster-Nietzsche, and after some time received a cordial, satisfactory answer. However, I was no longer in Italy when the letter arrived, so that it was impossible for me to personally visit the lady in whose house Nietzsche had once resided to give her in person the present which Frau Dr. Förster had intended for her. Yet although I was far away from the edge of the Ligurian Sea, through the kind offices in Genoa, of Mr. Theodor Blum, a nephew of the great Robert Blum, I succeeded after a long search in locating our philosopher's former landlady and establishing the [necessary] connection with her. And now the following thing happened: Carlotta Bianchi—that is the landlady's name—still had a suitcase of her former renter's from the time when Nietzsche had lived there. She had kept it faithfully and not forgotten to save its contents, namely two not insignificant manuscripts and a professorial diploma of the philosopher's. Now, very understandably she expressed the wish to be allowed to keep the suitcase as a memento of her *piccolo santo,* as she called Nietzsche; and Frau Dr. Förster, who for years has been managing all her brother's affairs, later gladly granted her this request—just as she also in a most friendly manner offered me the right to keep the original of the diploma until my death. But for the good Italian lady, the other items could hardly have had any value and so they came into my possession for the moment. But because they did not rightfully belong to me either, I soon informed Frau Dr. Förster of the remarkable discovery. She was very pleased, asked me to send her the manuscripts, and also invited me to visit her and the Nietzsche Archives. So I came to Weimar.

Frau Dr. Förster herself met me at the station and rode with me through the streets of the venerable city—toward the villa where she has now been living with her brother for two years, caring for him splendidly and unselfishly and observing from a high tower with a sharp eye the waves which Nietzsche's thoughts have long been causing in the sea of human life.

We had left Weimar behind us and now saw before us on the hilltop the great thinker's beautiful home, which overlooked the meadows far and wide. Before long the carriage stopped: we had arrived. When I entered the lobby of the house, a strange feeling ran through my entire body; I was now in the closest proximity to the prodigious man whose works had kept me awake many a night as a student in Bonn. But I could not surrender to this feeling for long. The servant came and showed me the room where I was to stay for several days.

What a splendid view from here over the whole city and beyond to the sumptuous crops and the green forests that covered the hilly landscape on the opposite side! Yes, of course, such a spot of earth is rightly designed for a man like Nietzsche to call his own in the last days of his earthly journey.

As long as I was there, the greatest silence prevailed in Weimar itself and hardly a breeze was felt. On the hilltop the wind played its mischievous games all the more wildly. In the Archives' new, quite large garden I saw leaves and twigs of the most varied kinds of trees in constant motion and activity; and the aromatic flowers in their beautiful beds found it hard to defend themselves against the tempestuous wooing of their lover pressing in invisibly from the North and East. But this accorded well with the fearless thinker's restless striving for truth, for, when his health still permitted, he had hastened out day after day to the primeval freshness of nature and with a fine sense observed its weaving and creation, its unending struggle. And that he is loved in return, even today, by the great mother of all things, to whom he was so devoted, is proven by the countless nests on his present home and in the shrubs and trees of his garden, which the singers of the meadows have built there in the happiness of their love. Yes, wherever one looks, there is a friendly meeting and greeting of a most gracious nature on all sides. And what seemed so remarkably and touchingly beautiful to me at the time of my stay at the Nietzsche Archives—every morning when I awakened and inhaled the fresh, aromatic air at the open window, I noticed quite close to the window where Nietzsche almost always stayed, a little cheerful bird which before its day's work always sang a pealing morning serenade to its sick friend. Truly it was wonderfully touching; and I must admit that a certain sadness sometimes tightened my heart when I saw this.

I also probably felt such a sadness when Frau Dr. Förster with her own charming way of narrating told one or another deeply moving tale from her brother's life. On the whole, however, despite his illness, I had no cause at all for feeling depressed in Nietzsche's house. There was, however, no loud, jubilant joyfulness or even youthful wildness. There were no children joking and playing their happy games; the servants are well instructed;—who else could disturb the quiet of this peaceful domicile? No, a really heavenly peace hovers throughout the lonely, sick philosopher's beautiful rooms.

This peace, however, seems to me quite proper there, because especially Frau Dr. Förster herself and the present editor of the new Nietzsche edition, the good, loyal Dr. Seidl, are weighed down by many tasks. The latter is constantly busy in the library and gives himself no particular rest, now that he has undertaken to solve a last great task by publishing the aforementioned works before resigning his honorable position in Weimar and becoming editor-in-chief of the *Münchener Neueste Nachrichten*. And as for Frau Dr. Förster herself, it is known at least in her circle of friends with what industriousness and endurance she often works till late into the night in the interest of her brother's great cause. When everyone far and wide is already sound asleep, then her lamp—the only light in all that darkness—is still shining in the window of her room, keeping company with the restlessly active woman who despite the hard, heavy suffering inflicted on her by fate still looks unbrokenly and actively into life and reveals no trace of brooding pessimism.

And this great joyous trait in Frau Dr. Förster is precisely what, combined with the gifts of indescribable kindness of heart and deep understanding for everything good and beautiful, inevitably charms and delights everyone who has the good fortune to work in the Nietzsche Archives. This opinion is unanimous among all who have ever stayed in the house of this philanthropic and noble lady—from the members of the Grand Duke's family down to the simplest male and female servants.

Did I not say that things are always very still and quiet on the Weimar hilltop? But how is that possible when so many guests arrive there in every time of the year? Now, first the work in the Archives is hardly influenced by visitors; and particularly Frau Dr. Förster has her specific hours when she cannot be disturbed. Her guests then easily find the opportunity to look around in the beautiful environment and to see the many memorabilia which Weimar offers to strangers in such great number. But that peace is not such that it may not be interrupted once or several times a week. For, since Frau Dr. Förster, out of consideration for her brother, rarely participates in outside parties, she likes all the more often to gather around her a circle of old and new male and female friends, and she is excellently skilled in giving all her visitors a splendid time. I once had the privilege of enjoying such a party. Representatives of the most various kinds of professions were present: painters and sculptors, writers and scholars, singers and musicians, philologists and philosophers, doctors and theologians; and of course the corresponding ladies were also not absent from the party. Even during the meal we had a lively time of it. Everyone had something interesting to tell. Frau Dr. Förster reported, among other things, about the visit of the poet Detlev von Liliencron, who had been at the Archives the week before I and had during his stay occasionally recited some of his best creations very beautifully. The famous art critic Bartels surprised us with news of the most recent events in the life of the famous Swiss author Mauritz von Stern. From someone else we heard personal experiences about the successful student performance of [Hermann] Sudermann's *Quitzows* in Vienna. Others gave more detailed reports on the last presentations in Bayreuth. In short, there was so much interesting and exciting in that pleasant and talented society that the pleasant evening went by probably too fast for all of us.

But significant as every moment of my presence in Weimar was, the most interesting event for me by far was when I got to see Nietzsche with my own eyes; and by chance that was on my birthday, of which naturally no one at the Archives knew anything. On that day, however, shortly after the noon meal, Frau Dr. Förster summoned me from my room and had me enter the room where her brother was staying. Anxiously I opened the door and walked softly toward the patient, who was sitting in a large armchair with his head bowed, looking at the floor. At his sister's nod I greeted him softly with the words, "Hello, Professor." And strangely, as if he had understood me he raised his head, with the high forehead, the bushy eyebrows, the noble, deep eyes, and the strong, hanging mustache, slowly toward me, and all by himself, but just as slowly, he laid his feeble right hand in mine, which I had held out to him. So our hands rested in one another for a moment. Then we each let go, and Nietzsche again stared into thin air. Immediately after me, a young psychiatrist, Dr. Rutishauser, who had been visiting the Nietzsche Archives on his way to Switzerland, as he had done once before, had the same experience with him. We stood there conversing quietly with Frau Dr. Förster for yet a while, and we were getting ready to leave the great patient's rooms; but before we could, Nietzsche raised his eyes once more and looked at me so sharply and piercingly as if he wanted to bore a hole into me. Then his features became peaceful again, as they usually are, and Dr. Rutishauser and I left him, kissing his hand gently and hiding deep feelings in our heart.

Soon afterwards a carriage rolled up, and we got aboard with Frau Dr. Förster to ride to the nearby famous Tilfurt, where we would meet many others. The pleasures we enjoyed there lie beyond the scope of our subject.

I will mention only that that evening—my last evening at the Nietzsche Archives—arrived too soon. I sat up alone with Dr. Rutishauser till deep in the night. We talked mainly about the great hero of the spirit, whom we both equally respected. We also touched on his sickness and at first disagreed about it. I agreed with Frau Dr. Förster, who from occasional rational statements of her brother's a short time ago at least, still believed that he could be cured. And indeed such a conclusion seems plausible to everyone who has seen Nietzsche himself. I noticed nothing crazy about him; on the contrary, his candid look and understanding response to my greeting startled me. Likewise, statements to his sister, such as, "Did I really write a few good books?" made one wonder. And yet Dr. Rutishauser considered it wrong to entertain optimistic speculations and said that Nietzsche might still occasionally speak and act rightly by instinct, but no longer consciously and rationally. I could not contradict him any further and concurred in his view.

The following day, I left in deep sadness. I say expressly: in deep sadness, for the hospitality which Frau Dr. Förster had shown me had been so cordial, so pure and great, that I had to admit sincerely to myself: I did not deserve it. And if at the end of this treatise I may recall once again the impression which that lady had given me of her pitiable but fortunate and suffering brother, then I must confess: he was a thoroughly moral personality, such as can rarely be found. His works also have to be seen from this point of view. Of course, they do contain some statements of dubious validity. But I am convinced that these reservations can be removed if we do not separate the man Nietzsche from his works. Other philosophers formulated their philosophies but did not act accordingly. Nietzsche, however, lived as he thought and wrote. May he only be understood correctly! (*30*)

83   Ernst Horneffer   *August 1899*

On a glowingly hot August day in the year 1899 I walked up Louisen Street in Weimar up the hill to Nietzsche's red villa. Frau Förster-Nietzsche, the great man's sister, led me into the Archives where two young scholars, Dr. Horneffer and Hans von Müller, were busy deciphering Nietzsche's manuscripts. Now Dr. Horneffer has come to Vienna to give lectures on Nietzsche, and we renewed our Weimar acquaintanceship. Dr. Horneffer, who came to Nietzsche's house one year before his death, has a lot to tell about the sick man, and the image he describes is totally different from what the legend says.

"Anyone who has seen Nietzsche as a patient," says Dr. Horneffer, "must consider himself lucky. At first thought, of course, one would expect it to be a depressing sight to see this man as a patient. Frankly, I myself feared this sight. But how impressed I was by his beauty! Nietzsche lay on a sofa, wrapped in a loose white coat—I always saw him only in this coat, which heightened his prophetic appearance—and the impression was powerful, indeed overpowering. I had pictured Nietzsche quite differently. I did not find the brooding, mordantly ironic Nietzsche of the sharp, cutting aphorisms. This was another Nietzsche whom I saw there, a prophet of divine simplicity, nothing fancy in his being, in a word: the Zarathustra Nietzsche. I stood still, awestricken with reverence. The first thing I saw was the forehead, the mighty forehead. There was something Goethean, Jupiter-like in its form, and yet delicate fineness in the temples. Peter Gast says that Nietzsche did not make this Jupiter-like impression in his healthy days. That is certainly strange! As a healthy man, Nietzsche's demeanor was so modest and shy that the idea of anything very extraordinary and high did not occur. With the illness, however, consciousness disappeared, and therewith the denial of his own greatness. No visitor could escape the impression of greatness which the patient made. A tremendous power lay in the forehead and in the strongly protruding lower face. The nose was very delicate and elegant. This elegance came out especially on his deathbed. His thick hair was completely black and silky-soft as a woman's. This silken hair seemed an expression of his entire sensitivity and of the femininity in his nature. His eye-sockets were deep but the dark-brown eyes were quite expressionless. He constantly drew his forehead in horizontal wrinkles, which was not a pretty sight; and when he simultaneously looked up with his sightless eyes, it made a terrible impression. It gave a gruesome view of his sickness. But when his eyes were closed and his forehead lay smooth, then the peacefully sleeping philosopher was of a wonderfully fabulous beauty. Sometimes he also moved his head gently like a quiet king. When he lay quiet, Nietzsche emanated a sovereignty that seemed to force a world to its knees.

There are two portraits of Nietzsche in his last years: the not very outstanding little statue by Cramer, and Hans Olde's excellent etching. But Olde's picture happens to show the sick Nietzsche with the wrinkled forehead. It does not render the Jupiter-effect, which was typical of him. In profile lay all his delicateness, all his elegance; *en face* he was power personified. I regret deeply that no one drew him at rest, with his eyes closed.

Despite his Olympian greatness, Nietzsche always looked like a German scholar, though heightened to the genial. And anyway, as a thinker he always was, in a certain sense, an armchair philosopher. In his room he soared above man, moved in a completely unreal world, and in all his ideas and theories was actually a Utopian in Plato's manner. It has often been said that he looked Polish. And a lot has also been said about his Polish ancestry. But there is no truth in this. My friend, Hans von Müller, proved that the name Nietzsche is not Polish but a good middle-German bourgeois name, which can be traced back to Reformation times. Nietzsche, in his great preference for the nobility, let himself be convinced that he stemmed from a Polish noble family. Nietzsche gave me the impression of a typical German.

I consider any reports that Nietzsche spoke in his last years of illness completely incredible. And if anyone says so, it must be the result of self-deception. Music made a great impression on him. When he was told that music would be played, he immediately was ecstatic and emitted ugly, unarticulated sounds, a dull, horrible groaning. After the music began his whole face was transfigured and beamed indescribably. But this expression of excessive joy was, in its sickness, no less terrible than the animalistic behavior just before. When I reflect on how the sick Nietzsche struggled for an expression and after terrible torments produced nothing else but ugly sounds, I cannot imagine that in this deep stage of mental derangement he can ever have spoken. At the beginning of the sickness, of course, he still spoke with visitors, and Peter Gast told me of a very remarkable conversation he had had with him on the intoxicating force of truth, in which Nietzsche coined the fine pun: *in vero vinitas.* But progressive paralysis silenced him. He grumbled with displeasure when strangers visited him.

His intellectual work came to a sudden stop, all at once, within a few, very specific days, in January 1889. From this point in time he wrote nothing more, and also formulated no further thoughts. It is remarkable how strongly the products of the last year 1888 seem affected by the approaching sickness. In this year he wrote *The Wagner Case, The Twilight of the Idols,* and *Antichrist,* and made the preliminary notes for *Revaluation.* As for the logical force and the scientific form of the ideas, he was never as clear as in these, his last works, but a certain nervous excitement trembles through all of them. Inner necessity compelled his development to follow the path of prophetic passion; but the future sickness was now determining the tone of his passion as if from the outside. Shortly before his complete derangement, all his vital energies underwent one more mighty upsurge. And his *Ecce Homo* benefited from this last flare-up. It is also remarkable how in the critical year 1888 his handwriting also changed completely. He suddenly uses the most incredible abbreviations, leaving out letters and syllables and finally writing almost only the consonants. You have seen these writings in Weimar yourself, where one can no longer speak of reading, but only of deciphering.

However often I saw Nietzsche, the impression was always the same. But he was mightiest, most beautiful, on his deathbed. There he truly looked like "a dead God." (*28*)

84   Health Commissioner Vulpius   *1899*

I too was deeply moved upon meeting the shadow of the man whose writings I had studied with lively enthusiasm as a student and had discussed with friends—especially the later assistant at the Nietzsche Archives, Dr. M. Zerbst. Later I learned to my utmost sorrow that this brilliant mind was insane and that its bearer had been committed to the sanatorium in Jena for observation and treatment. A short time before, I myself had been active there as an assistant doctor under [Otto] Binswanger and [Theodor] Ziehen and on occasional visits from the Leipzig University Clinic for the Insane I heard oral reports on the patient's condition. So it is understandable that I approached my patient not only with medical but also with psychiatric interest, which in turn led Frau Dr. [honorary] Förster-Nietzsche to entrust me with writing a critique of her brother's medical history and the unsavory controversy connected with it.

Nietzsche's eye ailment proved to be an inflammation of the left iris. The right pupil was considerably wider open than the left one, which was extremely deformed, but both showed no reaction to light. Slight adhesions of the somewhat discolored left iris with the front lens capsule were mostly dissolved after the insertion of a grain of atropin into the corner of the eye; and the pupil—though it remained irregular—could be kept open from then on with lesser dosages of atropin in droplet form, while at the same time the initially violent irritation-phenomena—redness and tear-flow—decreased when treated with warm poultices. Specks of pigment, which had obviously remained from earlier adhesions, could be recognized on the frontmost lens capsule under focal lighting. Mirror-examination proved to be impossible.

This treatment lasted, since occasional small boosters were required, until May 1900. Then the cure lasted until his death on August 25, 1900.

The widespread discussion of Nietzsche's medical history which began only years later was inspired mainly by the book written by the Leipzig neurologist, P. J. Möbius, *On the Pathological in Nietzsche* (Wiesbaden, 1902), which appeared in a second edition in 1904, and again under the title *Nietzsche* in Möbius' *Selected Works* (Leipzig, 1909). (Quotations will be according to the second edition.) In this pathological study, Möbius comes to the conclusion that Nietzsche's sickness had been a progressive paralysis—though it developed along an unusual course. As for the etiology of this sickness, he adopts the general view of more recent psychiatrists and neurologists who consider paralysis, as well as locomotor ataxia, to be a metasyphilitic affection of the central nervous system. Accordingly he sought information among Nietzsche's circle of friends and acquaintances as to when the "exogenous disease germs" entered Nietzsche's system, injuring him "in this particular way" (Introduction to the 3rd edition). He becomes very much clearer on pages 48 to 50, where he traces down Nietzsche's sexual relations. Although on the one hand he was convinced that Nietzsche's attraction for sex had been abnormally weak and that he had lacked the sex-urge which a healthy male needs in order to devote himself to a woman, on the other hand he calls it a myth that Nietzsche had had no sexual relations. He cites the testimony of unnamed witnesses from his Leipzig University days, although he also quotes a statement of Deussen's, who insisted with the complete conviction of a friend of his youth: *"Nunquam mulierem attingit"* (He never touched a woman). To harmonize this contradiction, he presents the strange explanation: "Nietzsche could have overcome desire, but not the curiosity to know."

If Nietzsche had been afflicted by his misfortune in this way, then it surely can be assumed that his most intimate friends would have learned of it immediately or in later stages of the disease's manifestation, or that the many doctors under whose treatment and observation he was would have seen and reported it. But the first group, most recently his friends of his youth, Professor Wachsmuth and Professor Roscher (in *Der Tag,* of January 14) have repeatedly protested against this supposition. They regard such an insinuation not only as a slur on Nietzsche's image, which they remember so well, but also as casting doubt on their intimate relationship with their friend. —But none of the doctors observed any externally perceptible luetic symptoms or used them as an explanation for their numerous diagnoses. Even the most thorough physical examinations which were made upon Nietzsche's delivery to the Basel and Jena mental clinics and later by Dr. Gutjahr, his personal physician in Naumburg, gave no basis for a post-luetic skin, mucous membrane, bone, or gland infection. The only suggestion of this that one might see is the repeatedly recurring inflammation of the retina, although specific proliferations were not observed.

Nonetheless—since, as we shall see later, the diagnosis of 'progressive paralysis' must be retained—the causal toxin must have once entered Nietzsche's system, namely without his knowledge. The most obvious and likely occasion for this assumption was his service as a volunteer medical corpsman in the 1870 campaign, and especially perhaps the final transporting of influenza and diphtheria

patients under the most unfavorable hygienic conditions. To overcome his lively disgust and probably in the belief that he was thereby
enjoying some disinfecting protection, he smoked in the ambulance.
How easily a transmission of the poison could have taken place if he
ever set down his cigar in order to help a patient in the crowded
vehicle! For afterward he himself became mortally ill, namely not
with influenza but with an infection of the jaws which was diagnosed
as diphtheria but could perhaps have contained an admixture of
syphilis. Even Dr. Hellpach in his essay "The Files on Nietzsche's
Illness" (*Der Tag,* January 22, 1910), in contrast to or in addition to
Möbius' deduction, pointed out this possibility, which upon a
detailed evaluation of all relevant sources, including Nietzsche's letter to Wagner from Erlangen, September 1870, is raised to a well-
founded probability, and then he continues: "Today we unfortunately know that a particularly close relationship exists between the
mildest, most inconspicuous infections, which often go unnoticed,
and the metasyphilitic (tapic and paralytic) diseases." Professor Ziehen also confirmed this in a personal interview in December 1922
on the basis of his own observations and those of others and he considers such an origin of the infection, which he treated in Jena but
also saw later, to be very possible. (*63*)

85   Isabella von Ungern-Sternberg   *March 31 to April 1, 1900*

It was a good day for the patient, and so Frau Elisabeth accompanied us to her brother's rooms, located on the top floor, aside from
any disturbance or noise.

How I felt when I saw him in the grandeur of his being, the
infinitely deepened beauty of psychic expression! The beauty of his
eyes especially, no longer concealed by any glasses, was practically
overpowering. These deep sad eye-stars, which roam in the distance
and yet seem to look inward, radiated a powerful effect, a magnetic
intellectual aura which no sensitive nature could resist.

Wrapped in white garments he rested on his sofa, which I
approached hesitantly, introduced by his sister's words: "Darling, I
am bringing you a dear friend, about whom we have often remi-
nisced together." With both hands I clasped his thin, emaciated
right hand—the same that had written down immortal chains of
thought—and whispered: "We met once, long, long ago, in Italy, in
Genoa and Pisa." Questioningly, reflectively, his eye rested on me

and then, with a shaking of his mighty head, his look directed a silent question to his sister, who whispered gentle, soothing, loving words to him.

Under Master Peter Gast's hands, the grand piano emitted magnificent sounds, mighty tones, which seized the patient as if with magic power and quivered through his organism like an electric spark. Blissful rapture transfigured his features, his whole body quivered with feverish excitement—and behold new life flowed through his transparent, lame hands. They broke the fetters of paralysis and moved toward one another as a sign of applause. He could not have enough of this manifestation of joy; the strings had already fallen silent—but eye to eye with his sister, seeking and finding eloquent empathy there—he continued to tremble with delighted excitement, a real storm of enthusiasm, in his facial expression and with a clapping of applause which did not want to stop. A spectacle for gods, which I was fortunate enough to observe.

With tears in their eyes, the witnesses to this psychic commotion, vibrant with ineffable feelings, withdrew quietly and with deep emotion. A handshake and tears released the psychic tension. (*61,* 41–43)

86   Anonymous

Friedrich Nietzsche's death, which gives the entire press—including abroad—the occasion to express itself *pro* or *contra* about the deceased man's intellectual legacy depending on their various aesthetic or religious beliefs, will certainly also arouse lively interest in the unfortunate man's condition before his death. Although there has been no lack of interviewers from a great many countries in the course of the last four years, during which the patient lay under the loving, considerate care of his sister (and biographer), Frau Dr. Elisabeth Förster, only a little was reported to the public about his physical health since the interviewers never saw this so afflicted man face to face. Since Nietzsche could become loud at any moment, without having lucid moments, a secluded villa had been bought (in Weimar topography it bears the name "Silberblick"), and in this building the poor unfortunate occupied part of the second floor, mostly bedded in his "mattress-grave" and surrounded with all kinds of protective measures to prevent his escape. Hardly any really lucid moments could ever be recorded in this so very sad medical history. In those rare moments he recognized his faithful nurse, rejoiced in her appearance, and thanked her for her love. But his mental derangement never receded enough for any oral readings to have aroused his interest, and though recently it has often been reported that this was the case, and even a few of Nietzsche's favorite authors were named (Guy de Maupassant!!!) this is sheer invention or lies. On the whole, his condition was desolate and hopeless. The patient even reached stupidly for every shining object to try to put it into his mouth. His appearance was, as is also shown by a recent sculpture, completely that of a mentally ill person. Physical functions were performed only with all kinds of difficulties, but on the whole Nietzsche was an obedient and cooperative patient. He rarely felt physical pains. His death came rather unexpectedly; the struggle with it was hard, but not very long. His constitution, which was imposing even in the coffin, could perhaps have struggled longer. The bushy mustache, which gave the head a somewhat gallant effect and markedly stressed the Slavic type, was still brown. When a somewhat bigger Nietzsche-community was invited to the funeral and it took place by the corpse, which lay in state on the ground floor, the head was covered with yellow silk cloths; flowers and wreaths covered the body. The rooms dedicated to the Archives now housed the four collaborators, Peter Gast, Arthur Seidl, Ernst Horneffer, and August Horneffer, who were arranging his spiritual legacy and preparing it for print. The furnishings and equipment of the villa show that the brother and sister's financial situation must be very favorable! (*3*)

87   Elisabeth Förster-Nietzsche   *August 25, 1900*

. . . On Monday, August 20, he suddenly fell ill of a cold with fever and heavy breathing; it looked like pneumonia was setting in. In a few days however the sickness seemed to have been dispelled with the aid of the faithful doctor; the doctor even believed that he did not have to return. But on the 24th, toward midnight, as I was sitting opposite him, his whole expression suddenly changed; he suddenly fell over, unconscious, from a stroke. A terrible storm was beginning and it looked like this great mind was to perish amid thunder and lightning. Yet he recovered once again, regaining consciousness toward evening and trying to speak. When I handed him a glass of refreshment toward two o'clock in the morning and pushed aside the lampshade so that he could see me, he cried joyously: "Elisabeth!" so that I believed the danger over. He slept for a long, long time; and I hoped it was a sign of recovery. But his dear face changed more and more, the shadow of death was spreading and his breathing became heavier and heavier. He opened his magnificent eyes once again. "He moved and closed his lips again, and looked like someone who has something more to say and hesitates to say it. And to those who were watching him his face seemed to blush slightly. This lasted for a little while: but then, all at once he shook his head, closed his eyes voluntarily and died . . . So it happened that Zarathustra perished." (*15*, 93–97)

BIOGRAPHICAL NOTES

(Numbers in parentheses refer to selections.)

Adelt, Leonhard (1881–1945). A pupil of Nietzsche's at the Basel High School, he later became a journalist and free-lance writer in Munich and Vienna. During World War I he served as a pilot and a war correspondent. A minor author, he wrote plays, novels and literary criticism, and also did translations. (19)

Andreas-Salomé, Lou (1861–1937). Famed woman of letters, of French-Huguenot and German Baltic ancestry, and daughter of a Russian general, Salomé grew up in St. Petersburg, then studied the history of religion in Zurich, starting in 1881. In Italy, she met Malwida von Meysenbug, Paul Rée, and Nietzsche, who made two proposals of marriage to her, one through the mediation of his friend Rée, and one in person. Nietzsche and Salomé were together repeatedly for about a year, until their friendship came to a stormy end, for which Nietzsche blamed himself and interference from his mother and sister. After this Salomé lived in Berlin together with Rée. In 1887 she married the Orientalist F. C. Andreas, and they settled in Berlin and Munich. Salomé also travelled to Paris and Vienna and she befriended many other famous men, including the symbolist poet Rainer Maria Rilke, with whom she travelled to Russia in 1899 and 1900, and Sigmund Freud. In 1912 she studied psychology in Vienna, and after 1914 she practiced therapeutic psychoanalysis in Göttingen. Besides poetry and short stories, she wrote literary criticism of her friends' works, including *Friedrich Nietzsche in His Works* (1894) and *Look Back at My Life* (published posthumously in 1951). (42)

Bachofen, Luise Elisabeth, wife of Johann Jacob Bachofen (1815-1887), a law historian and antiquarian, noted for his works on primeval matriarchy and on mythology. Acquaintanceship with Nietzsche during his stay in Basel. (27)

Bartels, Wanda von. Author. (67)

Benndorf, Otto (1838–1901). Famous archeologist, who taught at Pforta in 1862–64. After wide travels in Italy, Greece, and the Middle East he became professor of archeology in Zurich, Prague, and Vienna. From 1898 on, he was director of the Austrian Archeological Institute. Benndorf was one of the scientists who set the modern pattern of archeological work, which combines research and classroom teaching with expeditions and on-the-site excavations. His books include *The Ancient Statues of the Lateran* (1867) and *Greek and Sicilian Vase-Pictures* (1869). (8)

Bernoulli, Carl Albrecht (1868–1937). Pseudonym of Ernst Kilchner, a theologian and cultural historian, who studied under Franz Overbeck and taught Church History for one year at the University of Basel. He wrote many books, including three on Nietzsche: *Overbeck and Nietzsche* (2 vols., 1908), *Nietzsche and Switzerland* (1922), and *Nietzsche's Intellectualism* (1924). (66)

Bradke, Marie von. Acquainted with Nietzsche in Sils-Maria in 1886. (61)

Deussen, Paul (1845–1919). Philosopher and Indologist. A friend of Nietzsche's since their school days in Schulpforta. They studied together in Bonn until August 1865 and joined the "Franconia" fraternity together. Deussen devoted thirty-five years of his life to the study of Indian philosophy. From 1889, he was a professor of philosophy in Kiel. He was also the founder and president of the Schopenhauer Society. His last meeting with Nietzsche took place in mid-October 1894 in Naumburg. Deussen's masterpiece is his three-volume *Universal History of Philosophy.* (7, 10, 14, 72)

Egidi, Arthur. Acquainted with Nietzsche in 1882 in Tautenburg. (45)

Eucken, Rudolf (1846–1926). Philosophy professor in Basel in 1871–74. Advocate of an "active idealism." Author of *World Views of the Great Thinkers*, he won the Nobel Prize for Literature in 1908. (20)

Förster-Nietzsche, Elisabeth (1846–1935). Nietzsche's sister, biographer, and manager of his literary remains. In 1885, to her brother's chagrin, she married Bernhard Förster, a leading anti-Semite and proponent of the Wagner cult, and emigrated with him to *Nueva Germania*, the German colony in Paraguay, which he founded. In 1893, after her husband's suicide and the bankruptcy of his colonial scheme, Elisabeth returned to Germany, replacing her mother after her death as her mentally deranged brother's custodian, established the Nietzsche Archives, and devoted herself to promoting a legendary image of Nietzsche. Hitler himself attended her funeral. A scandal later erupted upon the discovery that she had suppressed and falsified documents to project her particular image of Nietzsche. (1, 2, 3, 4, 5, 13, 44, 65, 87)

Freund, Robert (1852–1936). Pianist. Concert pianist and piano teacher in Zurich in 1875–1912. Closer acquaintanceship with Nietzsche in the summer of 1883 in Zurich. (55)

Fritsch, A. Pupil in Pforta together with Nietzsche in 1863–64. Met him again while studying in Leipzig, and in Sils-Maria. (9, 59)

Galli, Eugenie. Reporter who recorded conversations with Nietzsche's landlords in Sils-Maria. (54)

Gast, Peter, pseudonym for Johann Heinrich Köselitz (1854–1918). A composer. Nietzsche's student (1876–78) and lifelong friend. He lived in Venice for ten years and there wrote his main work, the comic opera *The Lion in Venice.* He often helped Nietzsche as a sort of unofficial secretary, reader, and adviser. After Nietzsche's commitment to a sanatorium in 1889, Gast worked at editing Nietzsche's *Complete Works* and later (1900–1908) was a collaborator at the Nietzsche Archives. (30)

Gelzer-Thurneysen, Heinrich (1847–1906). Classical philologist. High-school teacher in Basel (1869–73), later professor of classical philology and ancient history in Jena. (23)

Göring, H. Acquaintanceship with Nietzsche in Basel in the summer of 1878. (38)

Granier, Raimund. Fellow pupil in Pforta with Nietzsche. (6)

Hausmann, Sebastian. Acquaintanceship with Nietzsche in Sils-Maria in the mid-eighties. (46)

Heckel, Karl (1858–1923). Philosopher. (22)

Helling, Viktor. Spoke with Davide Fino, Nietzsche's landlord in Turin at the time of his collapse. (69)

Horneffer, Ernst (1871–1954). Collaborator at the Nietzsche Archives beginning in 1899. (83)

Janicaud, Walter. Reports on Nietzsche's repeated stays at Janicaud's parents' house in Leipzig, for the last time in the summer of 1899. (47)

Jesinghaus, Walter. In the summer of 1899, he discovered Nietzsche's notes from Nice in the year 1883. (82)

Köselitz. See Gast, Peter.

Lanzky, Paul. Author. Permanent domicile in Italy since 1879. There he met Nietzsche in February 1884. (56, 57)

Lec, Heinrich. Reports on a conversation with Franziska Nietzsche. (75)

Mähly, Jacob (1825–1902). Teacher of classical languages at the Basel Pedagogical College. Full professor of Latin Language and Literature at the University of Basel in 1875–90. (24)

Meysenbug, Malwida von (1816–1903). Author. A friend of Nietzsche's for many years. Liberal and idealistic, she was exiled from Berlin in 1852 for corresponding with the leaders of the Revolution of 1848. After this she led a cosmopolitan existence in London, Paris, Florence, Rome, and on Ischia. For a time she was a governess in the house of the Jewish-Russian socialist Alexander Herzen. She was also a friend of Garibaldi's, Mazzini's, and Minghetti's. She wrote novels and short stories, but is best known for her *Memoirs of an Idealistic Woman*. As a Wagner devotee she stayed with the Wagner family in Bayreuth many times after 1872, where she met Nietzsche. In the winter of 1876–77 she stayed with Nietzsche in Sorrento. (26, 34)

Miaskowski, Ida von. Wife of the economist who taught at the University of Basel since 1874. Between 1874 and 1876 Nietzsche had close relations with her family. (28)

Miaskowski, Kurt von. Son of Ida von Miaskowski. (29)

Nietzsche, Franziska, née Oehler (1826–1897). Nietzsche's mother. She devoted herself to the care of her sick son from March 1890 until her death. (73, 74, 77)

Overbeck, Franz (1837–1905). Protestant theologian, professor of Church History in Basel in 1870-97, who believed in the incompatibility of Christianity and culture. A close friend of Nietzsche's all his life, he unofficially managed Nietzsche's affairs after his retirement from the Basel professorship, and he was the one who hastened to Turin after Nietzsche's mental breakdown. (25)

Overbeck, Ida, née Rothpelz (1845–1905). Wife of Franz Overbeck since 1876. She had already met Nietzsche briefly in Maderanertal in 1870. (15, 40, 41, 43, 48)

Piccard, Julius. Professor of Chemistry in Basel. (16)

Probst, Emanuel. Nietzsche's student in Basel in 1871. (21)

Promitz. Nietzsche's pupil at the high school in Basel. (18)

Reuter, Gabriele (1852–1941). Author, and pioneer of the women's rights movement, she wrote many novels about women's problems. (79)

Reuter, Richard. A member of Elisabeth Förster-Nietzsche's circle of friends in Naumburg. (33)

Ruthardt, Adolf. Pianist. Acquaintance of Nietzsche's in the summer of 1885 in Sils-Maria. (58)

Salis-Marschlins, Meta von (1855–1929). Swiss poet and women's rights advocate. She obtained a Ph.D. at the University of Bern and wrote many books of essays and novels about women's rights, as well as several volumes of poetry and a book on Nietzsche. Her acquaintanceship with Nietzsche began in 1884. (51, 63, 64)

Scheffler, Ludwig von. Student of Nietzsche's in Basel. (32, 39)

Schirnhofer, Resa von. Meetings with Nietzsche between 1884 and 1887, correspondence until 1888. (49, 52, 62, 78)

Schumacher, Fritz (1869–1947). Architect. Designed a Nietzsche monument in 1898. (81)

Seydlitz, Reinhardt von (1850–1931). Author and painter. Meetings with Nietzsche between 1876 and 1885. (35, 36)

Simchowitz, S. Medical doctor. In Jena in 1888–89 he was a student at Professor Otto Binswanger's psychiatric clinic, where he knew Nietzsche as a patient. (71)

Sophus. Pseudonymous Berlin journalist. (76)

Steiger, Edgar. A student of Nietzsche's in Basel. (37)

Strecker, Karl (1862–1933). Journalist, novelist, and dramatist. Reports on a conversation with Nietzsche's Turin landlord Fino about the time immediately preceding Nietzsche's breakdown. (68)

Stürenberg, Heinrich. Acquaintance of Nietzsche's during their student years in Leipzig. Like Nietzsche, a member of the Philological Association inspired by Ritschl. (12)

Ungern-Sternberg, Isabella von, née von der Pahlen. Met Nietzsche while on a trip to Genoa, in October 1876. (85)

Volkelt, Johannes (1848–1930). Kantian philosopher, concerned with problems of certainty and truth. (50, 60)

Vulpius, Health Commissioner. A specialist who treated Nietzsche's eye ailment in 1899. (84)

Wackernagel, Jakob (1853–1938). Philologist. Nietzsche's pupil at the Basel High School in Basel, he later studied under him at the university. In 1879 he became Nietzsche's successor as Professor of Greek Literature at the University of Basel. (17)

Walde, Philo vom. Pseudonym for Johannes Reinelt (1858–1906). Teacher and regional author. (80)

Widemann, Paul Heinrich. Composer and author. A student of Nietzsche's in Basel in 1876 together with his friend Peter Gast. (31)

Wisser, Heinrich Wilhelm (1843–1935). Researcher of Low German folk traditions and *Märchen*. Acquainted with Nietzsche in Leipzig during his university years as a member of the Philological Association. (11)

Zimmern, Helen (1846–1934). Translator. First met Nietzsche in Bayreuth in 1876, further meetings in Sils-Maria. (53)

SOURCES

1. [Adelt, Leonhard], "Der Herr Professor und der Luftballon," *Basler Nationalzeitung,* June 6, 1923. Also as "Gymnasialprofessor Nietzsche," *Frankfurter Zeitung,* August 25, 1910.

2. Andreas-Salomé, Lou, *Lebensrückblick,* ed. Ernst Pfeiffer (Zurich: Niehan, 1951).

3. Anon., "Der Tod Friedrich Nietzsches," *Allgemeine Zeitung* (Munich), August 31, 1900.

4. Anon., "Nietzsche in der Heilanstalt," *Frankfurter Oder-Zeitung,* July 4, 1908.

5. Bachofen, Frau J. J., in Hermann Randa, *Nietzsche, Overbeck und Basel* (Bern and Leipzig: Paul Haupt, 1937).

6. Bartels, Wanda von, "So sollt ihr Nietzsche verstehen," *Allgemeine Zeitung* (Munich), January 5, 1901.

7. Benndorf, Otto, in Anon., "Der Primaner Nietzsche. Eine Unterredung mit Hofrath Benndorf," *Neues Wiener Tageblatt,* September 2, 1900.

8. Bernoulli, Carl Albrecht, *Franz Overbeck und Friedrich Nietzsche: Eine Freundschaft* (Jena: Diederichs, 1908), vol. II.

9. Bradke, Marie von, "Begegnung mit Nietzsche," *Die Propyläen* 17 (1920), pp. 394–395.

10. Deussen, Paul, *Erinnerungen an Friedrich Nietzsche* (Leipzig: Brockhaus, 1922).

11. Egidi, Arthur, "Gespräche mit Nietzsche im Parsifaljahr 1881," *Musik* 1 (1902), 1892–1899.

12. Eucken, Rudolf, "Meine persönlichen Erinnerungen an Nietzsche,"in *Den Manen Friedrich Nietzsches,* ed. Max Oehler (Munich: Musarion, 1921).

13. Förster-Nietzsche, Elisabeth, *Das Leben Friedrich Nietzsches,* vol. I (Leipzig: C. G. Naumann, 1895).

14. Förster-Nietzsche, Elisabeth, *Das Leben Friedrich Nietzsches,* vol. II (Leipzig: C. G. Naumann, 1897).

15. Förster-Nietzsche, Elisabeth, "Nietzsches Tod," *Zukunft* 13 (1904), pp. 93–97.

16. Förster-Nietzsche, Elisabeth, "Nietzsche-Legenden," *Zukunft* 14 (1905), pp. 170–179.

17. Förster-Nietzsche, Elisabeth, *Der junge Nietzsche* (Leipzig: Kröner, 1913).

18. Freund, Robert, *Memoiren eines Pianisten,* vol. 139, *Neujahrsblatt der Allgemeinen Musikgesellschaft Zurich* (Zurich: Hug, 1951).

19. Fritsch, A., "Erinnerungen," 1932, unpublished.

20. Galli, Eugenie, "Im Wohnhaus Friedrich Nietzsches in Sils-Maria," *Deutsche Zeitung,* December 17, 1899.

21. Gast, Peter, "Vorwort des Herausgebers zur 2. Auflage," *Menschliches, Allzumenschliches* (Leipzig: Insel, 1908).

22. Gelzer, H., "Jakob Burckhardt als Mensch und Lehrer," *Zeitung für Kulturgeschichte* 7 (1900), pp. 1–50.

23. Göring, H., "Eine Begegnung mit Nietzsche," *Deutsche Zeitung*, January 12, 1924.

24. Granier, Raimund, in Friedrich Dernburg, "Neues aus Nietzsches Jugend," *Berliner Tageblatt*, November 24, 1902.

25. Hausmann, Sebastian, "Eine Erinnerung an Nietzsche," *München-Augsburger Zeitung*, July 4 and 6, 1922.

26. Heckel, Karl, *Nietzsche: Sein Leben und seine Lehre* (Leipzig: Reclam, 1922).

27. Helling, Viktor, "Nietzsche in Turin," *Neues Wiener Journal*, July 4, 1926.

28. Horneffer, Ernst, in Th. Thomas, "Der kranke Nietzsche," *Neue Freie Presse* (Vienna), February 1, 1903.

29. Janicaud, Walter, "Eine Erinnerung an Friedrich Nietzsche in Leipzig," *Leipziger Neueste Nachrichten*, August 25, 1910.

30. Jesinghaus, Walter, "Bei Friedrich Nietzsche," 1899, unpublished.

31. Lanzky, Paul, "Friedrich Nietzsche nach persönlichem Umgang," *Sphinx* 18 (1894), pp. 333–340.

32. Lanzky, Paul, "Friedrich Nietzsche als Mensch und Dichter," in *Unsere Dichter in Wort und Bild*, vol 5, F. Tetzner (Leipzig: Claussner, 1895).

33. Lec, Heinrich, "Bei Friedrich Nietzsche," *Berliner Tageblatt*, September 11, 1893.

34. Mähly, Jacob, "Erinnerungen an Friedrich Nietzsche," *Die Gegenwart* 58 (1900), pp. 246–250.

35. Meysenbug, Malwida von, *Der Lebensabend einer Idealistin* (Berlin: Schuster & Loeffler, 1898).

36. Meysenbug, Malwida von, "Der erste Nietzsche," in *Neue Freie Presse* (Vienna), September 18, 19, 21, 22, and 28, 1900.

37. Miaskowski, Ida von, "Erinnerungen an den jungen Friedrich Nietzsche," in *Neue Freie Presse* (Vienna), September 12, 1907.

38. Miaskowski, Kurt von, "Basler Jugenderinnerungen," in *Basler Jahrbuch 1927* (Basel: Helbing & Lichtenhahn, 1929), pp. 78–137.

39. Nietzsche, Franziska ["Gespräche mit Nietzsche," February 1891], unpublished.

40. Nietzsche, Franziska, "Was heute der gute Fritz alles gesprochen," February 24, 1891, unpublished.

41. Nietzsche, Franziska, "Aussprüche meines guten kranken Sohnes. January 1895–July 22, 1896," unpublished.

42. Overbeck, Franz, "Erinnerungen an Friedrich Nietzsche," in *Neue Rundschau* 17 (1906), pp. 209–231, 320–330.

43. Overbeck, Ida, "Erinnerungen," in Bernoulli, *Overbeck*, op. cit., I, pp. 234–251, 336–346.

44. Piccard, Julius, "Erinnerungen," in Bernoulli, *Overbeck*, op. cit., I, pp. 168–171.

45. Probst, Emanuel, "Empfang bei Nietzsche: Herbst 1871," unpublished.

46. Promitz, Dr., "Nietzsche als Gymnasiallehrer," *Schlesische Zeitung*, May 9, 1926.

47. Reuter, Gabriele, "Eine Nietzsche-Büste," *Neue Freie Presse*, October 31, 1901.

48. Reuter, Richard, "Ein Besuch bei dem jungen Nietzsche," *Die Kritik* 2 (1895), pp. 1275–1281.

49. Ruthardt, Adolf, "Friedrich Nietzsche und Robert Schumann," *Zeitschrift für Musik* 88 (1921), pp. 489–491.

50. Salis-Marschlins, Meta von, *Philosoph und Edelmensch: Ein Beitrag zur Charakteristik Friedrich Nietzsches* (Leipzig: Naumann, 1897).

51. Scheffler, Ludwig von, "Wie ich Nietzsche kennen lernte," *Neue Freie Presse* (Vienna), August 6 and 7, 1907.

52. Schirnhofer, Resa von, in Hans Lohberger, "Friedrich Nietzsche und Resa von Schirnhofer," *Zeitschrift für philosophische Forschung* 22 (1969), pp. 250–260, 441–458.

53. Schumacher, Fritz, *Stufen des Lebens: Erinnerungen eines Baumeisters* (Stuttgart & Berlin: Deutsche Verlags-Anstalt, 1935).

54. Seydlitz, Reinhardt von, "Friedrich Nietzsche: Briefe und Gespräche," *Neue deutsche Rundschau* 10 (1899), pp. 617–628.

55. Seydlitz, Reinhardt von, *Wann, warum, was und wie ich schrieb* (Gotha: Perthes, 1900).

56. Simchowitz, S. "Der sieche Dionysos: Eine persönliche Erinnerung," *Kölnische Zeitung*, August 29, 1925.

57. Sophus, "Von Friedrich Nietzsche," *Berliner Tageblatt*, October 18, 1894.

58. Steiger, Edgar, "Zarathustra auf der Schulbank und auf dem Lehrstuhl," *Das literarische Echo* 17 (1915), pp. 1349–1353.

59. Strecker, Karl, "Auf Nietzsches letzten Spuren," *Tägliche Rundschau*, August 23, 1925.

60. Stürenberg, Heinrich, "Erinnerungen eines Achtzigjährigen," *Dresdner Anzeiger*, Wissenschaftliche Beilage, May 13, 1930.

61. Ungern-Sternberg, Isabella von, *Nietzsche im Spiegelbild seiner Schrift* (Leipzig: Naumann, [1902]).

62. Volkelt, Johannes, "Einiges über Nietzsche," *Dresdner Anzeiger*, Wissenschaftliche Beilage, April 17, 1926, p. 67.

63. Vulpius, Sanitätsrath Dr., "Nietzsches Krankheit," 1923, unpublished.

64. Wackernagel, Jakob, "Erinnerungen," September 17, 1908, unpublished.

65. Walde, Philo vom, "Friedrich Nietzsche in Weimar," *Wiener Familien-Journal* 145 (1898), pp. 578–580.

66. Widemann, Paul Heinrich, "Erinnerungen an Friedrich Nietzsche," *Chemnitzer Tageblatt*, August 6, 1901.

67. Wisser, Wilhelm, "Ein Brief von Erwin Rohde," *Hamburgischer Correspondent*, August 26, 1925.

68. Zimmern, Helen, in Oscar Levy, "Nietzsches englische Freundin," unpublished.

INDEX OF NAMES AND WORKS

Abbess of Jouarre, The (Renan), 204
Achilles, 37
Adamus, Franz, 237
Adelt, Leonhard, 38–39
Aeschylus, 36, 74
Agostino, Patre, 227
Allason, Barbare, 219
Allemands, Les (Didon), 153
Altmann, Professor, 175
Alwine. *See* Freytag, Alwine
"Amid Birds of Prey" (Nietzsche), 218
Anacreon, 10
Andreas-Salomé, Lou, 124–127, 128, 129, 130, 147, 151
Angermann, Professor, 28
Antichrist, The (Nietzsche), 81, 96, 106, 110, 209, 256
Anti-Strauss (Nietzsche), 57
Apollo, 16, 54, 71, 97
Archilochus, 98
Aristotle, 63
Arnold, Matthew, 26
Astarte, 185

Bacchae, The (Euripides), 36
Bach, Johann Sebastian, 70, 139, 184
Bachofen, Johann Jakob, 227
Bachofen, Luise Elisabeth, 49–50
Bacon, Francis, 77
Baedeker, Karl, 218–219
Bagge, Selmar, 70
Bahnson, Julius, 176
Bartels, Wanda von, 213–216, 252
Bastian, Adolf, 227
Baudelaire, Charles, 163
Baumgartner, Adolf, 114
Beck, Johann, 26

Beethoven, Ludwig van, 32, 139, 186
Benndorf, Otto, 15–17
Bentham, Jeremy, 56
Berkeley, George, 113
Bernays, Jakob, 29
Bernoulli, Carl Albrecht, 212–213
Beyle, Marie-Henri (Stendhal), 153, 202, 203
Beyond Good and Evil (Nietzsche), 79, 160, 168, 181, 182
Bianchi, Carlotta, 249
Birth of Tragedy, The (Nietzsche), 17, 33, 36, 39, 41, 44, 49, 54, 60, 63, 77, 79, 97, 119, 138, 146, 173, 186
Biedermann, Alois, 125
Biedermann, Karl, 29
Binswanger, Otto, 222, 223, 224, 245, 257
Bismarck, Otto von, 44, 78, 223, 236
Bizet, Georges, 139, 150
Blum, Robert, 249
Blum, Theodor, 249
Bourget, Paul, 153, 202
Bradke, Marie von, 188–192
Brahms, Johannes, 93, 137, 185, 187, 189
Brandes, Georg, 154, 222
Breisig, Kurt, 248
Brenner, Albert, 83, 91
Browning, Robert, 169
Bülow, Hans von, 48, 138, 139
Burckhardt, Jakob, 37, 39, 40, 44–47, 58, 62, 63, 65, 67, 71, 76, 100, 102, 104, 119, 123
Byron, Lord, 62, 113, 186

Cadorna, Marshal, 169
Carlyle, Thomas, 204
Carmen (Bizet), 149, 150, 178

Cazotte, 154, 155, 163
Cervantes, 87
Chamberlain, Houston Stewart, 182, 205
Chamfort, Roch Nicolas, 112
Chamisso, Adalbert von, 233
Chopin, Frédéric, 9, 139, 182, 183, 184
Christianity of Our Contemporary Theologians (Overbeck, F.), 48, 55, 56, 60
Cimarosa, Domenico, 134
Clemm, Friedrich, 27
Constantine the Great, 62
Cornelius, Peter, 186
Corssen, Wilhelm, 8
Course of Philosophy, The (Dühring), 100
Cramer, Joseph, 255
Cranach, Lucas, 243
Cromwell, Oliver, 242
Curtius, Georg, 97

"Dance Song, The" (Nietzsche), 155
Darbes, Joseph, 201
Darwin, Charles, 153, 204
Daudet, Alphonse, 204
Dawn of Day, The (Nietzsche), 160, 173, 176, 177, 181
de Lisle, Léopold-Victor, 202
Desnoiresterres, Gustav, 57
Deussen, Paul, 10–15, 18–26, 30–31, 200, 225–226
Didon, Père, 153
Diederichs, Eugen, 213
Diogenes, Laertius, 22
Dionysus, 16, 54, 97, 98, 144, 222, 225
Dostoevsky, Fyodor, 193, 202, 209
Doudan, Ximénès, 202
Dräseke, Felix, 186
Dühring, Karl Eugen, 99, 100, 198
Durisch, Gian Rudolf (landlord), 212–213

Ebers, Georg Moritz, 204
Ecce Homo (Nietzsche), 110, 195, 256
Egidi, Arthur, 133–140
Eliatics, the, 85
Emerson, Ralph Waldo, 154, 204
Engel, Gustav, 135
Ephorus, 37
Erlenmeyer-Benndorf, Dr., 225
Eucken, Rudolf, 39–41
Euphrosyne, 243
Euripides, 36
Eusebius, 58

Faust (Goethe), 24
Feuerbach, Henriette, 33

Feuerbach, Ludwig, 25, 114
Fichte, Johann, 16
Fino, Davide (landlord), 217, 218, 219
First Love (Turgenev), 132
"Flaming Heart, The" (Brenner), 91
Fontenelle, Bernard Le Bovier de, 112
Förster, Bernhard, 201, 213, 231, 243, 245
Förster-Nietzsche, Elisabeth, 3, 4–6, 6–7, 8, 30, 41, 46, 48, 53, 58, 69, 77, 89, 124, 129–130, 131–133, 151, 163, 165, 166, 211–212, 213, 218, 226, 231, 232, 236–254, 257, 259–262
Freund, Robert, 172, 192
Freytag, Alwine, 229, 230, 235, 236, 244
Friedrich Nietzsche in His Works (Andreas-Salomé), 127
Friedrich Nietzsche's Collected Letters (E. Förster-Nietzsche), 48
Fritsch, A., 17, 187
Fritsch, Julie, 187
Fritzsch, E. W., 56
From an Unknown Soul (Andreas-Salomé), 128
From the Alps to Naples (Baedeker), 218
Fromentin, Eugene, 202
Froschammer, Jakob, 121–122
Froude, James, 203
Fynn, Emily, 195, 213

Gade, Niels, 185
Galli, Eugenie, 169–172
Gallwitz, Hans, 249
Galton, Francis, 153
Gast, Peter, 54–66, 68–70, 72, 74, 76, 102, 134, 192, 217, 227, 256, 260, 261
Gelzer-Thurneysen, Heinrich, 44
Genoveva (Schumann), 185
German Writings (Lagarde), 82
Gersdorff, Karl von, 59
Gevaert, François, 185
Geyer, Ludwig, 152
Gladstone, William, 92, 160
Gluck, Christoph, 57, 135
Goethe, von, Johann Wolfgang, 17, 24, 86, 87, 113, 136, 139, 155, 200, 201, 254
Goncourt, de (Brothers), 154, 202
Göring, H., 99–101
Gramont, Duchess of, 154
Granier, Raimund, 9–10
"Grave Song" (Nietzsche), 157
Grieg, Edvard, 185, 189
Grimm, Hermann, 154
Gutjahr, Dr. Med., 234, 235, 258

Haeckel, Ernst, 224
Hagen, Edmund von, 174
Hagenbach, Carl Rudolf, 40
Handel, Georg Friedrich, 137
Hannibal, 230
Hanslick, Eduard, 223
Hanson, Ola, 230
Hartmann, Eduard von, 99, 158, 176, 204
Hartung, Robert, 233
Hausmann, Sebastian, 115–124
Heckel, Emil, 43
Heckel, Karl, 43–44
Hehn, Viktor, 201
Heine, Heinrich, 77
Heinze, Max, 141
Helling, Victor, 218–220
Hellpach, Willy, 259
Hempel, 11
Heraclitus, 73
Herakles, 71
Heredity (Ribot), 199
Herodotus, 15
Herzen, Natalia, 124, 193
Heusler, Andreas, 34, 40
Heyse, Paul, 58
Hillebrand, Karl, 169, 177
Hobbes, Thomas, 113
Hoffmann, E. T. A., 184
Hofmiller, Josef, 165
Holbein, Hans, 71
Homer, 22, 29, 98, 119
Horneffer, Ernst, 246, 248, 254–256, 261
House of the Dead, The (Dostoevsky), 193
Human, All Too Human (Nietzsche), 79, 89, 91, 96, 101, 137, 138, 177, 178
Hume, David, 113
"Hymn to Life" (Andreas-Salomé), 151
"Hymn to Solitude" (Nietzsche), 59

Ideals of Materialism, The (Stein), 47
Immortal, The (Daudet), 204
Indian Summer (Stifter), 154, 202
Individual and His Property, The (Stirner), 240
Inquiries into Human Faculty and Development (Galton), 152
Insulted and the Injured, The (Dostoevsky), 202

Jahn, Otto, 21, 24, 25
Janicaud, Walter, 141–143
Janssen, Johannes, 154
Januarius, St., 144
Jesinghaus, Walter, 248–254

Joachim, Joseph, 185
Johnson, Samuel, 114, 115
Joyful Science, The (Nietzsche), 125, 131, 133, 138, 160, 163, 173, 177, 181
Jungmann, Emil, 29

Kālidāsa, 87
Kant, Immanuel, 81, 115, 143, 203
Keller, Gottfried, 47, 54, 58, 172, 200, 201
Kessler, Harry, Count, 248
Kiel, Friedrich, 8, 140
Kinkel, Gottfried, 28
Kirchner, Theodor, 33, 185
Kirschmann, Friedrich von, 99
Klindworth, Karl, 137
Klinger, Friedrich Maximilian von, 113
Klopstock, Friedrich, 15
Klose, Friedrich, 182
Koberstein, August, 8, 14
Kohl, Johann Georg, 27, 28
Körner, Theodor, 14
Köselitz, Heinrich. *See* Gast, Peter
Kowalewski, Sonia, 200
Kreisleriana (Schumann), 184
Krug, Gustav, 6
Krug, K. A., 6
Kruse, Max, 237, 238
Kuhne, Wilhelm, 234

La Bruyère, Jean de, 112, 126
Lagarde, Paul de, 80, 81, 82
La Harpe, Jean-François, 154, 155
Lanzky, Paul, 172–176, 176–182
Laocoön, 16, 225
La Rochefoucauld, François de, 112, 126
Las Cases, Count de, 154
Lec, Heinrich, 228–232
Leopardi, Giacomo, 176
Lichtenberger, Henri, 240
Liebmann, Otto, 224
Life of Friedrich Nietzsche, The (E. Förster-Nietzsche), 48
Life of Jesus, The (David Friedrich Strauss), 21
Liliencron, Detlev von, 252
Lion of Venice, The (Gast), 192
Liszt, Franz, 169, 184
Little Nocturne in F-Sharp Major (Chopin), 184
Livy, 11
Lohengrin (Wagner), 77
Lombroso, Cesare, 205
Lonesome Nietzsche, The (E. Förster-Nietzsche), 194

Lorm, Hieronymus, 136
Lucretius, 29
Luther, Martin, 142

Mähly, Jacob, 44–45
Manfred (Schumann), 138, 185, 186
Mansuroff, Madame de, 168, 182, 183, 184
Mascagni, Pietro, 93
Matthias Corvinus, 200
Maupassant, Guy de, 261
Maurepas, Count de, 153
Mazzini, Giuseppe, 88, 155
Meistersinger, Die (Wagner), 32, 51, 60, 77
Melzer, Professor, 12
Memoirs of an Idealistic Woman (von Meysenbug), 84
Memorial de Sainte-Hélène (Las Cases), 154
Mendelssohn, Felix, 70, 139
Menippus the Cynic, 29
Mérimée, Prosper, 202
Messiah, The (Handel), 6
Meyer, Conrad Ferdinand, 200
Meyer, Guido, 11, 12
Meyers grosses Konversationslexikon, 223
Meysenbug, Malwida von, 48–49, 83–89, 91, 124, 126, 146, 147, 151, 155, 199
Miaskowski, Ida von, 50–53
Miaskowski, Kurt von, 53–54
Michelangelo, 72
Michelangelo (Scheffler), 103
Miscellaneous Opinions and Sayings (Nietzsche), 173, 177
Möbius, August, 167, 257
Moltke, Helmut von, 230
Monod, Gabriel, 49
Monod, Olga, 48, 49, 124
Montegut, Emile, 153
Montesquieu, 142
More, Thomas, 56
Mozart, Wolfgang Amadeus, 135, 186
Müller, Hans von, 254, 255
Muriello, Bartolomé, 209
Musäus, Johann Karl August, 243

Napoleon, 143, 203
Natural Daughter, The (Goethe), 86
Nietzsche (Möbius), 257
Nietzsche, Erdmuthe, 1, 203
Nietzsche, Franziska, 18, 127, 199, 209, 213, 227–236, 245
Nietzsche, Joseph, 5
Nietzsche-Legends (E. Förster-Nietzsche), 212

"Night Song" (Nietzsche), 155
Nightfall (Lanzky), 176
Nirvana (Bülow), 139

Oldag, Friedrich, 21
Olde, Hans, 255
On Love (Stendhal), 203
On the Origin of Moral Feelings (Rée), 85
On the Pathological in Nietzsche (Möbius), 257
On Vanity (Rée), 126
Origen, 96
Origins of Contemporary France, The (Taine), 154, 163
Orlow, Nicolai, Prince, 182
"Other Dance Song, The"(Nietzsche), 156
Overbeck, Franz, 33, 45–48, 50–53, 55–58, 60–62, 108, 125, 146, 212–213
Overbeck, Ida, 32–34, 105–110, 111–115, 125, 128–131, 143–146

Palestrina, Giovanni Pierluigi da, 248
Parsifal (Wagner), 107, 120, 133, 138, 147, 190
Paul, St, 82
Persian Letters, The (Montesquieu), 142
Pestalozzi, Johann, 107
Peter, Karl Ludwig, 8
Petöfi, Alexander, 24
Phenomenology of Moral Consciousness, The (Hartmann), 158
Piccard, Julius, 34–35
Piccolomini, Aeneas Sylvius, 102
Pindar, 98
Pinder, Wilhelm, 4, 5
Platen, August, 72, 75
Plato, 17, 21, 24, 36, 66, 67, 72, 95, 96, 103, 104, 255
Poets and Artists of Italy (Montegut), 153
Prantl, Karl, 66
Preyer, Wilhelm, 224
Probst, Emanuel, 41–43
Promitz, Dr., 37–38
Prudhomme, Sully, 202

Quitzows (Sudermann), 252

Ranke, Leopold von, 16, 222
Red and the Black, The (Stendhal), 153
Rée, Paul, 83–86, 106, 124–127, 129, 147
Reinecke, Carl, 185
Rémusat, Claire de, 153
Renan, Joseph-Ernest, 33

Republic, The (Plato), 66, 104
Reuter, Gabriele, 236–238
Reuter, Richard, 76–83
Revaluation of All Values, The (Nietzsche), 256
Ribbeck, Otto, 26
Ribot, Théodule-Armand, 199
"Richard Wagner in Bayreuth" (Nietzsche), 43, 59, 79, 114, 205
Richter, E. F., 54
Ring of the Nibelungen, The (Wagner), 52, 135, 223
Ritschl, Friedrich Wilhelm, 21, 24–29, 40
Rohde, Erwin, 18, 26–28, 31, 98, 108
Romundt, Heinrich, 28, 50, 52, 53
Roscher, Wilhelm, 26, 28, 258
Rubinstein, Joseph, 185
Ruthardt, Adolf, 182–187
Rutishauser, Dr., 253

Saint-Simon, 137, 154
Śakantulā (Kālidāsa), 87
Salis-Marschlins, Meta von, 158–161, 195–207, 207–211, 243
Sallust, 151
Schaarschmidt, Karl, 21
Scheffler, Ludwig von, 50, 63–76, 101–104
Schellwein, R., 240
Schiess, Heinrich, 225
Schiller, Friedrich von, 13, 87, 88, 200
Schirnhofer, Resa von, 146–158, 159, 161–166, 192–195, 199, 239–242
Schmeitzner, Ernst, 55, 56, 59, 187
Schmiedbiser, Professor, 99
Schnabel, Ernst, 18, 19, 20
Schopenhauer, Arthur, 25, 31, 43, 47, 54, 55, 56, 68, 81, 85, 93, 114, 137, 176, 200, 226, 230
"Schopenhauer as Educator" (Nietzsche), 55, 56, 64, 86, 138
Schuhmacher, Fritz, 246–248
Schumann, Robert, 24, 70, 138, 184, 185
Secret Marriage (Cimarosa), 134
Seidl, Arthur, 251, 261
Seume, Johann Gottfried, 58
"Seven-Seal Song" (Nietzsche), 157
Seydlitz, Reinhart von, 89–93, 93–95
Shakespeare, 14
Shelley, Percy B., 113
Simchowitz, S., 222–225
Simonides, 22
Socrates, 22, 54, 232
Sophocles, 74, 86

Sophus, 232–234
Spencer, Herbert, 204
Steffensen, Karl, 40, 95, 96, 97
Steiger, Edgar, 95–99
Stein, Heinrich von, 47, 186, 198, 199
Steinhardt, Carl, 8
Steinhart, 11, 12, 17, 24
Steinhäusser, Karl, 71
Stendhal (Beyle, Marie-Henri), 153, 202, 203
Stern, Mauritz von, 252
Stifter, Adalbert, 154, 201, 202
Stirner, Max, 113, 114, 240
Stöckert, Georg, 22
Stoecker, Adolf, 134
Strauss, David Friedrich, 21, 55, 56, 99
Strecker, Karl, 216–218
Strindberg, August, 216
Struggle for God, The (Andreas-Salomé), 128
Studies on the History of the Ancient Church (Overbeck), 55
Stürenberg, Heinrich, 28–30
Stürmer, Maria, 19
Sudermann, Hermann, 252
Symposium (Plato), 21

Table Talks (Luther), 142
Taine, Hippolyte, 154, 155, 202, 203
Tannhäuser (Wagner), 77
Tempel, Wilhelm, 172, 173
Theognis, 15, 22, 27, 98
Thucydides, 38
Thurneysen, Rudolf, 37, 44
Thus Spake Zarathustra (Nietzsche), 17, 105, 106, 109, 112, 126, 131, 133, 141, 142, 144, 145, 151, 155, 156, 157, 158, 163, 167, 173, 177, 179, 181, 232, 237
Tristan und Isolde (Wagner), 48, 77
Triumphal Song (Brahms), 137
Truth and Poetry (Goethe), 113
Turgenev, Ivan, 124, 132
Twilight of the Idols (Nietzsche), 110, 204, 256

Underground Man, The (Dostoevsky), 193
Ungern-Sternberg, Isabella von, 259–260
Untimely Meditations (Nietzsche), 17, 33, 40, 43, 55, 59, 60, 63, 79, 99, 114, 146, 173, 177
Usener, Hermann, 29
"Utility and Value of History for Life, The" (Nietzsche), 138

Value of Life, The (Dühring), 100
Vanity of Human Wishes, The (Johnson), 114
Vauvenargues, Luc de, 112
Velde, van de, Henry, 248
Veronese, Paolo, 74
Victor Amadeus I, 220
Vigny, Count de, 202
"Vikings' Return Home, The" (von
    Seydlitz), 93
Virgil, 12
Vischer, Adolf, 39, 40
Vischer-Bilfinger, Privy Councillor, 34
Voltaire, 114, 169
Vulpius, Christiane, 243
Vulpius, Health Commissioner, 256–259

Wachsmuth, Wilhelm, 258
Wackernagel, Jakob, 35–37
Wagner Case, The (Nietzsche), 140, 208, 256
Wagner, Cosima, 43, 73, 135, 138, 210
Wagner, Richard, 25, 32, 33, 35, 39, 43,
    50, 51, 52, 54, 56, 59, 61, 77, 79, 90,
    93, 99, 114, 120, 121, 126, 133, 135,
    137, 138, 139, 140, 152, 163, 174,

    177, 182, 185, 186, 187, 190, 193,
    194, 199, 208, 218, 223, 259
Walde, Philo vom, 242–246
Wanderer and His Shadow, The (Nietzsche),
    173, 177
Wawroch Family, The (Adamus), 237
Wegehaupt, Professor, 27
Werther (Goethe), 113
Wesendonck, Mathilde, 99
Widemann, Paul, 54, 55, 56, 57, 60–63
Wilhelm II, Kaiser, 209
Willdenow, Clara, 161, 164, 165, 166
Windisch, Ernst, 28
Wisser, Wilhelm, 26–28
Wolf, Hugo, 193
Wolzogen, Hans von, 174, 186, 237

Young Nietzsche (E. Förster-Nietzsche),
    166

Zerbst, M., 257
Ziehen, Theodor, 257, 259
Zimmern, Helen, 166–169
Zola, Émile, 228